There is no need for me to write grandiloquently about the surging growth of writing by Māori nowadays in both te reo Māori and te reo Ingarihi because such a blooming boom is manifestly apparent throughout the pages of these two volumes, *Ngā Kupu Wero* and *Te Awa o Kupu*.

Yes, it has not always been this way, but I do not wish to dwell on past grievances, justified as they are — and as well-articulated in several of the pieces in both books. I want more to exalt in the sheer *presence* of fine writing by Māori across several originative genre and several challenging topoi.

I will, however, express appreciation of the seminal volumes of Māori writing assembled under the auspices of Witi Ihimaera and his co-editors, namely *Into the World of Light* (1982), and the *Te Ao Mārama* series commencing in 1992. Tēnā koutou katoa. Our new volumes flow from and beyond such creative beginnings, to the stage now where they overflow with a veritable flood of talent. Indeed the awa is rapidly becoming a transformative torrent throughout Aotearoa as more and more young kaituhi Māori plunge in.

Mai i te pūkaki manahau, te awa mārohirohi.

I also do not wish to get caught up in specious definitions as to what writing by Māori is. Suffice to restate what Witi Ihimaera, D.S. Long, Irihapeti Ramsden and Haare Williams penned 30 years ago: 'If the writer has Māori ancestry, his or her work has been considered, regardless of content.' He tino pono tēnei kōrero. Such has been our approach also.

Further gratitude to my fellow co-editor, Kiri Piahana-Wong. To all contributors. To Harriet Allan, the redoubtable fiction publisher at Penguin Random House. To Creative New Zealand for their munificence. And, above all, to Witi Ihimaera, without whom this project would have never existed.

E kore ēnei pukapuka e rere ki te kore a Witi.

Vaughan Rapatahana (Te Ātiawa)
Series Editor

A stunning new collection of poetry & stories by contemporary Māori writers

Te Awa o Kupu

Edited by

Vaughan Rapatahana
& Kiri Piahana-Wong

PENGUIN BOOKS

The different dialectal spellings used by the individual writers have been preserved and likewise any preferences for double vowels instead of macrons.

Cover art by James Ormsby, based on the phrase 'Ka rere tonu tēnei awa kaha.'

PENGUIN

UK | USA | Canada | Ireland | Australia
India | New Zealand | South Africa | China

Penguin is an imprint of the Penguin Random House group of companies, whose addresses can be found at global.penguinrandomhouse.com.

First published by Penguin Random House New Zealand, 2023

1 3 5 7 9 10 8 6 4 2

Design by Carla Sy © Penguin Random House New Zealand
Prepress by Soar Communications Group
Printed and bound in Australia by Griffin Press, an Accredited ISO AS/NZS 14001 Environmental Management Systems Printer

A catalogue record for this book is available from the National Library of New Zealand.

ISBN 978-0-14-377795-3
eISBN 978-0-14-377796-0

The assistance of Creative New Zealand towards the production of this book is gratefully acknowledged by the publisher.

penguin.co.nz

Mihi Whakatau

Tākiri mai te ata,
hura te ata,
kake te ata,
hura mai te ao,
hura mai te awa hei te ao Māori,
ki āna rerenga,
ki tōna kawa.
Tēnei te awa,
te awa o kupu,
kia rere tonu.
Haumi ē! Hui ē! Tāiki ē!

Contents

Introduction

Kia ora koutou katoa.

There is a river.

It has flowed throughout Aotearoa for aeons. Across and through Te Ika a Māui, Te Waipounamu, Rakiura. It has many tributaries, cascades, curvatures, currents. In places it is majestically serene, in places fierce and forbidding. It is forever mighty.

Its waters have always spoken, it has always been an oral river.

It is a river of words. Always ngā kupu Māori. More recently, ngā kupu Ingarihi.

Over time, several skilful fishers have carefully negotiated its waters, lovingly captured its trophies, selflessly displayed them for all iwi to share.

One of the greatest fishers is Witi Ihimaera, who not only collected and collated his own clever words, but also – in a series of strenuous expeditions – the words of others, which he named *Te Ao Mārama*.

Since his catches, the awa has grown wider, stronger, more powerful, and has so much new life within its depths – from vibrant toikupu through paki mōhio and creative non-fiction, to challenging and creative kōrero pono: ngā kupu wero. It is now verging on flooding the sometimes barren plains of Aotearoa letters.

So much so, that we – the curators of this prolific river – have not been able to grasp a few of the burgeoning kaituhi who inhabit it. Some were too busy, some escaped our attention, some are still growing in stature. Some seemed to have not quite made it to shore.

In this creative bounty titled *Te Awa o Kupu*, the evidence of such literary life, such voluminous vigour, is presented for everyone to plunge into, enjoy, reflect, savour. From the headwaters pūrākau, this pulsating flow twists across a topography of topoi – among them ngā tikanga, te tiriti, ngā takatāpui, te taiao, ki te ā mua. Springing ceaselessly from contemporary rural streams across widespread marae plains and into and sometimes over congested urban aqueducts.

Kei te tupu tonu tēnei awa kaha. Te awa o ngā iwi Māori katoa engari mō ngā tāngata katoa o tēnei whenua ki te kaukau.

Tēnā koutou katoa.

Vaughan Rapatahana rāua ko Kiri Piahana-Wong

Apirana Taylor

karanga

when on to the marae i'm called
my heart hears the words, 'karanga mai karanga mai',
taken back i am by the first woman
to the first woman to the first call
to the manu tīorooro singing
to the twelve heavens, 'haere mai rā, haere mai rā',
thus begins the journey back to the beginning
sailing the waka to the mauri Māori
on the marae ātea where the dust of Tūmatauenga whirls
in the waiata of kōrero seeking te ao mārama
opening like a bud
the people weave the light
from threads of memory
stories stitching weaving
everyone together with laughter tears and kōrero

Whiti Hereaka

Papatūānuku

In the end it was their son Tāne that separated them. She knows it's repugnant to admit that, even to herself. Those who say that it is not fair to blame the children have not met stubborn, tenacious, persistent Tāne. He was always a wilful child.

All of their sons, at one point or other, had come between them; but it was Tāne, who had pushed and pushed until they could no longer embrace each other. And Rangi had left.

Her boys are strong willed. Tangaroa, changeable Tangaroa – calm one moment, a tantrum the next. Tāwhirimātea, strident in his beliefs, always trying to stir something up. Tū is smart, cunning even, and is always looking for a fight. Haumia is tough and wild, she's given up trying to tame him; and Rongo, the quiet one, the peace broker; steadfast, stoic and stubborn.

Perhaps the relationship would have survived if she and Rangi had waited, had spent more time together as a couple alone. Been rational and cool headed: planned their family, prepared themselves. It makes her laugh. How could she have prepared herself for her children? You know what they say about best-laid plans. As if you can plan for love, plan for life.

Still, perhaps if she and Rangi had been strict with them. Brought them up to be . . . different. Six perfect little gentlemen, who wouldn't dream of raising their voices or arguing with each other, or – *heavens!* – their parents. It is a fleeting fantasy. Those docile, obedient children are blank faced in her mind, the thought of their cloying voices chanting *Mummy! Mummy!* makes her shiver.

Ah, my sons. I wouldn't have you any other way.

She can't blame Tāne. Not entirely. There must have been signs before. Sometimes she thinks of herself clinging to Rangi, her grip so tight that her fingernails dug into his skin. Maybe her intense need for him pushed him away. She can't remember the last time they actually talked, really talked. And they haven't been alone together since they had kids. Apart from their children, she doesn't know what they have in common. Rangi was always the one with his head in the clouds. She was always the grounded one.

Why didn't they fight harder to stay together? They should have held on until their fingernails were ripped from their beds. Maybe Tāne's pushing was the excuse they'd both been looking for.

It's strange to think about it, but perhaps they started separating the moment they came together. All their past decisions led here.

She has a terrible crick in her neck – has had it for years, but it's flared up again, from the stress, probably. Or maybe from the relief. She moves her head left to right and then back again, trying to release the muscle. She reaches for the knot just underneath her shoulder blade, trying to dig in with her fingers, but it is just out of reach. There's pain in doing nothing and pain in trying to free it. She's not sure which is worse. Her forehead tightens, another headache is on the way. She'll lie down until it goes away.

Her bed is vast and empty.

They were so cramped before, living on top of one another really. It was no place for growing boys. She heard them grumbling amongst themselves. Perhaps they thought that she couldn't hear them – their bickering and their plans.

We need more room!

I can't breathe here.

We should kill them.

There was a hush after Tū had said it. Of course she didn't believe he meant it – *although, there's a darkness to him, something in the way he stares like he's always plotting his next move* – of course he didn't mean it. Of course he didn't, what would Tū know of death?

It's irrational and paranoid to think that her children were plotting against her. Sure, sometimes it felt like they ganged up on her, but that's what children do, isn't it? They test the limits and push boundaries, that's how they grow.

She closes her eyes as if she is trying to shut the thought out. Why would her own children want to hurt her so badly? Hurt themselves? Because, despite their bravado, she knows that they miss Rangi too.

Her pillow is wet. She wipes her face with the back of her hand as she sits up. She never was a pretty crier – her eyes puff up immediately and hupe runs freely from her nose.

She shivers and pulls a shawl around her. She feels cold all the time now, more if she's been crying. Maybe the need for warmth is a comfort thing, mental rather than physical. Tāne gave her the shawl. He can be so thoughtful and generous that it makes her feel guilty about dwelling on his flaws.

Funny, she never thought that green was her colour but this suits her so well. Maybe she doesn't know anything about herself at all. She looks at herself in the mirror. Really looks – her own face is like that of a stranger, she has trouble recognising herself. She knew Rangi's face so well, his eyes flecked with light, his nose, his lips . . . almost every pore and whisker: she knew it so intimately. She studies herself – her smile, her frown. Looking at herself makes her think of what she is missing, his lips on hers, their shared breath. Does she have real sympathy for the woman in the glass? That woman is a stranger to her.

It is too quiet. With the shawl wrapped tightly around her, she goes in search of her boys. Surely their chatter will chase these useless thoughts away. *Where are they?* The homestead is empty.

The boys have scattered – did they hear her crying and flee? No, she can't imagine that they'd be so callous. They're exploring, the novelty of having so much room is still new to them. They've made this place their own; each staking out their territory, busy with their interests. Rongo will be nearby in the garden, digging neat furrows into the ground. Tāne and Haumia will be in the bush – Tāne has probably claimed the tallest tree and Haumia will be hanging out in the scrub land. Tangaroa will be at the beach. And Tū could be with any of them, it depends on his mood or if he's annoyed his brothers – which he often has.

She wanders around the homestead, checking each empty room until she's back in her own. Even if the old place was cramped, at least she wasn't alone. Who has she to talk to here? Her sad reflection in the mirror? She looks at herself again: tired and sad. Has she always looked this way? She reaches out and touches her reflected cheek: so cold and hard.

She had thought that her family was all that she wanted, all that she needed. She's devoted herself to them and now what? What is there left for her now?

She was happy before. They were happy before, weren't they?

She feels numb. She doesn't know who she is. She has always been defined in relation to Rangi – their love, their embrace, their children.

She can't remember life without him. Did a time ever exist when she was just herself?

She flops on the bed, stretches out like a starfish and stares at the blank ceiling. That's what her life is now. Nothing, wall to wall. She can't remember what life was like without Rangi, in her mind he was always there – before love, partnership and children. If she tries to think of a time when she was on her own there's a deep void in her memory. He was her light in the dark. There is nothing without him. She's nothing without him.

And yet, here she is. She still exists, even if their relationship doesn't.

The ceiling is so blank. She stares up at it, relaxing her eyes so everything is sort of blurry. There are no edges anymore. There is not an absence of a thing, but the potential for anything.

No, not yet. I am not ready to stop wallowing.

Ah, but there is a flutter within her. It is excitement and hope and . . .

'No.'

Her own voice surprises her. She didn't mean to speak.

The smell of rain is in the air. It reminds her of Rangi. It is the smell of their love, their lust. Petrichor, the musk of the earth and sky combined.

Rangi was her first love, her one and only love. But now she wonders if it was real. Had they simply settled for one another? Too scared to live without one another, too scared of the unknown?

Since the separation, she can finally see Rangi as another being. When they were together it was easy to think of themselves as one organism, or to be frank, one orgasm. Sex had always been passionate, they had always been hungry for one another.

She can still feel his fingers digging into her hips, the prickle of nerves running right down her spine from his breath on her neck.

She reaches out her leg and kicks her door closed, it would be just her luck if one of the boys wandered in now.

Eyes closed, she conjures him. Imagines that they are his rough fingers brushing her nipples, his hands squeezing her breasts. Even though she had been with him for so long, even though they had made love hundreds of times, she's finding it hard to keep him in her mind. She pushes a finger into the cleft of her vulva, seeking out her clit, her sticky pubic hair tangles around her fingers and a clenching warmth spreads from her clit to deep within her.

And then her mind wanders to all of the jobs she has to do and the moment is gone. She grinds the heel of her palm into her pubic bone –

trying to convince herself that it is his weight upon her, determined not to give up . . .

She groans and sighs, but it is not from pleasure. How long has it been? She's showing, so five or so months. Another sigh. It's been far too long.

They were never shy with one another. Their love was intense and oppressive. Is that why their boys wanted them to be apart? The disgust one has for the sex life of parents?

She was happy with Rangi. She felt whole. She was satisfied.

Now she is apart from him, she has the clarity to ask whether being filled is the same as being fulfilled.

She looks at her hand. The dent in her ring finger is still there. The skin is pale and smooth, like it is a scar. She supposes that it is.

Is it time to finally learn who she is?

She is a mother.

So she does what good mothers do – *isn't this what good mothers do?* – forgets her own feelings, forgets *herself*, and concentrates on her children. Focuses on how they are coping rather than how she still yearns for him.

Her boys are too young to understand, they have no experience of love that is all consuming. She loves their father still.

It would be so much easier if she hated him – at least then she'd have anger to distract her from the hole he's left. If she hated him then she wouldn't miss him right?

It is so lonely here. She has no one to talk to about her grief. She can't burden her children with it. Not that her boys have ever considered her feelings; she is their mother, a being who lives only for them.

Is that all she is, all that she's ever been: a mother? Now that she has the room to breathe, the room to think, will she find something more? She rubs her temples, guilt pinches between her eyebrows. What kind of mother wishes for something other than her children? She wishes she knew another mother so she could ask – though she never would, no one can know she doubts herself.

The love she has – *had* – for Rangi is dwarfed by the love she has for her children, and yet . . .

Sometimes she feels like her throat is constricted by resentment – she tries to suppress the part of her which hates those boys of hers. The boys that ruined her love. Her boys, her boys. The story will always focus on her boys.

No one can understand her loneliness.

As if in response, the baby in her womb turns; sending tremors throughout her body. She has named her youngest son Rūaumoko. He will be a son: she always bears boys. Poor Rūaumoko. He will never know his father. Not like his brothers have.

Her only comfort is the thought that it was good for her boys, the separation. Each of their reactions at the beginning had been so different. Tū had brooded, at times it seemed as if he was jealous of Tāne; as if *he* wanted to be the one who had separated his parents. Rongo had become withdrawn and when she picked up Haumia he held her so tightly, like he wanted to be buried in her. Even Tangaroa clung to her. He was always there: at her arm, her knee, her hip. Of course she's glad he's found his independence now, that they all have — but when she was focused on them she didn't have to think of her own pain. Now it seems like there is nothing else to think about.

Freed from his father's shadow, Tāne has flourished. He has made a life for himself. She can see that soon he will be ready to pursue a love of his own.

It is good for them. It is good for us. She repeats the words over and over until it is the truth.

Most of their boys had stayed with her. Only Tāwhirimātea has gone with his father. The look on his face as he followed Rangi. She had not known her son to be so angry before. He was angry at her, she supposed, he blamed her for the break-up.

Everyone is on edge when Tāwhirimātea visits. He takes pleasure in destroying his brothers' precious things. When did he become so cruel, so angry? She shields Rongo and Haumia from Tāwhirimātea, the older siblings need to work it out amongst themselves.

Tāwhirimātea goes after Tāne first, shaking the tree Tāne has climbed — trying to shake him out. Tāwhirimātea tries to get at his brother, ripping the lower branches of the tree. Tāne ignores him, which only fuels Tāwhirimātea's rage. Should she intervene? Tāne laughs and she's relieved: *Just brothers being brothers.*

Tāwhirimātea manipulates Tangaroa to fight against Tāne with him. They hurl water at Tāne, but he doesn't budge. Tāwhirimātea leaves to get more ammunition and Tangaroa looks at the tree in front of him and then up to his brother in the branches above him. Without Tāwhirimātea's encouragement, Tangaroa's anger quickly subsides and he wanders off down to the beach again.

It is Tū who fights back against Tāwhirimātea. While Tāwhirimātea is spurred by his anger, Tū fights because he enjoys the violence. Tū yearns for the bruises and the blood. The fight is vicious and physical – Tū punching Tāwhirimātea over and over again. She yells at Tū to stop and is grateful that he listens, she's not sure if she could have stopped him physically. Tū crows at his victory, proud that he has beaten his brother.

However, Tū hasn't finished fighting, it is like he just can't stop his rage now that he's unleashed it. Angry that none of his brothers stood with him against Tāwhirimātea, Tū finds any excuse to argue and fight.

She is disgusted by her sons – where did the love go? How has she let such cruelty take seed? She cannot bear to see Tāwhirimātea's rage and humiliation. She cannot bear to see Tū's arrogance.

Rangi calls to her, pleads for them to be together again. He pours his grief over her and suddenly she feels the weight of him again, pressing down upon her. She didn't realise that she had been drowning under him. That alone she could breathe again. She can't muster any sympathy – why should she be burdened with his pain?

She still loves him, will always love him, but she needs to put herself first. She's not strong enough yet to save them all.

Her arms are heavy. It's like she's spent all this time reaching out for him, trying to cling to what was. For now she must put the things that remind her of Rangi away. She packs the shirt that still smells like him into Tāwhirimātea's bag – he can take it back to his father.

She turns the photos of them together around. One day she'll be able to look at them again. Hopefully, one day soon.

When he comes to pick up Tāwhirimātea, she turns away before closing the door. She doesn't have to see him leave again.

She sits at the window looking out over her land. Her boys are out exploring again, it's nice to have a moment to herself. Time to think. It's getting dark, soon they'll come home and tell her about the things they made and discovered. One day, she'll tell them about her discoveries too. As the light fades she can see herself reflected in the glass. She reaches out to touch her cheek – the glass is still a little warm under her fingertips.

'There you are, Papa.'

Yes. It was good for them. It was good for us. We needed room to grow.

Hana Pera Aoake

My body is made of many

My flesh is made of the deep red clay of
Kurawaka.
It is the blood of my parents,

the blood is the sacrifice Ranginui and
Papatuuaanuku endured,

so that there could be life,
namely my life.
Gifted by Papatuuaanuku,
my bones are the bones of my tupuna.

Papatuuaanuku's guiding hand vibrates in my
blood and through my body,

it is etched in my bones.
The spirit of Ranginui flies through my mind.
My breath is the breath of Taane
deep in my lungs.
Haa
My breath.
The first breath of life.
Mine to hold.
Mine to release.
My body is made of many.

Arielle Walker

Here are all the ways the story is the same

The story always begins at the takutai moana, the shoormal
where sea meets sand [1]

The story always reminds us that there are
rocks
on the shore [2]
where they first meet
(The story always skims across the *how* and *why* of their meeting,
notes that *he* stumbles upon *her* by 'chance' [3])

The story always includes
  a seal-skin
  a sea-dress
  a cloak
  a cap or
  a kākahu
  a covering which means that

the story always tells us that she is *un*covered
on discovery

The story always gives her kind as *selkie silkie selchie seal-maiden finn-folk maighdeann-ròin maighdean-mhara* [4]
The story always lingers on how
álainn ātaahua beautiful bonnie bòidheach lovely
she is

The story always centres on an entrapment, a betrayal [5]

The story always reminds us that there are
children [6] she will leave behind [7]

The story always ends with her returning to the sea.

---

[1]
It is always night time, it is always moonlit, it is always
just dark enough

[2]
The rocks are where things can be hidden — people
and shed skins
and secrets

[3]
the intent, it's implied, comes later, so we can't assign fault

[4]
but never her name

[5]
Sometimes the betrayal is at the beginning
in the stealing of seal-skin, sometimes near the end
with the trickery and trap of cooked kai
but it is the same betrayal every time:
he stops *her* returning to her kin

[6]
The story forgets to remind us that children are made
of earth and saltwater
and belong to *both-worlds* & *neither-world*
always caught in between

[7]
The story forgets to remind us that sometimes
she takes them with her
The story forgets to remind us that
this is her choice to make

Te Kahu Rolleston

Te Rārangatira

Te Puna
Springs to mind when I reminisce on the initial gathering of all of us.
Together, at Paparoa, we were safe and secure within the Mauri of the Moana.
Natives! Feeding off the light and rising to the skies like the Kauri and Tōtara.

Together, we created moments.
Moments like . . .
When you step into the pōwhiri
And your ope begins to kōkiri.
Through the air and the earth,
The tīpuna of your iwi
Converse
And you reply with vibrations through your kōiwi.

We created moments.
That added to the muka kaupapa on which this Te RārangaTira korowai has been woven.

We were interwoven by the force of the the four winds. Ngā hau e whā.
A generation of natives with aspirations of going far.
Some peaceful warriors, others of Tūmatauenga.

Regardless.
Together as one we created moments.

Moments like . . . with these giants by my side.
Afraid of heights we walked the sky.

Skating on tree branches.

Feet planted 20 feet above the ground.
We moved through the clouds.
We moved in leaps and bounds.

In an instant, lifetime friendships were found.
Bonds were bound.
As we created moments.

Moments like on Te Tairāwhiti together as one, we shared the air.
We breathed the air and listened to whispers of our ancestors' actions that echoed stories that whispered in our ears.

We were guided along this journey. By some of its kaitiaki.
We were safe. Escaped away from the technological trap and life-sized hīnaki.

We created moments in a place before this.
To me was only a myth.

A place where the free reign of wairua exists.
A place that just is.

Preserved in the kōrero and waiata of my tīpuna. Mai i Ngā Kurī a Whārei.

I've always known where that is.
Now I can finally say I've journeyed to where Tihirau lives.
A place overshadowing Puketapu at Te Taunga Waka. The boundary of Mataatua's grips.
And we breathed its air.

We breathed the air, and shared the breath of our ancestors, salted by the ocean ever so slightly.
As we observed Tīrairaka dance in the light breeze.
We received stories of great voyages to and from Hāwaiki.

We watched Tāwhiri's breeze
Blow through Tāne's trees.

We watched Tangaroa gently greet Papa along the beach below.
In a frame preserved in the picturesque of centuries ago.

As we stood atop the maunga, listening to thousand-year-old history of waka,
We attempted to buffer the esoteric barrier for but a minute with haka.

As we scattered amongst the hills' peaks
We listened and allowed ourselves to hear the hill's peak.
And tell us stories only birds mountains and hills speak.

From atop this maunga.
Hungry, in search of new adventures we voyaged to Heretaunga.

Where we felt,
As if he cast us himself.
To uplift a motu. At least partly.
We pierced through Tangaroa's sea on Te Matau a Māui
Blinded but guided right and left, left and right, matau and mauī.

Basically what I'm here to ask is have you felt secure?
I don't mean seatbelt secure.
I mean safe to be yourself,
Within yourself, secure.
Because I have.

essa may ranapiri

One of the Great Ocean-going Canoes

on Tainui
the hull
leaps waves with their own peaks
one and a half millennia after Christ's
wooden diorama
(did it come after Māui's attempt at slaying death?)

the tohorā acts as a guide
wailing waiata
spraying notes
to the hook in the sky
as Tāwhirimātea spits
a gust to forward tāngata

they're silent carrying seeds of the
kūmara
sweet
ness
between their knees

arched mouth
with no dorsal fin and
no breath left
to pump a spray
it hits the land
before them

a safe wake for their great waka
beached

Ben Kemp

Kūmara

Sweet Potato,
Taputini,
a voyage to Polynesia east,
an offering of *kūmara*
brings tears to the eyes of *Toroa*.

Matariki,
behold the eyes of god,
clear and bright this constellation of stars,
a pathway of light to harvest.

Hutihuti,
the blessings of *Rongomātāne*
rest at the toes of spring,
tapu mounds of soil scatter the hillsides.

Rekamaroa,
a bed of hot river stones,
under the earthen blanket,
steam rises, the buttery smell of pork belly.

Houhere,
creamy fingers to open mouth,
mīere, mīere, oh *mīere*
upon a honeyed tongue, spirited *tīpuna* sing.

Rangi Faith

'. . . no one thing we wanted'

(Kāpene Kuki, Poverty Bay, 1769)

On the slash-littered beach at Oneroa
we look for shells,
and find them easily — pipi, tuangi, kuku;
we draw kete in the sand & add rimurimu for relish,
dig an umu, and tattoo the sand
with Te Maro's name and Te Rakau's name;
we heap up stones for their fearlessness,
build palisades of driftwood for their strength,
find a tall rock for the tribal haka;
we listen to the story
of giant white-winged manu coming into our bay —
emerging silently on the breath of the sea
with men in their claws
who paddle backwards towards us,
dip their white legs into the sea
& huddle together on the beach,
their red and blue kākahu glowing in the sun;
from their taiaha there is smoke, sound & fire —
we race to the rock Te Toka-a-Taiau
and pūkana our defiance.

Gerry Te Kapa Coates

The Promised Lands

Then — 1870s
Ethnic Cleansing — Pākehā Style

Must it always be about land or money
especially when they're ostensibly free?

It was also the same thing as the Cheyenne
or the Sioux in Amerika had to cope with.

The new settlers thought the land was free
for the taking by force, occupation or devious means.

Hadn't getting there in covered wagons been hard
enough on their families not to deserve the rewards?

So they called it Terra Nullius — unoccupied land —
as if the original indigenous people did not exist.

In Te Wai Pounamu we were also itinerant going
from kaika to mahika kai depending on the seasons.

Tuna from the awa, weka and raupō by the lakes.
Yet it was still a hard life living by the seasons.

Float the previous cargo down the mighty awa
Te Waitaki, our mōkihi steering clear of rapids.

Ferrying the settlers over the Waitaki, rain or
shine, flood or drought, these pastors or explorers.

Shortland or Taylor still wanted to stay the night
and talk, talk, talk then pick our brains for facts.

Eventually Pākehā owned all the land up the valley
but took umbrage at us still hunting and foraging.

Ownership, not occupation, was everything for the
Pākehā settlers so there was always going to be conflict.

Mantell, the Commissioner appointed by Governor Eyre
along with Kemp condemned Māori to a subsistence life.

Te Maihāroa, a 'miracle worker', had the spiritual mana to lead
a rōpū to the Hakataramea valley, finally occupying 'the promised land'.

He also performed miracles by stopping a train on the Waitaki
bridge at his command until all the carts of the rōpū left the bridge.

The rōpū finally reached Ōmārama, another 'promised land' and
re-established their rights of ownership, if only they could have
endured.

Finally it was the Māori dogs and their power and intelligence that
worried Pākehā

by challenging their assumptions that Māori were still just stone age
people.

The dispersion from Ōmārama came as the final straw — leave or be
arrested, so the 150 Māori

solemnly began the long trek back to the coast. At least we avoided the
fate of Te Whiti.

We ended up at the Waitaki river mouth but not with our tails between
our legs. But that

was when we knew what the meaning of defeat and being seen as
strangers in our own land meant.

Then — 1990s
Te Kerēme
The Politics Of Difference

This drawn out Tiriti process of redress and apology
is divisive and like life and death for us at the flaxroots.

Anything can be signed for under duress, it's like getting
army issue clothing, we would never be proud of.

Remember how the power balance changed after we
became the minority though we are still tangata whenua.

Yet the majority make the rules and it's those inside the
Tiriti process — largely Pākehā — who follow the rules.

Our tūpuna grew old and died with this cancer still in their
hearts, but the nine tall trees of Te Kerēme finally bore fruit.

Yet we accept our settlements under duress, whatever the Crown
deigns parsimoniously to disperse to us and we are expected to be
gracious.

The pale Apology matters too along with the dollars. Notice
they never apologise to the banks and airlines they bail out.

In the beginning Tiramōrehu said to Eyre 'should you return to England,
we shall never cease complaining to those who may hereafter come.'

Ake, ake, ake.

His prophetic words took 150 years to come to fruition, and the
settlement reached was a drop in the bucket of what was lost.

As the sandstone cuts the pounamu slowly with water raining like
tears, we will reach our goal. There is no true peace without justice.

Note: *Te Maiharoa and the Promised Land*, Buddy Mikaere, Heineman, 1988.

Witi Ihimaera

Te Hau Puru

1

As Totowera saunters the waterfront of Kororāreka he knows he turns heads. Not for being good-looking but, rather, scary. He is taller than most Pākehā and that is intimidating to them. Plus he has a full blood-curdling facial moko and is darkly complexioned.

'Not my fault,' he sniffs disdainfully, 'that Pākehā associate black with Beelzebub.'

Totowera must admit, though, that there are benefits to looking like the devil incarnate. Well-dressed, civilised, White folks step off the walkway and into the mud rather than require him to step around them. A little goggle-eyed blond boy, however, is momentarily shocked into stillness.

'Boo,' Totowera says.

'Mamaaa,' the child wails, scampering off.

Totowera laughs out loud. Appearances are deceiving. He may look frightening but he is a savage with a sense of humour. And today, in a top hat and silks, he's dashing.

It is late January, 1840, and Totowera has been in Kororāreka for two days. He has come to the riotous settlement on board the *Aaka,* the tribe's coastal barge, from the Bay of Plenty, with a cargo of kauri spars and flax. He is *very* pleased with himself. The local merchants know quality wood when they see it: Te Whānau a Roimata's forests provide spars 150 foot long, lengthier than most, and that alone brings the highest price from mast makers.

'Strong and supple, boss,' Totowera has assured likely buyers, 'guaranteed not to snap in the strongest winds. You can't buy better than Roimata kauri, no sign of rot.'

Oh, he has the gift of the gab, Totowera, silver-tongued as Satan!

'And feel the quality of the flax, pā harakeke, I have brought with me. Hand-picked from our swamps. Make strong ropes from strong reeds.'

Merchants, beguiled by Totowera's pitch, have vied with one another, upping the price until one astute emptor says, 'Okay, Blackie, name your price for the lot, I'll take your flax too. And I'll buy in advance your next shipment.'

What? Trust a Māori and purchase another shipment sight unseen? The other purchasers melt away.

Meanwhile, Totowera and his buyer, Donald Carey, shake on it. Young Carey is an eager, new trader trying to cash in on the new colony's growing export market in shipbuilding goods – 25 per cent and climbing. The new partners seal the deal with a bill of sale drawn on the Union Bank of Australia.

'Now a whisky to celebrate,' Carey says as they make their way to one of the harbourside bars. 'And then, what say you, Blackie, to a night of whoring?'

Kororāreka lives up to its sordid reputation as hellhole of the Pacific. Although the Pākehā prostitutes are too bony for his liking, and while Totowera has three wives and children at home, he does not say no.

2

Three days later, Totowera receives word that all the kauri spars and flax have been unloaded.

'Time to ship out and head back to Roimata,' he says to Carey, his new friend in debauchery.

The *Aaka* has been loaded with a return cargo of guns, booze, axes and other agricultural equipment, pigs and, of course, gifts for Totowera's wives. They will love the silk petticoats, dresses, boots and hats from the local millinery shop.

Then, 'He aha?' Totowera asks Carey, as they approach the coastal vessel.

When the *Aaka* berthed at Kororāreka a few days earlier there had been the usual assortment of whalers and sealers in the bay, some being refitted. Now there were more, some congregating at Kororāreka but most on the other side of the bay at sunlit Waitangi, northwest of Paihia.

Spearing across the water are numerous waka. The air resounds with chanting paddlers. 'Auē, tiaia! Auē, koia hoki!'

Carey spits at the sight of the distant tangle of sails. 'In a week's time, the British plan to appoint a governor and to extend the rule of law.

They will sign a treaty with your lot, all the Māori chiefs of New Zealand.'

'First I've heard about it,' Totowera replies. 'Why wasn't I told?' He stands on his dignity, his mana as a chief offended that he did not receive a personal invitation.

'It will be the end of free enterprise,' Carey adds with his own, increasing, ill temper.

Totowera's attention is diverted as he notices, more immediately, that a French whaler, *La Baleine Verte,* has come to anchorage next to the *Aaka.* It is a double topsail barque, manned by some 30 men, on its way to hunt cetacean pods further south. Totowera points out a group of brightly clothed clergymen waiting on the beach. 'More Wīwī,' he says, as they shout, '*Oui, oui,*' to the sailors on board the whaler.

Prominent among the clerics is Father Michel Cabanel, awaiting a special shipment from family in France. A member of the Roman Catholic Marist Order, Cabanel has followed Jean-Baptiste François Pompallier to New Zealand. The Congregation's blue capes, sashes and preaching crosses mark a distinct and colourful difference from the more sober black and white costuming of Samuel Marsden and his Anglicans.

And then, from the hold, emanates a huge, roaring, sound. Totowera's heart stops as a huge tipua emerges. Blindfolded and weak from confinement, the monster thrashes against the ropes which bind it. One of the sailors removes the mask and, as the quadruped moves from shadow into sunlight it bellows with outrage. *Where am I? What is this place?*

And then the taniwha looks straight into Totowera's eyes.

Āwhinatia ahau. Help me.

The warrior chief has seen equines before but this draught horse is a revelation. The stallion, at 17 hands high and weighing some 1800 pounds is, like him, a giant, with a square head, straight profile, strong neck and deep wide chest.

The hōiho nunui moves further into the light and Totowera is struck dumb by its beauty: the coat shimmers a startling blue as the sun gleams on the white hairs among the black.

The blue roan stands high on its rear legs. Though wasted and skeletal from the long sea voyage it summons up the last of its strength, *He pai kē ahau ki te mate,* and, lashing out with its hooves, breaks open a gap in the ship's railing. The sailors scatter as, with a shrill cry that splits the universe apart, the horse falls ungainly into the sea.

Totowera has been in love many times. He knows what the emotion feels like. How all consuming it is, like your heart can break out of your body. In an instant he has dived into the water to rescue the monster. He lifts its head to his, looks through the eyes to its soul, and sobs.

He has never felt as overcome by such aroha.

3

Nothing will stop Totowera from saving the horse and owning it.

'I will not leave Kororāreka without him,' he tells Carey.

He enlists Carey in bargaining with Cabanel for the cheval de trait Belge, a horse from the Brabant region.

Cabanel says, 'Non, absolument pas.'

'I will not take no for an answer,' Totowera answers. He offers Cabanel the entire income from his sale of spars to Carey.

'Le cheval n'est pas à vendre.' No sale. The cleric is somewhat offended that a mere savage would want to claim such a noble breed. After all, in medieval times, had not the horse's ancestor been, in 807, among the gifts sent by Charlemagne to the Abbasid caliph Harun al-Rashid?

'Then I shall steal the horse,' the warrior chief says.

'You could be tried for such an offence and hanged,' Carey, his new friend, warns him.

Although Carey turns Totowera from any thoughts of theft, the warrior chief redoubles his efforts with Cabanel. He shadows the cleric's steps night and day, turning up at all sacramental services.

'When will God give me my horse?'

His wild and lunatic appearances cause great disturbances, but Cabanel is unperturbed.

'Il ne changera pas d'avis.' God will not change His mind.

In Carey's eyes, Totowera seems to plunge into madness. He mortgages two future shipments and, 'I will give you the *Aaka* as well. I will walk home by my horse until he is recovered enough from his long sea voyage to ride.'

The ship as well? Cabanel's eyes flicker with interest.

The warrior chief follows up with an offer that stops Cabanel in his tracks.

'I will also tender my entire tribe to the Catholic Church.'

The vertiginous proposal takes the clergyman's breath away. 'Tout votre people? Your entire Māori tribe? Pour un cheval?'

Totowera is aware that the Roman Catholics and the Anglicans are in a bitter fight for Māori souls. He may have caught Cabanel at an opportune moment. What with the upcoming Treaty signing, Cabanel is momentarily diverted. Bringing an entire wild, barbaric, uncivilised Māori tribe to the Catholic god will stand him in good stead with his superior, Pompallier, and also look good in despatches to the Holy See in Rome. However:

'Mais j'ai besoin de ta garantie,' he says. 'A guarantee is required. You, chief-Māori, must be baptised a Catholic, comme garantie, as surety of your entente.'

Totowera readily submits. He takes upon himself a new name, Noa, the Biblical patriarch who saved animals in his own, Pākehā, ark. However, the newly baptised Noa requires a warranty too: a bill of sale for the magnificent horse. 'Otherwise,' he says, 'I might be accused of stealing it.'

'What will you call your Tipua?' Carey asks after the ceremony. He is aghast at Totowera's folly.

'He will be Te Hau Puru, The Blue Wind.'

Carey farewells Noa. As the warrior chief leads his great prize, Te Hau Puru, out of Kororāreka, he sees that Cabanel has already departed with Pompallier by sailboat for the Treaty signing. Noa raises his binoculars and scans the chiefly activity on the other side of the bay. He considers delaying and attending the event.

'No,' he decides. 'I will wait for the Pākehā to come to me and, on my own lands, I will talk to him on my terms.'

All of a sudden, puffs of smoke and the echoing sound of cannonade from Waitangi indicate that the chiefs have signed.

Noa watches as the British flag is raised.

Raina Kingsley

Museum Ethnographic Case No. 1

she squats by the fire
looks over the plains
one of the original inhabitants

the real dirt and dust
are sealed out
she has a haven of sorts

the glass does not protect her
from the onlookers who titter
at her exposed breasts

her own descendants slink past
she wonders when
they became ashamed of her

what she can't know
is some of her people
plan to take her back

end the cultural peep show

Briar Wood

Kuramārōtini

So the story goes
that trickster Kupe
cheated his friend
into diving overboard
to free the lines
then paddled rapidly away.

Some hoa.
Best to know that
legendary navigators take huge risks
and do not make the safest companions.

Ākuanei –
she asked herself –
what do I want –
home in Hawaiki
or the travelling years?

What does he want –
the waka my father gifted?
Matahourua and me?

Or maybe unhappiness
with the man she'd married
drove her to the coast.
It's possible –
she was curious and Hoturapa wasn't
the kind of man who liked a journey
so she chose Kupe.

Yet even an inveterate traveller
might become weary in a waka
on the open sea,
looking out for landfall.

Travelling direct to her destination –
as the future loomed towards her
she named that radiant land
on the horizon
Aotearoa.

Hinemoana Baker

He Kanohi Kitea

He kanohi kitea, he hokinga mahara
A face seen, a memory stirred

We are high contrast for the camera
black plaits down the fronts of our white shirts.
Behind us a door aches shuts.
Beside us gold buttons, Wi Parata's beard
the white bulbs

of the girls' dresses.
All is light, all light is removed.
The pounamu shine of the blade
and the sports team's shins, their shield.
The bright of the white-blue

behind Tamihana's head.
The heavy mere singing its
shape, singing the stone's skim,
the urge of birds.
You women, your tassels.

The weave is golden
and always at our throats
are collars, the moon. Pull my chin
towards you from your height.
Stroke my eyebrow with

the pad of your thumb and say
the word *perpetual*, the word *kneel*.
We are warm in your cloaks.
Unaiki, your skin's glow.
Huria, the listing ship behind you.

Kay McKenzie Cooke

Tuturau

In a gully's lonely gut, the monument
marks both
the skyline
and the end of the Musket Wars
in the middle of nowhere
                                        so far south –

the first victim to be claimed
the invader himself,
Te Pūho, asleep
in the porch
when the Motupōhue war party arrives
early dawn,
the chief, Tūhawaiki,
landing soft

onto the verandah roof,
surprising this place into history
with a musket's blast
                                        so loud it wakes a child who cries out.

Today a lamb's bleat,
the only ghost I expect.

Robert Sullivan

The Declaration of Independence

(for Moana Jackson)

The Declaration of Independence

in Aotearoa was not one. It was an assertion of mana
by our rangatira – not to mention of independence
as we were already there. Why are we talked to about
the Treaty when it is Te Tiriti that was signed by us
and He Wakaputanga spells it out so very clearly
in black and white with our nose moko
as signatures – can you get any closer?

He Wakaputanga

Nō roto o Aotearoa. Ka whakaputa i ngā reo,
i ngā mana o Ngāi Rangatira o te motu. Kāore e kī
i ngā kupu tūhāhā. Nā te aha i kore ai e pānui i tēnei
tirohanga. Kei hea te pai ki te kōrero mō The Treaty;
koia nei Te Tiriti i hainatia e mātou, kua mārama i ngā
hainatanga o ngā ngū moko – ka whakatata rawa ake
i te hā rangatira. Ka whakaputa i te mana Motuhake.

kani te manukura

Tricks of a treaty

article the first:
one good trick, that one
played by an empire
on our tīpuna
how could they have known
by making their mark
on that paper
we, the descendants of chiefs
would become palimpsest
upon the pages of this land
the signs of our
past present future
made so faint
we can barely see our own shadows
let alone that of the land
as both pass to the pākehā
upon whom the sun never
seems to set

stories that carried us safely
across space & time
now told by simple strangers
climb pine trees
upside down torn apart
by bush lawyer vine

it's fuck all really
but let my every word
be a stone in the mouth of the people
for those who do not know

the purposes of a pebble
at least it will help shut you up

for those who do
hold it long under your tongue
he mea hāpai ō:
provisions for the journey

because of the tricks of the treaty
we gotta long way to go

article the second:
you, the ran'atira
wo/men of great mana
have the choice of signing
or not signing
this trick of a treaty
with a mere messenger
distinguished from the rest of the syphilitic sailors
& crude whalers
only by his fancy dress
& the title it entails

they aren't even giving you the respect
of trying to cover their tracks:
you know what
a hobson's choice is, ay?

no?
oh, you're gonna have one good laugh at this . . .

article the third:
if your bent is more political-economic
you will sign thinking,
only the shadow of the land
will pass to the strangers

the substance will remain
let the queen govern for a time
we will trade potato pig flour
& grow our material power

if your bent is more spiritual-metaphysic
you will sign thinking
only the substance of the land
will pass to the strangers
but the shadow will remain
let the queen govern for a time
we will maintain the mana to guide her hand
and the stories that bind us to the land

either way you will be wrong

for the trick of a treaty
made with an empire
upon whom, for a time at least,
the sun never set,
is both substance & shadow
the strangers will get

article the fourth:
the truest trick
of a treaty
is to offer a lot
then
to the promises of paper
supply an antidote
bring it in by the boat

call it commerce,
call it provision of goods & services
according to the natural laws
of supply & demand
aw heck,

go to the full farce & call it a civilising mission

don't worry
the natives will give this powerful potion
one good name
something like
karaitianatan'a
or waipiro

whatever you or they call it
be sure
to dress it in red
that way
it'll go straight to their head

article the fifth:
among all the other mystical reasons
is this one:
you will sign believing

hei wakaritenga mai hoki tenei mo te wakaaetanga ki te kawanatanga o te kuini – ka tiakina e te kuini o ingarani nga tangata maori katoa o nu tirani
ka tukua ki a ratou nga tikanga katoa rite tahi ki ana mea ki nga tangata o ingarani

possesses sufficient authority moral weight
to protect your people
from syphilitic sailors whalers rapists rapacious missionaries
assorted riff raff
thrown to the farthest margins of empire

no one will admit just yet
the difference between
the ones transporting & those transported
is mere money power class
that is to say,

smoke, mirrors,
a simple trick of light

what you learn is
that a treaty signed with gangsters
is no kind of treat at all,
will not even provide a fig leaf
to cover your losses
even worse
hindsight will continually tell you
the lesson
has not been well learnt

article the sixth:
so clever of you
to not teach the natives
your tongue
before they signed
i mean, that way
how could they see the
double-crossed-cultural entendre
of 'nu tirani'

surely no accident
it sounds so similar to
new tyranny

Anahera Gildea

Speaking rights

My neighbour is learning te reo. Man he's proud
of his long body of white
flicking hair, conquering language. He doesn't feel
an inch of guilt. Nothing. He feels nothing. Man he's proud.
I've learned my mihi, he says,
where you say your mountain and stuff. He struts
and tells me his mang-ga. Then his moan-a.
He can tell me where *I'm* from too
he's found a site
that can trace my whakapapa for me. Shit that's good.
It's all on the internet now. Your iwi all the way back
to your waka.
Man, he's proud. Do you know poi e? he says.
Prince what's his name. The big guy. You'd like it.

Manaakitanga mutes my thunder,
my eyes wide, short stepping him out of my whare
frightening the fuck out of him, beating
my drums at him. Who do you think you are?
How dare you?
You butcher me. Still,
two hundred years on you insult my house,
pissing your kōrero everywhere.
You represent no one, and nothing
when you speak.

When I speak, my pepeha
is standing
is anchored
to speak with the consent of every single one of my ancestors;
she who nursed koroua through the pākehā fever,

he who married the forbidden,
she who plunged into the rapids to rescue children,
they who carried their pou, from hīkoi to hīkoi
across the motu
so we could speak, I speak, I call,
to the mountain that forged shelter for us,
the ground beneath that remembers every breath
loved here, lost here, fighting
right at your fucking feet.
Their blood the stratum that reaches forward into the future,
accumulating, hardening, speeding
into this exact moment,
into this very person who matters,
it matters what she says, it makes a difference every time,
not throw away, not nothing,
not ever alone.
I am held up, infused, risk taking
with the strength of a thousand hands
who demand, shout or whisper, that I dig in my toes,
that I make them proud.

If I do they surround me,
words, thoughts, hearts,
swell, swell up behind me, feet askance,
bodies wide open to the sky,
voices harmonising in waiata that resound, rise,
rise up,
no longer silent, the bones of Papatūānuku
afford speaking rights to all.

So, good on you, man, for learning te reo.
You must be proud.

Steph Matuku

Homesick

David Howe was our boss, a white guy in his forties who imagined himself as that guy at the end of the *Breakfast Club* film, fist held high, marching along to an iconic Gen X theme song. You could see it in the way he dressed, the expensive plaid shirts open over grungy band tees, the bone carving replacing the tie at his neck, the smooth kicks on his feet on Fridays. He had Pasifika-style tattoos up and down his arms which he showed off when he rolled up his shirt sleeves to indicate how hard he was working. He greeted us with a kia ora which was nice, even if he couldn't roll his r's. He tried.

The last few years had been good to people like him. He had a title now; he was an ally. He was a useful cog in the wheel against racism. He said he was going to start te reo classes as soon as his schedule allowed it, which was pretty much never, but at least he tried.

He had hired Te Rangi and me, the only two brown faces in a sea of white, apart from Dana who was Chinese, by way of Henderson. There was Paora too, and Terry the Samoan who both worked in the basement in Packing, but Te Rangi and I were the only tangata whenua upstairs in the office. We knew we were the diversity hires, but we didn't mind. If the business managed to tick a couple of boxes – women, check, indigenous, check – and we were those boxes, what did we care? At least we were getting paid.

Of course, it kind of sucked getting hauled up the front whenever visiting managers came, to smile, smile, smile and show off our keen browness, and it sucked when people came to us in a flap wanting to know how to do a pepeha because they had a work course and everyone had to do a pepeha, and would it be okay to sing 'Ten Guitars' afterwards?

And it really sucked whenever some politician or broadcaster would be all over the news pontificating about Mowrees being losers and druggies and ungrateful for the pittance the government gave them because they couldn't find work or whatever, with no mention of how colonisation was the creation and the cause.

Our colleagues would discuss the latest tirade in the staffroom, their words floating around and stinging our brown flesh with careless venom. Whether they agreed or disagreed, or thought it was okay because it was free speech, and wouldn't it be worse if we weren't allowed to say whatever we wanted, they didn't seem to understand that it was still Te Rangi and me who were the loser, druggie, ungrateful people being discussed. All Māori get sliced and stabbed by racist rhetoric, no matter if it's specifically directed at them or not. The words find us. They cut us. They force us to heal with a thickened callous. They make our souls harder.

And because we both had long wavy black hair and brown eyes and brown skin, people would mix us up, or assume we were related.

'I'm Ngāti Porou,' Te Rangi would hiss at them. 'Can't you tell?' and she'd jerk her hips from side to side and wiggle her bum at them, and they would back away, eyes wide, not knowing anything about the infamous Ngāti Porou hips but not wanting to admit it, and not wanting to be caught staring at that juicy bum of hers in case she slapped them with a MeToo hashtag.

'If you've got the hips, what am I supposed to be known for?' I grumbled.

'Your triangle head,' she replied. 'Just like your koro.'

She meant my mounga, of course, Mounga Taranaki. I loved that first glimpse of his white-topped peak emerging from the clouds in greeting whenever I flew home to visit. He made my heart leap and brought me home. My hand crept up to my head to check the bones of my skull and Te Rangi laughed, a booming chuckle that made me laugh too, and soon we were screaming and clutching one another, because our existence isn't entirely pain and struggle. It's joy too. So much joy.

It was our monthly staff meeting. The guys from Packing came upstairs, blinking under the flourescents like little owls in daylight. David Howe always had piles of fish and chips delivered for the meeting — he said it was the only way he could make sure we all turned up — and we appreciated it, even though the cloying smell would linger in the office for the rest of the day.

After we'd tucked in, scoffed the lot and thrown away our paper plates into the big garbage bag — 'not the office bins!' trilled Sandy, one of the bossy admin staff who thought she was running the Dow Jones or something — David called on the heads of department to brag about whatever they'd done over the past few weeks, and then asked for any other business. Somebody said something about parking in the garage, and someone else said it was the last day to put your name down for the indoor netball team. A couple of the lads glanced surreptitiously at Te Rangi, and I could tell they were imagining those Ngāti Porou hips bouncing around the court. No one glanced at my triangle head.

When silence finally fell again, David said, 'And to finish up, I'd like to make mention of a very special piece of art that's been donated to the office by the Woodruff family. As you know, they started the business a hundred years ago and as part of our centennial celebrations, they're donating a piece of greenstone named' – he squinted at a piece of paper – 'Tea Ah-tah-fy. Very old, very special. We'll put it out in reception later today.'

And he pulled Te Atawhai out of a shopping bag and put him on the table where the remains of the fish and chips lay so that we could all ooh and aah at the chunk of rock lying in a glass box.

Te Rangi blanched, and swept to the front of the room. I could see her lips moving, perhaps in a karakia, more likely in a stream of inaudible invective, and then she took the box up in one smooth motion. 'I'll put him in reception now.'

David Howe looked after her in some bemusement, but no one said anything. Māori people doing strange Māori things, you see. The rest of the team dispersed, lips still greasy, stomachs bloated. Sandy tsk tsked and threw open a window, waving her hand around as if she was magically disappearing the miasma of fish.

I went out to reception along with Terry and Paora and a couple of others and we watched in silence as Te Rangi carefully laid the pounamu on the shelf that held the awards the business had won over the years, another trophy to add to the rest. Then she said a karakia, for real this time, and Terry sang a song, but only a short one because he was due back in Packing.

'Kia ora, Koro,' I said. 'We hope you'll be happy here.'

'Would you be?' said Te Rangi. 'In a box?'

No, I wouldn't.

We leaned forward, our breath misting the glass. Te Atawhai was a clear forest green on top, with a webbing of yellow and white across the middle that traced his arteries and veins. The base was darkest green, like the deep, deep sea. He looked like a mountain, but not like my graceful ancestor. This mountain was stumpy and squat, stoic in his existence, all crevices and slopes and sharp valleys. When I looked closely, I could see the figure of a lizard, a taniwha, in the grain of the rock, crouched beneath winter tree branches.

'He'd look good all carved up,' said Paora.

Te Rangi gave him a wink and a poke in his soft belly. 'So would you.'

I greeted Te Atawhai every day after that. It was automatic. Say hello to Jillian the receptionist, check for messages, say hello to Te Atawhai, go to office. At the end of the day, I would say goodbye to Te Atawhai and then to Jillian and punch the button for the lift down. Sometimes I would brush my finger over his glass box as I passed, an affectionate caress to keep him happy in his prison. I wished I could touch him. If he was carved and worn around my neck, he would feel cool at first, and then warm under my touch, like a standoffish person thawing from attention. He would remind me of the sparkling tingle of flesh being dunked in cold mountain streams. He would hold whispered secrets and never let them go. He would bring comfort when I held him at night, and in the day, he would be a guardian against the sting of scathing white stares. He would hold the carver's essence too, a meaningful message in every line. The glass box didn't feel like that. Glass was impersonal, cold, rigid.

Te Rangi saw the taniwha in Te Atawhai's grain too. She said it looked as though he was crying. The speckles didn't look like tears to me. They looked like rain, or water dripping from the branches above.

'Those are tears too,' Te Rangi said. 'Sky tears. Mountain tears.'

She coughed and pulled out a tissue to wipe her mouth. She was always coughing these days, and very quick to say it wasn't Covid, she'd been tested. I didn't know if that was true or not, but it didn't sound like a viral cough. It sounded like a cough that came from deep within her, as though something was trying to get out. She threw the tissue in Jillian's bin, and beckoned me over to the trophy shelf to stare at the chunk of pounamu.

'He hates it in there,' she murmured to me. 'He wants to go back home.'

'Don't we all,' I replied. I liked Auckland, liked the sunshine and the busyness and the air of possibility in each new morning. Home wasn't like that. Home was a sleepy provincial town with smothering parochial pride, but it had its charms. The endless black sand beaches, the stirring wind, the cheap parking, and of course, my mountain.

'Look, he's crying again,' she said, pointing at a mark on the greenstone that had the gloss of moisture to it. I looked closer. It did look like liquid was seeping from the stone.

'Condensation?' I said, tentatively.

'If you say so,' said Te Rangi.

We went back to work, but I made a point of stopping by Te Atawhai several times that day, to check if more tears were falling.

The next day, Te Rangi's face was flushed with fever, her eyes dull. The coughing had worsened to a hacking bark.

'You can't work like that,' I said to her. 'Take the day off, stay in bed. You'll make everyone sick.'

'I've got that contract to do,' she said, but David Howe walking by caught the tail end of our conversation. He sent her home then and there, and gave me Te Rangi's contract to finish instead. I didn't mind; he said I could get a bottle of wine from his fridge afterwards.

As soon as they had all gone home, I went into David Howe's office and perused the contents of the fridge as if I was supermarket shopping. I wanted a nice Pinot Gris, an expensive one, but there was only a row of Sauvignon, clearly ones that no one else had wanted, so I took the sixpack of craft beer at the back instead. I wasn't a connoisseur of wine or anything, but the only way I would ever drink Sav would be if someone had poured it down my cold, dead throat.

I finished up my work, gathered my things, turned off the computer and the lights. Everything was very quiet with just the humming of electrical things doing what they had to do.

I went out into reception and put the keys in the office drawer. Jillian had long gone and when I turned to say goodbye to Te Atawhai, he was gone too.

I wondered about that as I went down in the lift. Perhaps David had moved him to another office. Perhaps he'd taken him home.

Perhaps someone else had taken him home.

Te Rangi lived in a suburban villa with a rotating group of flatmates. Right now, there was Wendell in the front room, Theresa and Sonya out the back in the sleep-out, and Doors in the tiny room off the kitchen that was supposed to be a mudroom or pantry or something. He only paid half rent because his room had no windows and the cooking fumes made all his things smell, but he didn't care. He was saving for his OE, although with the pandemic, it was unclear where exactly he was going to go.

I could hear Te Rangi coughing as I made my way up the stairs, armed with a bunch of flowers, the sixpack, and a thermos of the previous night's boilup. There were no bones, but there were still bits of meat floating in it and I'd added some fresh baby spinach to wilt in the heat. I pushed open her door and found her, not propped up in bed with a mountain of tissues on the bedside table next to her, but sitting on the floor, untangling a shoelace knot in a hiking boot. She was dressed in black tights and a big hoodie. A heavy backpack was lying next to her.

She started when she saw me. Her skin had a greenish cast to it, her eyes feverish and yellow.

'Where are you going?'

'For a walk.'

'With boots and backpack?'

'To the bus station. To the airport. Then to Christchurch.'

I blinked. 'What the fuck's in Christchurch? They don't like brown people in Christchurch. I brought you boilup.'

'Thanks.'

I handed her the thermos and she stuck it in the front pocket of her bag.

'When are you coming back?'

'As soon as . . .' her voice trailed off and a look of guilt crossed her face. She didn't have to tell me. I knew.

'Jesus, you didn't.'

She unzipped the bag and dug around inside, taking out a colourful parcel, a soft scarf wrapped around a hefty weight. She gently unfolded it and I reached out a hand and stroked Te Atawhai's cool head.

'You stole him.'

'They stole him first. I'm taking him home.'

'How do you even know where he's from?'

'I don't know. I just know.'

'He's making you sick.'

'Yes. That's why I'm taking him home.'

I nodded. Took out my phone. Dialled.

'Who are you calling?'

I shushed her as David Howe picked up. 'Hello?'

'Hi, David? It's Ana. I think I've caught Te Rangi's cold. I'll be off a few days.' I added in a cough for good measure and said goodbye.

I hung up, smiled at her. 'I'll drive.'

Anne-Marie Te Whiu

Smells like Colonial Spirit

always a man next door
clearing his throat
clearing the land
he has a dream for extensions
a need to renovate
a desire to reshape
his patch of turf
each meter controlled

sharp edges   tall fences   brick pathways
raising his leg
marking his territory
first it is drill   then saw   then hammer

measurements defined
as right as nails
map laid out

bricks hold down the plans on each end
trucks deliver planks of foreign wood
to make his man-shed

I want to burn it down in the middle of the night
                                        and spread the ashes in
                                        the carpark

Nicole Titihuia Hawkins

Tuia

Kia whakarongo au ki te tangi / have you ever sat at the foot of a stage / carved lectern / embedded / pāua / pūkana / clutching / sweat-worn notes / thought / I've never heard this karakia before? / Fingertips / wiri / voice carries / confident / calm / shining eyes / all teeth / just like Jacinda / good intentions / intonations / in all the wrong places / tu-i / tui-i / tuituia.

Tuia i runga / tuia i raro / don't recognise these words / Endeavouring / to be bi-cultural means / speaking / in present tense / colonial violence / It's not just / Tuia / i waho / blankets / smallpox / multiplying in the fibre / dogs raised / taste / human flesh / tuia / tuia.

Tuia i roto / weave / incompetence / peanut slabs / inside wharenui / manaakitanga / taking credit for someone else's mahi / haka / whakaaro / kotahitanga / karakia koha / reproduced / under school crests / whanaungatanga / strategic ignorance / refuse requests / kōrero / kanohi ki te kanohi / poho kererū staff haka / one day / obstruct karakia Māori / thank u next / the settler state must reinforce itself / convert / or kill / Tuia i te here tangata.

Bi-culturalism / busing / brown kids / NZSO celebration / Cook250 / no consultation / Māori are involved / whakaiti Horo's mana / if you mean it / Maisey thinks it's ok / who the fuck are you? / celebrate / rape / theft / genocide / peril of Pacific / peoples / perspectives are important / you say / you don't want to hear mine / stick to the facts / white supremacy / 250 / ka rongo te pō.

The karakia stops / here / a stuck cassette / spewing wet ribbon / all we have left / this pen / in my head / chant / Britney's tune / coloniser / coloniser / you're a coloniser / Ginger's Union Jack / hustles / Scary / Colonisers of the world / Spice up your life! / jammed / repeats / ka / rongo / te / pō / ka rongo / te pō / ka rongo te pō.

Try ignoring Tina Ngata / Moana Jackson / Dr Emalani Case / hyperlinked / hyper profesh email / this is why / she hasn't watched the uplift / stepped on the whenua / Ihumātao / strategy / left it too late / say / sorry / this is not process / you should have come earlier / plan / last minute Māori / process / push you to / put your foot down / paint you / the problem / pass / white / tissue / 2-ply / pity.

Tuia i te muka tangata / Ngāti Kahu / said / no / we won't celebrate death / destruction / colonisation / Cook / didn't land here / didn't discover shit / not welcome at Mangonui / Tūranganui a Kiwa / respectfully refuse / they're your / bloody / guests / you welcome them / descendants of colonialists / Cook / thief / Āe / he tata a runga / he roa a raro / i takea mai i Hawaiki nui / i Hawaiki roa / i Hawaiki pāmamao.

Hawaiki te hono i wairua / colonial violence / at kura / inviting Pania to present / to the kids / Timotimo too / keeping it a secret / you want to be the pātaka / and the wakahuia / you see magic in our mātauranga / and even you know / you can roll those r's / around your tongue / they'll never taste the same / as they do / in my mouth / I've fought 20 years / to feel these kupu / I'll spit them wherever / I like / don't you know who my ancestors are? / I'm a direct descendant of those / you could not kill / this is about / pussy power / big vag energy / I whakapapa to / Rongomaiwahine / no matter how big / your Crown jewels are / I can take it / ki te whaiao.

Why is one man's life more important than the lives of all those he murdered? /

Labour boosts / suicide prevention / 40 million / spends 20 / to celebrate Cook / Colonisation / cause of it all / Millenial Batallion / Māori men / at war / with themselves / ask the coroner / they won't give us our census data / erasure / strategy / 20 million / Lest we forget / hungry children / mouldy state houses / Pākehā process / Te Puea Marae / Pākehā progress / Mob at the Mosque / they are us / unless you're / Māori / pain does not diminish / with time / dismantle the doctrine of discovery / Tahiti to Tonga / Pitcairn to Aotearoa / Hawaii /

ki te ao Mārama /

Tihei! /

Mauri /

Ora!

Vaughan Rapatahana

Rangiaowhia

I pāhuatia ō mātou tūpuna i Rangiaowhia — our ancestors were killed unguarded and defenceless at Rangiaowhia
— Tom Roa, 2014

ko wai e mōhio mō ngā whakapiko o Rangiaowhia?
kāore te maha i tēnei whenua ināianei.
ko wai e mahara ngā tamariki mura?
kāore te maha i tēnei rohe.
ko wai e whakapono te kupu o ngā mōrehu?
he tokoiti noa o ngā tāngata i noho ki waho o tērā tāone.

auē.
  auē.
    auē.

i ngā hāhi hoki,
i ngā hāhi hoki,
te wāhi puaroa; te wāhi whakaruruhau —
tēnei mahi whakamataku o ngā pākehā.
tēnei tārukenga nā ngā tāngata mā.

kia mōhio ki tātou katoa.

Note: At dawn on February 21, 1864, armed cavalry, followed by foot troops, charged into the settlement of Rangiaowhia, whose terrified, startled and screaming residents ran for their lives in every direction . . . Rangiaowhia was a place of refuge for women, children and the elderly. It was an open village, lacking fortifications or defences of its own . . . For the Kingitanga supporters urged to fight in a 'civilised' manner, just like the British, the assault on Rangiaowhia was an almost incomprehensible act of savagery. They had complied with requests to move their families out of harm's way, only for the troops to deliberately target them in the most horrific manner possible.
— Vincent O'Malley, 2017

[Rangiaowhia, 1864

who knows about the murders at Rangiaowhia?
not the majority in this country nowadays.
who remembers the burned children?
not the majority in this district.
who believes the word of the survivors?
only a minority of people outside that town.
alas
  alas
    alas.
in the churches also
in the churches also.
the sacred place, the safe place.
this terrible deed of the pākehā
this massacre by the white men.

we all should know.]

Jacqueline Carter

Our tūpuna remain

Nothing like a lone-standing nīkau
in the middle of some paddock
owned by some Pākehā
to make you feel mamae

Surrounded by maunga
who serve to remind you
that once that whole paddock
had that same sense of tapu

It's a bit like that urupā
in the middle of that reserve
that used to be a papakāinga
till some Pākehā had it burned

So

consider yourselves warned

It'll take more

than a change of name
a chopping down of trees
a burning down of whare

to make us forget

our tūpuna remain

Donna McLeod

Ihumātao

Our first born
is holding the blue line.
Blessed by mana whenua kaumātua, Kīngitanga,
an eviction notice is served.
Houses can be built on confiscated
land, deals have been struck.
Our first born
is their visual might.

Our first born
is still holding the blue line
after the important people have left.
Those left holding space have woken.
They too form a line.
Kanohi ki te kanohi.
Our first born
is their pou.

Our first born
is holding the blue line,
standing fifteen hours,
no kaumātua, no karakia.
We karakia.
We hold him.
Our first born
is our heart.

Our first born
is holding the blue line
with Māori, with Pasifika
full-face challenges of kūpapa, told he isn't

Māori, whakaiti of whakapapa, lectured
on the Treaty. They stand as pou.
Our first born.
Puku stirs.

Our first born
is holding the blue line.
He tells his cousin, who stands before him,
he is proud of her and to be safe.
He texts his sister, as she gathers koha,
to dress warmly and bring him pizza.
Our first born
upholds our uri.

Our first born
is holding the blue line
He carries maunga, waters, whenua, whānau,
grew up knowing
he was born holding te Tiriti.
He stands as Māori
Our first born
is

Our first born
is holding the blue line
He is a child of Parihaka.
His blood runs with passive resistance.
He is a child of warriors
and men of God.
Our first born .
E tū, Tama.

Shelley Burne-Field

Pinching out Dahlias

I said to my husband, 'Māori children have different values, that's all. It's not their fault. You know?'

My husband didn't know. He couldn't figure out, for the life of him, why the school principal had allowed a student to speak to me like that today? He leaned over the kitchen table, pointing.

'That girl called you a Pākehā c**t,' he said. 'At the school! And you just took it.'

I turned away, my forehead hot, and bit into an ulcer on the side of my tongue. Bit it hard. The sting helped bring me back. Back to the taste of tea in my mouth. Back to my husband's beer belly. Back out of the memory of sitting in the school office behind the glass window, shocked, my mouth gaping like a hole in an empty sack. Of being called a c**t by a student . . . but not just any student: Ana had been our daughter's friend in primary school. She'd eaten at our house. She'd swum in our pool.

'Ana's never said anything like that before.'

'They always have it in them,' he said.

'Something happened to her aunt.'

'Jesus, don't make pathetic excuses.'

I never replied.

'Did you give her the yearbook?' His voice erupted, urgent. 'I hope you didn't give her the yearbook?'

I shook my head.

A squint pulled at his left eye, and he rubbed at it with the back of his hand. 'You do too much for that bloody school. And those mongrel kids,' he said, and walked outside. Dust swirled inside the house, before a rush of air pushed it back out the door. The smell of lamb casserole wafted past my shoulder.

My hand rested on the door frame. It was Thursday. The ute pulled away, its tyres silent on our asphalt drive. Not a rasp. Not a hint of roughness. The day had deepened, yet the Hawke's Bay heat continued to throb, rising into a familiar turquoise haze.

In the front garden, my peonies exploded into scented balls of fluff. I felt re-energised for a moment, the day's awfulness forgotten. The blooms had survived the November gusts which had sucked the region dry. Every farmer's prayer for rain shimmered above rooftops and stalked across rutted and parched hills. We were lucky. Last summer, I'd convinced my husband to install a grey water system. It was one thing we agreed on: keeping our gardens the best in our street. The street we'd worked so hard to reach.

The dahlias had soaked up enough moisture to push through days ago, but they needed thinning. Over the years, I'd learned how to pinch out the unruly shoots, leaving the best to thrive. I joked to my gardening group that I'd learned 'the pinch' from my mother's habit of nipping my fleshy upper arms as a punishment for speaking in shops or on serious occasions.

This was Ana's last year at school. She was a beautiful Māori girl. Thick black hair and burnt caramel skin. An excellent player in our top netball team. One of her poems had been selected for the yearbook. Her art blazed out from the cover, too. The painting showed a geometrical flower shape with Māori design, its leaves and thorns embracing the school crest. It was stunning.

'She deserves a copy of her own work,' I'd mentioned to Principal Burger.

'Ana missed the work day, Dora,' he'd replied. 'One rule for all. You and I know that a student won't receive the yearbook unless all fees are cleared.'

Over the 15 years I've worked in the office, the standards have remained the same. No exceptions. Cardboard-framed photographs and yearbooks were often left in boxes, never picked up by families. Or they were occasionally retrieved the following year, after they'd paid.

Knowing Ana, I tried to defend her, but it didn't help that her attitude had been shifting. Over the past few weeks, she'd missed classes – sometimes days at a time. I suppose after today, I knew why she'd been absent, though there was no excuse for Ana showing pure defiance towards Principal Burger, or the school. Or me.

I blame the aunt.

Ana's Aunt Pai, a lawyer, arrived from Sydney at the end of lockdown. She looked the part. A local law practice took her on, but she didn't last long there. Too coarse. I tried to welcome her back – for Ana's sake. After Covid, Pai spoke at our first women's group meeting, but it ended in disaster. She turned up with an intimidating tattoo on her chin, and ranted about re-naming our town streets to Māori names. It struck a nasty chord and I was completely embarrassed, considering it was my turn to organise the speaker. However, it was no surprise to my cycling friends.

'Her family is pure trouble,' Barb had said, straddling her e-bike. 'Re-naming Hobson and Grey Streets – if it wasn't for Governor Grey, there would be no New Zealand as we know it.'

'Agreed.' Judy pushed wisps of hair into the sides of her helmet. 'I shouldn't say this, but EnZed would be a banana . . . what's it called?'

'Republic,' Barb said, matter of factly.

'That may be true,' I said. 'But it's a bit harsh, don't you think? I believe New Zealand has done quite well, culturally. Much better than Australia.'

My friends shrugged. 'It is getting worse and worse, though,' Barb continued. 'Iwi want equality, and then they want special recognition? It's separatist.'

Judy agreed again. She glanced up and down the limestone track and lowered her voice. 'This town is getting far too Māori-fied. Have you seen the school buses?'

I had seen them. So had Barb. Māori designs looped down the sides, woven alongside foreign words none of us understood.

'I feel sorry for you, Dora.' The look in Barb's eyes was comforting. 'You, poor soul, have to answer the phone in the office. How can you possibly be expected to pronounce all of that? And changing street names? I've only ever bought houses on streets with English names.'

'Mmmm,' Judy nodded. 'Me too.'

Barb rechecked the iPhone strapped above her elbow. 'Anyway, I heard that Pai woman can't get a position anywhere in town now. Completely black listed.'

That wasn't all. Not long after she came back, Ana's aunt wrote a letter to the editor which caused *another* typhoon in the community, and this time it swamped the school. Her letter stated ridiculous claims that the school stood down or expelled Māori students more often than other races. Sometimes without any paperwork. The principal and the board of trustees were livid. I answered so many calls during the fallout.

After that, Ana organised a 'black lives' protest outside the school gate. Several students pinned up black fist posters in the common room. The posters came down barely an hour after they hit the walls. Ana had stomped into the office and glared at me across the counter, her eyes narrowed. She'd braided her hair like some sort of American. It was so unlike Ana to be aggressive. She'd always blended in well.

The bursitis in my left shoulder ached, and I bent my neck to the side. An odour of rotting fish blew out of the air conditioner.

'Miss, where did Mr Burger put our Black Lives Matter posters?' Ana asked, breathless, pulling up each white sock so they stretched towards her bare kneecaps.

'The principal told you they weren't permitted on school grounds. We can't be inciting violence,' I said. It rang true. We had to keep some sort of order. 'Radical protests do not have a place here.'

'We were expressing ourselves, Miss! I thought you might understand. Our lives matter. My life matters, Miss.'

'I do understand. I do get it.'

'So, where are the posters? We painted them ourselves.'

'Incinerator. I'm sorry.'

Ana's pupils had sparked then. I saw the change. She spat out the eff-word into the foyer where it bounced off the glass barrier.

'Language, please. I think you're lucky it's near the end of the school year, otherwise, you may get the leaver's form.'

'For protesting racism? Miss, he had no right to rip them down!'

'The principal didn't do it, Ana. He told me to take them down, and I did.'

'*You*, Miss?' Ana's lower lip trembled.

We stared at each other from either side of the counter, both remembering our shared past. Both flicking through the same deck of slides, sorting through the mist of years: Ana and our daughter, Sally, running through our sunflower yellow kitchen, laughing and snatching ANZAC biscuits off the counter, then shovelling them into their mouths. Both skinny kids somersaulting together on the trampoline. Both diving for rocks at the bottom of the swimming pool.

At the end of Year 8, my husband insisted we separate the two girls. I never argued. Especially after Ana introduced Sally to that activist poet. Wild poems about sucking and sex and chicken wishbones in margarine containers. It was a sign. We always knew Sally would attend a private secondary school. The sort of secondary school that shielded her from the wrong types of influence. All our friends' children had been on waiting lists for years. Both Ana and Sally had cried, but I was so pleased to help Ana every day at our local college. I enjoyed giving back to the community.

'*You* tore them down, Miss?' Ana repeated. '*You*?'

My lips pressed together. I wasn't sorry about taking down vile words that stained our student's minds. I wasn't sorry about destroying a sentiment that denigrated my own daughter's life. Sally mattered. Her life mattered just as much as a black person's life. She mattered more than some. Criminals, the gang members, drug addicts, the dishonest people.

A strange shadow flitted across Ana's forehead. A wisp of a frown. As if we were new strangers. As if I hadn't given her a lift every Saturday to the netball courts. As if I hadn't slaved in that office for years, helping *her* — helping every local student, whether black, brown, yellow, purple, or blue.

This 'black lives' thing was completely irrelevant in our part of the world. The mayor had it right when she wrote a post about being 'sick of apologising for being white'. It was about values.

Ana sloped into the office with two of her friends. I hadn't seen her for a few weeks. Her hair was still braided, but today it was tied back into a ponytail. She leaned on the counter to speak through tiny holes in the glass. Her eyes looked filmy and tired.

'Can I please have my yearbook, Miss?'

'You know I can't give it to you.'

'Why not?'

'School fees are still outstanding, dear. You missed the fundraiser workday.'

'So? It's my last year!'

'You missed all those days off school. Other students had to make the effort, Ana.'

'Days off? My aunty died!' Ana whispered. 'You remember her, don't you? She . . .' Ana's voice hitched and she covered her mouth with the back of her hand. One friend grasped Ana around the waist, while the other held her hand.

Died? When had that happened?

Ana lifted her chin. 'She hung herself. A month ago. I found her at the house. Aunty Pai, at the house . . . and, and all you care about is your school fees?'

Did I know she'd passed away? Did I? I thought and thought. Why hadn't anyone told me? Two boys bustled in the door, laughing and then whispering, before they galloped down the corridor.

'Are you listening?' Ana shouted. 'I want my yearbook? Please. I wrote her a poem . . .'

Principal Burger strode out of his office. 'Everything alright out here?'

'No! All I want is the Yearbook, Mr Burger. My poem about my aunty is in there. My painting is on the cover. Please.'

'I understand, Ana,' he said. 'But what message would it send to our core students who actually put in quality time? You've done well to make Year 13, but you've slipped recently. You'd agree with that?' The principal placed his hand on Ana's shoulder. She flinched away.

'You'd agree you haven't given your best this year?' he repeated.

Ana's mouth cracked open. I could see her arms shaking, and her fingers turning white as she squeezed her friend's hand. Why didn't she stop and think about what she was doing? The clock ticked loudly on the wall, and the telephone buzzed into life, making me jump in my seat.

'Why are you so racist?' Ana asked. Her words rasped. They were rough, as if her throat had closed in around swollen vocal chords. As if a foreign object was lodged in the centre of tissue and bone.

'Pardon?' said Principal Burger.

'Ana . . . !' I said when Ana opened her mouth to speak again. For some reason I started to pant. Sweat broke out on my top lip, as if somehow I was responsible for this child's hideous behaviour.

'She's sorry. She really is,' I said to the principal, in a panic. 'They have different values, that's all. It's not her fault.' I turned to Ana. 'I'm so sorry about your aunt, but you can't talk to Principal Burger like that. You must apologise.' The yearbook was suddenly in my fingers, held on top of the counter, waiting for Ana to concede. To push through.

Tears dripped from Ana's lashes. The other girls wiped their eyes too, yet they never backed down. Ana ignored the principal and stepped towards me. She saw me holding the yearbook.

'Please, Miss?' she asked.

I replaced the yearbook under the counter, she watched me do it.

That's when Ana called me that disgusting name. I'm sure she mouthed it, as she and her friends turned and walked out of the office. Just a whisper, mind you. A hiss under her breath. An insult that sparked up from the black stain at her centre. It shot up to her eyes, sharp and full of the future; prodding, accusing. Hot on my forehead. I swear on my dear mother's grave. I heard it. I did.

Well after nine o'clock, I drifted out to the garden to dead-head the peonies and deal with the dahlias. The evening had cooled off. Indigo clouds carved the sky into spiralling waves, reflecting the darker bay below. I caressed the best dahlia shoots then put on rubber gloves and pinched away the rest. Pinch, pinch, pinch. My teeth cut into the side of my tongue. The relief was instant, sending warmth to my navel and lower to the base of me. Pinch, pinch.

Alice Te Punga Somerville

Kupu rere kē

My friend was advised to italicise all the foreign words in her poems.
This advice came from a well-meaning woman
with NZ poetry on her business card
and an English accent in her mouth.

I have been thinking about this advice.

The publishing convention of italicising words from other languages
clarifies that some words are imported:
it ensures readers can tell the difference between a foreign language
and the language of home.

I have been thinking about this advice.

Marking the foreign words is also a kindness:
Every potential reader is reassured
that although obviously you're expected to understand the rest of the text,
it's fine to consult a dictionary or native speaker for help with the italics.

I have been thinking about this advice.

Because I am a contrary person, at first I was outraged —
but after a while I could see she had a point:
When the foreign words are camouflaged in plain type
you can forget how they came to be there, out of place, in the first place.

I have been thinking about this advice and I have decided to follow it.

Now all of my readers will be able to remember which words truly
belong in Aotearoa *and which do not.*

Michael O'Leary

The Burst Pipe

'Won't your boss be annoyed that you didn't
go in today, Hone?' 'No, he knows you're here.
He'll understand. He'll be pleased I've got a man
like you to start work tomorrow' as we drank

ourselves into companionship on the way to
oblivion, laughing and smoking and filling in
the spaces of our past few years since we last met.
Then, suddenly, with drink and remembrance

Hone's mood went angry. 'My father was in
the Māori Battalion in the desert war,' said Hone.
'He used to tell me that despite the whole
terrible time of the war, the years of fighting

and deprivation, the dead comrades,
the worst thing he ever experienced,
far worse than anything fucking Rommel dished up,
occurred on the ship on the way back, eh.

When the troop ship called into South Africa
on the way back from war the Pākehā soldiers
all went on shore leave. But the Māori Battalion
was not allowed on the fucking shore 'cos of

the colour of their skin. He hated the Pākehā
more than the Germans.' When Hone woke
him in the morning with 'Haere mai ki te mahi,'
Paul was glad to be going to work,

even though he had a terrible hangover from
the night before. As the bus pulled
into the Britomart Station it started to pour down.
'Won't be doin' much today,' said Hone.

'Sorry boys,' said the boss, 'but we've got an urgent job,
a burst water pipe over by Dominion Road.
The Council boys have got their hands full
so they gave me a call to see if we could do it.

'Of course, I thought we'd have a full gang,
but if I give a hand I'm sure we'll get it done!
It won't be for nothing either, you'll get a bit extra —
Rua, give me the names of those who didn't turn up!

'I think they'll be collecting their final pay tomorrow.
Stupid bastards, all it means is they have to go
back to Mt Eden to finish their sentences instead
of the freedom of the pre-release work . . .'

The burst pipe was really flooding the whole area,
and a couple of properties were threatened. Hone
& Paul got the job of digging around the break in order
to clear any blockage that was in the pipe.

It was really pissing down, and they got to work
to dig a channel in order to clear the excess water
that was building up behind a stone retaining wall:
half an hour later they had the water running

off down a local road and they had all but cleared
the blockage of clay and mud, and for the first time
caught a glimpse of the broken pipe, they had to
replace about a metre of pipe — can't just cap that.

They got the generator going, went up to the concrete mixer.
It was dangerous using one of these in this weather
even with a transformer, but it had to be done . . . .

Briar Wood

Skep

It’s by-election day. Buzzwords
are out on signs in country towns
Horeke, Mangamuka, Whirinaki.
The harbour’s still as a milk vat.

My bro and I are the first visitors
for a week and possibly the last,
in the trim rebuilt mission house.
Mary Anna Bumby’s home

is honeycombed with notes —
sister of the Wesleyan minister
she brought two hives of bees
stacked with cinders above

and ice below to keep them alive
on a spending spree in Sydney,
delivered safely to Mangungu.
Trees burst with ripe quinces

and rosehips litter the porch
where three thousand tāngata watched
a binding signing of Treaty papers.
Voting on the road, each small tick

skims into a vast blue morning.
Patuone, Heke, Rongo — tamumu
in my ear, tell me your whakaaro about
the sovereignty you did not sign away.

Atakohu Middleton

Wairua

Ka uru mai a Paratai ki te tomokanga o te whare pirihimana o Whau. Kāore i te tino pai ngā kare ā-roto; kāore anō ia kia oti ētehi rīpoata whakahirahira mā tōna pāhi, ā, ki te kore e whakaotia i taua rā tonu, ka rīria ia. Nōna e paneke ana i te taupaepae, ka karanga mai te kātipa kei muri i te tūpapa.

'Mōrena, Tāriana,' tāna kī me te tohu atu ki te taiwhanga. 'Kei te tatari tētehi tokorua ki a koe.'

E poko, te whakaaro tuatahi o Paratai, waiho mai au kia whakaotia aku pūrari rīpoata. I huri ia ki te tāne me te wahine e noho ana i te taiwhanga. He Pākehā te tokorua nei; e ono tekau pea te pakeke, pēnei i ōna mātua ake. He tarau tāngari me te poraka ō rāua kākahu. Mārakerake ana te kitea, i te pōkaikaha rāua. Te whakaaro o Paratai, kua kitea kētia te tokorua nā, engari kua wareware i a Paratai te take.

Kātahi, ka hinātore – ko te tokorua nei ko ngā rangatira o tētehi mōtēra i Te Hauāuru o Tāmaki. I te wā ka tūtaki a Paratai ki a rāua, kotahi tau ki muri mai, kātahi anō ka whakamata tētehi taitama ki te pū i tētehi rūma moe i te mōtēra. Ka tukua a Paratai ki reira nā runga i te whakaaro he kōhuru pea te take, heoi he whakamomori kē. He āhua poto tōna hononga ki ngā kaiwhakahaere o te mōtēra, heoi ka maumahara pai a Paratai ki ō rāua ohorere, pōuri hoki.

Ka hīkoi atu a Paratai ki a rāua me te harirū. 'Tēnā kōrua. Ko Nathan kōrua ko Emily, nē hā?'

Ka tū mai rāua, heoi kāore rāua i kōrero.

'Nō reira,' te āta kī a Paratai, 'e hiahia ana kōrua ki te kōrero mai?'

Ka mapu a Emily me te kī, 'Kāore māua i te tino mōhio mēnā e pai ana tā māua haere atu ki a koe. Nā . . . kei te maumahara koe, i haere atu koe ki tō māua mōtēra i tērā tau?'

'Āe,' te kī a Paratai. 'Ka aroha ki a kōrua, otirā ki te tama hoki.'

Hei tā Emily, 'Āe. He ohorere. Heoi, he nui ngā raru mai i taua wā, ā, kua pau te hau. Kāore māua e mōhio ana, he aha te aha. Tērā pea māu e āwhina mai.'

Ka ārahi a Paratai i a rāua ki tōna tari. Kei tāna tēpu anō āna kōpaki mahi e pupuke ana, e pūkana ana ki a ia. Ko tāna, he whakatītaha kōpaki me te kōrehu i roto i a ia.

Hei tā Emily rāua ko Nathan, i muri mai i te mate ohorere i Whare 5 o tō rāua mōtēra, he kino te haere o te pakihi. 'He nui tō māua āwangawanga,' tā Nathan. 'Mai i taua wā, he raru kei taua rūma rā. Ahakoa kua whakahoua, kua peitahia, kī ai ngā manuwhiri katoa kāore rātou i pai ki taua rūma.' Ka mapu ia. 'I ngā marama kua tata, ka kī ngā manuwhiri katoa ka rongo i te ngunguru i te pō, ka rongo ngā pereti e tukituki ana i roto i te kāpata o te kīhini, ahakoa kāore he tangata, he kiore, he paku aha i reira. I ngā wiki kua pahure nei, i tīmata tētehi raru hou – i te hokinga mai o ngā manuwhiri ki te whare, kua paraketua ā rātou taputapu, kua hūnukuhia ngā tēpu me ngā tūru . . . heoi, kāore he tangata i uru mai – he kāmera haumaru kei waho.'

Ka pātai ake a Paratai, 'Ka tāhaetia ngā taputapu a ngā manuwhiri?'

'Kāore – koirā te mea rerekē,' hei tā Emily. 'Heoi,' tāna tāpiri atu, 'he kino te hua. Ka wehe tōmua ngā manuwhiri, me te tuku arotake whakatakē ki ngā pae tukutuku tūruhi. Ka rere ēnei kōrero kino, me te aha? Ka heke te mana o te mōtēra.'

Kāore a Emily rāua ko Nathan e tino mōhio me pēwhea te anga whakamua.

He kaha a Paratai nō te mau kanohi pirihimana – arā, kāore he paku ohorere ki tōna kanohi ahakoa te momo kōrero. Heoi, nōna e whakarongo ana ki te kōrero, ka pewa.

Hei tāna ki te tokorua nei, 'Nā . . . he aha kōrua i haere mai ai ki a au?'

Ko te whakautu: kua kōrero rāua ki ētehi o ō rāua hoa me te whakaaro tērā pea e hono ana te raru ki te ao wairua o te Māori, heoi kāore rāua i mōhio pai ki ngā tāngata Māori. Heoi, i maumahara pai rāua ki te taenga atu o Paratai ki te mōtēra me tōna āhurutanga. 'Nō reira,' te kī a Emily, 'tērā pea ka mōhio koe me pēwhea te whakatika.'

I taua ahiahi tonu, i puta a Paratai i tōna waka i te taunga waka o te mōtēra, he takanga tērā nō ngā tau whitu tekau. He kanukanu te āhua o te mōtera; i ngā pātū e whakatākōkō ana te peita kahurangi. Kei mua, he māra putiputi ka whakakapia ki ngā putiputi muramura.

Ka puta mai a Emily i te tari i te taha o te taunga waka, me tētehi kī kei te ringa. 'Anei, Tāriana,' hei tāna me te hoatu kī. 'Māu e haere atu, kāore au mō te haere.'

Ka tuwhera a Paratai i te kuaha o Whare 5. Ka pāngia iho tōna ihu ki te rongo o tētehi wāhi kua kore te hauhau e rere mai. Ka ārahi te kuaha ki te rūma noho, ā, mai i taua rūma ka kitea ngā kuaha ki te rūma moe, te kīhini me te rūma horoi.

Ka huri haere a Paratai i ngā rūma katoa, te rūma moe te whakamutunga. Ka noho ia i te taha o te moenga me te titiro atu. He hou te whāriki kikorangi. He turipi whero te whakaahua ki runga i ngā ārai, he pēnei te papanga o te uhi ki runga i te moenga. He toroa kei ia taha o te moenga. He hāneanea te wāhi.

Ka noho, ka noho. Kāore he paku hoihoi i puta mai ki roto i te whare i tua atu i te ngunguru hīrea o ngā waka e hāereere ana ki waho. Kāore he paku aha i puta i te wairua o Paratai. Tekau meneti ka pahure, ka tū a Paratai me te whakaaro he moumou wā tana haere mai. Me pēwhea tana kī ki a Emily rāua ko Nathan?

Mea rawa ake, ka ahu mai i te kīhini te pakūtanga nui o ngā maitai e heke ana ki te papa, me te pakaru o te karaehe.

Ka ohomauri a Paratai. Tōtika atu ia ki te kīhini. I reira ka puare rawa ētehi o ngā kāpata, ā, kei te papa ngā maitai me ngā kapu karaehe kua potapota. Ka rongo a Paratai i tētehi hā kei tōna pāpāringa, heoi kāore te matapihi e tuwhera ana. He kōrero kēhua tēnei, tā Paratai ki a ia anō. He mahi tēnei mā Pāpā.

I te poupoutanga o te rā, ka haere a Paratai ki te whare o ōna mātua. Kua ritāia te tokorua; i ngā wā o mua, he nēhi a Niwa, tōna māmā, ā, he tumuaki wharekura a Rongo, tōna pāpā. Heoi kāore rāua mo te whakatā; e pokea ana rāua e te mahi hei hāpai i ngā kaupapa ā-hapū.

Ki a Paratai, mō te wānanga, kāore i tua atu i ōna mātua. He tāngata whaiwhakaaro te tokorua, he ngākau māhaki ō rāua ahakoa te aha.

I muri i te kai, nō rātou e kapu tī ana, ka kōrero a Paratai mō te raru ki te mōtēra. 'Ko te mea rerekē,' ka mea a Paratai ki ōna mātua, 'he nui taku mahi e pā ana ki ngā mate ohorere Māori, whakamomori rānei i roto i ngā tau, heoi kāore anō kia puta mai tēnei momo.'

Ka pātai ake a Rongo, 'Nā, e hine, mō te mate e kōrero nei koe, ka tukuna te wairua mā te karakia i te wā i hīkina ai te tūpāpaku?'

Te whakautu a Paratai, 'Te tikanga nei, āe – kāore au i reira i taua wā, heoi koirā tonu te tikanga mō ngā mate ohorere Māori.'

I tungou tōna pāpā. 'Ka pai. Māku koe e āwhina.'

I taua pō tonu, ka hoki atu a Paratai ki te mōtēra. I tōna taha ko Rongo e hari ana i tētehi pēke hākinakina. I te tari o te mōtēra, ka tūtaki rāua ki a Emily rāua ko Nathan. Ka tonoa te tokorua nei e Rongo kia noho i te tari.

I te rūma noho o Whare 5, ka huri a Rongo ki tāna tamāhine me te kōrero, 'E hine, me haere takitahi au ki te rūma moe. Tēnā, noho mai ki konei tatari ai. Heoi, he mahi māu. Kia katia te kuaha i muri i a au, purua tēnei i raro i te kuaha.' I tāna pēke i tango mai tētehi rohi parāoa.

Ka tungou a Paratai. Ina katia te kuaha i muri i a Rongo, ka tīhae a Paratai i te parāoa me te purupuru ki te whāruarua i waenga i te kuaha me te papa. Kātahi ka noho i runga i te hāneanea tatari ai.

Ka rongo ia i te matapihi o te rūma moe e tuwhera ana, kātahi ka tīmata tana pāpā ki te karakia. E rima meneti pea te haere o te karakia. Kātahi, ka ngū. Kotahi meneti, e rua meneti . . . he roa ake te ngū, he nui ake te manawa pā o Paratai. Mea rawa ake, i puta mai i te rūma moe tētehi ngawī e titi ana ki tōna ngākau me ōna taringa. Ehara tērā i a Pāpā, te whakaaro o Paratai. Kātahi, ka rongo ia i te reo kaha o tōna pāpā e rere nei: 'E haere, e tama, e haere! Kua wātea tō wairua kia rere ki te kāpunipuni o te wairua!' I pupuke ake te ngawī. I kupi a Paratai me ngā ringaringa ki ōna taringa. Mea rawa ake, ka keremutu te ngawī, ā, ka rongo a Paratai i te pakaru o te matapihi i te rūma moe.

Ka noho pakoko a Paratai i te hāneanea. Kātahi ka āta tuwhera te kuaha, ā, ka puta mai a Rongo, me te kī, 'Kua ea. Kua haere ia.' He ruha tōna kanohi.

Ka hoki a Paratai me tōna pāpā ki te tari o te mōtēra. I reira a Emily rāua ko Nathan e kapu tī ana, me te āwangawanga ki te kanohi.

Ka menemene a Rongo ki a rāua. 'Ki tōku nei whakaaro,' tāna kī, 'koinei te rā whakamutunga o te raru.'

E toru ngā marama i muri mai, e taraiwa ana a Paratai i te takiwā o te mōtēra. Ka tū tōna waka i waho o te mōtēra, ko te tirotiro noa te take.

Ka kite a Paratai i a Emily rāua ko Nathan e ngaki ana i te māra putiputi kei mua i te mōtēra. He koa tō rāua āhua, ā, e whā ngā waka i te tūnga waka.

Ka menemene a Paratai ki a ia anō. I ētehi wā, he rerekē te mahi a te pirihimana Māori.

Anne-Marie Te Whiu

Blood Brothers

I recite a karakia for my brothers
they would prefer I bring kebabs

I tell them about the Hokianga
they tell me about their bills

I explain tangata whenua
they turn up the TV

I dream of Tāne Mahuta
they roll cigarettes

I summon the names of our ancestors
they take their medication

I miss our marae
they put the bins out

Kahu Kutia

kids

When we were kids we used to go riding more. Either with Pāpā or Uncle Tonk. Usually I got my own horse. My brother Hemi would jump on the back of Kereama's horse. Kereama's our cousin. Sometimes we'd ride just up to the next house and back. Sometimes if we were with Uncle Tonk he'd take us further. Up some of the tracks that follow the river into the deeper bush.

Uncle Tonk is our resident kau-boy. If he's home, you will usually find him sitting under the tī kōuka tree that grows next to his house. Sleeves rolled up. Mending ropes and notching wood. There are initials in a heart on his forearm. S.K. Hemi reckons that they are the initials of Uncle Tonk's first girlfriend.

'He did it himself. Before he met Aunty Bubbie, of course.'

When we try to confirm the story with Aunty Bubbie she raises her tea towel and sends us running with a crack.

Uncle Tonk and Aunty Bubbie are a famous pairing. Everyone likes them. If there is mahi to be done at the marae, they can usually gather up the troublemakers to do some of the chores.

Hemi and I are hanging like pegs over the fence in the cattle yard. In the centre of the pen is Uncle Tonk. Wide-legged and looking directly into the eye of a horse. This one's new. Came in yesterday from the next valley over. The horse is still. Head tilted slightly to the left to stare back. I'd probably be shocked as well if I had to face off with Uncle Tonk's mullet. Six thin dreads hanging off the back of his head. The rest is kinda bald.

Aunty Bubbie is watching from the front deck. Gold hoops in her ears. Slippers. Tea towel in hand. She is the first to spot my pāpā coming down the road.

He's driving fast. Fast for him anyway. Puffs of smoke rise from the driver's window every five seconds.

He pulls in the drive and hops out of the truck in a singlet riddled with holes. One hole is three tiny threads away from exposing a nipple.

My dad is not a soft man, but he is a quiet one. At first I don't catch what he says.

'Bull's out. Jumped fence and gone. Uphill.'

Uncle Tonk asks when.

'Twenty minutes ago.'

I turn to Hemi, my eyes wide. I have hated those bulls from the minute they arrived. Uncle Tonk leaps out of the pen. He disappears into his house for a second and returns with his keys. I watch him say something to Aunty Bubbie.

Hemi and I jump on the truck with Pāpā. I don't really want to go, but Pāpā's eyebrows are mushed together. So I know I have no option. Aunty Bubbie is still standing on the deck. She calls out. 'Didn't I tell you those bulls were useless?'

She's got a bowl in her hand and she's been drying the same spot for five minutes. Her eyebrows have invaded the dark line of her fringe.

Pāpā opens his mouth to reply, but decides there's no time to argue with his sister.

Uncle Tonk gives Aunty Bubbie the same look that he gave his horse. She's just amused. She puts down her bowl though and heads inside to the telephone.

We travel in tandem back to our house, six kilometres down the road. Hemi and I are both silent. I try to think of an excuse that might get me out of helping.

Pāpā drops Hemi at the gate that leads off the road to the farm. Hemi's job is to point any reinforcements in the right direction. Pāpā and I continue down the dirt track. Uncle Tonk takes a left and goes to grab our horse. Cindy is another one that he had broken in. I think she resented us all for that.

Pāpā and I stop at the end of the track. In front of us is the gate that opens onto the river bed. The river is a little low from a dry summer. There's only one good swimming hole left at the moment. Across the river the mountain range rises on a steep slanting angle. Bald and creamy green at the bottom, and gradually rising through patchy mānuka and tī kōuka into dense native bush. I've only been up there once my whole life. There's five bulls in sight, grazing on the hill.

'Oh well Pāpā, at least we know where half of them are.'

He gives me a look that says my jokes are not funny. His cigarette from earlier is still hanging from his mouth. Only half smoked. I jump out of the truck and open the gate for him.

Pāpā leaves me at the gate, calling, 'Watch for the bulls,' as he drives past.

'Alright Paps,' I mutter, 'Thanks for the clear instructions.' I close the gate and pace for a minute. Not really knowing what to do. I stop to survey the land around me. I can see Hemi in the distance to my left. Straight ahead is the shed where Uncle Tonk is saddling the horse. My eyes trace the path I usually take from the river up to the house. Halfway down the dirt track then cut right, through three paddocks. Follow the third paddock straight up the middle. There is a natural path traced into the hill that follows all the way up to the gate. At the very top is our house.

My daydreams are interrupted when I see Uncle Tonk heading in my direction. I open the gate and watch him pass through. He directs Cindy across the river and up onto the path that Pāpā has taken.

Pāpā and Uncle Tonk used to work together, setting traps and minding huts all over Te Urewera. They were friends before Uncle Tonk married Pāpā's sister. Uncle Tonk saved his life once. When I asked him how he saved his life, Pāpā just sat there rolling a smoke in silence. Eventually he looked up.

'Uncle saved me from that big taniwha that lives near Crays Creek. It had its claws on me. But your uncle has a way with words, Bub. Sweet talked him into letting me go.'

'Didn't you tell us never to swim there.'

'Well yes, and now you know why. Uncle had to offer my firstborn to get me out.' I can't help thinking that maybe I would rather face off with that taniwha than one of these bulls right now.

It is a while before any reinforcements arrive. I am standing at the gate, watching clouds of stony white fold in and out of the trees on the maunga. I can hear Pāpā tooting his truck horn and the occasional swear word echoes across the valley. I can't tell if that is Uncle Tonk or Pāpā. Eventually I hear sounds from the road and turn around.

Hemi lets in a truck, closes the gate, and follows it down the road. I recognise this truck as one that is always parked on Uncle and Aunty's front lawn. I can't see who is driving but I make out at least five figures in red.

The truck pulls closer and now I know who it is. It's Kereama and his koretake friends! The help that Aunty Bubbie called in on the phone. Kereama is a year older than me, but everyone still calls him Kid. Two years ago he started spending more time with his hōhā cousins and now he has a patch. At 20 years old he thinks he's a real top dog, but they aren't really trouble to us. Kereama still lets me call him Kid sometimes.

He looks at me. 'Girl.'

'Hi Cuz.'

He looks scruffy like usual. The humble beginnings of a goatee have sprouted on his chin. They are all similarly dressed in gumboots and shorts. Three of them have their vests on. The youngest of them wears only a red bandana to show his allegiance, tied snug around his neck. It doubles as a buffer for the clouds of grey dust that fly off the roads this time of the year. Kereama doesn't have his vest on, but he's wearing a bright red shirt. I think to myself privately that I am glad to have them here. If only to distract any bulls that come my way.

I point at the hill and tell Kereama that I saw his dad disappear into the gully that spews out between two folds of mountain. Just five minutes ago. He nods and then all his friends jump out of the truck. I am still watching them scramble up the hill when I feel Hemi come up beside me.

'Reckon they know?' he asks.

'Know what?'

'They should just stand in the shape of a big red arrow. We'll have these bulls back in in no time.'

He grins at me.

Getting the bulls back across the river is hot and laborious work. Uncle Tonk and the horse leave dust trails behind them as they hoof across the treeline. Once a bull is pushed out of the trees, the aim is to direct it straight down the hill, towards a very specific and small opening to the river flats. Then you just have to get them across the water. I station myself in the middle of the river, just upstream. Kick and fuss whenever I need to. Hemi moves back and forward controlling the gate.

The bulls dodge and leap for any clear space. Pāpā prowls across the riverbed in his truck, turning tight wheelies in the dust and bouncing along at an alarming speed. Kereama and the boys are spread right along the hillside. Iraia, one of the older boys, ends up in a standoff with a bull. The bull hurtles down the steep slope, aimed straight for him. He's a big boy too. Hard to miss with his bright red puku sticking out.

The bulls trail shit and mud into the river. When they come close, I hold my ground in the river, and Hemi edges up the line of the fence.

Making as much space as he dares between himself and the bull. When they come through, he jumps for the gate and slams it shut.

After two hours of chasing, the last bull is nowhere to be found. Uncle Tonk disappears off into the hills again, says the bull is probably on the ridge. Kid and two of the boys come down to the river. Pāpā has stopped the truck and is rolling another cigarette.

I wade to the edge of the river and sit down.

'Been a while, Cuz.'

Kid falls down next to me. He's smoking a cigarette.

'So you're a smoker now too, aye.' I think about how competitive we were when we were little. How much I tried to be like him. Still, Pāpā would always go and pick him up when things needed to be done. That always bothered me, that he got to do things because he was a boy.

'How you been?' he says.

'Good . . . You?'

'Yeah I'm all good.'

He glances up at the hills behind us. Towards the spot where his dad disappeared five minutes ago. I don't really know what to say after that.

'There. There!'

Iraia calls out from the bottom of the hill. He is pointing towards the ridge.

On the top of the ridge is the last bull. His front and back legs kick forward and back like a seesaw. I know this one. He reminds me of a bodybuilder who has gone three steps too far at the gym. He somehow manages to keep himself up on bony white legs. This bull is darting from tree to tree along the ridge. Sometimes he stops to stare at Uncle Tonk who is in hot pursuit.

I don't believe that Uncle Tonk was raised by horses, but watching from the ground I understand why they say that. Cindy jumps from side to side across the hill, and Uncle Tonk moves intuitively with her. His feet are braced on the stirrups and his mullet of long brown dreads whip from side to side on the back of his head.

'Here we go,' Kid mutters. He pulls himself up off the ground.

This bull, I do not like. I know it's evil. I jump back in the river and slowly back upstream. Kid comes too.

The bull gets crazier and crazier. Uncle Tonk makes his way down as well, but keeps back as Pāpā takes the lead on the chase. Pāpā has his left hand on the driver's wheel, and his right hand banging on the outside of the truck as he does wheelies across the rocks.

When the bull jumps into the river my heart drops into my shoes and floats away down the river. I look at Kid. He's standing there in his shorts and red shirt. His left leg braced back. Arms bent in front of him like he's gonna push the bull away with his bare hands. His face is blank.

The bull is looking at me and Kereama. Pāpā is paused now, the truck parked up on the river edge nearest to us. I look at my cousin.

'Kid.'

Uncle Tonk is standing riverside now. I see Kid glance at him again. My voice is low and quiet. So quiet that at first he does not reply.

'Kid.'

'Cuz.'

'We need to move.'

'Move where!'

'Forward.'

'Fuck.'

'Ready?'

'Cuz, what are we –'

I slowly turn to look at him, which I know is a mistake. Kereama's feet are sliding on the river rocks.

I turn back to the bull. I realise my heart has returned to my chest because I can feel it rattling in my ribcage. I take a breath. Look this bull in the eye. Bulls can't see you if you stand completely still right? Shit.

The rocks beneath me are unsteady. My lungs take an involuntary gulp of air.

When your chest convulses and suddenly you are filled with oxygen like you haven't been breathing for ten minutes.

My spine arches back and I can feel the rocks slide beneath my feet. The movement attracts the bull. He leaps toward me, little legs pulling against the current.

'HURRRAAAAAH.'

I turn my slide into a twist and stomp backwards into the water. Plant my feet firm in the stones. I decide to go all out at this point. I'm about to be roadkill anyway. I look the bull in the eye and raise my hands above my head.

Everyone moves now, converging upon the bull in the river. Pāpā's out of the truck and standing on the edge. Two of the boys are by the water too. Uncle Tonk leaps forward in front of me and startles the bull towards the gate.

The bull goes in eventually, kicking and screaming. I am still standing in the river. I take a deep breath in and out. I can feel the water lapping around my knees. The current is strong and cool. I look back behind me. Kereama is sitting on the bank again, way up the river. He's rolling a cigarette.

Anne Waapu

a series of never ending beginnings

Ko te pū, te more

Sun drenched whenua, tipi haere
we run
my sisters and I
explore
running fair fingers over brown carvings
we trace edges and curves
not knowing names but
knowing

bloodline

from concrete statues
we sound out rolling vowels
seeing difference but not why
we belong to those vowels
as much as they belong
to us.
We explore all sorts
we run,
we find
connection
— to the smallest objects —
in the biggest ways

te weu, te aka

Silk boxers
on cold hall floors
dusty linoleum scratching
at exposed knees
        dial-a-pōwhiri
        invoked.

My usually truant classmates are here
school resources used
to ensure these school resources
are here
        herded
        into
        lines.
Borrowed school jumpers
adorned with achievement pins
— traded so we all reflect their mana.

Pakihiwi ki te pakihiwi
Tātou tātou ē
rhythmically we pull the waka manuhiri in.
Seats taken, breath caught.
Jobs done.

We sit.
We wait.
It's coming . . .

        'Tin of cocoa, car door!'

Haaaa . . .

Our tapu

tau

moment

bro
-ken
once more.

te rea, te wao-nui

Sleepless nights of visions
Tīpuna calling
wailing ensues
3am
in the urupā
clinging
to headstones
the rain
storms
my pores
cleansing
shielding
loving

My trained brain cries
'This isn't safe!'
shoved aside by
Puku knowing
here, exactly
'Exactly here, is where I am meant to be.'

Wairua connections normalised
clearly I see
Tīpuna safety
trumping 'common' sense
bigger, deeper lessons are pooling:

Remember the influence of example
Dad's epitaph says

Remember the success of perseverance,

Remember the value of time

te kune, te whē

Tipi haere anō
hoamahi side by side
we travel the motu
learnings
with each
lapping tide.
Kitchen table vision
4-wheel driving to hapū land
colonial building meeting rooms
libraries, museums
Koru Club infiltration
back seat taxi gossip
exchange knowing glances
and grins

kōhanga reo
marae
rūnanga
wharekai

Wānanga
weaving them all in

Prisons, in protest, Ministers' offices.

Kaputī-tītaora kōrero

with Our people.

Speeches on stage
some to our colonisers,
exposing the truth   of *their existence*
Most
to ourselves,
realising the
    Truth
    of our
    own
    Power

    Ka whawhai tonu.

te kore, te pō

We collect together
the Gathering

every cycle
needed.

We farewell
we cleanse

we expose wounds
in trusted circles holding space
for exactly this.
We wail, we call
ka tangi

generations healing

reflecting on past
lessons bubble
wayfinding wānanga
bearings aligned
We Are
the Ancestors
Descendants
Whanaunga
re-empowered by constant re-connection
nā te mana o te moana
ka tū kaha tātou
together

we replenish the energies
remind ourselves
We Are
so loved
so precious
given so much

and given so much
and given so much
and now, together
we can give more.
(And just like that)
we spark
another series
of beginnings

ki ngā tāngata Māori nā Rangi rāua ko Papa

Big kuia arm o u t s t r e t c h e d
while small eyes boggle at
e x p a n s i v e   rolling hills

ngā puke tapu

ngā maunga rongo

glistening in the morning rays.

'See this moko,
this is everything
you are.
This is *who* you are.
All your beginnings and endings happen here.

Everything you will be, you will decide.

Everything you will do, you will decide.

And along your way,
you will never be alone,
You can always come
to us, or call.
Just remember . . .
all your beginnings
and endings
happen here.'

Ko tēnei
te tīmatanga
o te
ao

Ko tēnei te tīmatanga o te ao

Hinemoa Jones

Kaikaranga

Dawn breaks
she wakes
to the sound of lists
forming
she gets up with them
ready to march
into the day

two loads of washing
tea towels soaking
lights fire
brews tea
stirs oats
feeds kids

lunches made
bags packed
notes signed
extra socks
get your hat
where's your book

at the door
line up
spit cleans
crusted mouths
pats down
stray hair
have a good day
give me a kiss
come home on the bus

call Rona
bring milk
lemon
for nanny's tea
no excuses
hurry up
pick uncle up on the way

unchains marae gates
unlocks the doors
fills the zip
butters bread
whips cream
cuts fruit
sweeps floors

opens the whare
fresh air
breathe in
greet carvings
brief them on the day's events

sets up chairs
linen laid
mattresses down
round the walls
breathe out

Stack toilet rolls
new towel
more soap
wipe sink
open windows

who's coming
that's right
they came to Eru's tangi
six years back
brought wild pork

$500
Mere's mother lived with them
till she was eight

Whakapapa
Who's their maunga
Where's their river run
Who're their dead
Pare kawakawa
Did we go
pay respects
who spoke
what's that song

Phone rings
It's Hemi
20 minutes
get a move on
no gumboots
good pants
have a shave

Cousins arrive
get to work
set the table
where's Rona
with Uncle
Hemi's late

Cars pull in
There's 30 plus
boil more eggs
defrost a cake
add more chairs
what's that song
who knows the words

Mihi atu
mihi mai

say a prayer
to the toops
ask for strength
to get it right

shoes off
blacks on
stand straight
don't whati
be clear
project your voice

keep them safe
bring them on
weave the words
uplift the tribe
sit them down

Uncle asks
What's his name
the one in the hat
Paora Tai
you remember
Hera's boy
sing the song

Wharekai
call them in
call again
have a seat
serve the tea

Out the back
call the farmer
pig scraps
slippers on
Cuppa tea
It's 9 am

Kai karanga

Marino Blank

Porotaka *Circle*

Ko Hikurangi tōku maunga
Ko Waiapu tōku awa
Nō Rangitukia ahau
My mountain is tall
i am small
my place in this landscape
a piece of gravel
i will complete the circle when i die
my body exposed to the heat of cremation
will reduce to the elements
that are found in the path of exploding stars
and there i will join
my mother the shooting star
my father the one who meanders
my new form hydrogen and helium
will form the next generation of the galaxy forever
Pōmārie *Good night*

Marino Blank

Tūrangawaewae

Waitangi Day 2019

The best calamari salad @ Poppy's in Whakatāne.

The best sweet corn pancakes @ The Emerald Hotel in Gisborne.

The hotel room looked out to the pool.

The landscape speaks, serendipity, I read 'Massey University Press publication by Deborah Shepard' The Writing Life Twelve New Zealand Authors interview with Witi Ihimaera in the hotel room. His photograph displayed in the foyer. Witi spent his school years in Gisborne, the connection.

I walk the main street. Memories come to life with the scent that drifts from the sea. Lists of provisions are discussed in Rangitukia with my grandmother. I am seated on a high stool in the kitchen. She is seated at the table, with my mother. My brother Anton, mother Arapera and I stay with my grandmother in the summer holidays. The kitchen at Whataamo bustles with life. My mother, her eleven siblings and cousins filled my grandmother's kitchen, breakfasts served in five sittings. Whataamo, seventy hectares of pastoral land edges to the sea. The lists of provisions are to be bought in Gisborne a two-hour drive away from Rangitukia. It was hot, it was humid, it was busy.

I am awake in the night. Stirred by an energy, the energy of belonging, the energy of knowing, the knowledge of being.

The scent of the landscape lingers on the drive to Te Puia Springs. My brother Anton and I are visiting to my aunty Keri who lives there at the hospital, iwi-owned. We visit, she is seated, she is well, she is dressed to greet visitors. There is dignity, there is laughter, there is wit. Seated with my aunt in the porch, a breeze flows, the spirit of my ancestors feed my soul. I am whole.

Ariana Tikao

To'u reo

I understand
your rounded vowels
your voice painting pictures
Poetry
    Aglow
My Tongue words
fail me
one big stop
repeated over and over
,,,,,,,,,,,,,,,,,,,,,,,,,,
[To'u reo]
My heart in sync
but words [disappear]
Language is a Tongue mine
                    Pākehā

Remember that time my karanga stopped midway through
in front of the whole of Aotearoa
a glitch
closed eyes, mouth askew
Tongue offline
Even though
I have a degree in you
two diplomas
countless hui in you
scratching my way back
nails splintering
from inside the lid
buried alive
in shame
'Why the hell am I not fluent by now, dumb fuck!?'

Then I remember the words of Hana O'Regan
'He ātaahua te reo i roto i a koe'
(the reo inside of you is perfect)
It's in my blood
Like lava
Like a fire
My Pōua said
mana is a fire
never extinguished

Rangimiria Ihakara

Kua Ngū

Mere sat back into her brown chair and stared at her swollen legs. Her skin was pink under the heat of the wood fire. Over her shoulder her children whispered to one another. They looked over at her and she could just make out snippets of their kōrero.

'We need to keep her safe.'

'But she won't leave.'

'She doesn't have a choice!'

Mere turned the dial and Radio New Zealand flickered to life. They were heading into 'four weeks of isolation' with 'many lives lost worldwide' said the radio host. Mere tapped a finger on the glass of the silver photo frame on the mantle. Manahi. Watch over me Manahi.

'I guess it's inevitable,' said Mere. Her children didn't look up from their frantic murmurs so she left for the bedroom and pulled a brown suitcase with orange lining from her wardrobe. She opened it on the bed and a dust cloud enveloped her. She sneezed.

'Geez, I didn't know it's been that long since I left this place.'

In neat rows she placed her purple scarves, skirts and knitted jerseys. Then her eldest daughter Hine came in and started throwing the rest of her clothes into cardboard boxes. Mere thought to stop her, but mumbled a karakia instead as she got into Hine's car. The 1994 white Honda took a swerve onto a gravel road driveway, avoiding the potholes.

Manahi. Watch over me Manahi.

Mere knew that she needed to sleep in the wharenui of Kura marae, under her beloved Manahi, hanging on the wall by the tāniko tukutuku panel in the right corner. She inhaled the wood and took in the faded photos of tūpuna, the tekoteko on the middle pou. It reminded her of when she was a little girl and she used to hide by the linen cupboard and listen to her whānau sing waiata and dance. Falling into her feather down pillows and double mattress bed, her eyelids grew heavy so she pulled up the black fleece blanket with a koru on it. The warmth sat heavy on her body.

She woke to the cackling of a tūī in the trees behind the wharenui. Something wriggled next to her, her youngest mokopuna Tuhi. She noted the orange sunrise before rubbing her worn hands together and tucking in the bed sheet corners. Tuhi scrambled away to join his cousins and she looked up at Manahi.

Standing outside the wharenui, a whoosh of cold air fluttered past her cheeks. She closed her eyes to take in the decomposing grass and the rushing awa next to the wharenui.

Mere arched her back and inhaled. Her elbow joints were stiff from scrubbing the ceiling and her thighs burned from bending to reach the cleaning bucket. As a child Mere was taught the marae roles so she knew what she had to do while she was here. She rubbed her elbows and thighs to cool the aching.

Looking around the marae, Mere was reminded of her māmā Ngāwhetu and her long black hair. Ngāwhetu the queen of karanga and forever remembered as a wahine of beauty. As far back as she could remember her māmā had worn a moko kauae.

Mere remembered the words of Ngāwhetu's karanga and how they would flow off her tongue, her voice powerful, clear and direct. She wandered the marae grounds and thought of whether she was living up to her mother's legacy of karanga. Ngāwhetu had never seen Mere's karanga. Te Arawa women aren't allowed to karanga until their mother or older sister has passed on.

As a child Mere was taught the marae roles so she knew what she had to do while she was here.

Her moko Puti joined Mere at her side. They picked the purple berries and squashed them between their teeth. Mere had no shoes; she enjoyed the damp of Papatūānuku on her toes, the grass tickling her soles.

Through the windows, Mere peered at Hine in the wharekai. She thought of how she'd always made an effort to kōrero to her eldest daughter, to kōrero about life, the colour of the sky, the sores on her fingers and of course Manahi. Hine was loud and hardworking, just like her father. She remembered the time Hine came storming through the wharekai to the kitchen. Both doors had swung open and nearly took out the kuia standing right behind them.

She was like a tornado. 'Clean the bench, wash and dry those dishes! Why are those plates over there, they need to be over here. Start getting the cutlery ready to serve dinner.'

Mere knew Hine was not the type of woman to want to carry on her legacy of karanga but she was proud of the role she had given herself.

Mist lay wrapped around the trees in the front gardens. The tune in Mere's head was interrupted by her moko Waiiti and partner Hau yelling at each other.

'I don't have any more money left, Hau.'

'Why not? I only gave you my card the other day! I need some cigarettes.'

'Well, we can't afford any can we . . . 'cos you were laid off!'

'It's not my fault I lost my job! Where's all my money gone then?' The door slammed.

'Well, you've been drinking every day since lockdown started. How do you think the kids are being fed?'

Mere had seen Hau's orange and blue uniform from the meatworks on the back seat of their car. Now Hau and the others were spending their evenings in the meat shed by the wharekai. Through the cobwebbed windows Mere stared and watched them empty bottle after bottle. Most nights they wouldn't even make it to their beds.

Ngāwhetu the queen of karanga and forever
remembered as a wahine of beauty.

Mere got up and walked onto the mahau of the wharenui. There was a darkness infiltrating her mood. It was just her on the mahau now and she realised that there was no one to call to, no one to welcome onto the marae, no one to lament the death of anyone. There was nowhere for any uri to express their pain. The sound of her mokomoko laughing and running across the ātea distracted her as the words of her call scrambled through her mind.

She yelled at the mokomoko, 'Kāti! No running across the marae when there are whaikōrero!'

Her moko stopped playing and looked back at her, their kui, and ran off to find their parents. She continued to watch the entrance to the marae. The sun dipped over the mountain onto the front of the marae.

The air was afire with the sound of tūī, kea and kākā. Mere watched the kaumātua give their orders to present in an orderly fashion and the people darted around as cars filled the car park. She was strong in herself, as she had rehearsed this karanga for years – a celebratory karanga to welcome her cousin Aio's future husband Kiwa and his whānau to the marae.

The nod came from the paepae and her heart started to beat faster. Blood rushed to her cheeks and her nerves stumbled her through the first line. Mere was shocked at how her voice carried through the air and echoed through the trees as she called on the Ihaka whānau to welcome them. Then before she knew it, her job was done and the speeches could begin.

As she took her seat, she felt the eyes of someone on her cheek. A fit young man with a strong jawline, big lips and brown eyes was gazing towards her. Her cheeks burned, he wouldn't stop looking at her and she felt hot under his stare. When the time came to harirū, Mere stood and with a brisk pace headed toward the wharepaku.

It was just her on the mahau now and
she realised that there was no one to call to

The guitar was pulled out after the ceremony and kai. Mere heard her note and led a trio of iwi anthems. The drinks were flowing and whānau were dancing, singing and eating. Mere noticed the man who had been staring at her earlier coming towards her. He was wearing a fine brown hat and black suspenders hooked over the shoulders of his white dress shirt. His shoes reflected the light of the wharekai they were so flash. She turned away and placed a hand to her cheeks – they were hot – and then jumped a bit when he touched her shoulder. The man cleared his throat and introduced himself. He was Manahi, the best man for Kiwa. His eyes dropped and he told her of how in awe he was of the song she had sung to welcome them to her marae. Ever since hearing her karanga, he had wanted to talk to her. Mere averted her gaze but he grabbed her hand and she took in a quick breath as he guided her onto the dance floor.

Her eyes affixed to the entrance to the marae and Mere began to sing the celebratory song she remembered from the day she met Manahi. Her mokopuna heard her karanga and gathered around, she felt their hands on her shoulders and the curves of her back, offering comfort.

The heartache of watching her mokopuna fight with each other had left a heavy feeling in her chest and she'd realised everything she'd lost. Only karanga reminded her of who she was, a strong wahine Māori. Karanga was the gift she liked to share with the world, her spiritual connection to those she had lost. Through her call she grieved for Manahi.

Mere wiped the sleep from her eyes. Another day and the sun no longer looked so beautiful but pulled at her heart. She couldn't hear the trill of that tūī, the birds had stopped their singing and the grass was frosted over.

Mere had received many kaumātua packages from the iwi and these were uplifting but she yearned for the comfort of her cousins and friends. They would understand how she felt sitting here with the melody of her song yet to be sung. Instead she felt the plastic of a broken white chair beneath her fingers and looked on as her kids and mokopuna drank at night and slept most of the day. She shook her head and went to bed.

Karanga was the gift she liked to share with the world, her spiritual connection to those she had lost.

The next morning Mere took her time getting ready. Something was urging her to dress up and so she pulled over the wool of her favourite purple and black jersey and felt the warmth of her black stockings on her toes. She dragged her armchair to the mahau of the wharenui and relaxed into the folds as her mokopuna tuarua ran around the marae grounds playing, just like she used to. Mere motioned to Hine and her moko to come and sit. She wanted to tell them a story. Hine groaned and said that she was sure she had heard all Mere's stories before.

Mere ignored her and called over the rest of the whānau. 'E noho.' She paused and waited for them to gather. 'Let me tell you,' she said, 'of the day I did a karanga to our Kuini Māori on this very marae.'

'The Kuini Māori came here? To Kura marae?' shouted her moko Te Kahu.

'Her visit was to maintain whakapapa and unity between our iwi.' Te Kahu looked up at her.

'I spent all morning choosing a skirt to wear. But of course I chose the one your dear Koro Manahi gifted to me. For a whole year your Koro must've saved his pennies from the sawmill to buy it. It had black pleats and red, black and white stripes at the waistband. Your koro told me it was made for his Queen and I was to go out there and represent my tūpuna with my mana and pride.' Mere looked over at the empty concrete. 'By 2 pm the car park was full to the back fence at that treeline. Then a flash car pulled up and parked by the entrance of the marae. A man opened the doors and the ope surrounded the car in a protective embrace. Then they walked towards the marae.'

The Kuini Māori came here?
To Kura marae?

Mere's stomach twisted as she remembered the emotions of that day. 'I was so nervous that even my forehead was sweating and my throat closed up. Then Aunty Wai pushed me forward from behind and I knew it was a sign, I had to begin.
'Haere mai rā te Kuini Kahurangi o te iwi Māori e
Te hākui Te Atairangikaahu e
Ki runga i tēnei marae o Kura e
Haere mai, haere mai, haere mai rā.'

The grounds of the marae were silent as Mere's whānau listened to her. Karanga was her legacy and she had been lost without it during her stay here.

She continued, 'I've appreciated your love and support to protect me during this time. But my wairua isn't right here. I'm becoming tired and I'm ready to go home.'

Her whānau started screaming at her. 'You can't' and 'We're here for you!'

Mere stood. She told them that was enough kōrero for the day and she would pack her bags in the morning and expected Hine or one of her mokopuna to take her home.

As she stared up at the roof of the wharenui Manahi again floated into her mind. Then just like that first morning, she heard the call of the tūī and looked around to see all the beds were empty. She thought that they must still be drinking.

'Koretake,' she muttered to herself and in her sheets and pulled on a grey tracksuit.

Mere's hands trembled as she rammed kākahu into her bag and then she stopped for a moment and could hear the murmur of singing coming from the kitchen. She could tell who it was from the tone, her daughter Hine, doing a pao, a karanga practised to let the manuhiri or whānau know when kai is ready. She listened to the words of the pao and realised they were for her.

She listened to the words of the pao
and realised they were for her.

Mere entered the bright-lit dining room and her mokopuna started beguiling her with her own songs. She was guided to a seat with a scribbled note with 'Kui Mere' on it. She sat upright as a sense of pride wriggled from her toes and all the way up to her hair. The table was covered with kōura, creamed pāua, raw fish, mussels and boil up with watercress and rēwena. Her hands gripped her fork and she realised they were all of her favourite dishes. One of her mokos stood and said karakia. Although she was unsure what this was all for, her wairua was starting to feel normal again as she watched her whānau talking and laughing and helping themselves to the kai.

Mere put her plate to the side and her puku pushed up against her waistband. Tuhi, Mere's piri pāua mokomoko came over to Mere and asked her to teach them to karanga and Mere jolted with a wave of electricity. The whānau flowed out onto the grass and Mere called all her moko girls to her, Tuhi, Puti, Te Kahu and Waiiti. She told them the story her māmā told her about the beginnings of karanga and said that the words for karanga come from deep within the heart and then the melody follows. Mere asked her four moko girls to each practise a karanga welcoming manuhiri to their birthday. The words took her back to Manahi's last birthday.

He was sitting on the old chair in their lounge. It was his eightieth birthday and as the speeches came to an end, Mere knew it was time for her karanga. His shining eyes looked at her as she launched into a song she had never sung before. It spoke of their travels together around the country, the birthplaces of their children and her mokopuna. The words flowed from her heart and a waterfall streamed down her face. She wished she could forever keep that moment of him sitting there at the main table, wearing his favourite buttoned black suit, chequered red tie and white dress shirt. His mouth was wide and laughing, the same smile he'd had for her the first day they met.

The crackle of the radio sounded behind Mere's shoulder. The strict measures of the government had got a hold of the virus and a decision had been made to go from alert level four, to three and then two. Mere sighed at this announcement. She had been looking forward to returning home, but Hine said that she was still locked up for her own protection.

Mere wondered how her group of kaumātua were doing. She would call them as often as she wanted, but it wasn't the same. At times, she would sneak down to cousin Pare's house and sit by the fence and they would talk about how they couldn't wait to play housie.

The radio was on and the host announced that they were back in level one. Mere gripped her hands tight. She was allowed back into the world again. She folded her kākahu back into her suitcase and cardboard boxes and told Hine to take her home.

the words for karanga come from deep within
the heart and then the melody follows

The next morning, Mere put on a long floral dress with warm black stockings and flat black shoes. She felt for the length of her long hair and tied it into a plait. She wrapped a black scarf over the top of her head to keep her ears warm and waited on the porch for the kaumātua van.

The dark blue Toyota grumbled up her gravel driveway. As the door slid open her throat dried up. All her cousins and friends were in the van and ready to hit the town together. Suddenly, the van took a wrong turn and instead of heading towards town it began to trundle down the gravel road to Kura marae.

They slid to a stop and then Mere asked Ariki the driver why he had stopped there. One of the kaumātua opened the door and just as Ariki was about to answer her, a karanga began, one of the kaumātua kaitiaki. Mere walked to the front and with her head held high she replied.

This was Mere's sense of belonging in this world, her gift of karanga that connected her to her whenua. As the still air around Kura marae was pierced by her powerful voice she walked down to the mahau.

As she called she could see her Manahi. There he was at the door of the marae, looking just as she had always remembered him.

Mere was at peace once again.

Frazer Rangihuna

Piro

I'd be winning if it took me this long to stink! Hey, I'm not saying I'm a paru fulla or anything. I'm just saying if I wanted to be one of those breethas who sprays Lynx Africa up his t-shirt sleeves when his pits stink, I could be. Especially now that my Nan — the only person to get close enough to have a sniff — has gone to a rest home.

Anyway, I'm not talking about how people can be stink. What I'm talkin' 'bout is that kānga piro, rotten corn porridge stink, and it's making me all hōhā! Because every time I visit Nan she's forever saying this kind of kānga piro karakia. If someone gets her just a bowlful it will make her whakaaro pai, she reckons, and then she might want to think good things about ngā tāngata katoa.

So that's why I'm out at the stream every day, pulling her old kete filled with corn cobs out of the water. Hoping for a hit of what my cousin says — he's heard — smells like dick cheese.

I never wanted to be a kānga piro DIYer. I've been searching high and low at the Flea Market every Saturday since there was a rumour this kuia was dealing frozen blocks of it out of a chilly bin. Turns out though, she was a kuia but an Asian one, and the stuff she was selling was some shit called congee. Even my horiest uncle was no help. He just slurped a kina tongue into the gap where his front teeth used to be and reckoned, 'Ew, Boy. How would I know? I don't eat that shit!'

So finally, I had a nosey online. I asked Kōkā Google. There were instructions on the Rotten Corn Fan Club page on Facebook and I got some tips off Stuff, too, from Matua Marty, the rotten corn man. How shame it must be to be him, I thought, but then I thought, you can talk, Kīngi Piro!

At home, Mum is on the phone, again.

'Does she need anything?' She stretches the phone cord. 'Will she let me visit her yet?' She lets the phone cord go. 'OK, let me know when she does . . . straight away. Mā te wā. I said Mā te — oh, never mind.' She hangs up then walks over to the bench. Rubs at scratches in the stainless steel.

And I'm listening to my boy Tupac in my headphones with just one bud in my ear so I can hear if I go flat because Māori are supposed to know how to sing. It's Tupac feat. Me and we're rapping about the shit we're going through and about injustice and I'm mouthing the words at Mum's back until she turns around with this look on her face that says I know shit about injustice.

'Knock, knock,' a voice says without knocking. It's Aunty. She sits at the table and with her eyeballs she pushes me over to the kettle. 'Hey, why so quiet, Girlsie?' she asks Mum.

'Just having a bad day.'

'Oh, how come? Why's the house so quiet? Where's Te Kuini?'

'In a home.'

Aunty winces, sucks in air between her lips. It makes a sore, whistling sound. 'But the last time I saw you, you said you were only thinking about it.'

'I feel bad enough as it is, so if you're going to make me feel worse then buzz, alright.'

'Alright, alright. I just don't get it, that's all.' She looks over at me now lip-synching Whitney. 'And look at that one's face! Can't you see he's hurting? Aren't you, Boy? I remember when she used to push you down the street in your pram and the second someone's jujus kissed you she'd hiss, reach for this soapy flannel she kept in a plastic bag and she'd wipe their germs off, right in front of them! Me included. You were her little prince, nē?'

She's looking at me like I better agree because she has even more embarrassing stories she could tell. Straight away I think of the whānau favourite – when I forward rolled in dog shit. So I just nod. Tuck the sweaty hair at the sides behind my ears.

At the stream there's something black in the water. Something that catches my eye then it disappears and then that episode of River Monsters comes back to me. When those eels are corkscrewing their way through a cow dropped dead in the water – and knowing Nan's huckery old kete wouldn't have a shit-show – I start to wander around, looking for something to protect it, when something else says,

Over there!

And I say, 'Over where? I can't see shit.'

And in this doongie voice it says, Open your eyes dummy, you're looking straight at it!

It turns out to be an old fishing hand line and I know just what to do with it. Pulling the nylon loose, I start to weave it through the holes in the kete. In and out, in and out and what I thought was in and out. Yeah, Aunty's right. I am Nan's little prince and Nan's a hāti lady except when it comes to kānga piro, she loses it. When she's eating it that haka action comes to mind – the one I've seen her teaching – where she curls and wriggles her fingers by her mouth as if she's eating someone else's mana and she forgets about her own.

Weaving done, I imagine a taniwha's clenched teeth.

Cleaned up I go to see Nan at the rest hole. I can see she's sitting in her armchair. Her back is to me but I know it's her. I can see her toetoe hair is sticking up above the headrest and even if I couldn't see her I'd know she was here, know she's still with us because the air is warmed by her Oil of Ulan. As I get closer she unhitches a poi that was tucked into the side of her track pants. She swings one poi over her shoulder then thumps it on her back. And again. When she sees me she stops.

'So, Darling, have you found any kānga piro yet?'

'Nah Nan, not yet, but I'm still looking for it everywhere, eh.'

She does that thing all of the Ngāti women in my life do so badly; she tries to hide her disappointment.

'I will find some. I promise.'

'That's what I'm holding on for, Darling! Did I ever tell you my dearest Aunty loved kānga piro as much as I did? She lived next door to us so when I was cooking it the smell would be this kind of smoke signal for her to come over for a kai. It was one of the few times my mongrel uncle let her go anywhere alone. He hated the stuff! He said that if she eats that crap then he better watch his back or he might be next. We'd laugh about how safe he was since we'd never, ever eat snake! Auē, my dear old Aunty.'

In the silence that follows I look down at her hands. Don't realise I'm playing dot-to-dot with her age spots until she speaks again.

'And another thing. Your mother. Tell her to stop calling every day. Tell her I'm still alive and not to worry about me.'

And I want to tell her to try and stay alive but I also don't want to jinx her. My mind wanders off to her kete in the water and the little white puffs of particles are the little parts of herself she's losing. So the big things haven't killed her, not her heart problems or this rest hole – yet – so what about the little things then? The little things that build up and finish old people off? If not eels then what about those tiny maggoty things? Are they even things?

I tell her I have to go. I rush off home and back to the stream.

I'm glad there's still enough light outside to see the kete is all there. Sitting back on the grass I look over at the water, the heads of trees rippling on its surface, the way the reflection of pines would ripple up the windscreen as Mum reversed the Morris Minor out of Nan's driveway. When I'd sit there and wail, turning into dry sobs when my angry, Drum-smoking uncle said he'd put me under the tree to cry to the acorns if I didn't shut up. And after I'd performed to the acorns I'd go inside, pull down Nan's orange-tasselled bedspread and snuggle into her.

Before I could say anything about wanting to go home she'd pop a blackball lolly in my mouth. We'd do crosswords and with these wide, loopy letters she'd spread my four-letter guess across a seven-letter space. Sometimes Nan and I used to fight – well, I fought with her, really. Just the thought of my brother at home, the small of his back, sighing into the extra space in bed was enough to get me going. An almost breathless Nan would ring Mum and say, 'Come and get this blimmin' kid, he's driving me nuts!' But we'd always become friends again by the time Mum arrived. Nan would meet her on the doorstep, look her up and down and say in Māori, 'What are you doing here? Go home.'

From my backpack I take out the rest of the roll of nylon and start to weave all over my old weaving again – it makes all of these little scales as I go. Threading, threading, the kete is now this kind of glittering, robo-fish. And again I tell myself why I'm doing this and how I might not get anything for it – even though I've suffered – and how that has to be OK. Although, now and then I think about what my saint name might be.

I step out into the next blue day, so bright I have to squint. The sunlight has turned a tiny speck of dust on the end of my eyelashes into this fragile green bubble floating before my eyes and I reach out my hands, not knowing if I have to try and grasp it or just let it go. But when I turn my back on the light into a less light place where I can really open up my eyes, really open them, the bubble has left without me having to do anything.

It's dark by the time I get home. Mum has done mince two ways this week and tonight makes it three ways.

'Hey Ma, I've got some good news.'

'What?'

'I said I've got good news, about Nan.'

'Yeah, what?'

'She wants you to visit her, maybe in a few weeks.'

'Oh, I'll ring and ask if she needs anything!'

'No, no, no, no, don't do that! She just wants to see you, that's all.'

'Oh, OK. Far out, I didn't think she'd ever want to see me again . . . after.'

'Well, she must be over it.'

I actually feel older – say, sixteenish – when the corn smells the way it's supposed to. And I think if this is what dick cheese smells like, my cousin needs a hot wash with a steelo pad. To my Nan it's gold, though, so I try to get over myself – tie her scarf over my nose and I sniff hard where she had patted the rose-scented powder on her neck. The mushy kernels come off the cobs easily.

It's Saturday and Mum says she's put on a bra and I've put on my least hori t-shirt. Sneaking into the kitchen I go to the back of the fridge where I've hidden the container of kānga piro and I put it in my backpack along with a small bottle of cream. From the cupboard I take out some sugar and wonder about the kind of hiding I might get for lying to Mum, or how Nan might see Mum and do a Matatini performance, starting with the whakawātea. If Mum said I couldn't visit Nan anymore, I'd die, somehow. I don't want her to be one of those old ladies in that rest hole who hardly see their mokos. Who just get sent those grainy print-outs of photos I've seen them stick on their wall. On the drive over, I'm willing to say the stink is me if Mum asks. But she doesn't say anything. She lets me change the gears so I push it up into third.

When we're walking down the hall at the rest hole I'm still not used to the smell. I want to do the dabbin' dance but to really jam my nose into the inside of my elbow but I'm too worried about Nan's reaction. So I just walk behind Mum, my head floating above her shoulder. Nan is talking to some old Pākehā man wearing war medals. He's pissed his pants. He's not even calling Nan by her right name. She looks over in our direction, first at Mum and then at me. When our eyes meet I plead with her with my face and she tries to look less shocked – isn't exactly putting on a pōwhiri for Mum but she's not cutting her off either. Well, not in a whāngai cousin whose mamae made her stand up at the marae, only to be told that she'll be mamae alright if she doesn't sit down again way. But close.

While Mum and Nan are stuttering sentences at each other, I think it's safe enough to go and look for a kitchen, where I blitz the kānga piro in the microwave for a minute at a time. I'm not sure if it needs any salt but there's no way my lips are going anywhere near what now stinks of hot vomit. So I just sprinkle it with sugar and swirl cream over the top. Suddenly it feels still in my head. Everything that had been beating against my skull has stopped. This has taken a few months out of my life I'm never going to get back. I could've been getting myself liked for my flash comments or likes for one of those pics I post now and then, where I look shy but skuxx at the same time. But I've been making – making – kānga piro!

Nan is having a lie down in her bed when I get back to her room. Peering around the door frame it seems all is forgiven. Mum is sitting next to her, her hand on top of Nan's and both women are smiling. When I walk in I'm hiding my hands behind my back, holding the bowl of kānga piro, waiting for the right moment. I'm not sure how to do this, what style I'm going to go for other than knowing from past mistakes that whakahīhī styles is never the way to go, when Nan sniffs at the air.

'Hika, what is that smell? It can't be!'

'Surprise!' I shout, bringing the bowl out in front of me.

She takes the bowl from me, but she's not hoeing in the way I've dreamed. She doesn't even eat. I get the feeling she's waiting for someone, someone she's missing. She just sits there for a while, seasoning the kānga piro with her tears.

Tayi Tibble

4 The Dead Homies

We cut watermelons on the doorstep while the uncles were smoking imported cigarettes and cheap meats. I was thinking about when we were small enough to run blind between what we thought was wheat and speckled wildflowers and I remembered the poor Bratz doll

one arm, hair hacked, green felt mono, that we buried a week after we returned from the dead up north, still haunted by the tears that ripped our parents' faces, we prepared for our own funeral. We didn't know anything then. We were protected by witchcraft.

Several lengths of daisy chains. A palmful of Papatūānuku. A salt circle. Fake cries. Neither of us knew how to give eulogy so we sang the same old Māori songs twice. Trying on emotions the same way we tried on our mothers' makeup. Now the grass

is rarely neglected and if it was it would barely graze our waists. And we wear lipstick in ripe colours that our mothers never cared for. Now we can care for them in small ways, cut the fruit and feed our cousins. And the day it actually happens, we can always sing those songs.

James George

Whenua to Whenua

Vick is quiet for most of the drive down. A couple of times she touches the buttons on the dash display to flick some music on, but as soon as she does she seems to want to talk over it, so I turn down the volume to listen and she goes quiet again.

'Vicki? You okay?'

'What do you think?'

I flex my fingers against the steering wheel, glance to where the reflection of her eyes skitters among the sunlight and shadow on the windscreen. We pass a couple of furniture moving vans perched in driveways, moving in or out I can't tell.

We stop at the supermarket for essentials that Vick thinks Ella won't have, a list she's fingered to a crumple since we got the light rail to the airport up home.

'I don't think she's eating right,' says Vick. 'On top of everything else.'

I should've swallowed some painkillers before I started driving. The light is harsh here. We got up early for the flight down, picked up the rental car on arrival, stood by the plastic flowers in the agency's showroom, glancing through the tinted glass at Vicki packing the wagon I'd ordered, me passing the time of day with the sales woman. When I mentioned where we were headed, the woman stared blankly at me for a moment, then at the other sales person next to her. Her face stiffened.

'You'll need the full insurance cover,' she said, reaching for a stern looking little booklet on the countertop. 'And here's a list of all the places and circumstances you won't be covered for. You need to read it all the way through, initial each box and sign it at the bottom.'

'We're not going all the way,' I said.

'Even so. We've had cars just disappear.'

'Christ, we're not going to bloody disappear.'

'No. I mean —'

I signed, flipped the pen onto the counter. It bounced off onto the carpet.

'What was all the conversation about?' said Vicki when we set off in the wagon.

'Just small talk. Let's make tracks.'

When we get to the supermarket though, it's a shock. Shelves half empty, labels trumpeting *'Limit of . . .'* when there's nothing there at all. Vick stands in the middle of an aisle that looks like it's been attacked by rats. She just circles with the list in her hand, the top of it tipping over.

'Half of what Mum will need's not here,' she says.

I nod.

'I said we should've stopped in town when we picked up the car,' she says.

I nod again.

'I said that, didn't I,' she says.

'Vicki,' I say, 'it's okay. How about we head to the coast, out to the house, and I leave you there with what we bring and you can stay with your mum while I head back to town and pick up what they don't have here.'

'That'll take you two or three hours.'

'Okay. I can live with it.'

'That's time you don't have to spend with her, I guess.'

'That's not it and you know it.'

Vicki turns away, the list gripped tight in her hand. I can see the skin blotching red.

'I'll start at the other end of the shop,' I say. 'Let me memorise a few things.'

She passes me the sheet to glance at.

'Sorry,' she says. 'You know. It's just —'

'Yeah. I know.'

'Shit,' she says.

I grab another trolley. In five minutes at most, I've put mental crossouts through just about everything. When I was half a dozen aisles from Vicki I could still see her through all the gaps in the shelves, shaking her head at the overhead signs that were just empty promises. Like she could change them, change everything. Last night in the dark she lay there, just the quiet wariness of her breaths, then she started talking to the darkened ceiling about Ces and Ella and a bunch of people I know only as verbal sketches and shadows, names that crisscross Ella's rambling family stories like rivers that have lost their way. She mentioned some real estate guy named Greg, who stood at Ces's letter box in a pressed blue suit and vermillion tie, and his offer to buy the house and how Ella said, 'Pop, maybe we should hear him out,' but old Ces just hunkered down in that squared way of his, in the chair with the little table next to it with his tobacco and papers and his tins of boot polish that smelled like whiskey and old motor oil. That was the end of that. No one bothered Ces or Ella about the house again, at least not to her face, until Ces was gone to glory and all the agents who had left smiley flyers in her letter box began showing up again in person.

'The astronomical sums they were quoting,' said Vicki, in the dark, 'when the coast was booming. They grew each month. All around Mum's, even down past the village and the marae. Beach location, beautiful ocean views, development potential, your own private getaway. Lifestyles of the future. Boltholes for the monied!'

'She should've sold then, maybe,' I said.

Vick didn't answer. I took a fold of sheet between my fingertips, drew it towards me a bit, the rest was caught beneath Vick.

'Would you have sold?' I said.

'We weren't all as keen to get away as you, Daniel!'

'I know. But would you have sold?'

'I don't know,' she said, rolling over to face the wall. 'Stop asking me.'

I let go of the fold of sheet, walked a wary couple of fingers towards her pyjama top. I felt her slip deeper into the mattress, away from me.

In the aisle where stacks of bread should be there's one loaf of raisin toast. I exchange glances with an elderly chap leaning on a walking stick, then nod to him. I push the trolley back to where Vicki stands raking her hand over her pitiful haul. She looks at my near empty trolley.

'Thanks anyway,' she says, reaching with a hand to touch the back of mine. 'That'd be great if you can head back to town for, hell, you might as well get everything.'

'Yep,' says the checkout girl when we set the few items we have on the conveyer belt. 'It's just been confirmed. Couple of weeks. So we're just running everything out before they lock the place up.'

'What are you going to do?' says Vicki.

'We have a counselling session scheduled for Monday.'

'Counselling?' I say.

'Grief, I think,' says the girl.

I'm sorry I asked.

'To put it in perspective,' says the girl. 'Someone from head office is going to talk about placement elsewhere.'

'Where?'

'No idea. Somewhere where the people haven't left in fucking droves would be nice.'

I laugh at her irony, then realise she's not being funny. Vicki touches her hand against the girl's, who has rings on pretty much each finger and both thumbs, and a spider's web tattooed in the webbing between thumb and index finger. Above it is what looks like a mermaid. On the road I check the battery mileage left before we need to recharge. I can get to Ella's and back here. I wonder how much closer to the village the first of the warning signs will start, then the roadblocks. The For Sale signs for houses that will never sell. I guess also when we'll see the first of the religious nutters standing with their *Apocalypse-is-nigh* signs, not as funny as they used to be. And the gawkers and salvagers and other assorted grifters who think abandoned houses and shops are fair game to just wade in and take whatever.

'I hope she hasn't got much thinner,' says Vicki. 'She doesn't have much more to lose.'

'Is she keeping up the appointments?'

'She says she is.'

'You don't check?'

'No. Why would I check? Christ, she should still have the dignity of privacy, of not being second guessed.'

I ease off the gas, glance at Vick. She meets my eyes for a moment. I look back at the road and think of Ella. Choriocarcinoma. Jesus, what a word. Ovarian cancer.

Ella was always more of a force of nature than someone's mother, even someone as singular and strong-willed as Vick. I can conjure her out of the jumble of my kid's memory, like the assembled shrapnel a boy carries in his pockets. Rough hewn memories, from a rough hewn coast, axe swings and seagulls' wings in time and place. Ella standing straight as a door frame on the side of the footie field in her gumboots, which I'm sure she wore as a kind of sartorial wink, for rural ambiance. She'd been a travelling scholar, not a farmer, back in the day, when people were still cool with blatting everywhere on jet airplanes. Paris. The Sorbonne, they said. That would've been after the first big sickness but before the second, and before the food crisis and riots and the street battles over fresh water. She was a visiting fellow in Milan, then to Venice well before the flood tides became the new permanent water level and all that crumbling elegance became a strange new reef system.

She got pregnant with Vick somewhere among the boulevards and canals, so cut it all short and came home. Vick never talks about her old man — ever — and I never ask. It was just Ella and old Ces, Vick's grandfather. I never thought Vick and Ella looked much alike, except for their eyes, so there's always the silhouette of some stranger, her father's whakapapa and whānau from who-knows-where, ghosting at the edge of her outline when I watch her sleep. Something not known, but there anyway. A present absence. It's there in the way she goes quiet and just withdraws, in the way she carries an icy river in her sometimes, weighted with it, weighted like she was with our baby daughter, which is another thing we don't talk about but which shouts its silence at us in the worst times.

'I guess I'm going to spend most of this trip apologising to you,' says Vick, as we take the turn off to the coast.

'There's no need. I get it.'

She shapes to say something else, but doesn't. For the next couple of k's I drive in silence, trying to sense her. Over a rise a brand new roadside sign beckons.

'First one,' says Vicki.

'I see it.'

'They used to say "Welcome" and all that. "You are now entering . . ." '

'They still say *you are now entering*,' I say.

'But it means something different,' says Vick.

We both spot the upcoming roadblock at the same time. I stop and wind down my window. A guy in a hi-vis vest and holding a tablet computer raises his chin at me. I see they've replaced the plastic fences and drums with huge concrete barriers since we were last here. The asphalt on the other side of the barriers has sand and weeds blowing over it.

'We can't go into the village at all now?' I say.

Another guy, with a two-way radio, chuckles.

'There is no village, mate,' he says. 'Unless you're a seagull, or a fish.'

I nod towards the smaller road, branching off at forty-five degrees. 'We're heading on up the ridge a bit,' I say. 'Then over to the far shore.'

The first guy leans forward, looks into our rented wagon, raises his eyebrows at Vicki. She gives him her best 'I'm not a looter, honestly' smile and he nods.

'There's not much out there now,' he says, 'but I guess you know that. You got family? We're not supposed to let sightseers through.'

'My mother,' says Vicki.

'She won't leave?' says the guy.

I look at the road ahead.

'They had to drag my Uncle Buddy out,' says the guy. 'Dudes in hard hats and uniforms. A woman in a two-piece charcoal city suit, holding her hair in place and trying to quote regulations over the wind. My bones are here, the old guy said. Our urupā. They did the same thing all up the coast.'

'So your people were from around here?' says Vicki.

'Up the road a bit, yeah,' he says. 'We were in and out of here as kids.'

I think Vick is going to ask him more about his whakapapa, but she doesn't.

'That's tough,' I say, and then I'm overwhelmed by the sheer inanity of what I just said. The guy is half-turned away now, glancing over the dusty asphalt and down the hill to where the school he probably went to sits half submerged in sea water, where the fish and chip shop he loved like a mother has real fish swimming in a metre or more of ocean swirling over its rotting vinyl floor and up against the counter. He closes his eyes to all that, to his family's flooded house, his hapū's urupā and all their original 'last resting places' now underwater. At their marae where the papa kāinga stood with feet rooted into the whenua like the pōhutukawa on what used to be the shore road stood rooted in the soil and stones among the other, older, roots. Through time, through the proclamations and land confiscations, against the crappy news home from two world wars, against the influenza epidemic that filled a whole corner of their urupā, against the Great Depression and the loss of so many of the young people to the big smoke. Against fly-by-nighters, developers and politicians.

And then their own ocean came for them.

Hi-vis vest guy doesn't answer me, just gestures towards the branch road.

'Just make sure you stick to solid ground,' he says. 'Some of the edges of the slopes are crumbling and we don't want to have to call for a helicopter and a rope ladder for your asses.'

He steps away. 'You take care,' he says.

'You too,' says Vicki.

The road over the ridge is a bit worse for wear, potholes and piecemeal patches and weeds growing from the ditches out onto the disintegrating asphalt. I guess there's not much use in upkeep. The first time we see the ocean from the ridge it's still a beautiful sight and I think of all those real estate adverts promising people with no real connection to Papatūānuku *an adventure playground by the sea* and I notice that some of the houses up for sale are three or four times the size of others, but they're all equal now in their redundancy, after the second and third seawalls didn't hold.

The land itself is what songwriters and poets and painters used to think of as golden, basked in the welcoming egg yolk of sunshiny days when sunshiny days were a good thing, mixed as they were with other days when promised rain kept its promise. In the before.

'On the way,' I say, 'let's call in and see Beth and them.'

'I was about to ask,' says Vicki. 'Thank you.'

Beth and Tere and the twins live on a little offshoot out towards a promontory not as prominent as it used to be. Far enough up to not get your windows wet except in the heavier storms. Vick was telling me the people from the ministry of whatever sent a couple of geologists – pressed jeans and coiffured beards – to look at the effect of the insistent ocean on 'natural subsidence'. Beth put them up in their yard in the two caravans which Tere keeps having to shift further from the old shore. They stuck things in the earth to extract soil samples and put the findings in long perspex tubes.

Beth's at the door before I've even turned off the engine. A black and white bitsa dog stands and stretches on the rust-coloured grass.

'You two finally come to take Ella away?' she says, squinting into the sun.

I'm standing behind Vick so I shake my head, trying to get Beth to cool it. Vick seems to sense that and turns and looks back at me and I find a spot on the scrabbly yard dirt to study. Quick as a wink Tere appears, hands me a beer. I rip off the tab as Vicki steps up onto the verandah. Beth's girls come out and Vick leans and kisses them both, sets down her bag and sits on an old sun chair.

'There's only two of them left on this road now,' says Tere, nodding towards where we're headed.

'Who else is still there?' I say.

'That tattooed and studded young thing that run away from her folks. She's in the fibrolite cabin halfway down towards Ella's.'

'Doing what?'

'Running away from her folks.'

I laugh, but not for long.

'Kid's too young to be in that ghost town,' I say.

'I know. Beth tried to talk her out. She doesn't trust anyone, I reckon. Long story, I reckon.' Tere takes a sip of his beer.

'We're out too, end of the month,' he says.

'Shit. Really?'

'Yep. Packing up. Me, Beth, the girls and dogs and cats. Heading inland. I've been offered a job.'

'When are you gonna tell Vick and Ella?'

'Ella already knows, and I'm guessing Beth's telling Vicki. Right. About. Now.'

I look back towards the house. They've gone silent on the verandah. Vicki has her eyes pointed down between her sandaled feet, and she's nodding.

I swallow hard. I want to say something to Tere, get on his case about bloody holding on, making a stand. Me, who left here as soon as I could. A few days after the last schoolbell I was in a cadre of three unlikely lads burning rubber to town. Then a few paypackets later got on a plane to the real 'Smoke'.

I'd asked Vick to come with me, all of eighteen she was, but already well qualified for uni in the city. We had each been our 'firsts', secretive and fumbling and giggling and nothing like a movie but beautiful all the same. The day before I left the village I pumped up the courage to ask her. She lay listening, resting her head against my thigh as we sat against a driftwood log. The tips of her redgold hair sunlit against the sand, like I'd lit a match in the marram grass. She tapped a couple of fingers against my knee and rolled over to face me and gave me the widest smile my flimsy heart could stand without splintering and I said 'how about it' again, and she sat up onto her heels and looked down at the sand.

'Mum and Poppa and the whole whānau and everything are here,' she said.

I looked out at the sea. I knew she was still looking at me but I just watched the waves. The next day I left, just with the cuzzies.

That was the summer before the first of the sickness circled the earth, seeding droplets in its toxic orbit. They said it was a great leveller, same shit they also say about wars. But it wasn't. It never is. There are those pushed out in front, with solemn thanks given to their sacrifice. And then those who can, withdraw, garbed and gated away in their exclusivity.

I thought about her every day, and then three years or so later when Ces died, Vick's cousin Henare phoned me to tell me and to say, 'I thought someone should tell you, Boy. To, you know, give her a call.'

I didn't.

I faffed about at work for a few days then put my tools in my kitbag halfway through an afternoon and washed my hands and headed home and grabbed a backpack on the way out the door. I drove day and night, all the way down, sleeping in lay-bys and washing at the sink and eating in truck stops until I parked my car outside the entrance to the marae and took my jandals in my hand and walked down the beach and that was when I saw Vick, twenty-one and all-grown-up and still redgold and unmissable amid the dunes. She was wrapped in a sarong, soaked through, her hair wet and gleaming, eloquent and electric in the twilit sea wind and I just walked up the beach waiting for her to see me and then, well, it would be what it would be. And she did. At first I couldn't read her face. She raised the edge of her hand to shield her eyes from the slipping sun. Then:

'You came back,' she said.

I nodded.

'I guess you've heard about Poppa?' she said.

'Yeah. I'm real sorry to hear that.'

She turned back to the wind.

'I'm not brave enough to ask if you came back for me,' she said. 'For us!'

'I did.'

She took a long breath, stood within the moana's warm whispers.

'You look like crap,' she said, 'by the way. You should get more sleep.'

I laughed. She looked at me, reached a hand and bopped me on the nose.

'Daniel,' she said. 'No bullshit. Did you really?'

I tried to think of something debonair, or at least less monosyllabic to say than 'yes' but I had nothing, but then the sea shallows speaking through the green and hazel of her irises and the warmth of the nearness of her after so long were like ointments on my skin and I just stepped to stand next to her and we stayed there, looking out at the horizon.

I billeted for a month or so, helping with carpentry work around the marae, while Vick made arrangements to extract herself from her Mum's house — her Poppa's old house — while leaving the flaxweave of her whānau intact and strong enough to be both her sail and her anchor, wherever and however we might turn out. Ella gave me a slow, royal, wave as I got in the car, and I felt the weight of history on me, taking her daughter away. I knew Vick would one day want to return here, maybe for good, and I also knew *she knew* I wouldn't. But I figured that'd be a battle for the future.

A couple of years after we settled into a flat in the Smoke the news snippets starting piling up, just a faint and ragged pulse of them at the start, then an artery, cut and spilling everywhere. Amazing sights of green islands in the Arctic, Indian summers where decent summers had been a rarity. Forests were turned to fire. Closer to home, sea levels rising, coastal land disappearing, climate scientists' projections – this model and that. There was a once-in-a-century drought, followed by another. Then some other once-in-a-century phenomenon. Vick caught a plane and bus back here every six months or so, every year for Ella's birthday and sometimes also for her own. On occasion I'd go with her and the whole whānau would get the guitars and waiata out and we'd have a great couple of nights, with the sea getting louder and closer in the background, parts of the beach already being closed off.

There were subsidences, slips and rockfalls, due to 'increased wave activity'. Walkways maybe centuries old were no longer safe. Up at *Sunseeker Acres* or whatever the fuck it was called, a hedge fund banker threw a tantrum when his helipad began to slip away with the wave cycles. In the next bay they had to move the surf livesaving tower, next the cinder block public loos. It was sub-optimal to stand peeing at a urinal while ankle deep in ocean. By the coast, on the shifting shore, roads became instant boat ramps without trying, letter box slots were always damp and unusable. King tides were the harbinger, fanning out one or even two streets inland if the land a settlement was built on was flat. After a while when you waded into the surf, instead of watching out for the rocks and slippery seaweed you'd always been wary of, you had to be careful of what were once kerbstones, or rocks from what had been pebble gardens.

I stand watching Vicki and Beth and their girls on the verandah. Beth is crying now. Tere swirls the beer in the bottom of his can.

'Never thought I'd be a Leaver,' he says.

'What the hell do you have to stay for?'

'You would ask it like that.'

'Like what?'

'Like it doesn't mean anything to you.'

'That's not how I meant it and you know it. Why does everyone think like that?'

He squints into the harsh sun. His face has aged a decade since I was last here a couple of years ago, I swear. And it's not just the bitter sunlight.

I look further on up the ridge road, towards where we're headed.

'I know what you're thinking,' says Tere.

'She'll really be alone now.'

Beth and Vicki are in a hug on the verandah, rocking each other, as if the silent music of their slow swaying can speak back to all this. They kiss each other on the cheek and step apart and Beth raises a hand, goes inside and comes out with a string bag of what looks like store-bought veges and hands it to Vick. When Vick joins me at the car I lift the bag from her hands and sniff into it and it actually smells green, the only thing green on this spit of land so dry the frazzled stalks of yellow grass just seem to hover over the dirt.

I shake my head.

Water from the sky that won't come.

Water from the sea, that won't stop.

The sun is three-quarterwise to the western hills by the time we get to the first of the empty letterbox poles slanting stark and bony like skeletons of wading birds that just died and hollowed out where they stood. At the same time the half-circle sweep of the bay and the sea and what used to be the shore open up below us as we turn straight into the wind for a bit and Vick takes a sharp breath as we see the village now, down to our left, the abandoned buildings half submerged, the coast road gone, the kura and playground where its kids used to run about a jumble of walls and roofs shrouded in cresting waves and spray. The school's rugby goalposts just pale stalks casting rippling shadows in the circling swell. The old RSA hall is gone, the urupā too – the remains of tūpuna exhumed and tagged and taken away on trucks – the marae grounds not even visible at the lowest tide.

I turn away, steer us on down the lane, slow again when Vick leans against my shoulder and I feel her shudder.

'Fuck it, Daniel,' she says, 'I'm pushing forty years old and my childhood will soon be underwater.'

It hits me, for the first time in, Christ, I don't know how long. It just hits me and I stop on this road with no traffic, and lean towards Vick and take her in my arms and nestle against her hair and we just sit with the hum of the motor and the sound of seawater swirling all over the four square court where we first met when we were kids, over the little cabin by the sand where we first made love. Me, the guy who couldn't wait to see the back of here, and Vick who has spent almost twenty years with her heart cleaved in two, straddling two homeplaces.

The baby, our daughter, was supposed to be a kind of bridge between the worlds, I guess. A little piece of all of it. But then the pains came, wrong pains, and I leaned against Vicki in the hospital where she just lay watching the digital numbers on her monitor. As if she could lend some to our daughter, a heart rate, a tiny piece of pulse. We had her cremated and keep her ashes safe until one of us goes and she'll go into the whenua with them.

We never came close to a child again.

I sit holding Vicki, just holding her, like if I don't she'll float out of this rental car and out the window and down the hill to join the echoes and the ghosts.

For long minutes we don't move. Don't say a word. Then:

'You know I have a choice coming up,' she says.

'Yes.'

'You haven't said anything.'

'I'm not going to try and persuade you.'

'Thank you. But I need to know where you stand. Where we stand.'

I lean back for a moment, still holding her, then reach and flick the ignition key.

'Ella will be wondering where we are,' I say. 'And I still have to head back to the city where they have supermarkets with stuff on the shelves.'

'Can you do that tomorrow?' she says.

'We're leaving tomorrow.'

'We can stay on another night.'

I look on down the road.

'Sure,' I say.

A little bit along the ridge road we come to the rickety old fibrolite cabin that was rickety and old way before any of this started happening and the tattooed young thing that Tere mentioned is out by the fence, hanging some clothes on the line. She stiffens when we approach, not recognising the car, then Vick waves and the young woman's stance relaxes and she waves back and picks something else from the basket.

'They play chess,' says Vick.

'No?'

'Yes. Mum taught her. Apparently she's a quick learner.'

We get to the house at the end. Ella's place, Vick's Poppa's place, old Ces, and Bonnie, Vick's grandmother. The paint is faded and flaking and a couple of the roof tiles look broken and even though the windowglass is sandblown and dusty, the curtains behind them look newly hung.

We're only just out the door when I see Ella standing on the sunscorched grass, looking down to the sea. She half-turns, glances over her shoulder and smiles a quick greeting that I go to nod back to but then remember isn't for me.

'I'll get the bags,' I say to Vick, 'you go on.'

'No. Let's go in together. We'll get our gear later.'

Ella is in the kitchen when we get there and she and Vick hug then Ella steps to me and I get a hug too, which would knock me back if she didn't feel so thin beneath her baggy top and swirling skirt. Her hair is proper white now and tied back with a mauve loop.

'Great to see you again, Daniel,' she says.

She points to some scones and cream and jam on plates on the benchtop, opens the kitchen's door to the patio with its corrugated perspex on two sides, and we go out to where she has a little glass-top table set up with some wicker chairs.

I volunteer to go back when the kettle boils and from the kitchen window I see Ella and Vick sitting toe to toe, leaning into each other with their right hands clasped and their foreheads touching in silence. I go to the doorway but they don't move and I decide to go and get our luggage and put it in the sitting room.

I'm struck as always by how big the house is, built by Ces for a big family they never ended up having. The rimu-floored corridors are like avenues, the bathroom big enough to park a car, two sitting rooms, one for best when the minister called in or for visiting whānau from far away. I walk to the end of the hall where the door still has the faint trace of lettering in a careful stencil: *Victoria's Room: Private.*

I push open the door and it creaks a little. The single bed is tiny, the wooden legs and metal feet still sturdy though. The table by the wall has a desktop computer, its screen and keyboard a little dusty. There are framed photos of Ella, in her twenties maybe, another at fortyish. Ces on horseback, another with Ces and Bonnie and a young Vick eating ice cream. And half a dozen others of Vick. In one she's sitting on the sand, one tip of a half-circle of kids, smiling across at the other end of the crescent of children to where a boy sits cross-legged, looking back at her. Holy shit. It's me. I have no memory of any of it. I stare, willing it to be born again in my mind. The door creaks again and I look up.

Vicki is standing in the doorway, one hand grasping the door frame.

'I need to know,' she says, coming in to sit beside me on the bed.

'You asked her?'

'Yes.'

'And?'

'I need to know, Daniel.'

I look back up at that semi-circle of kids in the photo.

'This place will be swimming in a metre of water in five years,' I say. 'Maybe deeper. Maybe sooner.'

'Yes.'

'Ella might not see a year of that time.'

I feel her stiffen and I put my arm around her back.

'That doesn't really change anything we have to do right now,' she says.

'We need to make this decision together,' I say.

'Yes,' she says, running a fingertip across the bedspread of her childhood.

'You made a choice to come with me, once,' I say. 'You took a risk.'

'And I've regretted it a hundred times.'

'I know.'

We laugh, just for a second, and I firm my arm against her back, take a fold of her blouse in my fingers.

I close my eyes to the sound of her breathing, and the incessant waves beyond. When I open my eyes Vick is looking out the window to where Ella has stood from the table on the little patio and walked out onto the yard, staring towards what was once a path down to the sea, but where the surf now flicks up strings of spray, where ragged swirls of sand and seaweed from high tides have climbed over the sandbags they laid as defences a decade or so ago.

I stand and watch her, this woman who rewound the string of her journeying, back across the world to come home to have the baby who is now the woman who has shared my bed and my life for two decades, far from her papa kāinga. Her home.

I move towards the door and Vicki follows me down the passage and out onto the grass to where Ella stands by a small stand of nīkau and a pōhutukawa tree, the branches all bent and gnarled but still strong. Ella gestures to the earth, then half-turns to face me. Not Vick, but me. She points beside her to a small circle of grass, ringed by rocks. She steps closer and stares at me, still pointing, and within the shells of her eyes the skin is all dappled, crinkled like ancient parchment, but her irises are greygreen, centred with a spoked wheel of hazel, like a sunflower floating in sea water.

'My whenua and pito are buried there,' says Vicki and kneels next to the grass circle and reaches for her mother's hand. 'And Mum's. And Poppa's and Nan's. All over here.'

Whenua and pito: placenta, umbilical cord, in the soil, in the earth. Whenua to whenua.

'And our daughter's would've been too,' says Vicki.

I sit next to Vicki on the grass, and Ella does also. l clip off a sprig of grass with a fingernail and hold it in the palm of my hand. Ella reaches and rubs it against my skin and the grass and dirt is warm. I turn to glance over her shoulder to the ocean.

'Mum,' says Vick, 'we have something to tell you.'

Robert Sullivan

Rock Art

The sign said Maori Rock Drawings
so no wonder the mature male cyclist
said to the group of women
what makes the pigeons Māori?
He cackled at his own joke.
I allowed it to ruin my drive
to Ōmārama — I nearly turned
around to talk to him,
but then allowed the land,
the other limestone cliffs
with our tupuna art,
our taonga tuku iho,
remind me what was what
and who was who.

Airana Ngarewa

A metropolitan tangi

Koro died yesterday. We buried him this morning. The whole w'ānau came to say their goodbyes, those who live close by anyway, and left soon after. There are only five of us now. His children and Nan and me.

Nan is inside, in the living room, a long-cold cup of tea nested in her hand, her coming-and-going gaze fixed on its top, the edge where the red color of her lipstick is smudged against its ceramic. The last two days have aged her more than a decade. Even so, she is doing well. She hasn't spoken, hasn't eaten, slept, but Uncle said she is doing well.

He is drinking in the shed with Dad and George. They were laughing earlier; they are not laughing anymore – made quiet by the guilt of burying their father against his wishes. Three days on the pā, a poroporoaki, a 'ākari. George all but insisted they all go back, do it the right way, he said, but the older boys, Koro's real sons, vetoed him. Can't afford it, they said. That was that.

George was a gift to Koro and Nan from a family friend. A w'āngai child. He never met his real parents. Koro and Nan have had him since he was born, raised him alongside Dad and Uncle. He was the youngest, the favourite, his brothers would protest. Koro called the other boys mischief. They were always wagging school and going where they didn't belong. George was everything they were not, everything a parent could hope for. A good student, a good athlete, a good son. I think he felt he owed Koro and Nan for taking him in. He must have meant to make them proud.

When he was old enough for college, he was picked up by a private school for his talents in the classroom, offered a full scholarship. He was going to be educated with the rich kids up north. Nan thought he might even go to uni. Not bad for a *snot-nosed maari boy* raised on a farm.

Koro moved the whole family for him, left the pā and his ancestral lands so his w'āngai son could go to a *better* school. Dad and Uncle don't speak much about it. I think they resented him. Anything for *Georgie Boy*.

Koro was a ruthless father to his own blood. Uncle has shown me the scars. If they did resent their brother, I would get it.

He was buried with strangers, said George.

With his people, answered Uncle. The Christians.

They're not his people. Not his tūpuna. He never stepped foot in that church. You read those stones. Those names ain't Māori.

You knew this day was coming, George. What'd you think was gonna happen? We ain't got the time nor the riches to drive halfway across the country just to bury the old man. We couldn't even get the day off work, let alone three. We ain't rolling like you. Our work don't wait for us. If we don't show up, we don't get paid. And if we don't get paid, we don't eat.

George stood from the table.

We came all this way for you, Bro. For you, George. No one else. If it weren't for you, we'd be back home already. This wouldn't even be an argument. If you want to blame someone –

I didn't choose this. I didn't want to move here. I was happy back home. These people, they don't know me. They don't walk like me, don't talk like me, they don't even look like me, look at me. He slammed his fist against the door frame.

C'mon, Georgie Boy, said Dad. None of us fit in here. None of us wanted to move here. Not even Dad. But he did what was best. And today, we did what was best.

Best for who?

For everyone.

Best for Ma?

I wavered between the living room and the shed, between Nan and her children. I never let any of them know I was there. It was easy to remain unnoticed. Everyone was busy with grief.

Mum left before the boys started drinking. She knew this was a family affair and didn't want to get involved. She took the kids somewhere to eat, would not get back until late. If there was another seat in the car,

I would've gone with them. In this way, I understood Dad and Uncle. It was hard not to be resentful. The eldest always draws the short straw.

She is mourning, said Uncle. It'd be no different here or there.

There she'd have time, said George. She'd be surrounded by her family. By his. And not for a day. But three. She could've looked upon her husband. She could've had a night of stories. She could've eaten and laughed. Don't tell me it would be no different.

He is already in the dirt, George. What would you have me do?

He shook his head. There must be something. If not for him then for her.

I wish there was, said Dad. But like the brother said, if we don't work . . .

The men of the shed fell silent and they drank from the bottle, waves of reggae filling the room, the biting voice of Bob Marley reverberating off the tin walls, an old CD skipping on occasion, a cobweb-ridden light bulb swinging from a string shining just enough light to stop the shadows from swallowing the room entirely. A temporary escape.

Nan was inside watching an old film. A different kind of CD, a different kind of escape. Had life become so ugly no one could face it directly? I gathered a pillow and a couple of blankets from the cupboard. On screen, a sorry group of children sang songs of sad goodbyes. I made Nan's sofa into a bed, and she did her best to get comfortable.

Every light in the house was turned off, except the light in the hallway, an exception made only in case she needed to use the bathroom in the night. Night, Nan, I whispered. She smiled a gentle smile.

Nan's 'bout to sleep, I said, announcing myself to the drunken brothers in the shed. Reckon we should turn it down?

Go ahead, Neph, said Uncle. How's she anyway?

I halved the stereo's volume. Dunno. But she smiled when I said good night.

The room breathed a hard breath. Wanna drink?

Dad fixed his gaze upon me. Nah. I'm all good.

You know, said George, your father used to steal your Koro's beers. He and your uncle would climb on top of the house and drink them dry. Even after Koro caught them, they wouldn't stop. They'd raise their drinks and howl like dogs.

We were going to get a hiding anyway, said Uncle. The room roared with laughter. Thought we might as well earn it.

Weren't scared of the old man, aye Bro, said Dad. He was oldschool, but he wasn't scary. Your nan though. I'd rather a hundred hidings than one of her lectures. The room roared again.

Would've paid for her silence back then, said George. He laughed and sighed and bowed his head.

Maybe we should've taken the old man home, said Uncle. A night of stories, laughs and tears would've done us well.

Not to mention a feed, said Dad. The room laughed a gentle laugh.

We should go back, said George. I mean, look around. Are any of us really happy here?

Nah, but work, you know?

Maybe we start with a weekend. Or a couple of weekends a year. You bring your w'ānau and I'll bring Ma. Who knows what'll happen?

The farms are always hiring, said Uncle. Don't pay us well but living's cheaper back there anyway.

A car pulled into the driveway. A small light in the distance. Mum and the kids. The men of the shed put down their drinks and sobered themselves. Tell me, my brothers, do you blame me for all this, for the family moving here?

Nah, no one's fault, said Dad. The old man did what he thought was best. Guess you don't know until you know, you know?

I think I blame myself sometimes. Your w'ānau –

Our w'ānau.

I just, I mean, your lives would've been simpler without me.

Simpler, said Uncle. Nah, Bro. Without you, Ma would have to move in with one of us.

C'mon, Georgie Boy. Listen to this guy. We need you here. My kids need one good uncle.

The tension of the room broke with a bout of laughter, Dad and the others rising from their seats and kissing their brother, his face filling with a youthful joy. Love, bliss, an absence of doubt. Then they went again for the drink, raising their bottles high and howling like dogs into the night. The kids ran down the driveway and joined them. I stood back and swallowed the moment, and Mum snuck up, kissed my cheek and wrapped her arms around me.

The howling continued until Nan came out of the house. You boys better cut it out, she said. Just because your dad's gone don't mean I won't whoop you. The brothers smirked and smiled and laughed a gentle laugh. Mischief.

Ruby Solly

Untitled

When you first told me
about *the white man*
I saw him as one great entity,
crushing villages with each step,
pushing chiefs to the ground
with his heavy tread.
Pulling entire species from the sea and land
only to crush them
between lake-sized fingerprints,
leaving only fossils.

When you first told me
that you believed
that even Pākehā should have
a little bit of Māori in them
to be counted as part of our world,
I asked if that applied to Mum.
You told me it did,
and that you'd always think of her
as an immigrant
even though her blood had circled here
for six generations
and counting.

When you first told me
that you gave me the name of our tupuna
so that I would be strong enough
to hold our family inside my ribcage,
I believed you.

Here you are.

Here is how I saw you,

trapped in your own amber.

Now it's time

for you to believe me.

Brian Potiki

Rowley's Tangi Down the Road

Ō-A-Tia, highest point above Ōruanui. You reach it up the well-maintained hard-packed dirt road that leads to the old house where Rowley was born and to where he was taken by his whānau from Taupō, after being found, still warm, by his wife, Birgitte. Dead of the heart attack he always expected would finish him.

They took him through the kitchen window, past the red table and forms, the wood-fire stove and into the front room; setting him hard up against the bay windows looking past a couple of distant houses, down the road to Te Waapu urupā where his mother and father lie together.

He and his whānau planned these things – the moving of the homestead from below (where his grandfather, then father ran a store servicing the passing traffic and sawmill communities) and his final resting place on a small grassed ledge – the sort of space where we'd all like to have our end, facing north so the first sun awakens many tūī thriving in trees lining the road. As dawn broke I sat there – six hours before the burial – and saw the same rosy-fingers that Homer described, appearing over the distant hills.

Hoani was the man. Rowley's close friend, shaven-headed (and ex-Vietnam he later told me) with loving memories of our mate – including Rowley's strong intuition. But it was Rowley's nephew Dean I spied first – standing outside the house watching us arrive, strumming one of the hardest-strung guitars I've ever played. Dean was one of Rowley's late touchstones – he'd read him one of his stories and if Dean said, 'that's good, Uncle', Rowley knew he'd nailed it.

There he was – our mate – or at least his shell. All bodies in coffins hold the merest trace of our loved ones (I first saw that with my mother, Jean). We – Jill and I with the others – were gathered to fulfill the most ancient contract, to ensure that wolves or enemies did not violate this remnant, this case of mummified flesh, this palimpsest. And we were gathered to kōrero and sing to assuage this shared grief.

House poroporoaki for a man who formerly loved the dangers of swimming in deep waters and who often strained the patience of his whānau with his whims, his stubbornness.

Candlelight flickered, firelight – a cold early-autumn night needing fires burning in this room, in the kitchen and outside.

Older sister Rose and fond daughter Tangimoana by his head on soft mattresses. His son Rere too. And sisters Evelyn and Joyce. And wider whānau. A rōpū from Hamilton arrived late (Ō-A-Tia is not easy to find) to tautoko Tangimoana, a doctor in their work practice. They couldn't stay and after their whaikōrero and waiata rich in harmony, the man Hoani took the guitar and responded with a sweet ballad by Engelbert Humperdinck which was a bit more my – and Rowley's – style!

The cooks were up tending their fires early next morning (when I was enraptured at the urupā). Without electricity it resembled a peasant scene from Bruegel. Laughter, women's voices and peeled vegetables, while below at nephew Greg and wife Nella's new house the men prepared the hāngī.

Walking back from the urupā, I got a bit lost in the bush seeking one giant rimu that can be glimpsed from the road. In a couple of letters, Rowley, you wrote of the close escape (you loved these phrases, nē?) you had when you once couldn't get your footing in Taupō's swift-flowing waters (where it rushes to the Huka Falls and where you loved to dive). You thought you were going to drown. I'd have written about this in my next letter and you'd have known exactly where that bush was and how close *I'd* been. Came out scratched and muddied . . . you'd have understood, made a generous comment.

So . . . no more exchange of letters, sharing of private adventures.

I was a pallbearer, solemnly helping to get you through the narrow doorway and out the window again, lying you tenderly on the verandah. The sun shone on you there and on your sisters and daughter by your side, the verandah of this old house, a paepae.

It was 11 am and there was now quite a crowd.

This is what we're going to do, said Hoani: a kaumātua's poroporoaki, a brief service, his son and daughter and sister Rose, Taupō's mayor (who brought condolences from the Governor-General), then the rest of us could speak.

Jim Moriarty made the connection with Wellington theatre in the 1970s. I read from one of the hundreds of letters you'd sent me, Rowley, over more than thirty years, showing your deep love of literature and the pleasure you took in writing. Many speeches honoured you, creative, child-like, friendly man.

Then lifting you into the station wagon and everyone following, most walking and chatting, the day clear and sunny.

And up, up to the tiny, old urupā. I'd never held the rope before – white, synthetic, thick. It bit into my hands as I – bird's eye view – saw you go deep into the ground.

Hoani led it all – the ceremony, the respect, the care taken.

And finally, a gay feasting, the food most delicious. And the catching-up that happens more rarely now. Some singing. That guitar though, metal strings unyielding like a medieval torture instrument. And Hoani was the man.

Colleen Maria Lenihan

Nerissa

Twenty years after the Greek ship *Nerissa* sank at the entrance to the Hokianga Harbour in 1928, eight lives lost to the deep, I was born. Due to the Māori proclivity at the time for naming babies after tragedies, I was christened Nerissa.

My mother was an excellent honky tonk piano player and a terrible drunk, and she made no bones about not wanting me.

'When you were a baby, I didn't give you the tit,' she slurred, wild-eyed from another night on the waipiro. 'I gave you water from the ditch. Straight from the side of the road.'

My grandparents took me in when I was five and raised me on their small dairy farm deep in the Hokianga, far from any sealed roads.

'Nerissa pisser!' the kids jeered, while a dark stain bloomed around me on the tattered cloth seat. I had wet myself on the school bus again. I turned my face to the dusty window. Māmā was waiting by the side of the road. She wore workmen's trousers and a blue gingham scarf tied under her tattooed chin. The bus came to a halt. I hobbled off it. Years later, a doctor in Auckland would ask if I'd been in a car accident, as my pelvis was so out of whack. If only.

Māmā dried me off without complaint and hoisted me on to her back for the long walk home. Every day she carried me home from the school bus and gave me a mirimiri, until I could walk again.

Māmā and Pāpā took me to the Courthouse at Rawene for a hearing about my custody. I have a photo from that day. It was my seventh birthday. I am wearing a hat, ribbons in my hair, a hopeful smile. My mother never came.

The creak of bed springs woke me. I peered out from beneath my faded feather quilt. It was still night. Māmā was sitting bolt upright in the old iron bed by the window. A rope of thick white hair hung down her back and shone in the light of the full moon. It illuminated everything: the rocking chair with its peeling green paint in the corner, the grandfather clock that no longer chimed, the walls papered with yellowing pages of the *Northern Advocate*. 'Did you know? To be a wife of Solomon you would need perfect teeth. Try Cole's Dental Cream.' 'Drought In Northland Worst For Years.' 'NAGASAKI IS BURNING LIKE A VOLCANO'. The war was long over, but Māmā and Pāpā were still deathly afraid. 'If the Japanese come, we will run up into the hills.'

My gaze settled on a long whisker on Māmā's chin that caught the moonlight and glowed in high relief against the bluish green spirals etched on her skin. I didn't want to look at her eyes. They'd be staring into nothing. Māmā was silent. She was talking to the spirits of the dead.

I clung to my doll, Kuini. She was a faceless bundle of rags and the only toy I had. I told her my secrets.

Outside it was very still. I could hear every rustle. The forest was waiting. Māmā got up, drew her shawl around her shoulders and entered the night. She went deep into the ngahere to gather rongoā while the moon was high.

It felt like no time at all before Māmā was shaking me awake for milking time. I put on the grey pinafore I wore every day except Sundays and pulled on my gumboots. No time for breakfast. The cream had to be ready for the milk truck to collect by 5 a.m. or else it would sour at the gate. We'd eat after mahi. Tin mugs of strong tea, parāoa takakau with dripping, perhaps some fruit preserves.

I trudged through the wet grass with Māmā and Pāpā to where our small herd of cows was waiting. They were always ready, stock-still, with doleful eyes. I felt sorry for the cows come weaning time. They would cry for weeks after their calves were taken away.

After the herd had given up their milk, Māmā and Pāpā poured it into the separator. I watched as the blades spun round and round. The rhythm of the machine and the scent of warm milk made me long to climb back into bed. Once all the cream had been siphoned off into shiny metal cans for the factory, we pulled the machine apart and scrubbed it down thoroughly. Pāpā always made sure we were meticulous about everything, but it was especially important today. It was inspection time.

The Pākehā man from the factory peered over his glasses and his clipboard.

'The cream is still low grade. No improvement from last year,' he said.

Mr Jessop had crepey skin and jerky movements.

I stared at his shiny pink head. None of the men I knew were bald. Pāpā, my uncles, all the kaumātua on the marae had thick, full heads of hair.

Mr Jessop wrote down the price the factory would pay for our cream. Pāpā spoke little English, and couldn't understand how the Pākehā came up with his numbers. I didn't trust him. I was sure he was hoodwinking us.

That night as we warmed ourselves by the fire, Pāpā said, 'Who's sick?'

'They told me to see the Maxwell girl, and make a poultice of tūpākihi for her arm,' said Mama. 'Lucky I did. She'd had a nasty fall. It was badly swollen.'

'Good,' Pāpā said. My grandparents only ever spoke of Māmā's night-time excursions between themselves by the fire at night. They were devout Catholics. The church would not approve of such things.

'Get the horses, girl,' Māmā said. I went down to the paddock bearing carrots and caught the horses. We rode down the peninsula bareback. We dismounted and sat on a grassy bank that overlooked the harbour for a while, and then Māmā slowly gathered herself up. She seemed to unfold and expand herself, until she was standing. She appeared even taller, somehow. Eyes closed, she leaned into the breeze rolling off the water and gave it a good, long sniff.

'Me haere tātou,' she said.

Māmā could smell the wind and know whether it was a good day for fishing. She was always right, which meant we never had to waste a day. I didn't know anyone else like her. I wished I could be special like her.

We pushed our wooden dinghy out onto the water and rowed out until Māmā said to stop. She carefully lined the boat up with the shore and the cardinal directions to find our fishing place. We had to stick to our spot. Māmā said a karakia to Tangaroa, and then she spat on the bait. 'Te māunu, te māunu,' she said to the fish. 'Tikina mai.' We cast the hooks into the sea.

Pāpā had a strong nose and was good with a gun. He'd brought back a pig that morning. After he'd dealt with it, he gave me a package, with a glint in his eye.

'From Santa,' he said. It was already January. 'Santa got lost. He had to drop it off by aeroplane.' I tore open the brown paper. Bright blue mittens with stars on them. Although it was summer, I put them on and wore them until Māmā ordered me to scrape the fur off the pig. Santa had flown an aeroplane to the Hokianga just for me.

—

On my twelfth birthday, Māmā sat me down in front of the house and chopped off my long hair with rusty dressmaking scissors. I felt like I was being punished, but I didn't know why. That night, I had the same dream as I'd had the night before, and the night before that. It began with me sound asleep in my bed. When you dream you are doing what you are actually doing, it feels like real life. It's the scariest thing ever. In the dream, I wake up to a sense of dread crushing me like a stone slab, in the deepest, darkest of nights. A night so intense it can be felt. A night where nothing can be seen. I will myself to get up and turn on the light. I inch barefoot across the cold dirt floor. I have trouble walking again, like when I was little. When I finally make it to the wall, I flick the switch, but nothing happens. The night still envelops me. I want to cry out but I am struck dumb. I want to flee but I am nailed to the spot. No matter how many times I try to turn on the light, I am alone in the darkness.

—

I loved English; especially poetry. It reminded me of the way the kaumātua speak on the paepae. My teacher, Miss Kingi, took an interest in my poems and loaned me books from her personal library. We didn't have any books at home.

'You'll go pōrangi if you keep looking at those Pākehā books!' Māmā said.

She truly believed that, and feared for me, so I would read in an old pūriri tree, perched in its branches where she couldn't see me.

Māmā thought I was still out with Pāpā cutting tea tree. After he and I had cut a big stack for the fire, Pāpā whistled for the dogs and headed into the bush with his gun. That was my chance to retrieve a book I'd hidden in the woodshed.

I liked it up there in the tree. I imagined it was my house. Each limb was a different room. I sat on the widest branch, which was my parlour. It had a plush red couch and a record player in the corner. There were pictures on the walls of classical Greek ruins in gilt frames. My doll Kuini was wedged into the branches.

I opened up the worn blue volume of Shakespeare's plays with my teacher's handwriting scrawled in the margins, and read a couple of lines for Kuini:

> Full fathom five thy father lies;
> Of his bones are coral made;
> Those are pearls that were his eyes;
> Nothing of him that doth fade,
> But doth suffer a sea-change
> Into something rich and strange.

'The photographer from the *Northern Age* is here,' said Miss Kingi, smiling. I smoothed my hair down. I had washed it last night, starched my school blouse and mended the loose binding on my blazer.

'So, is this the poet? Lovely! Hello, dear. Now, stand over here by the door, that's a good girl,' said a Pākehā man with a bulky camera around his neck. I stood there looking at the ground while the other kids gawked and pointed.

'Miss! Why is Nerissa getting her picture taken? What about us?'

'Her poems have been published. If you apply yourself to your studies, Hohepa, maybe you'll get your photograph in the paper next.'

I wished everyone would stop talking and go away. 'Now don't be shy, dear. Show us that lovely face of yours,' said the photographer.

I lifted my chin and looked into the camera.

I ran down to the letterbox after breakfast. Pāpā read the newspaper to study English. Sometimes he'd invite Pākehā over for a cuppa so he could practise. I snatched the paper up and ran all the way to my tree and climbed up into its reaches. There it was. My picture in grainy black and white, and my poem, with my name underneath. I read the opening lines aloud to Kuini:

> Spade
> Dig your sharpened edge into the flesh of the soil
> let it turn over the soft turf and
> fling it high upon mounting mud.
> Let water find its way through
> the disturbed earth . . .

Pāpā and I had been fixing fences at the far end of the farm. We rode back on our horses in our usual silence. I wondered how I could steal away to read a book of poems by Hone Tūwhare, but when we got back Pāpā sent me straight inside.

'Māmā wants you,' he said.

I tilted my head. There was something in his tone.

Māmā was standing by the wood stove with something in her hand. She fixed me with a hard look, and made sure I was watching as she opened the black mouth of the stove. I knew what she was holding. I'd had several poems published by now, in several issues of the *Northern Age* and even a couple of magazines. She fed the fire with my only copies. The flames burned brighter for a few seconds as the words on the page dissolved into ashes.

I sat on the back of the milk truck with all my possessions in a satchel beside me. I'd left Kuini in the tree. I couldn't take her with me to St Anne's Hostel for Māori Girls. The others might laugh. Pāpā stood at the gate alone, straight-backed and forlorn. I watched him recede into the distance through clouds of dust.

Anahera Gildea

Black Shroud

I have not coped/I have
dug my burrow in handfuls/dirt beneath
my nails cut back to the bone

this flag of formaldehyde/heads
stuffed with the fat of extinct/muscles seize
become tough when fear cuts the throat
you would think/terror shock-collision hysteria-collapse
fight
/fists crunching – fight back
would be visible/since
it is etched into forever
by raupatu

There are stretchmarks on my 'pātaka' whakairo
'maungarongo ki te whenua, maungarongo ki te tangata'

This is the year of facing. Where
we ruined the soil of our dreams
and turned the earth. This
to where we pray on our knees to gods
ignored by the haunted sound of others we cry,
face down, we. This is where
we lie defeated, tearing the soft breast of our mother,
the last place. Us, responsible, we stand alone
on the scorch of the earth and weep at our own stupidity –
stand sideways choking the throat of the indigenous
warning: this is fire in the day, the blood of pointed stars
slicing the curtains of the sky. The seams of the land
ruptured as resource, the
breath of rabid dogs, those lost

among wires and bars
where apples that stink like cider come rolling,
an avalanche from the maunga,
to pool at our feet and rot
as we lament for summer, the cicadas missing.

I see her in the flax, machete from her wrists.
She will uproot you if she wants.
She is immense.

The damage she has taken,
her body, fists in capitalist dirt to do it.
Maybe this is the handle of her kete
her massiveness,
the age of the return to the body

I will need salve, and paint,
I need windows. Bigger windows.
and other places to put guns
I need the squeezing of my puku to slow
until I can breathe properly
deeply
without dust, without ash

no birds can fly in this house
without choking
the earth we have forgotten how to carry
as we hold our indigenous breath.

Vaughan Rapatahana

hā pīwakawaka

hā pīwakawaka
kei whea koe ināianei
taku hoa iti?

he manu me he waha rōreka
he whaikōrero pēnei i te waiata,
te wā katoa

he aha tō kōrero e hoa?
he aha te tikanga
o tēnei kōwetewete karawhiti?

kāore ahau he mōhio
nō te mea kua nunumi kē koe
ki tētahi atu he wāhi

kāore ahau he kite i tō whatu kanapa
kāore ahau he rongo i tō pūrākau roa,
kua ngaro koe ināianei
me kei te ngere ahau i a koe,

hā pīwakawaka
kei whea koe ināianei?

[hey fantail
where are you now
my little friend?

a bird with a dulcet voice
an oratory like a song,
all the time

what is your story friend?
what is the meaning
of this one-sided conversation?

I do not know
because you have already disappeared
to another place
I cannot see your glistening eyes
I cannot hear your long tale,
you are lost now
and I am missing you

hey fantail
where are you now?]

Apirana Taylor

to write

to write of the mountains
to write of the rivers
to write of the lakes
to write of the seas
to write of the land
to write for the poor
that is the dream

Ariana Sutton

The Right Whale to Talk to

When Tiwai Smelter finally closes:

A giant data centre could land there,
on the back of a Hokioi.
Hokioi is the innocent one.
He's flown in from the 7th Heaven,
just for the opening night.

The men will unload themselves, slide
down one feather at a time. Washing away
sin stirring ants, their hair will be stroked with oil free,
cyanide free, pāua gel.

The next day consultations will begin
first with the wandering Weka,
who have not been sighted here for decades.
The partnership plan will take 3 days, but
if there is food in it for them, it could stretch out for 3 months.
It would be opportune to plant pellets, of quiet speak into little holes,
analyse their tongues and translate to
possessives and pronouns, with haste
inject into the *Official Information Act* and act like you know
it's all ok, just because it is
and other poisons have been here forever, and never
ever killed a single fly.
From consultation and partnerships, Tarata could bloom.
We could sell that too. Make a sultry billion,
on the lining of French underwear.

After translations have passed the water bearers, they could stimulate
the machinery of corporate activity, activating waves

upon despondent nerve endings, that shimmy across the Strait.
Consult with the devil. See if he is willing to part with his horns.
Consult with the winds, see if they could dance elsewhere.
Investigate the soul of cyanide, it's not so bad
it naturally occurs in almonds, yes that's what they told me.

When Tiwai Smelter finally closes:

The mice in the council tower could gather in a blue lit alley.
Feast on the Tuatapere Sausage and narrow wedges of dairy full cheese.
Devour red liquid; potentially Pinot noir, rat blood or cranberry juice.
That's not the point here; the point is to trust your leaders and not tire yourself of critical thought or the need to contribute to the community.
Stand at the point of no return warrior
and there will be no need to worry anymore.

When the madness of navigation depletes us
we will wait, rest and wait some more.
When the last koru on the waka is carved,
the sky settlement can read it backwards
Ki Te Upoko o Te Moana
The *Southern Right Whale.*
Yes, He is the right one to speak with!
Him and that code breaker beak, can crack the tides
to tell the truth and you can trust the tides
to keep rolling in, the sea to rise insistently
to meet our will power and all the right choices
and all the fragmented hopes will rise to be tested
and then Hokioi, who will fly, shimmering across
Foveaux Strait, glimmering in his sunlit suit.

Kōtuku Titihuia Nuttall

Food

We get the permit on Wednesday, so on Saturday we're able to make our way up into the hills to find something good to eat. I'm trying to see all the new treasures I've missed

on walks before, like the tender hearts of cabbage trees and chick-and-hen ferns — the kind we grow at home but always forget to water, so the leaves become dry and translucent but spring back into succulence with a hearty drink.

I especially love the rhizomatous ferns and spleenworts. They move by themselves through the undergrowth, make their way up tree trunks if they so desire, and feather off the wood like ostrich boa. There aren't really any berries here, especially not at this time of year, but we are surrounded

by bitter and herbaceous plants — Jurassic trees that stretch their new growth away from the earth, to keep their fresh green hearts away from giant birds.

We put knife to branch, stalk, stem; smell fresh weeping sap; put catch in appropriate bag. We keep the dog on

a leash to avoid poison traps for pests, but she pulls and whines at the sounds of birds snapping twigs in the distance. There is a dense, acrid, sour taste; light falls in thin shafts through tops of tree ferns. Above, sky runs quickly, cloud passing over canopy with shaky speed. The wind sounds, but underneath such trees it is just a gesture of wind, a faint howl.

Kaikōmako flowers fall onto muddy track as tiny perfumed stars. The whole forest is sweet musky springtime. Tawa berries drop – fat, oily olives – from finely leaved branches. Orchids push up through the earth beside the path, fresh shoots with unusual flowers yet to open.

You need to meet a tree just once to remember the different ways it can be your friend.

After the rain the streams are heavy and fast, falling down the earth towards the ocean. Farther along the track are the dried-up beds of older streams, slopes of rocks the same shape and size – like foreign burial mounds. The clay around the water is covered in growth that's hard and green and scaly. The root systems of punga colonise the waterway, fresh roots growing into the still water in the ditch.

This isn't the place we thought we would end up, but it's the only way to heal the things we're hiding from. I crouch to snap a leaf or branch, thank the plant, be grateful for the weather and the car that got us here, and for waking up today. The small treats we take home to consume are the things that will keep us going for the rest of the week. Sometimes I feel weak and fragile in a way I'm certain isn't physical, but I appreciate being able to try to fix myself in such a corporeal way.

We carry an assortment of bags and jars and knives. We take very little of any one thing, except for when the tarata blossoms with heady lemony bursts of flowers – then we pick as much as we can carry from the towering bushes, to take home and soak in gin.

It makes plenty of sense to me now, but for a long time it didn't. Each no-dig hāngī we make in the oven with cabbage leaves sutures a different part of me back together. Every time we collect and cook something together, with love and joy, makes up for every time I ate until I was sick. We take a small moment each day to stand in my parents' garden in the sun. To nourish ourselves, we harvest the earth and the beings that spring from it. All our small attempts to care for ourselves and each other wash away

some of the shadowy figures that have followed us around for so long.

I have a knife, a basket, and two legs. He kai kei aku ringa.

Hinemoana Baker

December

December make me forget May.
Walk with me in the summer mist under powerlines
where the loud tūī bells out over the valley.
December I dream about you with your harbour
face in your sunshine hands.

Here we go again writing to each other, December.
On the other side of the aisle you lied about your list.
Mine was all porridge and salted fish, yours
was machetes and Christmas ornaments
drilled with holes and filled with salt.

December, in August the Hutt River flooded but
not for long enough. August went clucking off with a bottle.
In September you walked lightly off the ferry into a drift of
  soft night rain.
In this yellow square of light above Waiteata
I am a dark bird opening and closing its beak.

Robert Sullivan

Ruia

These ripples circling outward in the first instance
belong in the language of our ancestors, ruia ruia tahia tahia
as the bar-tailed godwits fly from Manukau to Alaska

and we step into the soil of the harbour floor.
Each step quickly fills on the lifting squelch
as the land from the hillsides covers our old sandy shores.

We can repair this I know. Patiently and with care
bring back the sandy beaches, end the oil draining
into inlets, the plastic, the chemicals, and endless rubbish

by thinking a little harder with our hearts soaring up
with the kūaka, and singing like them, in squeaks
rather than arias, so we travel further.

Peta-Maria Tunui

Noho mai

e ngā manu nui, manu iti
i te ata hāpara aro atu rā
ki te hihi whero
o te pae tawhiti

i reira rere ai te karoro
inuhia te tai
ka mānu te pōkai
i ngā kapua nui
e paroro ai

i reira rere ai te karoro
kaihororangi
ka hikina ngā parerau
e te puna hau a Tāwhirirangi

rere atu rā

mā te waiata aroha a tōu iwi e kawe
mā te tirohanga o tōu maunga e whakamanawanui

rere atu rā

mā te kākara o tōu moana e manaaki
mā te kōrero a ōu tūpuna hei huruhuru

hoki mai

e ngā manu o te ngahere
i te awatea, whāia te iti kahurangi,
i te ata pō
hoki mai anō
ki te kāinga
te kōhanga
tukua, kia ngā tōu manawa.

Hinewirangi Kohu-Morgan

Five kuia/grandmothers ago

Five grandmothers/kuia ago
I awoke in my Whare Tangata/womb
Hearing the voices of whānau singing my oriori/lullaby
I awoke to the voice of the Pūtātara/conch shell calling Wainuiatea

The goddess mother of all atua ō ngā wai/the god/desses of the water

She the first hoa rangatira/partner of Ranginui
To open the waters within, so I could safely pass
Into Te Ao Māori.

Five grandmothers/kuia ago
I sprang from my Whare Tangata/mother
Into the arms of my Uretū/father.
I became the taonga/treasure of my tribal peoples.
My kuia/koroua/grandmothers/grandfathers raised me, while all abled bodies

Went to their natural world mahi/work for the wellbeing
Of all the tribal people-collectives/whānau.
I was loved, and I learnt to love.
He taonga he mokopuna.

Five grandmothers/kuia ago
I understood the Pūrākau/ancient stories
Of atua/god/desses.
I understood that I was Atua having a human experience
I began my journey of Te Reo Rangatira/Māori language
I began to understand my whakapapa/genealogical links with Tūpuna.
I was sent to Te Whare Kōhanga/the birthing house
Where I sat upon moss, collected, cleaned by our kuia.

Within this sacred whare/house, I learnt the sacredness
Of my body, the sacredness of the Whare Tangata/the house of
Humanity.

I understood my preciousness and was loved in that space.

Five grandmothers/kuia ago
I learnt the love of my whaiāipo/sweetheart, Hoa Rangatira
With him, and his sacred seed, Te Uretū ngā kākano mai i Rangiātea
My uretū/father carried the sacred seeds 10 million of them.
And I would be the 'one in a million' to race into te Pae ō Tiki/cervix

To cling to the Āhuru Mōwai, a gift of the Mareikura.
We concieved in the whare tangata a beautiful child.
I felt my completeness, the circle, of love.
I understood the intrinsic knowledge was passed down by the wāhine

In the waiū/breast milk of Te Whare Tangata.
As I was raised, so would our baby, by the kuia/koroua.

Five grandmothers/kuia ago
I understood the esoteric world, the whaiāio carved
Into my rae/forehead.
The kuia of the Whare Wānanga taught women's stories
Schools of learning, for the tohunga karakia/prayer/chant specialists,
Tohunga Kōkōrangi/astrology specialists, tohunga tito waiata/
composers, Tohunga Kōhanga/birthing house.
I was chosen to walk in this world as a child and I knew my place.

Five grandmothers/kuia ago
I walk on Papatūānuku where sacred mountains and rivers,
Trees and rocks marked the demarcation of my tribal area
I was Tangata Whenua, I knew that.
I understood my role in taking care of the Papa/mother earth.
I bathed in the pristine waters of Wainuiatea, nourishing waters of
Parawhenuamea I went to the
great ocean of Hinemoana to take sustenance for my whānau.
I knew the balance of life, I was born into a world of balance.
Where we knew our roles as men and women

There was a balance and we worked together.
We lived in papakāinga/villages
Where our support systems were intact.

Five grandmothers/kuia ago
I knew where I could walk, I understood the wāhi tapu/sacred places
And walked tenderly, with respect.
I knew how to keep sacred the taonga gifted by tūpuna.
I understood my grandmother self and knew I
Would soon be five grandmothers going forward.
Because five grandmothers ago in 1847 Hinewirangi was born.
In 1947 Hinewirangi was born again.

Five grandmothers forward,
Only one hundred years later
Five grandmothers forward, what do I leave them now,
The mokopuna, kōtiro, wāhine, tāne, grandmothers, grandfathers
What sacredness can I teach them about
I must walk back five generations to bring that knowledge forward.
Five generations, five grandmother/fathers forward
And like both grandmother/father five generations ago,
Be loving but strong, be kind, but harden up.
Our grandmothers'/fathers' lives are at stake.

Rimurimu, tere tere,	*seaweed drifting. drifting,*
E rere ki te moana.	*floating on the ocean.*
E tere ana ki te ripo	*drifting into the whirlpool,*
I waho e.	*out there.*
Tirohia i waho rā	*when I look out there*
E marino ana e.	*it is so calm.*
Kei roto i ahau	*while within me*
E marangai ana e	*everything is storm tossed.*
Kei te tio te huka	*the snow is biting cold*
I runga o ngā hiwi.	*on the ridges.*
Kei te moe koromeke	*and lying curled up asleep*
Te wairua e.	*is your spirit.*

Tina Makereti

Whare Tangata

The Queen was buried the same week Josie buried her uterus in the grove of kahikatea near the urupā. Given as she was to reading signs in everything, Josie tried to see some cosmic meaning in this confluence of burials, and even though she couldn't, for there was no real relationship between the two events, she would forever remember the Queen with the same affection as she remembered her uterus.

The Queen had died a few days before Josie's surgery, and she hadn't felt anything about that. It was just the news, and on the scale of things the news had been serving up lately – flood, fire, pestilence and famine – it barely registered as significant. But later, after she had been wheeled blearily from recovery to the twilight of a private hospital room, she had switched on the TV because that was the easiest thing to do, so she didn't feel alone and bored when the nurse left. She was grateful for the room, the remote control on a small dresser beside her, the sunblinds closed on a view that consisted of doctors' and administrators' offices next door. There had been some luck in buying private health insurance when she had, on her 50th birthday, six months before the symptoms began. By the time she had been through all the diagnostic procedures, found the fibroids and the adenomyosis and suspected endo, been put on hormones and taken off them again when they didn't help, and decided hysterectomy was the answer, she was 52 and had been bleeding without much respite for 29 months.

She stuck with light news and special broadcasts in that hospital room, morning and evening. The other programming didn't interest her, but there was something comforting about all those scenes from castles and cathedrals in Edinburgh and London. The bagpipes and the crowds, the snaking queue of commoners camping out overnight just for a glimpse of the Queen's coffin, just for some kind of contact with collective emotion, for proximity to something grander than themselves. She liked that. Not that people didn't always have proximity to something grander than themselves. All they had to do was go to a marae, a park or festival, a forest, the ocean, a nursery. But this collective desire for the witnessing of *a big thing* – she liked that people were willing to commit to that.

It gave her a faint glimmer of that feeling from childhood – whenever there had been a telethon, a 40-hour famine, Live Aid, Christmas even – all time stopped and everyone focusing together on this one thing, something about goodwill and collective wellbeing. She wasn't sure she ever really bought it wholesale, but she'd been willing to believe, as much as she could, that such things existed. And then she turned 15, or maybe it was 14, and the possibility of magic had been replaced by the glint of hard cynicism – partly because it was cool, partly because she had seen too much, partly, she thought, because she inherited something cold and steely from the English ancestors who had walked onto the Māori ancestors' land and never walked off it. She wasn't very good at applying the proper societal blinkers after that. She saw things a bit too clearly, that was her problem. That, and her big mouth.

It was a good distraction, this show. She couldn't absorb any of the regular news, couldn't face social media, which told her in no uncertain terms that she shouldn't be feeling what she was feeling, that nobody should, that this was the opportunity for the colonisers to be kicked out. She got that, completely, but she didn't *feel* it, and she didn't quite believe that getting rid of the monarchy would get rid of the colonisers. Or that the Queen was really evil. Or that during her reign she could have changed much. It was, Josie thought, like most things: tangled up in a whole lot of greater and more intense forces than this one woman who had been brought up to believe that being queen was her biggest duty in life, and that following the rules of that queendom would allow for the most stability and prosperity for her people. It hadn't, not by a long shot, but Josie was sure that the royal family believed they were the goodies in the great cosmic game of cops and robbers they were all playing.

She wasn't much in the mood for reality. She didn't actually care about the larger ramifications of this moment in history. Her body had had one of its precious organs removed, and wasn't sure it would survive. Her mind knew she was fine, of course, but her body was too busy attending to its own trauma to enage with anything beyond itself. As far as her cells and blood vessels and reproductive system knew, something vital was missing all of a sudden. A violence had occurred. Her abdomen had been the victim of a crime. It was all emergency systems go down there, and the effect this had on her was that she couldn't care less, in a larger sense, about anything. She was on respite leave.

The morning after the operation, her surgeon had turned up at breakfast and told her all was well – there'd been no accidental puncturing of other organs, they'd gotten all the problematic stuff out. A bulky uterus, she'd called it, you should feel much better without it. Josie said she was very happy, and she was – elated in fact. She was happiest most of all to find herself awake and in good working order, given the procedure, the time under anaesthetic, and the small but significant chance of complications. She was happy to hear that her ovaries were healthy, now bereft of their lifelong fallopian companions, but happily pumping out the hormones for a bit longer yet. Or unhappily. Who knew?

The surgeon was right – she was glad it was gone, given the trouble it had caused her. She'd woken up grateful the procedure was over and so was the bleeding and pain, forever. She hadn't been conflicted about the operation at all. Her womb had done its job: housed three beautiful children before expelling them into the world and never caused her much concern before she reached a certain age. She would honour it with a burial, same as the kids' whenua, and in the same place. But before that there was recovery to get through.

Pete came later in the morning, with a coffee and the newspaper and flowers.

'How is it today?' he asked. He'd been there the night before, but she didn't remember much of that.

'It's good,' she replied, 'I can't feel much. I'm walking around. Tired.'

'You look good,' he said. 'Pale. But – you've got lots of movement, eh?'

'Yeah,' she hadn't expected that either. The nurse had commented on it. She'd been up and down to the loo all night.

'What are those?' Pete inclined his head towards her legs, which were wrapped in air-filled legwarmers that massaged her legs rhythmically.

'Circulation,' she said. 'It's quite nice.'

He nodded. One of her favourite things about Pete was how little he required of her. He was the least demanding man she'd ever been with. They had a simple relationship: companionship, sex, friendship. He was a man of few words and he required few from her. They kept their own lives: houses, jobs, kids, who were all grown anyway and didn't require step-parenting.

The screen flickered between reporters who were circulating amongst the crowds and images from St Giles Cathedral, where the Queen's oak coffin was raised on a catafalque, a word Josie had learnt from the broadcast, and draped in the royal standard, onto which had been placed a velvet cushion and the imperial state crown, adorned with 2,868 diamonds and a sapphire, set in the centre of the topmost cross. Josie had been absorbing all the most intricate details from the reports, not for their importance but because they reminded her of her mother's women's magazines from the eighties, the historical novels they both loved, and the way such things once had held currency. Perhaps she was nostalgic for nostalgia, for the comfort of a reliable system, the potency of symbols of unity, despite or maybe because of their emptiness. She was old enough to have been taught correct manners under the admonishment of what she would do if she ever had tea with the Queen, as if that was the highest one could aspire to in life. There would be no tea with the Queen now.

Pete was reading the paper he'd brought her, which was exactly what she'd expected. He'd probably stay for half an hour or more, in companionable silence for most of it, then kiss her cheek and get back to work. She turned up the volume a bit and leaned right back. She appreciated that he was always himself, wherever he was. It meant she could be herself too, watching this silly broadcast, falling asleep if the need came over her, texting him later to bring her things in the evening.

The main reporter kept saying 'thanks friend' in Māori to the other reporters as she guided the broadcast between locations, except she pronounced 'e hoa' with the lack of clarity common to Pākehā pronunciation, so that it came out sounding like 'Ihoa' every time. Josie wondered if the reporter knew she was actually saying 'thanks Jehovah' every five minutes. When a different reporter started giving facts and figures about the royal symbols of office, she wondered if his description of the crown would mention the history of the Koh-i-Noor diamond, property of other rulers for hundreds of years in India and Persia before it somehow found its way into the hands and headgear of British monarchs. She supposed it might lower the tone to go into the details of British imperial looting. To be fair, the diamond was at the centre of bloody conflict long before the British, but that's what made it a symbol of power.

Of course the reporter didn't mention it. Such things don't exist as long as they aren't mentioned, after all.

—

Before the surgery, she had set up her bedroom with her drugs and drinks and comforting books and the telly, so it was all ready for her when she was discharged. Pete went about his business as usual, since she was able to move around the house for essentials, but he spent the nights watching over her. He made her dinners that she couldn't finish, and they watched old movies together, ranging wildly between *The Godfather* and *Hunger Games* trilogies, and the entirety of Will Ferrell's oeuvre.

During the day, she continued her vigil, alongside the Queen's children, grandchildren and other subjects. The coffin was transported to Buckingham Palace, then Westminster Hall where the Queen lay in state for five days, and where the main news seemed to revolve around how long the queue to see her was. There was nothing more British than a good queue, everyone knew, so this seemed the most fitting tribute her people could give her: 19 hours in line for a one-minute audience, the tūpāpaku hidden beneath flag and crown and oak.

Josie could appreciate the need for a good tangi, several days longer than the usual. In this, the royal family finally seemed to have something in common with her own. You had to respect that. She could imagine all her nannies nodding in agreement that it was only fitting. Her own mother, who Josie had not told about the hysterectomy for fear the worry might upset her already fragile health, would be watching all of it too, tutting and commenting on the arrangements. If Brits knew how to queue, Māori knew how to mourn. It was gratifying, even, to see Charles cry, to note the weariness and sorrow etched into the faces of the older royals, the dignity with which Princess Anne executed her duties. When the grandchildren came to stand vigil, Josie teared up quite unexpectedly. Imagine this being the only way you could show emotion, standing still and stiff, facing away from the loved one instead of toward her, buttoned up tight in military uniform or formal attire, eyes downcast. How could anyone expect much from a culture that found such a display fitting? Yet, she was moved. Maybe she was a traitor then, or an idiot to be taken in by all of this. Maybe she was just her mother's daughter in more ways than she thought.

She started to walk twice a day — ten minutes at first, then twenty. She'd gotten so used to lying in bed reading and watching TV that the bright outdoor light felt harsh on her face, shocking, then invigorating.

It was always a pleasure to walk around her ruined and rebuilt city. She liked that about it: the contrast between old and new. Even on her own block – she could look out one window and see recently built townhouses, look out the other and see an abandoned house that hadn't been occupied since the quakes. The abandoned buildings closest to her own were grand old ladies: two or three storeys, clearly built a century or so before. Pink and blue paint peeling from their sides, corrugated iron roofs rusting and loosening with every storm, windows broken. Occasionally someone would come and mow the lawns, a strange exercise given the houses themselves remained untouched, as if this concession to respectability would maintain the illusion that they still made sense on this street. Nothing could hold back the inevitable ruin of the old mansions. She tried to see the ghosts of prior occupants, but she was no matakite.

There was only one way for the houses to go, really. Any day she expected to see someone arrive and begin demolishing them. Every year, she watched it happen to two or three old houses or sections in the neighbourhood: full demolition followed by new builds. The compact houses and apartments that sprang up in their place were immediately occupied by younger, browner, more international residents than had been here before. And yet the city still seemed abundant with abandoned buildings. Her walks took her through Latimer Square, past all the new apartments to the city centre, where graffiti still crawled up the façades of boarded-up and gutted high-rise remnants. So much was so recently built that the city was disorientating for anyone who didn't live right at the heart of it as she did, yet the remnants of its past losses still dominated the skyline.

In between these walks, when news reports got too repetitive, Josie watched the documentaries that had suddenly became prominent on TV streaming sites: *Elizabeth and Margaret* . . . *The Unseen Queen* . . . *Young Elizabeth* . . . the Queen as a chubby toddler, a smiling child on a pony, a gawky preteen, draped in jewels and finery for the coronation, her first speech, her changing wardrobe and aging face. Josie's interest might have been described as anthropological if it weren't for the comfort she felt at these images. She was back in her own childhood, her own chubby preschool years, black and white TVs and glass cabinets holding fine china that could only be used on special occasions, the glamour of princesses and ponies and dedication to countries that were greater than her own. Parents who seemed all-knowing, despite the casual cruelty that came with their affection. She yearned for the time when she believed all of that to be the correct order of things, the sweet naivety of the illusion. Her father was gone and her mother was frail. What she wouldn't give to go back to a time when they seemed all powerful. And now she was heading towards her own old age and the world seemed every day on the brink of ruin and collapse, even though it also seemed full of bright new things.

Josie and Pete watched the funeral procession while they ate ice cream, mesmerised by the particulars of the marching sailors who pulled the Queen along on the state gun carriage.

'Look at the ones in the middle,' Josie pointed at the screen, 'are they actual giants?'

They peered at the screen.

'They're at least a head taller than all the others,' said Pete.

There were six of them, or maybe eight. They debated it for the entire march – whether it was just an optical illusion or not. And then they watched the faces of the pallbearers intently.

'Imagine the pressure,' Josie said. It was bad enough at home, making sure it was done properly, but in front of the world? 'They must have been drilling for this all week.'

'There's Jacinda and Clarke,' said Pete, 'and here comes Biden.'

They kept watching the procession of dignitaries until the family arrived. Josie imagined it felt like arriving at a tangi – the centre of attention for a moment, self-aware but wracked with grief, pulled through by the ritual. But it was nothing like a tangi.

The royal family found their pew in that vast and beautiful tomb, and then it was gone, the thing that had held her, it was over.

'Let's switch it off,' she said. 'I'm tired.'

Pete turned off the TV and climbed into bed beside her.

A few days later, they took the little box they'd picked up from the lab and drove out to the marae. Pete dug the hole and Josie put on the gloves the lab had given her to handle the preserved remains. She'd thought this was the right thing to do, but the paperwork had explained how the organ had been preserved in harsh and toxic chemicals and now she was worried about placing it in the earth. It wasn't a pleasant business, once she got down to it, not the romanticised ritual of farewell she had anticipated. She placed it in the hole, and they said the karakia, and she felt better. It was done now. She was grateful. It was time to think about other things.

Teoti Jardine

Kuihi

My Great Great Grandmother
wove her korowai with clouds.
She braided bull kelp lines
to hold the tide.

When I stand to speak
I see the fire in her eyes,
and choose my words
most carefully.

She knew no fear,
reaching beyond
the blue, she daily
tidied up the sky.

Kahu Tumai

Tūrangawaewae

i missed out on boil up & fry bread as a kid.

my mother didn't like the taste
so every hour i take pictures of my own face
check the photo of my grandmother for proof
— am I my tūpuna's wildest dreams?

different angles give different results:
sometimes i look like a coloniser
like, yesterday i made a pipe with a kombucha can
smoked half a nug through split pink aluminium
i coughed on the last toke, ran ash over my wrist
& remembered how much my dad's funeral cost

e hine, taupiri te maunga
repeat it every hour
one day i'll sink
back to the whenua we're from
like i wish my placenta had done

instead, it burned in a concrete coffin
in an institution that continues to
          burn me
so tonight i'll jump in the ocean
cleanse off the year

i want the back of my throat
to taste of tangaroa & plastic
as my tongue curves around hine raumati's
thighs, later and later she comes
a threesome, we hongi
to ward off the coloniser condition

fuck you, don't tell me to diet
when we're just struggling to survive

Arihia Latham

(i) rui ruia, (ii) kapakapa, (iii) tui tuia

(i) rui ruia

Should I feel discomfort here // Te Rauparaha battled my tūpuna
for a decade // It is very hard when the tangata whenua are smiling
and singing // When the kai is glazed carrots and cream lamingtons
// Am I a lazy descendant, where is my fight // My nervous system
ticks over //
I recline on the mattresses beneath another Arihia, surely that's a
sign //
A sparrow flies inside the wharekai and my heart flaps // A sign //
Does it matter that it's the wrong bird // It was the colonisers
that brought the muskets // Perhaps the thing to lay to rest is this
genealogical trauma, to notice the elepha . . . sparrow in the room //
After all it's not a pīwaiwaka bringing a tohu of the past or the future
// Is time linear and do birds care // My cousin Ruby is a songbird, we
are sparrow and pīwaiwaka //
Why can't I sing like her // She flings her arms and the sparrow finds
the window // I am carried by the current of wānanga // I wonder how
the awa can keep cleansing us // How does it keep on flowing to sea //
I am eddying // The karaka berries make the air sweet and fragrant //
The poison is in the seed // Our poison was in the seed //

If you know how, the river can wash it away // Dusk // Women gather at the awa // To cleanse the poisoned kernels of colonisation, of the patriarchy //
I miss the swim waiting for my baby // Mokemoke māna //
He kākano, he kākano // These last precious moments with my thoughts going to seed // Wanting, waiting, eddying // The night curled like fruit to her seed // I hold my baby as the whare begins to shake // Ru rui ruia //
The young ones out front with blankets said lightning came first // Whaitiri conducting Rūaumoko // She flings her arms // The windows rattle //
Seriously did we need another sign //
I pick figs at Tukorehe // Their flesh spongy beneath my fingers // We pull them open and they are full of pollen //
More flower than fruit, stillborn // Is it a sign of my impatience // Genealogical friction // These fruits have no scent //
The smell of the karaka wafts // Tempting our female senses //
Forever the putiputi and the poison fruit//

(ii) kapakapa

I see the poisonous teeth of ongaonga
And I want to clutch them
Swelling my fingers to a throb
To drown my feeling of failure
To know how to be
Am I angry or resigned
Am I a peacemaker
Or a warrior
Clearly a fucking libran laughs the group
When I leave the marae
I feel woven into something intricate
Like only wāhine can
And on return I can feel he is extracting himself
Cutting ties, severing the muka

Packing belongings in bags
Silently, tāna ongaonga
If I try to speak to him
The sting would swell
my lips closed
I ask him to take our daughter
Because my son is in trouble
He says is trouble
So I take my poisoned love
The fragrant kernel sits on my tongue
Pecked at by pīwaiwaka and sparrow
Who could die by fruit or pane of glass
Bringing messages of the past, of the future
Where is the window, where is the river

(iii) tui tuia

The ambulance didn’t come
My foot kisses the accelerator
This is too close to frantic
Wings vibrating at the window
I will not let this be the tohu
My mind feels anaesthetised
A coping mechanism
Fight or flight
Fucking flight
Wing me away
But I am drawn back, tethered
To the rhythm of ED
The metronome of
Electrolytes
Reviving
My son’s sunken cheeks
The hum of insulin
Alkalising his blood
The space between his brow and hairline
Is the same as when he was
A tiny baby and my hand could cup his skull, birdlike
Now this body spills

Off the hospital bed
Limbs like vines
Searching for a better host
Everyone says time
Is the most deceptive thing
I know deception and it's poisoned fruit
But my son looking like a man
Smelling of sweat and cigarettes
Instead of baby's milk and honey
Or child's dirt and spit
This metamorphosis is blinding
Distressing, I flap
I still feel a novice
I fling myself at the window
Holding tight
Unlatched, set free
Letting him go
Watching his eyes flicker
Lightning on the hills
His heart zigzagging on the screen
Steadying my own
Coaxing it down from my mouth

to the bony cage where it belongs
I want to lock him up, keep him safe
His wings are beating in here
I want to set him free
watch his debut into the world
Rere atu rere mai
Perhaps we could settle on a tether,
a muka string on my wrist
Above, a bird
my tohu
darting freely

My middle child is flying
literally, en route to the airport
she glides into the hospital
whispering to her brother
things he will not remember
Her mind is sure
ready to fight for us all
Her stance is poised, calming
She has always
steadied her siblings with
unwavering navigation
Did she get this way

from being after and before
the past and the future
Did I even have a hand in it
Or was she thrown
from Rangiātea
Not confused or lost
Fight and flight
Sparrow and pīwaiwaka
Warrior and peacemaker
And together, my children
Rui ruia, kapakapa
Tui, tuia
tug at the muka
from before and beyond us
The fine plaits in my fingers hum
bind, release,
Release.

Stacey Teague

Hineteiwaiwa

there's an affinity between the weaver
and the plants that she gathers
harakeke, pīngao, kiekie
the flax scraped with a shell
then washed and dried
the muka prepared on her thigh
the weaver works downward

*

under, over
holding hands in place
she pulls at the threads
two up, two down

*

we women go about our women's activities
reach out to Hineteiwaiwa
to give us power
she prays over us
sits like a mountain
beneath the cycles of the moon

*

with her face lit up above us
she cradles mother and child
we trace our lineage back
as far as it goes
it ends with her

*

under, over
two up, two down
with your small flax
weave us into life
we summon you

Nicole Titihuia Hawkins

Titihuia's Moko

We sit in the
twilight of your lounge
the sofa now a bed

You search my face for your kuia
I've carried her name
for almost thirty years

It's good I've come
It's good I'm learning
there isn't much time you say

You insist, hold my hand
fingertips trace the valleys
between protruding veins of memory

Once were ringa raupā
feel the supple weight of it all
the fleeting pulse of all things

You show me a photo of her
taken before she got the
moko kauae I didn't know she had

There isn't much time
There are things now
that I will never know

You use every laboured breath
to pass whakapapa from memory
to tongue to ear

Stop only to make jokes
about flirting with the nurse
It's good you've come
Āe, I'm the last one

You still refuse
to use my first name
call me only Titihuia
a name you won't see
me live up to

Kelly Ana Morey

I'm So Happy I Could Die

It occurs to Annie, as she walks out into the sunshine on a blistering hot February day in 1953 with her brand-new husband at her side, that she's just made a terrible mistake. And this is big, because although Annie is no stranger to mistakes even though she's barely 20 (one could even say she has a talent for finding trouble), those mistakes and their consequences have largely been a mystery to her. It's like there's something in her brain that has the ability to wipe the slate clean and begin anew each time something goes wrong. She'll be well into her 70s before she discovers that there's a word, well two words, for this, thanks to her clever grand-daughter Pax.

Tabula Rasa.

But this, this marriage to a man she knows well enough to understand that she will never love him . . . well, it's too late to change her mind now. Legally if not in the eyes of God, she and Drago Devich are tied together.

Happily married.

Just for a moment, as she stands there on the street outside the Registry Office, Annie considers slipping off her new-too-tight shoes and making a break for it. Quick as can be. Across the road and away. Or into the path of a bus, a tram or speeding car. She closes her eyes and imagines the meaty thump of a moving tram . . . no, truck hitting her. The exquisite pain and bloom of dark blood on the road. Her final shuddering breath as people stand around her body in the silent rictus of horror. She startles as Drago takes her arm. 'What?' she says turning to look at her new husband.

'Happy?' he asks.

'Yes,' says Annie, looking up at him with a bright, brittle smile. 'Blissfully,' she elaborates, because she's a bride on her wedding day and this is what brides in the romance novels she loves so much always say when asked this question on their wedding day. *Blissfully. Wonderfully. I'm so happy I could die, darling.*

Drago's brothers Teo and Marin join Annie and Drago outside, having delayed to use the facilities. They are the only members of Drago's family who have agreed to come and stand by his side. His mother and sister Mia had settled for cursing the union in Croatian from afar. Not that Annie cares, she reckons she has more witchcraft in her little finger than those two Croatian hags put together.

'Where to now, Chief?' Marin asks Drago.

'Annie and I are getting our photo taken at a place on O'Connell Street,' Drago says. 'But that won't take long. I thought we'd have lunch at the Great Northern.'

When they reach Vulcan Lane, Annie and Drago turn right to make their way to O'Connell Street, while Teo and Marin continue down to the waterfront, keen to get a few rounds in before the newly-weds join them.

'Where you going for your honeymoon?' asks Marin, after the four of them are seated in the dining room and an overly officious waiter has taken their order.

Four roast beefs with roast spuds,
cabbage and gravy
followed by plum duff with custard.

'Rangitoto,' Drago says, lighting a smoke. 'One of the potters from the factory has a bach there and has loaned it to us for the weekend. I thought about driving us up to Ōmaha or Snells, but since it's only a couple of days I thought we should stay close. Annie wanted to go up to her mother's, but there's no time for that. Gotta be back at work on Tuesday.'

'Where you from again, Annie?' asks Teo. 'Bay of Islands?'

'No,' Annie replies. 'Further north. Right at the very top originally, a place called Te Hāpua, but my mum lives a bit north of Cooper's Beach.'

'We'll go up next Christmas when the factory closes for the holidays,' Drago says.

'But that's almost a whole year away,' Annie says, the words so soft that they go unheard. The food arrives, and the men tuck in while Annie, who feels queasy, nibbles on a potato and pushes her beef, which is still red with blood, around her plate.

'Are you not going to eat that, Annie?' Marin asks hungrily.

'It's just too hot to eat,' Annie says, pushing her plate towards him.

Once they've finished lunch, Annie and Drago depart, leaving Teo and Marin, who intended moving back to the public bar at the Great Northern until closing time. It's just a short walk to where Drago left the Studebaker. They retrieve their suitcases and the box of food and wine that Drago had put together that morning in preparation, then head to the ferry building. Drago's friend has assured him that the bach is stocked with the basics like tea, sugar, salt and flour, because the family had spent their Christmas break on the island.

'Nice weekend for it,' the ticket seller says, tearing off two returns and handing them over to Drago. 'Don't lose them or you'll have to buy another when you come back. You've got a bit of a wait for the ferry,' the seller continues. 'I'd get myself a cup of tea from the kiosk for you and your daughter if I was you.'

'Will do,' says Drago, as he pockets his change.

'He thought I was your daughter,' Annie says as they walk through the gate and onto the wharf.

'I have ears,' Drago says. 'Do you want a cup of tea?'

'Yes please. I'm parched.' Annie likes this.

Parched.

Famished.

Ravenous.

Gasping.

Darling.

Gasping.

That's what people in books say. The racier ones the girls at the hostel hide under their mattresses because even though they're not forbidden they also are. The books they share around under the cover of lights out.

Ravish me, Chad, you know you want to, she said as he laid her down on a bed of freshly cut meadow hay and wildflowers.

Giovanni's eyes caressed Lucia. 'You are more beautiful than I remember,' he said, lust thickening his voice.

Darling [Bianca said, sitting up in bed, a sheet covering her bare breasts] *be a dreamboat and make me a martini. I'm simply gasping.*

Annie doesn't even know what a martini is but she's sure she would love them.

Annie sits down on a bench and ponders briefly on how she's going to tell Drago she doesn't want to live out west where the Devich name is known by all, in the house he shared with his wife, and in the bed in which they slept and did other things for almost thirty years. This is not something they have discussed. She just knows that this is his expectation.

Drago returns with the tea, which is in cups that he recognises as Crown Lynn and very probably fired by him. He hands both cups to Annie. 'Hold mine while I roll myself a smoke,' he says, sitting down next to her. Once he's lit his smoke, he takes back one of the cups and has a big slurp. 'Pretty decent cup of tea,' he says appreciatively.

'Yes,' agrees Annie, wishing she could have a smoke too. Of course, she could if she wanted to, but those lessons like how only the lowest of women smoke in the street have been ground into her by the kaiako at Queen Victoria School for Girls. Because a Queen Victoria School girl would never smoke in the street, not like the common Māori girls.

'Happy?' Drago asks once again, looking at this woman who's barely more than a child and who is inexplicably now his wife. Would he have married her, he wonders, if it hadn't been for those moments of weakness while Anka was dying. When she had allowed him to bury himself inside her as he wept for his wife, his tears soaking Annie's long fine hair.

'Yes, of course, Darling,' Annie replies, raising her cup to her lips.

Blissfully.

I'll tell him later, about the house, she decides. When we're on the island.

The afternoon is turning golden in preparation for the dying of the day when they finally arrive at the little wharf on Rangitoto. Another couple, both middle-aged, and an older woman weighed down with two bags of provisions also alight. Fortunately, the bach that Drago and Annie have been loaned for the weekend is an easy walk along the shoreline from the wharf. Annie's feet in her new-too-tight shoes are killing her, and under her wool crepe skirt and jacket suit, sweat is trickling down her spine and prickling under her arms. On the doorstep of the bach is a dead tūī, its head on a funny angle.

'Oh,' says Annie. 'The poor thing.'

'Probably flew into the window and broke its neck,' Drago says, pushing it to one side with his foot. 'I'll bury it later.'

'Poor thing,' says Annie again. 'I hate it when birds die. It always seems like such a bad omen.'

'Oh,' snorts Drago, 'that old Māori rubbish. You don't believe all that, do you?'

'Of course not,' Annie lies. 'Of course not.'

Hocus pocus.

Drago opens the door of the bach, releasing days and days of trapped heat. Even though they have been as close to naked as you can get with each other, it has always been under the cover of darkness and there's a degree of shyness still between them so Drago lets Annie use the tiny bedroom that has a double bed crammed into it to change first while he opens a bottle of wine. He takes two tumblers down from the shelf above the sink and turns the tap on. The water belches out, warm and rusty at first, before turning clean and cold as the pipes flush out. He rinses the glasses and fills them with red wine.

'That was quick,' Drago says when the bedroom door opens and Annie comes out dressed in a cotton dress so faded you can barely make out its pattern. Her feet are bare.

'So lovely and cool,' Annie says, lifting her arms and slowly spinning around in front of the open door, which is allowing the last rays of reddening light to pour into the interior of the bach along with a faint murmur of a breeze.

Drago smiles. Leaning against the kitchen bench at the back of the bach in the shadows, he enjoys the show as Annie twirls, her body a dark shadow in the dress that the light had turned transparent. There she is, he thinks, there's the girl who I fell in love with. He wonders as he watches her whether her actions are deliberate and it's all just part of a game Annie plays. He also wonders who else she's danced for just like this, though she swears there's been no one else.

'Annie,' he says. Annie stops spinning and looks at him. 'Come here,'

Drago continues softly. He's amazed anew at how docilely she complies and how she's taken to matters of the flesh and pleasure with such enthusiasm. Anka, his wife – *Rest In Peace* – had never much enjoyed his attentions. She told him once that she had wanted to be a nun, but her family had made her marry him.

'I thought I'd go fishing. Catch us a snapper or two for dinner,' says Drago the next morning after a breakfast. 'They say the fishing is good around here. All you have to do is throw a line out and a few minutes later you've got dinner. Fresh fish for dinner sounds pretty good, yes?'

'I might go back to bed,' Annie says, scratching her arm. 'I slept rotten last night. It's the heat. And there was a mosquito in the room.'

Once Drago has left, Annie walks into the already stifling hot bedroom that smells of sex, sweat and Drago's smokes and turns around and leaves as her stomach heaves in protest. The driftwood bench under a pōhutukawa between the bach and the shoreline is an infinitely more inviting prospect. Annie ventures back into the foetid bedroom long enough to throw open the window and get a book out of her suitcase. She's just got to the part where Lady Jessica has been kidnapped by the pirate king and is being taken to his hidden island lair. Of course, Annie knows they will fall in love and rule the seven seas together, but, with three quarters of the novel left to read, there was no way she was leaving it on her bedside table at Hepburn Street. Some of girls at the hostel had laughed at her for taking a book on her honeymoon. 'You'll have no need for that,' they all said.

'If-you-know-what-I-mean.'

Annie had known exactly what they meant, but had pretended she didn't because why would a girl from Queen Victoria School know about such things? This is one of the reasons why she's liked less than she thinks by the other girls at Hepburn Street. 'If only you'd got married on the weekend, Annie,' Mahina and Kitty, who she considered to be her friends, had said when she had asked them if they wanted to be witnesses. 'I can't pull another sickie at work,' added Kitty. 'And if I don't work, I don't get paid,' explained Mahina, who works in a garment factory and is paid by the piece. So, she had married without friends. But Annie's used to being alone.

It's nice outside, sitting on the bench, under the trees with the sound of water lapping soothingly on the shore. She's been happily transported to the captain's cabin, where Lady Jessica is lashing the pirate king with words, giving as good as she gets, when the sound of a voice brings her back to the present.

'Lovely day, isn't it?'

'What?' Annie says looking up and seeing a young man wearing only some faded blue shorts standing on the pathway that winds itself around the rocks on the shore linking the baches. He is, Annie notes, very handsome. Almost pretty with his sun-bleached curls and slim, tanned body.

'The day,' he says again. 'It's a nice day.'

'It is,' Annie says. 'Lovely.'

Ravishing.

Glorious.

Spectacular.

'Are you one of Len and Radha's crew?'

Annie correctly assumes that Len and Radha are the owners of the bach. 'No, no,' she replies. 'A loan. Just here for the weekend.'

'Are you with that old bloke fishing on the wharf?'

'Probably,' Annie says.

'Is he your dad?'

'No,' Annie replies. 'He's my husband.'

'Oh,' the man says. 'He's a bit long in the tooth for you, don't you think?'

Annie knows she should be affronted. I mean, how rude. But he is such an attractive boy it's hard to be properly cross, and Drago is so terribly old.

Positively ancient, Darling.

'Maybe,' she agrees.

'I'm Harry, Harry Percy. My family owns a bach on the other side of the island.'

'I'm Annie Novak,' Annie says, then stops. 'Oh, silly me, I'm Devich now, Annie Devich.'

'Dallies, eh, we don't see many of you lot around this side of the city.'

'No,' Annie replies. 'I think they all live out west.'

'Well, nice to meet you anyway, Annie Devich. Sorry about that "old bloke" crack. I didn't mean anything by it.'

'Oh, it's alright,' Annie replies. 'He is old.'

'Bit of a waste, a good-looking girl like you, if you don't mind me saying.'

'Cheeky,' replies Annie in a way that indicates she really doesn't mind at all. She loves to be told she's pretty.

'Well,' Harry says. 'Maybe I'll see you around then, Annie Devich.'

'Maybe you will,' Annie replies.

In the end, it's not until Sunday morning, the day before they're due to depart, that the subject of where they're going to live now that they're married comes up in conversation, and it's Drago not Annie that gets it started when he casually mentions the two of them going home tomorrow. And by home he means his house, the one he lived in with Anka. It's never occurred to Drago that they wouldn't live there. It's a nice house on the fringes of Glen Eden and Oratia. Big place, four bedrooms with a sunroom, and the kitchen was redone a few years back, not that Anka had much time to enjoy it, and the bank owns none of it. Any woman would be happy to call it her own. It's close to work at the pottery in New Lynn, the family orchard is just down the road, and he has his vegetable garden and his chickens and vineyard, all there in the big backyard. 'Almost an acre and a half,' he tells people when they comment on its expanse. He's spent decades working on the soil. Seaweed, fish frames, possums and manure have all been dug in, layer after layer until what remains is a rich black soil heaving with worms. It's no wonder his vegetables, which are sold at the stand at the Devich Orchard front gate, are the talk of the locals. To Drago, it's not just a house, it's his home, his castle, his kingdom, and there's never been anything he's wanted more than to fill it with children, though God saw fit not to bless his and Anka's union. But that's all changed now.

'Oh,' Annie says. 'I can't live there. I promised.' She says promised, but what she really means is the place is cursed for her. That Anka had wielded her dying woman black magic with the last of her strength.

'Who did you promise?' Drago says, rolling himself a smoke as he stares at his wife across the bach's kitchen table.

'Anka. I promised Anka I wouldn't.'

Drago snorts. 'Why would Anka say something like that?' he demands.

'Oh Drago,' Annie says sadly. 'She was dying, not stupid. She knew. She knew exactly what you were doing with me.'

'Liar,' accuses Drago.

'It's the truth,' Annie replies, unmoved by the anger she sees building in him.

'You told her. It was you. You couldn't help yourself. You couldn't leave it, could you?' *Bitch*.

'I didn't tell her.' And this is the truth. As Annie said, Anka was dying, not stupid or blind or deaf. They all knew. All of them. Vesna, Mia, Marin, even stupid old Teo, they all knew that Drago was carrying on with the girl, Annie, who he had got in to nurse his dying wife.

'She just guessed then?' Drago says as if this is the most improbable thing he's ever heard.

'She saw it all with her own eyes. Ask Mia and Vesna, they'll tell you. She made me promise that I would never live in her house.'

'Why would she do that?' Drago demands.

'To punish you,' Annie says, though this has never occurred to her before, but as soon as the words come out of her mouth she instinctively knows that this is true. That this is the reason. His paradise is the price Drago has to pay for all the times he had fucked Annie on the single bed in the spare room next door, when he thought the morphine had knocked Anka out for the night. Drago had bitten deeply into the apple Annie had offered, and now he must leave the garden of Glen Eden.

'Anka would never do that,' Drago protests. 'She was a good woman. An honourable woman.'

'I'm sorry,' Annie replies.

'Why, Annie? Why are you doing this?'

'Because I promised,' Annie reiterates because it's easier than saying a dying old Croatian woman with the glitter of madness in her eyes had cursed her and this thing she was doing with Drago. Not that she had paid it much notice, because in truth she hadn't envisaged the thing that had started between herself and Drago as having any longevity. He's old. So old. It's just fucking. Same as it was with the others. Annie doesn't dream of children and a home of her own or a husband with a good job. She's too young. Her head is filled with impossible expectations, fuelled by the nonsense of romance novels. It's adventure and love, excitement, anticipation and sex that fill her twilight thoughts. When she falls into sleep, in all her dreams she's running. Though she can't be sure, she somehow knows she is running away, rather than towards something.

'Get out,' Drago says quietly. 'I need to think.'

'Fine,' Annie says, standing up, the legs of the chair making a harsh scraping noise on the uneven wooden floor. As she walks past Drago, she puts out her hand and takes the smoke that Drago's left smouldering in the ashtray.

Drago grabs her wrist, squeezing it tightly. Annie freezes and glares at her husband with such venom that he lets go. 'Take it then,' he says.

When Annie returns to the bach a few hours later, Drago and his suitcase are gone. She's not dismayed that he's left. She's almost relieved in a way.

It's just me and you now, kid.

She doesn't even care that there's barely anything to eat. She's been hungry before and suspects she'll be hungry again. Already she's making plans. She'll go north eventually, home, but she needs to stay on at Hepburn until she's too far along for Kaa to send her up to Te Hāpua to Nanny Bird and her old Māori woman black magic. She's not going to let her mother take this one from her.

My baby.

Annie touches her belly, trying to divine whether it's a boy or a girl asleep deep inside her. She knows Kaa won't be well pleased that her clever daughter, the one who went to Queen Victoria School for Girls, the one who was doing her nurse's training, yes that girl, is back under her roof with a baby on the way. But this feels safer than marrying an old man who she barely knows.

That night for the first time since Drago insisted that they would marry, Annie realises that she feels happy, and because of this she sleeps well, sprawled out on the bed by herself with the moonlight streaming in the curtain-less window.

The next day, Annie tidies up the bach and packs her bag. She's looking forward to getting back to the home comforts of Hepburn Street. Her little light-filled room with its pressed-tin ceiling, the deep cast-iron bath that they're not supposed to fill above a line scratched in the enamel, and dinner. Monday night is always mutton chops, gravy and mashed potato. The thought of dinner makes her mouth water. She hasn't really eaten since Saturday night when Drago had placed a plate of pan-fried snapper and boiled new potatoes in front of her.

When she arrives at the wharf, she's delighted to see Harry Percy.

'Hello. Fancy seeing you here.'

Such a treat.

Harry smiles. 'Off home already?'

'I am,' Annie replies.

'Where's your husband?'

Annie shrugs. 'I don't know.'

'Oh,' Harry says. 'Did you have a blue?'

'Yes,' Annie replies. 'Something like that. Anyway, it's over.'

Finished. Kaput.

'Surely not,' Harry says, a little taken aback by both Annie's candour and her apparent lack of concern that she's lost her husband. 'Couples have blues all the time. It'll work out. You'll see.'

'Maybe. Maybe not. It can't be helped.'

'It will work out, I promise you,' Harry says.

There's a part of Annie, a silent voice in her head, that is of the opinion that it would be a shame if it did work out. That maybe she's made yet another of her lucky escapes. 'Well,' she concedes. 'We'll see.'

'Do you have somewhere to stay?'

'Oh yes,' Annie replies. 'I have a little room at a Māori women's hostel on Hepburn Street in Freeman's Bay. I'm all paid up until the end of the month.'

'I'm sure it will work out,' Harry reiterates.

'Oh look,' says Annie having grown bored with the conversation already, 'here comes the ferry.'

Harry checks his watch. 'Right on time.'

'Are you going home too?' asks Annie.

'Just for the day,' Harry says. 'I have to go and see my dean up at the university and complete my enrolment, then I'm back here for another week before my holidays end.'

'What are you studying?'

'The law,' Harry replies. 'We're all lawyers in my family. I'll join the family firm once I graduate.'

'Will you defend murderers?' Annie asks, as they walk to the end of the wharf where the ferry is coming in to dock.

'Oh, we're not that sort of lawyers,' Harry explains. 'We do conveyancing. Wills, contracts, that sort of thing. Not very exciting. Well, not as exciting as murder trials. Not that we have many of those.'

'No, I suppose we don't,' Annie says, mounting the gangplank that the two crew members have just dropped. A murder in New Zealand in 1953 may not be unheard of but it's still rare enough to shock the nation. 'I often wonder if my mother killed my father.'

Harry, who's followed Annie onboard, gives her a funny look. 'What makes you say that?'

'One day he just wasn't there anymore. And Kaa, that's my mother, said he ran off with his fancy woman, but I don't know.'

'More likely to have run off,' Harry surmises quite reasonably as they settle in beside each other on one of the benches on the prow of the ferry. 'Murder is an unusual response to an extreme set of circumstances.'

'Yes,' says Annie. 'You're right. Husbands run off all the time, I suppose. Mine has after only three days. But I suspect I'm particularly unlovable.'

'Does he have a fancy woman?'

'My father?'

'No, your husband.'

'Oh, yes,' laughs Annie. 'Me.'

'Gosh, right,' says Harry a little shocked. He's dying to ask why she became an old man's wife, though it's probably because of money, because it's always money. Though this slightly strange young woman doesn't appear to want her husband back, so perhaps she's discovered there is no money and that's what their blue was about.

'It doesn't matter,' Annie says as the ferry, its diesel engine throbbing beneath them, noses its way out into the bright silvery expanse of water between Rangitoto and the city.

Annie opens her handbag, gets out her purse and checks her money again. There's just enough for the ferry trip and a tram fare up to Ponsonby Road. Tomorrow is pay day at the greengrocers where she's been working since she finished up at the Devichs when Anka died. And like with Hepburn Street, Annie hasn't burnt her bridges here either, having not handed in her notice or mentioned that she was getting married. It's not much of a job and the owner tries to touch her on the sly when his wife is out the back, but Annie's used to that and simply dances around his greedy hands. She'd love to say something, but she knows the wife will pin the problem on her and she'll lose the job, which she needs if she's going to make it through the next few months before she goes home.

She'd only said yes when Drago asked her to marry him because she didn't know how to say no, and right up until they were pronounced man and wife she was so very sure that the marriage wouldn't happen. She'd been almost surprised when he had arrived at Hepburn to pick her up the morning of their wedding. Though not that surprised because she had been dressed and waiting on the front stairs with her suitcase.

Annie and Harry disembark together, with Harry carrying Annie's little suitcase, because that's the way he's been brought up. As they get to the gate, Harry fishes a fare card out of his pocket. 'I'll pay for you.'

'You don't have to.'

'But I want to,' Harry replies. 'And it's hardly anything at all.'

'You're a knight in shining armour,' Annie says.

My hero.

A lifesaver.

'I don't know about that,' Harry says, 'it's just a ferry fare, but it just occurs to me that you could do with a little help.'

Annie smiles. 'I'm alright, you know. But sometimes a little help makes it a bit easier. Perhaps you could give me an address and I could post you the money? I get paid tomorrow.'

'You don't have to.'

'But I will,' Annie says as the man clicking tickets click-clacks Harry's ticket and waves them through. They pull out of the flow of people journeying to-and-fro so Harry can write down his address.

'I used to work in Remuera, looking after a rich old lady,' Annie says, reading the address after Harry has handed it to her. 'It was nice, the house, not the old lady, she wasn't so nice.'

'Is that what you do?'

'Yes,' Annie says. 'I'm a nurse.' It isn't quite the truth, but it's close enough, and easier.

Harry looks at his watch. 'Best I get going,' he says. 'Don't want to be late for my meeting; the Prof is a real curmudgeon when it comes to punctuality.'

'Well, thank you,' Annie says, smoothing out the creases in the piece of paper between her fingers. 'You've been a godsend, Harry Percy.'

Harry smiles. 'Pleased to be of service, Annie Devich. You look after yourself.'

'Oh, I will,' Annie promises, putting the scrap of paper in her handbag.

After Harry leaves, Annie stays, leaning against the wall, deciding what she's going to do next. Go home to Hepburn or go in search of something to eat first. Because she's suddenly starving as the last 36 hours of deprivation finally catch up with her. Annie doesn't notice Drago, who has been watching from across the quay, since she and Harry had come through the gate, until he is standing in front of her.

'That's the boy from the island,' he says in way of greeting.

'Drago!' Annie exclaims, genuinely surprised to see him. 'What are you doing here?'

'I came to bring you your ferry ticket and pick you up,' he explains. 'But I was running late. I saw you. With him.'

Whore.

'He paid for me,' Annie says. 'Because he's a gentleman. A lawyer from Remuera. Well, not a lawyer yet. But soon.'

Bitch.

'What was it that he gave you? I saw him giving you something.'

'He was giving me his address so I could pay him back,' explains Annie.

'Give it to me,' Drago says. 'I'll take care of it since it's my fault you didn't have your ticket. No need for you to worry yourself about it.'

Annie reluctantly opens her handbag and gives Drago the piece of paper. He shoves it in his pocket without even looking at it, and picks up Annie's suitcase. 'Come on, I've parked the car in front of the Post Office,' he says walking off. 'Time to put this silliness behind us.'

Annie follows Drago out of the ferry building. They wait together on the footpath for a break in the traffic so they can cross the road and head to the Central Post Office. It's always busy down here at the wharves on a weekday. People everywhere and the trams and cars and trucks, clattering and roaring up and down Quay Street. Places to go. Things to do.

People to run over.

'Happy?' Drago asks out of the blue. 'Annie?' he says, touching her shoulder a few seconds later when she makes no response to his enquiry.

'Oh, sorry,' Annie says, turning to look at him. 'I wasn't listening.'

'I was asking if you were happy.'

'So happy I could die,' Annie says after a long pause, because it's easier than explaining to Drago how intensely she wants to run out in front of the truck that's just about to barrel past on its way to the wharves.

The meaty thump of body meeting steel. The shocked faces of the driver and the onlookers as they look at her broken body. The scream of the approaching ambulance. The boy-from-the-island never knowing that she's died.

It would be worth it, she thinks. To stop this story right here before it even begins.

'What the hell is that supposed to mean?' asks Drago. Because the story must continue.

'Nothing,' replies Annie as the traffic comes to a standstill and they cross the road. 'Nothing at all.'

Jack Remiel Cottrell

Reasons why I called in sick rather than go to the mihi whakatau for new employees last Friday

1. When I did kapa haka at primary school, one of the leaders asked who in the group was Māori. I raised my hand and a teacher told me not to be silly.

2. When I was 11 my cousin Justine, who attended kura kaupapa, laughed at my accent after I said a karakia.

3. In my first year of uni the RA asked if anyone on our floor was Māori. When I said yes, a guy yelled, 'What tribe are you from, Ngāti Ginger Ninjas?'

4. The aunties at my marae have always told me I don't know anything. I'm not sure if they're right, but I believe them.

5. Two years ago, my journalism class had a lesson on te reo Māori in the news. We prepared our mihi, but when I spoke, I tried to sound more Pākehā so no one would think I was pretending to be something I'm not. Then I sat down and burned with shame.

6. Last Wednesday, I told the organiser of our mihi whakatau that I had been to pōwhiri before because I'm Māori. He laughed at me.

7. Because I didn't want another reason.

Kiri Piahana-Wong

Nō hea koe?

I'm in my grandfather's English village, where the pace of life remains slow and houses still have thatched roofs and wide brick chimneys. The fishing fleet is small now, but, as always, departs at dawn, seeking cod and bass across the narrow North Sea. For dinner at night, mackerel or cod, oysters, stewed vegetables and mash. I am visiting the village, Faversham, with my mother, but she has no known connections remaining here. So, we just walk around for an hour and then eat at the local pub. I've never had mackerel before. It tastes both strong and sweet.

I'm in my Māori grandmother's town, where the Crown took our land and on it built the city of Tauranga and, in return, gave my tūpuna new land to occupy by the town rubbish dump. In my great-uncle's whare, my father and 15-year-old me drink tea, and the men have a kōrero about the state of our remaining land, which is currently leased to a Pākehā farmer, and disputes within the hapū about the way forward. There is a pending Māori Land Court case because of bitter internal disagreement.

I've travelled to my marae with a cousin as our iwi is hosting the poukai of the Māori King. It's been some years since my last visit. In the wharekai I sit next to one of our foremost kaumātua. I nod politely and greet him but he turns his back and engages the whaea on his other side in conversation for the rest of the meal. 'We haven't seen your father here in a long time,' another woman says to me. 'Is he well?' For the remainder of the visit, I focus on sweeping floors and washing dishes.

I'm with the Chinese side of my family, a gathering that always involves food and lots of it. At Yum Cha on a Sunday afternoon in Wellington, the restaurant is buzzing while big groups of people are gathered at round tables all eating with gusto and talking over each other at the tops of their lungs. My cousin, who grew up in Maktin, Guangdong, and who has now emigrated to New Zealand to further her prospects and education, orders for the table in a confident and brisk manner. Plate after plate of food arrives. As I reach for an unfamiliar dish, my cousin bats my hand away. 'Don't eat that!' she advises. 'It is fried chicken feet. You have to grow up with it to like it.' I gingerly try one anyway and find that she is right. It is the most disgusting thing I have ever eaten.

I'm with my sister's family to celebrate the new Matariki public holiday. We sit down and eat together — me and my little son, my mother, sister, brother-in-law, and small niece and nephews. This is only a tiny part of my immediate whānau and we are quite a crowd. If we ever got the whole family together we'd have to hire a hall. My sister and brother-in-law don't have seats at the table because there aren't enough chairs. 'It's ok,' my sister says, as she hovers around attending to her baby. My son loves the dinner. He is four years old and does not suffer from any of the identity crises that plague me: he is with his cousins, he belongs. I smooth his wheat-blond hair and eat a third serving of fried rice. It tastes like every Sunday night of my childhood. My sister is reading descriptions of the stars of Matariki to the children while they eat. 'Hiwa-i-te-rangi is the star associated with granting our wishes,' she reads, 'and realising our aspirations for the coming year.'

Kiri Piahana-Wong

New Year

For Chinese New Year,
my grandfather cooks fried rice
and sweet 'n' sour pork
My Māori grandmother
prefers sweets
She bakes: rich plum cake,
preserves, biscuits, whipped cream
Matariki passed us by
Just another month of cold,
nothing special
And now my grandparents
have passed on too
None of their children can speak
Chinese, their father's tongue
Only one can speak te reo
My grandmother believed this:
English is the way forward
And she moved her family of nine
off tribal land in Tauranga to
Auckland, where there were
more opportunities
In some ways, she was right:
all of her children found work,
they flourished
In the 1990s, my dad and brother
and I went to te reo classes
We built stories with the coloured
rākau, we tried to speak
We were shy and I
have green eyes
Now it's 2016 and I can barely

remember anything but
my dad still cooks my grandfather's
fried rice, and every year
we gather plums
to make jam

Hāora Hema

The Whitest of Nan's Mokos

Without a [Māori] past, without a [Māori] future, it was impossible for me to live my [Māoriness]. Not yet white, no longer wholly [a Māori], I was damned.

Frantz Fanon, *Black Skin White Masks*
Note: 'Māori' in brackets replaces 'black'.

Part 1

In my Professional Studies class at teachers' college in 2002, there were two Māori students, myself and one other. Near the end of the course, our tutor singled us out, and told the class, 'these two will have it the hardest . . . all of the Māori problems, and all of the problem Māori children, will be their problems'. Our tutor meant that sympathetically, and somehow at the same time, encouragingly. Earlier in the year, she asked us to tell the class about our upbringing, to highlight that we were different – a fact she believed our Pākehā counterparts were not aware of.

In my first job in a New Zealand high school, I became the Kaitiaki or guardian of Māori students. This affirmed what my teachers' college tutor thought – that all the Māori problems would become my problems. The role of Kaitiaki (as it was conceived by some well-intentioned person) was to deal with the particular problem of Māori achievement, but put more accurately, Māori under-achievement. Learning to assert my agentic self, and my rights to self-determination, I began affirming my own definitions. I decided my role, as Kaitiaki, was more about the care and wellbeing of Māori students.

The Deputy Principal that I reported to was very supportive, but also had to 'deal with me', and try and understand the basis of my assertions that us Māori shouldn't have to always conform to the school; couldn't the school conform to us sometimes, even just a little? Couldn't teachers at least say our names properly? I did get hauled into her office on more than one occasion to 'please explain', but generally she was receptive and did her best to get 'the Māori thing'. One day she said something that really struck me. She said I was 'complicated'. At first, I was taken aback, but really I can't disagree. I am complicated. It is necessary that I at least try to explain my complication(s).

I was born Joshua Karl Browne, 1975, in Wairoa. My father is a Pākehā (family name Browne), and my mother a Māori (Hema). '*Injected with bastardy*', my complications probably start here. My parents divorced when I was seven, and both left town — my father went to Australia, and my mother moved to Wellington. My sister and I stayed behind. Initially I lived at my Pākehā grandparents' (henceforth Nanna Browne's), and my sister with my Māori grandparents (the Hemas). I went between the two households: '*2 poles of a world . . . 2 poles in perpetual conflict.*'

Between the ages of 7 and 12, when I lived in Wairoa, and while going between family members, I was not fully aware of the things that made me Māori. 'Real' or brown-skinned Māori, like the rest of my Māori family, were '*over-determined from without*'. Being very white-looking, I was (and am) '*over-determined from the inside*', where the Pākehā world has injected me with '*extremely dangerous foreign bodies*', as you shall see.

One day, around the dining table at Nanna Browne's, I recall my grandfather announcing and rejoicing in his calculation that I was apparently only 1/8th Māori, not even a 'quarter-caste!' Despite this, I was usually referred to as 'a Māori', or 'the Māori'. One day I was hiding (as Māoris do), and overheard my grandparents talking. My grandfather was telling Nanna Browne how well I had played rugby that day, 'even better than Allister'. I remember feeling very happy about that first bit. But! Nanna Browne was astounded! How could I possibly be better than Allister? Because in her exact words . . . 'but he's a Māori'.

One day we were on the veranda as we had visitors — family from out of town. Jeremy (a cousin of the same age) was getting rowdy and seeking too much attention. An adult suggested Jeremy should go to the town baths. Jeremy exclaimed that he didn't want to go to the town baths because, 'there are too many Māoris there.' Laughter. '*I slip into corners, and my long antennae pick up the catch phrases strewn over the surface of things . . . I remain silent.*' Uncle Stu interjected: 'You better be careful, Jem,' he warned, 'Joshie will give you a hiding.' Uncle Stu was fucking a Māori woman at the time, and no one could say her name properly — except me. I felt some sympathy from Uncle Stu in this, and that was probably due to where his penis had been, or where it was going to go next . . . exploring, colonising. *'I strive for anonymity, for invisibility'*; *'I slip into corners.'*

One day my mother visited from Wellington and explained she was moving back, and that we would be living with her in Nūhaka. Whaaat! My grandfather was enraged, fisted the table and yelled, 'I will not have my grandchildren travelling on a bus with Māoris!' Oh, so I'm not a Māori then? At Nanna Browne's, we sat at the table, properly. My mother never did move back.

From then on, I lived at the Hemas'.

I can't really explain why I have more affinity to my Māori side, *'I turn away from these inspectors of the Ark before the Flood,'* or even why I would ever want to choose to be a Māori given the *'existential deviation'* and the *'metaphysical misery'*. Life at the Hemas' was hard, the differences stark. At the Hemas', our house was small, bedrooms were full, and beds spilled out onto the living room floor. We bathed on Sundays (only) when Poppy lit the fire and boiled the water. Being the youngest, I was last in, 10th into the lukewarm water.

Food and the eating of it was different. At the Hemas' we rejoiced, clambered over each other, and got excited about food. We all helped Nan with the cooking and the 'clear up'. If we asked Nan: what's for tea? She'd say 'shit on toast!' If we complained we got a 'clip around the ears'. We could eat with our fingers, pick up bones, and suck out the ngoro. We could have more, 'as long as we ate it all'.

At the Hemas', we could 'stay up late' (or so Nanna Browne thought), play card games, and gamble. The language we used exposed the limits of our world. We could say things like, 'Uncle Pep's done a big shit, and it's clogged up the shit hole' . . . *'to make him talk pidgin is to fasten him to the effigy of him'*. People would laugh. We fought hard and fought all the time. I never heard Nan and Pop speak though — to each other. Nan yelled, and screamed, and ordered; Pop grumbled and mostly ran away. We could steal from the shop (although I never did) because 'the bloody Pākehā' had stolen from us.

Everyone's photo was on the wall. There were a few I didn't know; Uncle so-and-so didn't come back from Vietnam. Uncle so-and-so (we think) is somewhere in Australia. Uncle so-and-so has gone away, 'Bloooody iiiidiot's in jail, agaaaiiin, clooowwn!'

At some point I realised there was more than one photo of me on the wall – and Nan favoured me. I knew for sure my aunties pitied me, and were 'pissed off' with my mother for 'buggering off'. Nan couldn't understand why she'd left, 'ungrateful bitch', my father had 'bought her a washing machine'.

Nan would take all the photos down when someone died. She showed me things – spiritual things, signs when someone died, moving things, a kind of astral travel, mākutu. Her grandfather, Haora Ngarangimataeo, was a tohunga – a kind of Māori priest or spiritual chief. I was the whitest of all her children, Nan would say, 'but the most Māori'. Not sure how.

Nan's other grandfather, Haenga Paretipua, was a chief of Wairoa. Another ancestor owned the whole of the lake (Waikaremoana), and the area that is now the golf course, which the 'bloody Pākehā stole', and they are still 'stealing our whitebait, bleeming huas'. I sometimes went with Nan to land meetings. We went to the marae, directly to the wharekai, where it seemed people hovered around like ghosts, and spoke in whispers about land, and what they thought they owned.

Once when Nan was a Māori warden, she jumped in and stopped a gang fight. Another time, when Uncle Moot came home in a patch, Nan took it off him, and burnt it in front of him. I figured you didn't fuck with Uncle Moot – he'd been away a few times. You definitely didn't fuck with Nan. A 'Sheila' did once, with a knife, and came off second best. But Uncle Moot was kind enough to me. One day I was fighting with Jamie and he broke us up and said, 'Stop fucking fighting.' Another day, in front of all of the mobsters, he bought me an ice cream. I licked that ice cream and 'the bugger' fell off. Uncle Moot cracked up, went back in, and came out with another, in front of the mobsters. But one time at a party, a mobster took Uncle Dove's leather jacket, and Uncle Moot just stood by and watched, 'fucking cunt'.

One day I went to the courthouse with my favourite uncle, Uncle Dove. Uncle Dove had stolen a car – and got caught, 'Egg'. We took a crowbar to the courthouse, just in case. Uncle Dove had smashed up a mobster for smashing up the stereo at a party. All the mobsters would be at the courthouse that day. And apparently, 'mobsters don't forget'.

One of my classmates was laid on the train tracks for 'ticking up' and not paying up. He ended up with one leg, but even still he joined the mob. Another mate, Albert Brown, the best rugby player in town, was with the Black Power by intermediate, aged 12. He started scrapping with Leroy Grant, who was with the mob. We were all best friends once. My other mate Reg from down the road is in the mob. When we were four years old he stole my marbles – but he probably just won them from me. My father went down and got them back. I saw Reg at Nan's tangi, I hadn't seen him in 20 years. He gave me the Māori hello – slow raise of the head and slight lift of the eyebrows. I wondered if he wondered about marbles.

There is a saying from where I come from . . .

'Wairoa – Frasertown. Cousins killing cousins.'

Lucky I left then, when I was 12.

To Australia.

Part 2

Australia was by no means an awakening. My best mate Timmy was an Aboriginal, and we both liked Bob Marley equally as much. White Australian kids liked Kylie Minogue. Now, doesn't that say something? Timmy and his family, they knew what it was like, without ever talking about it. Timmy's uncle had died in prison. I hear Aboriginals have it worse than us Māoris. I couldn't really say, but probably, because I've never heard of a Māori getting bashed to death in prison by the police, not lately anyway. Not since maybe Te Kooti and some of my people were jailed on Wharekauri (without trial), or Rua Kēnana and his people who were shot up by the police at Maungapōhatu. The New Zealand police pointed their guns at the whole of fucking Tūhoe just a few years back – they just didn't pull the triggers, 'fucking baldheads, pig shits!'

For me, Australia was some sort of sanctuary, a place where no one knew I was Māori. It can be helpful being white. In Australia, the confusion was masked and hidden, mostly by my age and ignorance – although I could still feel the pain, deeply. I drank and smoked from far too young, and was way too violent. But I did survive, and even finished school – the first on my Māori side to do so. When I came back to New Zealand at 17, apparently from then, I could speak English. So, I suppose, thanks Australia.

I didn't go home to Wairoa, but to the city, Wellington. My mother lived there, but I couldn't stay with her – she was with yet another Pākehā, how many was that now? Not that I gave a shit. Fanon, tell me again why black women want white cock? Was it something about an '*inferiority complex*', or a '*wish to be white*'? Perhaps if you can't be one, appropriating by fucking one comes close. Here's one better, how about having a half-caste child, or what was I again, 'not even a quarter-caste', not accepted by no one. Mother, what were you trying to do, be white through me? Actually, I take some of that back, Nan accepted me. I lived at a university hall.

Now. Victoria University had a marae! Wow, now isn't that choice! A place for me? Hmmmm, nah, not really. I was studying maths and physics, so I'm not sure why I took Māori language. Nan and Pop Hema were native speakers. Nan would sometimes watch Te Karere, the Māori news on television, and rarely you might catch Pop hiding in the backyard speaking Māori to a mate. But everyone knows this story . . .

'. . . *White society has smashed his old world without giving him a new one. It has destroyed the traditional tribal foundations of his existence and it blocks the road of the future after having closed the road of the past . . .*'

Apparently one time, my mother was visiting from the city, saw Pop, and said, 'Kia ora.' Pop cried. He told my mother about the beatings at school. When I heard this, I couldn't believe it. Not about the beatings, but rather that he had cried. Pop, even at 70, had huge biceps, and was called Lofty for good reason. The original Lofty was a champion wrestler, and Pop, like Lofty, could handle himself, and other people. Pop didn't seem to care when Nan fed him shit, although I knew he did.

So, as it was, and as is usually the case, I didn't know a lick of Māori, and was doing Māori 101. Although, as you may recall, I could say Aroha – the name of the lady that Uncle Stu was fucking. Now, who knows what that means?

I hated Victoria University and the marae there. Supposedly I did learn something though. I learned about the things that should make me Māori. I should be able to sing (I was stuffed from here), haka, play guitar, play rugby, speak Māori, speak on the marae, handle my piss, and, fuck . . . . , look brown. (You thought I meant fuck, as in fuck like a Māori, didn't you?) Being so white, I was never going to be, or get that lucky. (Could I have some of that white privilege please? You know the one where I get to fuck Māoris.)

I was at the university pub in my first year, still three years underage. I saw a Māori in the toilet and said, 'Bro, got any dope?' He looked down at me, like he was looking down on me, and said slowly, deliberately, 'I'm not your bro.' '*I attach myself to my brothers . . . to my horror, they too reject me'*. I wish I could fight like the rest of my Māori family — I would've punched that cunt in the face.

I'm not sure where my salvation came — or if it ever has. I like women, but I loved watching Jamie Belich strut (back in Wairoa, I once stood between a homophobe, his butcher knife, and a gay man). I had a history lecturer who openly derided Belich. Belich was a 'wog' (I learned this word in Australia) or something, which must've made him sympathetic. He told a different story, as he strutted around. He told us that Māori resisted, and resisted superbly well, won (but ultimately lost), and that at times we were ingenious. Tītokowaru proclaimed, 'I shall not die', until his people ditched him, right before the final victory, for perhaps being a paedophile, a faggot, or maybe sleeping with another chief's wife. Who knows? Jamie! Did you ever ask Tītokowaru's people? Not that they'd ever tell you — and not that I hold it against you — for being a sympathetic Pākehā. Make up all the history you want, if you want to — that's what Pākehās do anyway — to keep New Zealand's '*mythology intact'*. Jamie, fuck it — keep strutting! But perhaps Tītokowaru was just a savage Māori after all.

Ranginui, the distinguished gentlemanly Māori scholar, seemed way too gentle to be so radical. His book told us about our struggles, and that it was a struggle without end. Moana Jackson, the intelligent intellectual, told us about the treaty, tino rangatiratanga, and our sovereign rights, that we NEVER ceded. Māori marched and occupied, the way we've done since Te Whiti. Fuck, how about we blow some shit up? I lived with Bruce Stewart, the freedom fighter, who built his own urban marae. I've wondered if Bruce ever got his freedom before he died. I met Eva Rickard, the activist, at Bruce's. I kissed her on the cheek, as I thought was acceptable. She pierced me sternly: 'What's wrong with my nose?' she said. '*From the opposite end of the white world a magical [Māori] culture was hailing me*.' I learned to hongi.

'*Unable to assimilate he associates with the dead*.' There is an idea in Māori that we move backwards into the future, confidently, presumably by learning about and looking back at the past. I experience this more like a spinning, like trying to catch something while off-balance. When I look back, or rather stumble off-balance backwards (or was it forward), I learn about death, then fall forward, more death, and my own, shedding of white skin — a death, that is coming. Is it time to take the photos down? In 1865, my people were murdered at Ōmaruhakeke. A year later, the New Zealand government confiscated, but a better word is stole, our land, despite most of my people being loyalists, but more accurately materialists. I have been learning, but now I'm frozen . . . and I still can't sing.

And, I'm not even started. There is so much more to tell you, for you to know what it is like, frozen, cold, spinning backward, falling forward, nauseous, spewing, vomiting things I'm told, but just don't feel. But I'm just too tired, and tired of it, to talk about it any longer, to confront it and struggle with it any further: the contradiction that exists in New Zealand society, Māori this and Māori that.

In a '*society that makes his inferiority complex possible*', a place that, '*brings about the emergence of a mass of illusions and misunderstandings*'. In New Zealand, it's like this. When in, say, a park, speaking Māori to my kids, 'staunch' Māori accept me. Most Māori shy away, almost frightened, hide away from me. Good-natured Pākehā fuckwits (a higher percentage than you might think), curious, may hypothesise something like, 'Oh, they're from Spain, speaking Spanish', until they gain the courage to ask, and I tell. Now confused and no longer curious they slip away, not into corners, but into spaces they dominate, just not mine, clearly. In a professional context, like a school (you might think), when I speak Māori, and I do, and I will . . . I know . . .

'Ka mate ka mate . . . it's death, it's death.'

. . . that I will probably never have an authentic conversation with a Pākehā in that context, ever again. This is how it is. '*To state reality is a wearing task*', and I feel the weight of New Zealand bearing down on me. I'm tired, dying of tiredness, from being Māori — but I can be thankful, for being white — at least security doesn't follow me around the supermarket, right?

'Ka ora ka ora . . . it's life, it's life.'

But what kinda life is this?

Tania Roxborogh

Rapurapu / Searching

Rapurapu weaving

Five of us sit, *harakeke* strips at our feet.
Threads of conversation tangling into a problem
Ko wai koe?
I shrug: *Aua*
I am the middle of them, middle aged, middling, choosing to knit not weave, my balls of black and red wool stuffed into the handbag beside my feet safe from the snag of flax leaves.
He aha ai e noho ana au?
Choosing something I can do in their company: these women, older and younger, fingers thick and soft and fast, their laughter too, *tā rātou mahi* making new things from old *mātauranga*.
We share our stories but I realise once again that my stitches, like me, are cast by *te pīpīwharauroa* a cuckoo bird: foreign to them, familiar to me.
While they select the leaves and join and fold and twist to create a part of a magnificent whole, the lineage of their families connected, *kōmitimiti*, secured in place by mountain, *awa, marae,*
Too late, I realise that I am
An unfinished row
A broken thread
Kāore e mau ana
Unanchored to anything certain.
Nō hea koe?
Neither here nor there
Ko wai ō tāngata?
Neither us nor them
Kei te pātai rātou anō: nō hea koe?
Neither theirs or ours

I tipu ake au i wīwī, i wāwā so
No unity for me
No *iwi* tribe
No family or *whānau*
Kore pungatia ki tētahi wāhi ki ētahi tāngata
No surety of every *hea* where I came from:
the way forward filled with
tangled, knotted narratives, *te mutunga*, ends
(plot) holes filled with *taniwha* and resentful *kuia* saying:
'Who are you to
    kī ana i tēnei
        speak that truth
            claim that name?'
I pick up the wool and set the needle to dive into the knitting. It digs into my hand, pricks my thumb and I say:
Ko wai ka hua ko wai ka tohu?
who knows?
'*Kaua e āwangawanga*; it is no matter,' says one, handing me her half-finished weaving. 'I started this for you. *Haere tonu*. Go on from here.'
I put down my needles and hold it, *tēnei harakeke* in my lap, her hand on mine, showing me how to join and fold and twist.
'Keep your fingers here,' she says, *ōna ringaringa* pressing lightly *ki waenga pū* the centre threads, *te aho tapu*. 'This is your anchor. If you muck up, *me tīmata anō*, you can always come back to this point.'

Searching *raranga*

E noho ana mātou, kei te papa i ngā *flax* mātātara.
Pōwhīwhiwhi haere ngā miro kōrero, raru ana.
who are you?
He hikihiki pakihiwi taku whakautu: *Who knows?*
Kei waenganui au o rātou, kei ahua taipakeke ahau.
Kāore au te kōwhiri te raranga, ka nitiniti kē.
Ānei taku wuru whero me taku wuru pango kei roto taku kete,
haumaru ana i ētahi mātātara.
why am I sitting here?
Ka taea e au te mahi nei te mahi ki a rātou: ētahi wāhine, pakeke mai,
taitamāhine mai. Ko ō rātou ringaringa he mōmona, he māenene, he
tere hoki. Katakata ana, *their work* e whakahanga ana rātou i ngā mea
hou mā ngā mea tāwhito *knowledge*.
Ka toha mātou i ā mātou kōrero paki engari, ākuanei, ka marama anō
ahau ka whakamautia aku kaui i te pīpīwhauroa *the shining cuckoo*.
He maitai ki mātou, he waia ki au.
Kei kōwhiri ana rātou i ngā mātātara, ā, te tūhoto, ā, te whātuitui, ā,
te kārure hoki hei te whakahanga i wahanga o tētahi mea whakahira
(ka whakamaua ō rātou whakapapa *blended* ki ō tōna maunga, *river,
village*)
tureiti, ka marama au ko au
he raranga hukihuki,
he tui pakaru hoki
Not fixed
kore pungatia ki tētahi wāhi ki tētahi tāngata
Where are you from?
Kore tēnei, kore tēnā rānei
Who are your people?
Kore mātou, kore rātou rānei
They ask again: whose are you?
Ehara i te tangata.
I grew up all over the place nōreira
kāore kotahitanga maku
Kāore he *tribe*
kore he *family*
Not anchored by a place or people rānei
Kore kore rawa te mōhio au nō hea *place* au, ā,

kore rawa te mōhio pēhea e haere tonu ai.
Nā to mea (te ara nei) ka puta mai te ara nei i ngā puna ki ngā kōrerorero pōwhīwhiwhi, *the finish* me ngā *monster* taniwha *and elderly women* me ngā kuia nihoniho, e kī ana
'Ko wai koe *to speak this*
ki te kī tēnā kōrero pono,
te kokoraho i tēnā ingoa?'
Ka tangohia te wuru e au, ā, whakareri i ngā taputapu hei te tīmata i taku mahi nitiniti. Kei te kō ia, te oka i tōku kōnui, ā, ka kī au:
Who can say?
Ko wai ka hua ko wai ka tohu?
'*Do not be anxious*. He aha', e kī ana tētahi wahine, e takoha ana ia i tona raranga hukihuki ki au. 'Kua tīmāta au i tēnei ki koe. Haere tonu! *Keep going.*'
Ka tuku au i ngā taputapu, ā, ka mau au i *this flax* kei runga taku waewae ki tōna ringaringa kei roto tōku, ako ana ia ki au pēhea te tūhoto, ā, te whātuitui, ā, te kārure hoki
'Kia mau o ringaringa ki reira', e kī ana ia, romiromi ana *her fingers* i te pukapūtanga, *the sacred first line*. Ko tau toka tū moana. Mehemea ka whakahē, *start again*, ka hoki mai koe ki tēnei wāhi.

J. Wiremu Kane

Tha Ara Rīpeka (*Crossroads*)

Paengawhāwhā, eleventh lunar month of the Māori year (approximately equivalent to April) 1997

A Bad End to a Good Day

Mum's head emerged from behind the laundry door. Kotahi froze as she looked him up and down, from his thick, black-brown curls to his bare, mud-spattered feet.

'What have you done with your school shoes?' she asked.

What have I . . . ?

Kotahi's body reacted before his mind could catch up.

A smooth, cool lump swelled in his throat like he'd sucked a pebble into his windpipe.

ASPIRATION

His heart buzzed against his ribcage. He couldn't have. He couldn't possibly have lost *another* pair of shoes.

The first pair had been six months ago. A pair of black leather imitation Doc Martins, complete with thick golden-yellow stitching and black and yellow laces that reminded Kotahi of bumble bees.

On that hot October afternoon, Kotahi had felt the grey wool of his socks growing thick with sweat. When it became too much for him, he abandoned the shoes on a bench in the enclosed deck of Room Seven. At the 3 pm bell, he hadn't given the shoes a moment's thought as he raced barefoot across the hot asphalt for the bus.

'They'll still be there tomorrow,' he said to his parents that night when he realised.

Dad shook his head in that annoying, slow way he did when he wanted to make you feel bad.

'Those were good shoes.' The corners of Dad's mouth drooped lower than usual.

Kotahi wanted to defend himself. Wanted to say they weren't even *real* Doc Martins, and he hadn't left them behind on *purpose*, but a look from his oldest sister Awhina warned him it was better to remain quiet.

'Plenty of room left in them.' Dad was still going on. 'Rua could've had them when you outgrew them.'

'Sorry,' Kotahi mumbled, his eyes fixed on the floor.

'Look at me when I'm talking to you, please,' Dad said.

Kotahi couldn't meet Dad's big green eyes. He focused on the space between them. There was a long, stray hair in the otherwise empty space between his thick eyebrows. Kotahi had a strange urge to reach over and pluck it out.

'I'm sorry,' he said again, his voice a little louder.

'Don't be sorry,' Mum said. She always said that, her voice weary and put-upon, fine-tuned to extract maximum guilt. 'Just try to be more careful in the future. *Please*.'

'I'll try.'

And he had tried, he really had.

Mum was still looking him up and down, as if wondering how she had given birth to such a slovenly child.

SLOVENLY

What a wonderful word. Miss Whittle had put three big ticks next to it when he used it in his story about a hedgehog that could talk and became best friends with a boy a bit like Kotahi after the boy scooped it from the swimming pool with the leaf net before it got sucked into the churning filter.

It had been a good story and the word felt good to say, even if it was too close to *slob* for his liking.

'Rinse your feet off before you get into bed,' Mum said at last. 'Or you'll be muddying up your sheets. And your toenails need cutting too.' Her head disappeared back into the laundry.

Kotahi followed her into the tiny room. It smelt like detergent and static electricity. He squeezed past her to the high sink, climbed onto the dryer, and sluiced his muddy feet under the tap. Cold tickled the blue veins on the soles of his feet. His toenails *did* need cutting. His left big toenail had a jagged cutting edge that could tear through socks and duvet covers.

He was always wary of cutting them too short, of blood clots sticking to the swollen tender skin.

Mum looked up from detangling wet clothes, her mouth open in dismay.

'I meant in the bathroom!'

'Oh.' Too late it seemed obvious that's what she had meant. 'Sorry, I didn't think . . .'

'Your shoes?'

ASPIRATION

He'd been having such a good day until then . . .

The morning had been as clear and sharp as broken glass. Kotahi and his younger brother Rua blew plumes of steam at each other while waiting for the school bus.

'I'm Smaug the dragon!' Kotahi cried, spreading his arms out like wings as he blew clouds at Rua.

'I'm not up to that chapter yet!' Rua complained. 'I'm still at Mirkwood.'

The late April air smelled like rotting fruit and just snuffed birthday candles. Kotahi wrinkled his nose at the bucket of overripe feijoas Rua had collected to share at school. There was something acidic and vomity to their perfume.

Glary light bounced off the wet asphalt of Riverside Road and the rainbow edges of oil-slicks on the autumn puddles.

Kotahi and his best friend Maz had even found a tiny patch of frost in the shadows between the back of Room Three and the rubbish skip. He tested the strength of the collage of ice and dead leaves on the surface of a puddle with his foot. It cracked in a millisecond. Frigid water filled Kotahi's shoes and his toes curled away from the wet wool of his sock.

He remembered wanting to kick his leg out like a dog trying to flick away mud. He wanted to flick away the wet sock, the wet shoe, maybe his whole foot. But he had still been wearing them through the morning . . .

'They got wet,' Kotahi said, towelling off his feet and lower legs. He climbed down off the beeping dryer and pulled out the load of staticky towels. He wasn't much good at folding washing, but he felt under the circumstances – he should try.

Mum heaved sodden washing into a basket and began piling the next load into the machine. Kotahi folded a stiff towel in half then into thirds, no, half again, *then* into thirds.

'Is Dad still at the hospital?' he asked.

'Him and Aunty Maggie are trying to sort out getting Granddad home,' Mum said. 'It'll be nicer for everyone that way.'

Kotahi wasn't sure what she meant. Nothing about Granddad's long illness had been nice for anyone. Not the late-night phone trills that made Kotahi's chest squeeze like an accordion, pumping and squishing his organs. Not the frequent visits from his aunties and uncles from around the country who came without the usual kisses, drinks, and laughter. Just hushed, half-heard conversations full of scary words like hospice, morphine, and

PALLIATIVE

A word Kotahi had scoured his dictionary to find the meaning of. A meaning that confirmed what he had long suspected but that no one would say out loud. One that he pushed to the back of his mind because he didn't know what else to do with it.

'There've been gastro outbreaks on two of the wards,' Mum went on. 'We'll take you and Rua to see him as soon as he's home with your grandma.' She looked at his growing pile of wonkily folded towels. The lines on her forehead relaxed a little. 'Oh, thanks,' she said, defeated. 'How wet are your shoes?'

Kotahi swallowed a mouthful of built-up saliva.

ASPIRATION

He could hear rain outside on the corrugated plastic awning that covered the back deck. Heavy rain.

'They got muddy too . . .'

Rachel B said there was frog spawn in the ditch that ran the length of the playing field.

'Really?' Kotahi asked. The last time it had been a major disappointment – a roll of old bubble wrap tangled in waterweed.

But as he'd crouched on the squishy mud of the bank, he could just make out tiny, wriggling tadpoles like black grains of rice in a patch of thickened water.

'Let me see!' Maz elbowed Kotahi in the ribs, and Kotahi slipped down into the shallow brown of the ditch.

The sun was high and hot by then. Kotahi left the shoes to dry in the sun until the end of lunchtime, when he shoved them into the bottom of his schoolbag, careful not to get mud on his black jacket or emerald-green Bishop Pompallier Catholic Primary jersey. Green was supposedly the colour of Bishop Pompallier. Kotahi wondered who had asked him.

'Scrape the mud off and put them in the hot water cupboard overnight.' Mum's instructions sounded like a sigh. She dropped the lid of the washing machine and stabbed at the buttons until it shuddered into life. 'And chuck your socks in before the machine finishes filling.'

She took the towels from Kotahi and smiled.

'Thank you, love. I'll finish these off.'

Kotahi opened his mouth to speak. If there was a good time to admit the full truth about his shoes, this was it.

'Mum, I –'

'Mum!' Awhina shouted down the hallway. 'Tell Terina that it's *my* sleepout! She's got her own room inside and I *never* get any space to myself.'

'Terina!' Mum was already out the laundry door. 'Sleep inside tonight, please!'

'You know she won't listen,' Awhi went on. 'She doesn't listen to *anyone*. Jesus, can you imagine if *I* tried to ignore you and Dad the way she does.'

'Terina! Where are you? Awhi, don't say Jesus like that please, it's not nice.'

Kotahi swallowed a burp. It somehow tasted of feijoas. He needed to clean his teeth as well as cut his toenails.

'You know his name was really Yeshua, right?' Awhi said. 'Which is just Joshua. Is it okay to say *Josh* like that instead?'

'Awhi, please!'

He hadn't *really* lied to Mum. And he knew exactly where he'd left his shoes. They'd still be there the next day.

He hoped.

Thug Life

That afternoon, Kotahi had had permission to go to his best friend Maz's house after school. He drummed his feet on the bus seat in front of him in time to Rua's rapping.

'And I pray, and I pray, and I pray, and I pray,' Rua's head bobbed in time to his singing. '*Everyday, everyday, everyday, everyday . . .*'*

Kotahi knew he'd have the song stuck in his head for days. He mostly remembered its terrifying music video, with a black angel of death collecting souls, seemingly at random. He also remembered the angel's bare and extremely muscular back when his wings were revealed at the end.

'Those aren't the right words,' Kotahi said.

'They're not?' Rua didn't seem bothered. 'I like my version better. Don't you?'

The bus rattled to a stop.

'Let's go,' Maz said.

'Bye!' Rua's bottom lip jutted as Kotahi and Maz exited the bus. It wasn't the closest stop to Maz's house, but the nearest to the real reason for Kotahi's excitement.

The Gully.

A little slash of green between the older suburb of Prince's Wood, with its established magnolias, cherry, and plum trees, and the boxy, samey houses of Harveston, where the slender trees were held up by stakes.

Kotahi and Maz skidded down the gravel track that crisscrossed the steep gully wall and skirted tufts of cutty grass and gorse bushes taller than houses. Kotahi's backpack rattled against his back and the corner of a hard-cover book poked him right under his shoulder blade.

Looking up at the eye-stingingly bright sliver of sky, Kotahi felt in a different world, a different planet from the surrounding city. A city his out-of-town cousins pulled faces at when named and gave their most devastating insult ever. *Boring*.

'At least we don't live out in the wop-wops,' was the standard reply, though a part of Kotahi wished he lived closer to their far north marae.

They followed the dirt path that wound along near the stream until they reached a wall of gorse. Even though they were clearly alone, Kotahi looked around before ducking under one of the bushes. He crawled through a tunnel of dry, brown needles, emerging into a green and gold glade they called their 'secret place'. The stream formed an unexpected loop away from the track, hidden by the prickly, peppery smelling gorse.

Weeping willows overhung the chittering brown stream. The sharp scent of onion weed sent sparks of confusion down to Kotahi's stomach. It grumbled and churned.

'Want a feijoa?' Maz pulled two out of her bag.

'Nah.'

'Ew!' She spat out a mouthful. 'They've got moth eggs in them!' She threw the feijoa at the trunk of a willow that had fallen like a bridge across the stream. The little green grenade exploded in a shower of yellow flesh and the vomity perfume smell Kotahi hated so much.

'Lemme have a go.' His feijoa missed, landing in the brown water of the stream with a plop.

'A tuna can eat it,' he said.

'Chew-na? The fish?'

'Tuna,' Kotahi repeated. 'It's um, what we call eels.' He paused. 'What did you call eels in Iraq?'

Maz shrugged.

'Don't remember,' she said. 'Probably just eels. We spoke English there too.'

Kotahi nodded. Maz never liked talking about Iraq and tended to squirm when asked about Arabic, though he heard her speak it to her dad, who hadn't moved out to New Zealand yet, on the phone sometimes.

'We live here now,' she would say, and Kotahi didn't like to push her further.

They followed the dappled sun as it shifted across the glade, clambering across the willow bridge. Maz had her head buried in the Goosebumps book Kotahi had loaned her. *The Cuckoo Clock of Doom*. It was a good one, one of his favourites, though the idea of reliving the same disastrous birthday party where his crush catches him in just his underpants, over and over, made him squirm inwardly.

Kotahi's own book was a nonfiction one about the water cycle. He glanced down at it every now and then and filed away some interesting words. EVAPORATION. CONDENSATION. TRANSPIRATION. All the green around them was TRANSPIRING. He mostly just sat, taking in the green and the onion smell, imagining invisible water all around them.

A flock of tiny waxeyes swept into the glade like a passing shower. They stripped a bush of its seeds and flowers then vanished. Kotahi wasn't sure if he'd imagined them. If he'd blinked just a little slower, turned his head a fraction, he might have missed them altogether.

Kirikiriroa, the stream gurgled. *Kirikiriroa*.

Kotahi imagined water being sucked up out of the ocean, EVAPORATION, rained down onto the swampy green of the Waikato, PRECIPITATION, trickling into the stream and finally emptying down into the massive river, DISCHARGING, like a tiny venule entering a thick vein.

'There's a taniwha at every bend of the river,' he said aloud. 'Waikato-taniwha-rau.'

'Really?' Maz looked up. 'Like, the monster?'

'Not *really*,' Kotahi said. 'Mum says it's Tainui boasting about how strong their chiefs are, but also a warning against like currents and submerged logs and stuff.'

'Utterly unforgiving' were the words Mum always used to describe the river.

A pair of pīwakawaka kamikazed through the air, snatching bugs that were barely visible in the filmy beams of light. They chinked and chirruped at each other as they spiralled overhead. Kotahi held out a hand, but the birds flitted away.

'I guess we should go,' Maz said as the tilt of the sun left the gully in shadows that were suddenly cold.

'Yeah.' A breeze ruffled the weeds and Kotahi's stiff brown curls. The trees sighed. He pulled his shoes and socks out of his bag and leaned them against a tree stump while he shook out his jersey and jacket to put on.

And that's where he'd left them.

They have *to still be there.*

He should have missed them when he had been packing up his things to leave Maz's house for his own. But there had been a distraction.

HOMO

'Is your mum home?' Kotahi called from the doorstep. He brushed as much mud as he could off his feet before entering.

'Nah!' Maz's voice was muffled by her closed bedroom door as she changed out of her uniform.

There was a strange man in the kitchen. He was shirtless and Kotahi's eyes darted down to where several centimetres of red and white satin boxer shorts showed above his low-slung jeans. Kotahi forced his gaze up, taking in the sparse, dark hairs below the man's belly button and around his brown nipples. At his face, Kotahi felt a jolt of recognition.

'Yousef.' Kotahi's voice sounded high and boyish.

'Hey brother,' Yousef said. He couldn't be fourteen yet, but his voice was as deep as a grown man's. Deeper than Dad's.

Kotahi hadn't seen Maz's older brother since he'd finished at Bishop Pompallier at the end of last year. Yousef's pudginess had stretched out. His severe bowl cut had been replaced by two greasy curtains of black hair either side of his centre part.

At eleven years old, Kotahi knew he had big changes coming soon. He'd read the pamphlet about 'Our Changing Bodies' with a mixture of horror and excitement, as the pictured children grew from compact and smooth to huge and hairy with massive drooping boobs, scrotums, and huge dangling penises. Bodies were interesting, but he knew he wasn't supposed to look too closely at other people's.

HOMO

But Yousef looked like his entire body had been replaced.

'Were you two playing down in the gully?' He turned back to the bench where he was slicing limes. His back and shoulders were red and shiny with pimples. Kotahi's own back itched in sympathy.

'Yeah.'

Yousef licked lime juice off his fingers. Kotahi could smell it over Yousef's body spray, Lynx Africa at a guess, and something else he couldn't place. The mystery scent burnt the inside of his nostrils and made his brain hum and rattle against his forehead.

'Huh?' he said to Yousef's expectant look.

'Water?'

'Oh, yeah. Thanks.'

The glass bobbed with lime wedges and mint leaves.

'You there, Yoose?' Maz entered the kitchen and rolled her eyes at the sight of her brother. 'Put some clothes on, you egg. Kotahi doesn't wanna see that.'

POOFTER

Kotahi forced a laugh.

He wasn't sure why he followed Yousef into his room. Two posters hung above the unmade bed, the map of The Wild from the front of *The Hobbit*, and the dead rapper who'd got shot last year.

'You read it?' Yousef nodded at the map.

'Yeah.' He wanted to say he pretended the gully was Mirkwood, that he half expected to stumble across feasting elves, or see giant spiders in the trees.

'You like Tupac?'

Kotahi took the excuse to study the second poster. Tupac too wore his jeans well below his boxers, though his were plain white. Kotahi wished he could ask his parents for boxers, his brightly coloured Jockey underpants felt suddenly childish. He couldn't wear sagging jeans with *those* underneath.

The dead rapper's muscles formed a deep V-shaped groove right below the T of THUG LIFE as it arched over his navel. His angular face was so beautiful Kotahi felt like he might cry.

'Yeah,' he said at last. 'I like, um . . . *Dear Mama*.' He hoped he'd got that right.

'Nice Bro.' Yousef raised his arms in a stretch that elongated his whole body. Kotahi could finally make out the pattern on Yousef's boxers, the Chicago Bulls basketball team logo. He found that he couldn't look away. He found himself wanting to play basketball, even though he hated how sweaty and uncomfortable sports made him.

PANSY

'Who else do you listen to?'

Kotahi liked dancing and lip synching to the Spice Girls with his older sisters. He liked Posh the best, even though she was the worst singer. But his sisters looked at his blue eyes and round cheeks and immediately assigned him Baby. He liked listening to his mum's Carpenters CDs. When Karen sang 'A Song For You', or 'Superstar', the sorrow in her voice sliced him to pieces. But he'd already learned that those weren't the right answers.

QUEER

And I pray, and I pray . . .

'Um, I like Tha Crossroads,' he said. 'You know, Bone Thugs-N-Harmony?'

'Right on.' Yousef mimed emptying a bottle onto the floor. 'Pour one out for Eazy-E.'

'What?'

'He died too, that's what that song is about.' Yousef looked up at the poster. 'But heaps of people say Tupac isn't *actually* dead. Just in hiding.'

Kotahi met Tupac's liquid brown eyes. They bored right through him. He couldn't imagine them not being alive. 'Did Eazy-E get shot too?'

'Nah.' Yousef gave Kotahi a look he didn't quite understand. 'AIDS.'

HOMO

'What?' Kotahi half-choked on his water.

ASPIRATION

'Eazy-E,' Yousef said. 'He didn't get shot. It was AIDS that killed him.'

Kotahi should've checked for his shoes before leaving Maz's. But they would still be in the gully the next day. They *had* to be.

The rain on the roof sounded louder than ever.

Waikato-taniwha-rau

Kotahi woke with a pebble in his throat, writhing tuna in his belly, and an aching jaw.

Rua sat at the window of their room, the curtains open, pale light shining on his round face through the wet glass.

'You were grinding your teeth in your sleep,' he said.

Condensation formed rivulets and pooled on the swollen wood of the windowsill. Kotahi imagined it wicking up the curtains and blooming into black florets of mould.

'I don't grind my teeth.' Kotahi rubbed the knotted angle of his jaw.

'Look how foggy it is!' Rua said, rubbing the window with his sleeve.

Kotahi could barely make out the red of the cherry tree leaves through the thick fog beyond the smudged window. He imagined standing on the pedestrian bridge that spanned the gully, white in every direction. He could be crossing a high pass over the Misty Mountains.

He took a deep breath. He had a plan.

He made sure to rush out to the bus before Mum could notice his still bare feet. He couldn't hide them from Rua though.

'Where are your shoes?'

'Doesn't matter.'

'Aren't your feet cold?'

Kotahi's feet were on fire with every touch of the gritty, wet concrete. He fished his spare school socks and summer uniform, brown roman sandals out of his bag.

'Hold this will ya?'

Rua held Kotahi's school bag and watched in silence. Kotahi balanced on his left foot, hopped into his right sock, and shoved his socked foot into its sandal. His toes pushed well through the straps and hung over the end.

How could his sandals already be too small?

'You lost your school shoes?' Rua's voice was awed. It was barely a question.

'Shuddup,' Kotahi said, switching feet and trying not to tip over.

'You lost *another* pair of shoes?'

Kotahi hadn't cut his toenails. His big toenail razor tore through the thin wool of his left sock. His entire toe erupted into view.

'Pokokōhua!'

ASPIRATION

Rua let out a gasp that turned into a giggle.

'That's a bad word!'

Maz wasn't on the bus. She wasn't in the classroom either, so she hadn't been dropped off by her mum, who always smelled heavily of musky perfume and was the exact opposite of SLOVENLY.

Kotahi could barely spare Maz a thought. He imagined everyone in the school, the city, the *universe* was staring at him, transfixed by his incongruent sandals, holey sock, and exposed toe.

You have a plan.

He wished he could share his plan with Maz and see what she thought of it. He didn't trust any of his other friends enough. When they asked why he was wearing sandals he repeated the sort of lie that his shoes were too wet and muddy. It had rained all night. They wouldn't just be wet; they would be drowned.

ASPIRATION

Kotahi sprinted for the bus when the 3 pm bell finally rang. He heard and felt a snap and stumbled, pitching sideways into a hedge of glossy camellias.

The strap of his right sandal had broken.

CHOKE

The fog had given way to half-hearted rain. He dumped the socks and sandals into the nearest bin. Rain spattered his face. He hoped it hid his brimming eyes.

'*And I pray, and I pray, and I pray,*' Rua rapped next to him. Kotahi couldn't even be bothered correcting him.

The bus reached the edge of Harveston. At the last possible second, Kotahi lunged for the closing doors. Rua's cry of protest was cut off by their hiss. Kotahi pulled the hood of his jacket down over his face against the now persistent rain and ran.

A stitch dug its sharp fingers into the soft bits under Kotahi's ribs. The inner seam of his shorts rubbed hot against his thighs. Gorse needles tried to rip away his schoolbag and jacket. His feet were numb.

They had to be there.

ASPIRATION

Rain filtered through the trees of the glade in a fine spray, studded with fat compound drops.

They had to be there.

ASPIRATION

That couldn't be the right tree. The twisted willows all looked the same.

It was the right tree.

CHOKE

His shoes weren't there. Had the stream broken its banks overnight? Were tuna giving them a wary sniff, wondering if the worn leather was worth nibbling? Had they made it all the way down to the mighty river? Or the ocean?

ASPHYXIATE

His first thought was that he could never go home, ever again. Maybe if these were only the second pair he'd lost?

But the second pair had been back in January.

A pair of almost new Reebok cross trainers, fresh white with the logo in aqua and lime. They had spent a magic afternoon splashing in the frigid water and cold, mineral smell of the Kaniwhaniwha stream with his siblings and cousins. He had clambered into Aunty Cate's little car, towels spread on the back seat, leaving the trainers in a little pile under the picnic table.

'We could drive back and get them,' he forlornly suggested to his parents.

'Drive all the way back to Pirongia?' Dad's voice was full of the sort of hot rage that would peter out before long. 'Do you think petrol is free? And they might not even be there! The last pair weren't where you said you'd left them!'

And when he had started crying.

'Do you have to be so *sensitive*?'

Sensitive had been a compliment once.

'*Two* pairs of shoes! In two months!'

It was much closer to four months, Kotahi had wanted to say, but he didn't need his older sister to tell him that would be the wrong thing to say.

Mum's near silence had been much worse. Her sad face struck Kotahi much harder than her angry one. She very slowly shook her head as she spoke.

'I thought you'd make more of an effort than this.'

Kotahi couldn't imagine the escalation of a third lost pair, with the added crime of running to the gully without permission.

KIRIKIRIROA! the stream roared. *KIRIKIRIROA!*

He wondered how long he would need to be missing in the wet for his parents' relief at him arriving home safe to outweigh their anger. Weeks, probably. Maybe months.

He imagined Mum leading a search party, everyone in fluorescent yellow and orange, torch beams useless against the rain and thickness of the gorse bushes. He imagined them shouting his name.

'Kotahi!' his mum and dad would shout. Maybe Awhi would be with them too, while Terina and Rua stayed at home in case he turned up there or someone phoned. Like the police.

'Co-tahi!' the search and rescue people would shout, despite them hearing Mum and Dad say it right.

'*Ko*-tahi!' he would whisper, sure that no one could hear him. 'It's *Ko* like apple core.'

He imagined them turning the dirt track to mud as they marched up and down it, missing the secret glade just beyond the bushes that no adult would think to crawl under.

A pīwakawaka chirruped near his head. It sat rigid, its wings folded like a stern pair of hands on hips, white stripes of feathers arched like aggressively pencilled eyebrows.

'Tēnā koe,' Kotahi whispered to the tiny bird. 'Can I live here with you?'

It chirruped again, a metallic warning.

KIRIKIRIROA! the stream thundered.

Without thinking, Kotahi scrambled over the willow bridge, up the steep bank, over a wire fence and into a blackberry-choked paddock. He looked back.

The stream was a wall of brown-white that tore across the glade. For a fraction of a second, Kotahi saw the stream as the biggest tuna in the universe, fat, brown, and muscular. Too big for the little streambed, it surged through the trees, swiping limbs and entire bushes, black eyes rolling, enormous jaws wide. Its eyes met Kotahi's.

KIRIKIRIROA! it roared. Its voice sounded like when water was released from the Aratiatia Dam, the hissing roar of too much water being forced through too narrow a gap.

It bit the willow bridge in two and swept it away, leaving a muddy stump and a few dangling roots.

Kotahi blinked.

Whatever he'd heard about mighty chiefs or unforgiving currents, he was sure that he'd barely escaped one of the Waikato's hundred taniwha.

Hummus bi tahina

Kotahi's feet were as heavy and useless as rocks when he reached the back gate to Maz's house where it opened onto the park. He heard a few muffled swear words over the steady thrum of the rain.

'Yousef?'

The gate opened. Yousef wore a black hooded sweatshirt over his baggy jeans and held a packet of cigarettes.

'Kotahi? What are you doing out here?'

'Maz wasn't at school . . .' Kotahi's voice cracked. 'And I lost my shoes and –'

He couldn't hold it in. He blubbed into Yousef's chest.

SENSITIVE

'I haven't had a great day either,' Yousef murmured. He steered Kotahi through the gate. 'You smoke?'

Kotahi shook his head.

'Good. Filthy habit.' Yousef tossed the smokes over the fence. 'A guy gave them to me, and I thought they might be spliffs.'

'Guys give you stuff?' Kotahi asked.

Yousef let out a short laugh.

'The smart ones do.'

Kotahi wasn't sure what that meant, only that he didn't want Yousef to clarify.

'Come inside. It's freezing and you're soaked.'

There were cardboard boxes stacked in the lounge and more in the kitchen. Kotahi's stomach clenched.

'You're moving?'

'Yeah.' Yousef's voice was dull. 'My uncles wanna sell this place, so we're moving to Morrinsville with them.'

Morrinsville?

It might as well be the moon. Kotahi felt tears pricking again.

SENSITIVE

'Take all that wet stuff off and jump in the shower. I'll put on a quick wash and find you something to wear while it dries.'

Kotahi went into the bathroom and stripped to his blue underpants. They were somehow wet too. He peeled them off, opened the door a crack and shoved the bundle of wet clothes out.

The shower was much bigger and cleaner than the one at home. It had nice liquid soap, not slippery, hair-covered bars made up of the squished remains of old bars. The shampoo and conditioner bottles looked and smelled expensive, so he left them alone.

The water felt scalding on Kotahi's feet. His skin turned bright pink all over.

Yousef had already taken the posters down from his wall. On the bed he'd laid out a grey marle tracksuit, black t-shirt, a pair of purple and green Charlotte Hornets printed satin boxers, and two pairs of Bishop Pompallier Catholic Primary socks. Grey wool with two of the bishop's favourite emerald-green stripes around the top.

'I knew I had those around somewhere,' he said from the door. 'I can't help with the shoes though. You're just gonna have to fess up to your olds about those.'

'Thanks!'

'Those haven't been worn,' Yousef added as Kotahi picked up the boxers. 'They were already too small when Mum bought them for me. You can keep them. Might as well keep all of it.'

'Really?' Kotahi shuffled into the boxers without dropping his towel.

'Of course! Come get some food when you're ready.'

Kotahi paused by the phone in the hall.

ASPIRATION

He couldn't put it off any longer. Mum would have passed angry and be approaching frantic.

Rua answered after only two rings.

'Mum and the girls went to be with Dad up at the hospital.' Rua's voice was a breathless pant. 'They say it won't be long now, so they're organising getting him home tonight. Mum said . . . Mum said we'll be able to see him back at Grandma's tomorrow.'

PALLIATIVE

'Oh.'

'Yeah, everyone started arriving here this afternoon.'

Kotahi assumed by *everyone*, Rua meant Mum's family within the greater Waikato. The rest would trickle in over the next few days. It didn't matter that it was Dad's dad who was dying, the Matawhaorua whānau never failed to show up.

DYING

Kotahi couldn't decide if that word was scarier than *PALLIATIVE* or not. Not that it really mattered.

'When Mum called I told her Maz was off school so you went to take her your homework. Pretty good, right?'

Kotahi felt the pebble in his throat shrink down to a speck of dust.

'You're a legend, Rua.'

'Do you need someone to come pick you up? Aunty Cate said she could.'

'Nah, I'll walk when the rain stops.'

'See ya soon. We're watching *Labyrinth* out in Awhi's sleep out! Cousin Sian said she'd warn me before the scary bits so I can shut my eyes.'

'Cool,' Kotahi said, hanging up.

Dying, he thought. *Granddad is dying.*

He couldn't remember much about how their other koro had died six years earlier. It had been summer and Nanny had been worried about Koro's body lasting in the heat. He remembered his great-uncles being angry that Koro wasn't being buried up north '*where he belonged*'. He remembered Awhi and Terina crying, which probably meant that he and Rua had cried too. He and Rua couldn't help crying if they saw their sisters cry.

SENSITIVE

He had been to funerals beyond count. Students from Bishop Pompallier would often have to fill up the pews at the attached church when elderly parishioners had sparsely attended funerals.

The blender whirred from the kitchen over the sounds of hip-hop. Kotahi made sure his new clothes were hanging just right before following the sounds.

Yousef was moving a little in time to the blaring music. It took Kotahi a few bars to recognise his supposed favourite song, Tupac's *Dear Mama*. Yousef must have remembered.

Yousef stopped dancing when he saw Kotahi.

'Try this.' He held out the bowl of the blender. Kotahi stuck his finger into the beige goop and licked it. It tasted savoury and earthy.

'Yum, what is it?'

'Hummus bi tahina. Hmm.' Yousef licked his own fingers. 'Needs lemon juice.'

Kotahi realised some of the griping in his guts might be hunger. He'd barely eaten all day.

'Out of lemons. Limes will have to do. Grab one for me?'

Kotahi took a lime from the fruit bowl and rolled it on the bench the way he'd seen Maz do. He sliced it in half, and with a nod from Yousef, squeezed the juice into the blender. Acid found tiny cuts on his fingers. Gorse prickles and blackberry thorns. He licked it off.

'Try it now.'

The paste zinged and almost felt alive in Kotahi's mouth. He tasted garlic and salt he hadn't before.

'It's good!'

The front door clacked. Maz stormed into the room, her black hair frizzed in a halo around her head. Her face lit up at the sight of Kotahi and she burst into tears.

They were moving away.

SENSITIVE

Kotahi cried too.

Kotahi balanced his now dry school uniform on his knees in the back of Maz's mum's car. There were no free parking spaces on the street outside his house. Cars were illegally parked on the grass verges and straying over the neighbour's driveways. A string of coloured lights swayed between the cherry trees. He heard the wail of Mariah Carey from Dad's big stereo speakers as she and Boyz II Men tried to out riff each other. There would be dozens of pairs of shoes scattered along the front deck.

'Thanks,' he said to Maz's mum. 'Thanks, Yousef. Bye, Maz.'

'Bye, Kotahi.' Maz didn't cry this time, so Kotahi didn't either. She would probably be at the funeral. That was something.

'Take these too, brother.' Yousef passed a rolled-up tube out the car window, and they were gone.

Kotahi peeled the edge back and smiled.

The Hobbit map would make a perfect thankyou gift for Rua. And Tupac with his bare chest, bulging muscles, blasphemous tattoos and exposed underwear would look great hanging over Kotahi's bed.

HOMO

If he was brave enough.

Light was pouring out the open front door.

He'd looked into the black eyes of a taniwha and made it out alive.

He was brave enough.

*Misquoted lyrics based on 'Tha Crossroads' by Bone Thugs-N-Harmony, Copyright Sony/ATV Music Publishing LLC. Universal Music Publishing Group

Miriama Gemmell

gimme a bone

can't tell if you're
Māori are you
M ā o r i —
how will I know
to let you take up
space with nō te
raki ramblings of
lived s o m e
things or to c o n
fisc a t e the
blither blather hei
give v o i c e to
tētahi a t u —
how will I know
to roll my eyes or
be i n f i n i t e l y
patient for tētahi
a n ō struggling
to separ a t e a
c o l o n i s e d
self from deeply
t ū t u r u
one — how will I
know if I like you
as a p e r s o n
or by default —
gimme a b o n e
that a b r a'
m a t a u round
your neck there
or tourist taonga
— how will I know
whether to beat
myself late r for
g r a t i n g your
every word or if
we hono through
the w a o and
o c e a n waves
i h o matua and
Papa t ū ā nuku
who sustains us?

Nadine Anne Hura

The Garage Party

The stones were not yet in the hole when Leah turned up. She immediately regretted arriving so early. The street was quiet and the curtains were still drawn inside the house. She had expected to find the place humming with activity, potatoes a-peeling and jugs a-boiling, but when Leah stood still and cupped her ear to the front door she could hear nothing but the gentle suck-wheeze of slumber. The family, she realised in alarm, were still asleep. She dithered at the top of the stairs, cursing herself for not confirming the exact time she should arrive, assuming that 'putting down a hāngī' meant dawn. She was tiptoeing down the steps in an attempt to slip back to her car unnoticed, when out of the garage came a large man in an orange hi-vis jacket and work boots carrying a box piled high with shiny, just-washed cabbage leaves.

'Kia ora kia ora!' he said, stopping in his tracks and lifting his eyebrows towards her. Leah cleared her throat and put her shoulders back. She was determined not to be whakamā with her reo like she was in the classroom. Why else was she doing all this study, if not to use it in the real reo-speaking world? She came down the steps waving, then quickly remembered that a chin-lift looked more natural, so lifted her chin as well, giving her the appearance of an excited puppy. 'Tēnā koe,' she said breathlessly.

The man shifted the box under one arm and held out the other in greeting. Leah leaned in with her lips but he was lining up her nose like a plane above a runway and the whole thing ended with a headbutt and the unnatural sound of a kiss landing in mid-air.

Leah groaned internally. How many times had she practised the hongi in the mirror? A hongi always begins with eye contact!

The man smiled. He had dark, ropey skin and dimples so deep they might have been carved into his cheeks. It made her think of all the laughter that had shaped his face, like a chisel tap-tap-tapping away day after day, shift after shift. The green eyes, combined with the hi-vis jacket and work boots, reminded her of the photo of her father standing next to her pale English mother. She'd found the old Polaroid in a box under the bed while hunting for the Christmas tree and when she'd brought it out and asked her mother about it, Janet had scoffed and said, 'Biggest mistake of my life, that was,' barely looking up from the sewing machine. Though Leah had never met her father, or this man for that matter, it took all her self-control not to reach out and wrap both arms around him and sob into his vast reflective chest.

'I think . . .' Leah stammered. 'I think I'm a bit early. I came to help with the hāngī.' She smoothed down her jeans which suddenly felt too tight. 'I wanted to help but . . .' She gestured to the house and stated the obvious. 'Everyone's still sleeping.'

'Just us up at this time,' the dimpled man said, nodding towards the back of the garage where tendrils of smoke were curling towards the sky. 'Fire's got to burn down. It'll take a few hours.'

He began to walk and, not knowing what else to do, Leah followed.

'Nō hea koe?' the man said, looking sideways at her. Literally speaking, he was asking where she was from, but Leah knew that what he really wanted to know was who she was, and why she'd turned up here at the crack of dawn looking like a foreign exchange student on a tiki tour. Leah wondered quite the same thing. All she could think of was the man with tattoos.

'I'm from . . . nō te Nōta,' Leah said, trying to copy the casual tone of her mate Tarns. 'Ko Ngāpuhi te iwi. Engari, i tipu ake ahau i Te Awakairangi. I study with . . .' She hesitated before saying his name. 'Taneora.'

'Ahhhhh,' the man said. 'So *you're* his new flame?' He seemed to be looking at her now with different eyes.

Leah blushed, feeling the conspicuous weight of her Deadly Ponies handbag and the sleek whiteness of her shoes. She knew she didn't look like the kind of woman Taneora would be with, although she wasn't exactly sure what his type would be. He was hardly what you'd call a *typical* Māori, whatever that was. She'd first noticed him at a noho marae, standing outside the wharenui wearing a headscarf and kandura like he'd just walked out of the desert. She half expected to see a camel hitched up to the waharoa, so bare were his tattooed feet. But the words that came out of his mouth were Māori, not Arabic.

They became friends, bonding over a mutual appreciation of books and language. For some reason, when Leah spoke to Taneora, she didn't stutter or stumble over her words. The language of her ancestors seemed to flow from her tongue without thought or effort, the way it did in her dreams. What's more, Taneora understood everything she said, no matter how many mistakes she made. Their connection was spiritual, Leah was sure of it. She liked his teeth. They were tall and straight like a white picket fence inside his mouth. When she looked at his teeth she wanted to swing open the gate and move in.

Leah's mother was shocked when she turned up with him at the house one weekend for Sunday roast. She'd started telling everyone that Leah was going through a 'phase', emphasising the words 'reconnecting with her roots' while holding up two fingers on either side of her face. She acted like Leah couldn't hear her when she added 'mid-life crisis' and a knowing wink. Of course, Janet had been through a similar phase herself, once upon a time, which is how Leah came along. But that was an accident. Janet was really only trying to get a rise out of her father, a cruel and brittle man who hated anyone who wasn't white and English. Leah's grandfather had spent four years in a POW camp in Japan and the idea that one of his own offspring might have the blood of another race pumping through them was enough to push him over the edge. He'd left his pregnant daughter on the doorstep of St Mary's home for unwed mothers in disgrace.

Leah knew all of this. For years she'd lived with the knowledge that half of her was flawed and better off hidden. She was Māori but not a real Māori. And yet. And yet! Here she was about to put down a hāngī. At dawn!

When Taneora saw her approaching he leaned his spade against the fence and came over. She wasn't sure if his expression was one of surprise or embarrassment. She waved. He lifted his chin.

'Kia ora.'

'Kia ora.'

Taneora pressed his nose to her nose, holding her in a half-embrace that seemed to carry on for minutes rather than seconds. One of the men grinned and said something in an off-hand way and although only one corner of his mouth moved, the inflection of his voice together with the rapid twitch of his left eyebrow filled his short words with innuendo and all the men rocked in their boots with laughter. Leah joined in, not because she understood but because she wanted to be part of the laughter, not standing on the edge of it. She stole a glance at Taneora, who rolled his eyes as if to say *Ignore them*, then took her around introducing her one by one to his brothers and uncles and cousins. Each one squeezed her hand and smiled politely as though on their best behaviour. It made her feel, she realised uncomfortably, like the Queen.

Oh, but how everything changed once the beers started flowing! With the hāngī served and eaten and all the work done and cleared up, everyone began to relax. The rāhui on drugs remained but Cody's in moderation was perfectly fine. By the time the sun began its lazy retreat Leah could feel the alcohol filtering its way to her heart, simultaneously slowing it down and speeding it up. The whole garage seemed to be aglow in the warmth that was now sitting snugly inside her chest.

Taneora reached out and put his thick, calloused hand on her knee. 'Kei te pēhea?'

Leah nodded back with a wide smile. 'Rawe,' she yelled above the sound of Aunty Mavis crooning in harmony with her niece. She didn't know how to tell him, in any language, that she felt more relaxed here in this garage than she ever had at her cousins' house eating scones with jam and cream. She wanted to say that she felt like she belonged here, that she felt a rightness to the world she always knew was missing. She wanted to tell him that she wished she had a family like this, but it was a silly thing to say because she knew she was only seeing what she wanted to see and that Taneora's family had their dramas, plenty of them, too. Only a few minutes ago the cousin with the dreads had been told off for pulling his knife out on the dance floor, an act that seemed far more harmless in the moment than it would have looked to anyone standing outside the garage looking in. But even that – the way Tina had come up to him and put her arm around him gently and said, 'No more nephew, put the knife away,' was done lovingly. Everyone else had laughed but Leah . . . Leah had to fight to hold back the tears.

Just then, one of the uncles – one of the older ones – started playing the ukulele upside down. With the cousins egging him on, he got up and shimmied into the middle of the garage, strumming his fingers at the wrong end of the shaft. 'Play it, Uncle, play it!' yelled Taneora's sister.

Leah wondered what the neighbours must be thinking and an image of her mother flitted briefly across her mind, sitting at home on the couch watching *Dancing with the Stars* right now. The mere idea of it made her feel lightheaded.

'*That's the way, Uncle does the hula*!' the crowd was singing.

Taneora groaned and rolled his eyes. 'Ahh, sheet,' he said, leaning over to Leah. 'You're gunna have to dance.'

Leah's eyes widened. 'What? No!'

'Yeh. Sorry.'

Leah watched as Tina got up after Uncle, swinging her hips and gyrating down to the ground and up again while everyone sang '*That's the way, Tina does the hula!*' After Tina came Moana, flossing hard out, while the kids all cheered and whooped in approval.

Next was Charlie, who dropped to the ground in one swift movement and started doing one-armed press-ups. The crowd went ballistic.

Leah felt sick. There was no way out.

With one arm held high and another slapping her backside, Aunty Mavis rode into the middle of the circle and the crowd fell about wolfwhistling. Taneora was next, moonwalking across the garage and ending in a mighty pūkana in Leah's direction. Leah squeezed her eyes shut and took a deep breath. She could feel everyone looking at her, watching, waiting.

The next day she woke on a mattress on the floor with a pulsing headache and a sore back. She had a vague recollection of dancing the hula with a broom. Taneora was awake, sitting cross-legged on the verandah with his face inclined towards the sun. She couldn't tell if he was meditating or thinking. It was always hard to tell, with him. She got up and tiptoed to the bathroom. Her throat was dry and raspy and the memory of singing *Islands in the Stream* with Aunty Mavis came back to her in snatches. She could have sworn she could still hear laughter coming from the garage, but the party couldn't still be going on, could it?

Leah turned the tap on and splashed her face with water. She looked up at her reflection in the mirror. Her hair was frizzy and wild, untamed and free. It was the strangest sensation, but for a moment she almost didn't recognise herself.

'How was the party?' Janet asked that night on the phone.

'Great,' said Leah, as if settling a bet.

'Hmph,' came the reply.

'What's that supposed to mean?'

'Well,' said her mother, with a little puff. 'They're not always who you think they are.'

'Who?'

'The Maoris.'

'The . . . the Maoris? Jesus, Mum. *I'm a Māori.*'

'Well, yes,' said Janet. 'But you're not a real Maori.'

'How would you know? What does that even mean?'

'I just mean that you're not one of them,' said Janet. 'Are you?'

Leah looked out the window towards the moon, a slim crescent, barely there. She knew it had a name; every phase of the moon had a name and precise tikanga, everything from when to go out with the nets and when to stay in and watch your back. For some reason, though, no matter how many definitions she memorised or wānanga she sat through, the words just wouldn't stay lodged inside her Pākehā-thinking brain. It was as though certain knowledge had an untouchable quality, protected by a boundary or a threshold that she could feel on some molecular level but could not step across. In her mind, she could see Taneora, walking barefoot across the stones, and dimpled men in hi-vis jackets laughing at jokes she couldn't hear. The visions were intermingled and meshed together with her own reflection in the mirror, an intricate knowledge of the shape of mistakes, and the dead-weight of a designer handbag hanging from her arm like whakapapa unclaimed.

Leah sighed, feeling the final afterglow of the previous night fully dissipate. 'It's just that . . . I suppose . . .'

'Exactly,' said her mother.

Kahu Tumai

A Karakia

Kotahi:

I thank Tāne
        for the flesh of a manu on the
Tip of my tongue
        it curves its way down the
Back of my throat
        writhing, it falls into the
Pit of my stomach
        I rejoice in its sustenance
I thank Tāne

Tuarua:

Ancestors Tōtara, Miro,
Hōmai tō rākau
I need those knotty fingers
In the sinew of my lungs
Ahi / ahi / mārie
Set me on fire and breathe
Ki roto, ki waho
I want to be renewed

                Takahi / tinana

Lift it, lift all of it
The pot plant, the card, the pūtea
Let it all burn
        Light a cigarette with me
                Light a room with me

                    Whakanoa this whole

Fucking Body.
    Tihei, Mauri Ora
        Breath of life, breadth
            Of life.

I want to be with you

Tuatoru:

I have a question:
    will I ever stand
        like you, tupuna
            will my feet ever be cradled

                in our red earth again

The whenua has changed me but
Whiro's pupil gleams in the pores of a white man
Hoi anō I may as well be in Taupiri already
'Dig my grave shallow'
I say to my only son
'In case I want to see the river'

Tuawhā:

I wake to my Mother laughing
Hot summer hair a wheke
Te poi o te Tūī in her mouth
I cry into her hands like rivers
Through mountain ranges
And she never breathed again
I still have too much breathing to do

Ka tangi, ka tangi, ka tangi ahau

Tayi Tibble

Hine-nui-te-pō

Half caste daughters
of half castes
about to fall into quarters.

Cast out into cities
and universities
and forgotten about.

Their umbilical cords cut
and dumped in a sludge
of hospital waste.

The fake lobotomised smile
on their faces while bumping
a line off the back of

a phrenology textbook.
Shook at all the colours
you can find in a skull.

Taking boyfriends
like appointments with a doctor.
A finger in the mouth and

wanting to say
ah or amen
or ugh, men.

The migraines.
The light coming in.
The inherited trauma of

deeply existing in the space of
separated parents.
The long nights and the

sleep paralysis. Lying
on your back and pushing
the sky from your chest

with thighs that kill demigods.
The violence of divorce, the space
it leaves. The shock of the light

coming in. The distance.
The difference between
Heaven and the knowledge

that your first mother was hell
and chose to be.
Reconciling

what it means to be her daughter.
Getting her magic bible bashed
out of you. Running away to

cities and universities downloading
Tinder and getting assimilated in
white minimalist bedrooms.

Imported plants from Bunnings
overgrowing and infecting the whenua.
When it was my turn to come clean I said

I grew up tacky and hungry and dazzling.
I grew up neck deep in the dirt
but all I needed was a good pair of eyes

to see the stars first
which meant I got a lot wishes.
But I only had one thing to wish for.

All my fathers are in the sky anyway
I know I don't have to say it
But Mum you should have tied me

to the ground.
Instead I was given
to this city freely

Friends on benes.
Crown apologies.
Wannabe it girls at parties.

I wonder how it must feel
to be tethered somewhere
by a sense of home. To be buried

in your urupā and to find that when you die
you have been waiting
for yourself, this whole time, all along

Tayi Tibble

Identity Politics

I buy a Mana Party t-shirt from AliExpress.
$9.99 free shipping via standard post.
Estimated arrival 14–31 working days.
Tracking unavailable via DSL. Asian size XXL.
I wear it as a dress with thigh-high vinyl boots
and fishnets. I post a picture to Instagram.
Am I navigating correctly? Tell me,
which stars were my ancestors looking at?
And which ones burnt the black of searching irises
and reflected something genuine back? I look to
Rihanna and Kim Kardashian shimmering in
Swarovski crystals. Make my eyes glow with seeing.
I am inhaling, long white clouds and I see
rivers of milk running toward orange oceans of
sunlit honey. Tell me, am I navigating correctly?
I want to spend my money on something bougie,
like custom-made pounamu hoop earrings. I want to
make them myself but my line doesn't trace back
to the beauties in the south making amulets
with elegant fingers. I go back into blackness,
I go back and fill in the gaps, searching through archives
of advertisements: Welcome to the Wonderland
of the South Pacific. Tiki bars, traffic-light cocktails &
paper umbrellas. Tell me, am I navigating correctly?
Steering through the storm drunk & wet-faced
waking up to the taste of hangover, a dry mouth, a strange bed,
shirt above my head is the flag fluttering over everything.
What were we celebrating? The 6th of February is the anniversary
of the greatest failed marriage this nation has ever seen.
In America, couples have divorce parties. We always arrive
fashionably late. Tell me, am I navigating correctly? The sea
our ancestors traversed stretches out farther than the stars.

essa may ranapiri

Māui Becomes Who S/He Was Meant To Be

After Tāwhanga Nopera's 'Huka can Haka'

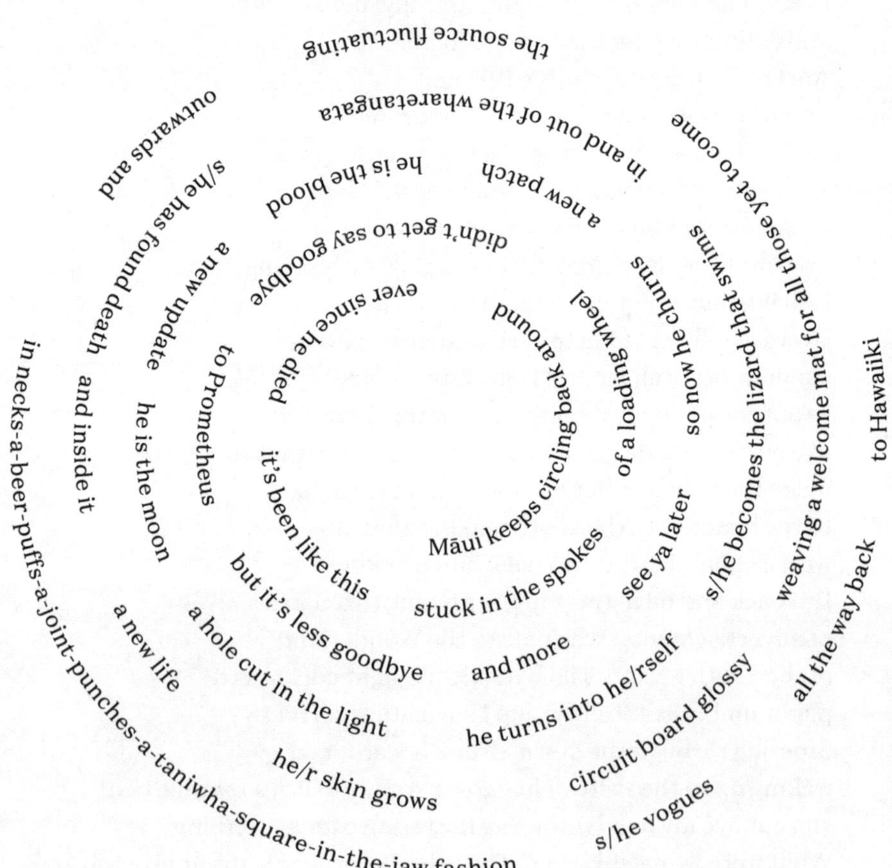

essa may ranapiri

knot-boy ii

an open space where?
not here   not here   knotboy!   that's me   sat behind the
                                    turbine of   brain
                                    exposed to water
                                                  ungalvanised

it turns   how i turn in a dress
sat behind a counter with   gabble
asking questions like   these questions
                         what kinds of   jokes
                         spin   in focus behind their mouths

it's telling
they're telling me it's not
alright   to b

wood clap on wood   if they see me alone   i am

gay man   or transvestite   or drag queen

if they see me with u   i   am

straight man   or nothing else   or lying to myself

---*---

— just smash me to pieces brave boys! just fucking have at it!
and at it and at it and at it   till i am meltdown   complexity
is a devil   horned   and writhing

my body is something I would like to see in writing that flat
and perfect and dead

---*---

the beetle pushes shit along the ground it knows this to be true because it
feels the object
on parts of itself it makes to move it tells itself it smells nothing

if the dress is short i get an ironic version of the
attention cis women get
u r so hot
what do we have here
those legs
u need to shave

scribble furious shapes onto
swollen board
the pen will be knife before long the letters will turn into splinters
before my body turns into a song

---*---

i can not be my self without verbal communication but my
mouth is turned inside out
doughnut meated inadequacy walk down aisle at
countdown
hold up mixed veges under the light
what nutrients are left in frost

people passing
from the rotting avocadoes black and soft
to the fresh-baked bread held in sheaves of cardboard
demarcating price and contents labels if you're able

push a week's worth of survival around in a cage   with

a look that shakes my spine   a look
on so many different faces   but still
the same fucking   stare   a snare

that hooks the lip
or a smirk that
highlines the forehead

---*---

wet saws battling themselves out chains clacking to the ground when will we realise the door is unlocked and a corpse is holding it closed when they realise they're utterly outnumbered way too late   //   severed ideas floating back into a vacuum where nothing is written and nothing lives the sun screams with no air to carry its screams   i speak with nothing to carry my—

---*---

the stars are all out   of their comfort zones here
sweaters cover   a wetness   of intent
a specific cast   lasered into the stone
we wear around broken bones   and broke-ass wallets
key chains hanging from flayed minds

a clatter   a   tear   in the eye   drop
in the ravenous   gloom
in the titan   of dust
smote in the memory of burying itself alive to feed

the earth a story

gut me for chances gut me for clever designs gut me or cut me
smudged
on the wood that he grew
from his spine
a whole fucking tree how could you miss it???

---*---

trick question is a tired coda
or a code to crack before the chemical hit

it takes to the sky on the polish of promise
leading a bull on a leash made of tissue paper
to the very centre of the circle where there /
any place could be

Zeb Tamihana Nicklin

Iti te Kupu, Nui te Kōrero

'He aha rā, e Tama?'
'Karekau hoki!'
'Tēnā rūkahu tēnā!'
'Taihoa ake, e Pā.'
'E hē, kōrerohia mai!'
'I . . . i . . .'
'I aha rā?'
'Kua raru au — karekau he putanga māku!'
'E hē, ahakoa te aha, he ara whakaputanga.'
'Engari . . .'
'Kia kaha rā, e Tama. Kōrero mai!'
'Kai te aroha mai koe ki a au, e Pā?' me te heke iho o ngā roimata i ōna pāpāringa.
'E tama, nāku koe!'
'Tēnā, whākina mai, e Pā!'
'He mahi whakaatu nāku ki a koe i ia rā.'
'He mana tō te kupu, nē?'
'Ehara oti ia, he nui kē te mana o te whakatinanatanga.'
'I mate whakamomori a Whai!'
'E Timi, ka aroha kē hoki.'
'Kāre ōna mātua e whakaae kia nehua ia ki tōna urupā.'
'Nō ao kē tēnā, ehara nō te whakaaro Māori.'
'E Pā, mōhio au he aha ia i whakamomori ai!'
'He aha kē hoki, e Timi?'
'He moe tāne kē a Whai.'
'Haramai, kai te pai noa.'
Ka awhiawhi tahi rāua ki a rāua, ā, ka tangi hotuhotu nei a Timi.
'Me nehu ki tō tāua urupā, e Pā?'
'Ehara, ehara! He aha ngā mahara o ōna mātua?'
'Kia tahuna kē a ia.'
'He tikanga Pākehā kē, me mūrei e tāua tana tūpāpaku.'

‘I nē!’
‘Āe, me whānako mai.’
‘He aha i kore ai i whakaae kia tanu ia ki te urupā?’
‘He tikanga Pākehā, hāhi kē tēnā, e Tama.’
‘Kai te aroha mai koe ki a au, e Pā?’
‘E tama, kāti rā!’
‘E Pā, ko Whai taku hoa tāne!’
‘Mōhio kē ana au, hai aha hoki!’

Paula Morris

Brussels

Kit Henare lived in Brussels. He had not been home for four years, not since his sister's wedding. His parents paid for his ticket. The visit was not a success. The wedding was crawling with smug cousins and disappointed aunties. All that university, and for what? Kit hadn't made it in Europe. He'd made nothing. Auckland was too expensive now, people told him; he'd 'missed the boat'. The property ladder had been whisked away and propped in the high branches of a tree. He had nothing in Europe to sell, nothing to leverage. He had no career. He had no capital. He had no assets. He was losing his hair: so many people told him that, with biting jocularity, as though he may not have noticed it himself.

'Europe's fine for a holiday,' his cousin's husband told him. The husband was a lawyer and wore tight shirts; he kept his phone in his hand at all times. 'But if you haven't got a big job there, there's no point. Here you've got the lifestyle.'

The lifestyle. If he moved home, would Kit have the lifestyle?

He spent a few days in London, staying with James, his oldest friend from Auckland. James had a corporate job that involved money and the media: Kit had no idea what it was.

'They all keep talking about the lifestyle,' he told James. 'It's the thing, apparently.'

'All they mean is going to the beach after work maybe twice a year,' said James, 'and walking into a dairy without your shoes on. Big deal.'

The train back from London was crowded, everyone sitting around Kit absurdly cartoonish. Although the weather in both cities was damp and cold, the guy across the aisle arrived without a coat, wearing sunglasses and carrying a giant fruit smoothie. He was dressed in a navy blazer and V-necked white t-shirt, his jeans artfully slashed across the thighs and shins to reveal the denim's stringy white innards.

Just before the train pulled out a woman in a fur jacket bustled up to claim the window seat next to Kit: she could have been any age between forty and seventy. When he stood to let her pass, she clambered onto his seat to stuff a shopping bag overhead, so he had a good view of her wine-coloured leggings, her wedged black sneakers studded with diamantes. Where did these people live? Who did they know? How did they spend their time? Where did they buy their clothes, and what made them dress like this, in winter and in public?

Perhaps this was part of their lifestyle, one that did not involve beaches after work and barefoot shopping trips for milk. The people who talked most about their lifestyle, Kit decided, were those who could afford to choose one over another.

From the Gare du Midi, Kit walked home to St-Gilles in the dreary twilight. In Brussels, in the winter, entire days could be twilight. When he first arrived in Europe, this was the most depressing thing – the long dusk of January and February. Night pounced at four pm. He had to keep the lights on all day.

He'd seen a number of spacious flats in Brussels, but Kit didn't live in one of them. He rented the smallest, darkest room in a flat of small, dark rooms. The place was owned by Jules Renard, who said he was a playwright, although he'd never had a play produced and possibly – Kit was unclear on this point – had never written one all the way through. Jules used to work as a teacher, until, as he said, the left-wingers drove him out; then he worked in a lobbying firm, where once again he was driven away, but this time by right-wingers. He was in his late 40s now, and had owned the flat for twenty years. Belgians, he told Kit, were born with bricks in their stomachs, which meant they bought property as soon as they could, and stayed put.

The next afternoon, Saturday, Kit walked out to meet Alejandra for her weekly English lesson in L'Ultime Atome in Matongé. Kit quite liked it in the café: there was something about all the brown wood that suited his mood. Still, he didn't want to blow all the money Alejandra was paying him on a *lait Russe* or a beer. He particularly didn't want to spend it on water. He didn't want to sit looking out at the street, because then he was forced to watch all the men around him who were doing things. The grizzled guy in the orange jumpsuit pushing a giant vacuum cleaner over the cobbles; the guy with the silvering ponytail parking his VW up on the pavement and dashing into a shop building site, keys dribbling from his fist. The guy herding his chubby toddlers along the street, cloth shopping bag in one hand, bike helmet in the other.

But if Kit sat facing into the café, there were the guys carrying trays, and making coffee, and clearing tables. All the men of Brussels seemed to be engaged in honest or dishonest labour, especially the ones who were thirty-eight years old and had been to university and had moved all the way from New Zealand to Brussels in order to work at the heart of the new Europe.

Alejandra arrived, her long hair impossibly glossy, wearing one of her many tight Puffa jackets and a pair of bejewelled ankle boots.

'Is OK,' she told him when he didn't order a drink. 'What you want – I pay.'

'You have to say *it* is OK,' said Kit. 'Remember? So, tell me what today is –'

'Is Saturday.'

'Today *it* is Saturday.'

Alejandra did not appear to be listening. She kept glancing over at the doors, or maybe at the case with revolving glass shelves of mousse and crème brûlée.

'You know what?' she said, still looking away. This was one of her favourite idiomatic expressions. She'd mastered it before they met, so Kit couldn't claim the teaching honour. But she didn't understand that it was a prelude to another sentence, a sentence that must hustle along after it before the listener grew bored. Alejandra always waited for a response.

'What?' he said, his irritation audible – though probably only to himself, because the blender behind the counter was mashing something like ice.

'No,' she said, and turned back to him. 'I think, that is a man I know. But I don't know this man. The man I know, he is bastard.'

'He is *a* bastard. That's how you'd say it in Spanish, wouldn't you? Someone would be *a* bastard.' Kit wondered if her English was getting worse. Why was she speaking like an old-time movie gangster's moll?

Alejandra's coffee had been delivered, and now she was staring at the inch of froth. She still hadn't removed the Puffa jacket, though the café was warm.

'So, let's talk about this man, the one who's a bastard. Tell me about him. Where did you meet him?' He generally built her lessons around gossip.

'I don't want to speak. He hurts me.'

'OK. I understand. But you should tell me that "I don't want to speak about it". Or really, "I don't want to talk about it."'

'Always *it*.' Alejandra twisted her mouth.

'And you could say "he hurt me", which is past tense. He hurt you in the past, not right now.'

'He hurts me now.'

'So maybe you could say "I am still hurt because of what he did". Or "I still feel hurt".'

'I tell you, I don't want to speak!'

'Yes, you did. I'm sorry. So why don't we talk about what you're going to do this weekend? That way we can practise talking about something in the future rather than in the present.'

Alejandra drew crosses in the froth with her spoon.

'All weekend I stay at home.'

'All weekend I *will* stay at home. Though you're out here now, with me, and not at home. So let's talk about other things going on this weekend. What else *will* you do this weekend?'

Alejandra shrugged.

'I don't know. Nothing. Feel sad.'

I *will* feel sad, Kit thought, but he didn't want to nag her. And anyway, not only was he making Alejandra's English worse, he seemed to be transforming her life into his own. He was sucking the joy out of her, like the street cleaner outside with his giant vacuum.

'You might feel better if you went out this weekend and spent time with your friends. Sometimes it's good to go out, even if you feel sad.'

'Where?' Alejandra asked, looking straight at him, spoon still poised in the brown scum of her coffee. 'Where *you* go, when you feel sad?'

'Where *do* you go?' He was playing for time. Where did he go? 'Well, sometimes I go for a walk. A long walk, through the streets.'

'Shopping?'

'Just walking, really. Looking at buildings and people.'

Alejandra appeared unimpressed. Outside, the VW guy was back in his car, talking on his phone and smoking what looked like a joint.

'Walking is not fun,' she said. 'I walk and I still feel sad. I walk and I think about this man.'

'Well, sometimes I go to a museum,' Kit lied. 'Maybe we could have a lesson in a museum one day? Walk around and look at paintings or sculptures, and then talk about them.'

'Maybe,' said Alejandra. 'When?'

'Soon.' He would need to find out when the various museums had free entry. 'I'll work out a good time to go and let you know.'

'But not a sad museum,' she cautioned him. She still hadn't taken a sip of her coffee. She only wanted to play with it.

'Not the Lace Museum, then,' joked Kit, but Alejandra didn't smile. 'Don't worry. I'll find a happy museum. I *will* find it and we *will* go to it. Together.'

This seemed to alarm her. She wriggled straight in her chair.

'But for class, yes? For English. Not for date.'

'Lord, no!' Kit rarely heard himself laugh. He sounded like a rabid seal. 'For English only. English lessons, I mean.'

'Good.' Alejandra smiled. 'You are too old.'

'That's right. Well, I know what you mean, but – really, I'm not an *old* man. You should say, "you are too old *for me*."'

'You are too old *for me*.'

'Good,' he said. 'That's right. Very good.'

Across the intersection at Little Tokyo, a girl with dark red lips was cleaning the glass of the door. Kit was too old for her as well. He was probably too old for the young mother in a striped sweater riding by, a waving child perched in front of her. If he'd been more sexually active back in his mid-teens, and if he'd grown up in Belgium then rather than Auckland, he could be the father of the waitress who brought Alejandra her coffee.

'You have no wife?' Alejandra asked him. He shook his head. 'No husband?'

'No. I'm not gay.'

'It hard to tell, with the English.'

'It *is* hard to tell,' he said. 'That's what you should say. "It *is*." Though I don't think it is, really. And I'm not English. We talked about this, remember?'

Alejandra looked puzzled, then she smiled, for the first time that day.

'Yes! You are Dutch. From Zeeland. But you speak English very good. That is why you are my teacher. So, I can live in Amsterdam.'

Her phone buzzed and she answered it without apology, and spoke to whoever was calling in high-speed Spanish.

Some days Kit wished he were Dutch, because then he might be able to get a better job, or at least move somewhere picturesque, like Antwerp. The sad truth was that Alejandra spoke better English than he spoke Dutch. He should have learned it when he first arrived, but he thought that his patchy French would be enough. Now it seemed too late. He was old. Really, he should either learn Flemish, improve in French or just go home where everyone spoke English all the time. Apparently, he spoke English very good. This was his most ringing endorsement of the week, tempered a little by the announcement that he was old, and by the suggestion that he looked gay – this in a city of men who wore Capri pants and floral scarves and carried their wallets in shoulder bags.

When the lesson was over, Alejandra took another call and pushed her way out of the café, pausing in the middle of the street to re-drape her scarf. She seemed oblivious to the looming presence of cars or the position of a nearby pedestrian crossing. Kit wished he could be so removed. Today the city beyond the window seemed raw and hostile, the flayed trees spiky, the cobbles as uneven and slippery as rocks in a stream. He could feel bricks scraping his knuckles just by looking at a building. The man reading *El Pais* at a nearby table was a dead ringer for Lenin. Didn't Lenin spend hours at European cafés much like this one – Marx as well, somewhere in central Brussels – stewing in politics and philosophy, conjuring up revolution? What did Lenin live on, all those years in pricey non-Russian places like Zurich? How could he afford a *lait Russe?*

Kit had nowhere to go but home, but the thought of sitting alone in Jules' flat didn't appeal. Walking was his usual distraction. Whenever the sadness felt unbearable, when Kit's profound disappointment in himself and his skulking, shadowy half-life, the utter fraud of his great European adventure, pressed on his insides like a tumour, he went walking. All those paving stones and little balconies, the dog shit-smeared pavement, the tumble of chairs at a corner café, the great intake of breath that announced an approaching tram: this was Europe, and he lived here.

In the final week of his last job, typing up testimony from asylum seekers, Kit spent over an hour with a Nigerian client – always a 'client', though they were buying no goods and receiving no services. She said she was from Nigeria, anyway, and it seemed true enough to Kit, from her accent and what she was wearing. She was swathed in something brighter than summer, a fireworks burst of yellow and red, her hair obscured by another stiff swirl of fabric. That she was also wearing a dour blue parka didn't diminish her flame. It looked like something she'd acquired since she arrived, the gift of some well-meaning agency that collected sad old clothes from locals and offered them to new arrivals as dimmer switches, something to make them fit in a little more in somewhere as grey and damp as Brussels.

'Nigeria,' Kit said. He tabbed to the next box on the form, the one that could grow to accommodate the longest testimony, and paused in case she changed her mind. The interviewers were told to do this, to give the client time to get his or her story straight. Maybe someone would say Nigeria but then change his mind, and say Mali instead; maybe Ethiopia would become Eritrea, or Somalia would become Sudan, or Sudan would become South Sudan. It didn't matter, apparently, as long as the story was straight, and detailed enough to be plausible. But if someone talked about coming from lush mountains in a country that was largely arid desert, then there was a problem. It would compromise the testimony and therefore the integrity of the narrative.

It was surprising to Kit, how so many people, when asked the story of why they left the place they were from, and how they'd come to be here in Brussels, struggled to explain. One morning he'd had client after client with almost identical stories, as though they'd all agreed on a party line out in the corridor, and even though – by dress and looks and accent – they were clearly not all from Eritrea, as they'd claimed, and not all of the age where military conscription, their stated reason for fleeing, was viable. His colleague Jackie, a frowning woman from Birmingham, always tightening her ponytail and tugging at her cardigan, warned him about that.

'They'll try to tell you they're refugees,' she said, addressing him from her desk by the office's one window. 'They're all escaping war or political persecution – that's what they'll say. They don't want you to think they're an economic migrant. Economic migrants get sent back.'

Kit wondered how they could be sent back, and where, if no one would admit where they were really from. How could anyone be sent back to Tripoli, when no international flights landed there anymore? Would the police or the army force everyone onto boats, to tow them back across the Mediterranean or tip them into the sea? And what was the point to all this, the writing down of testimonies, if some of the stories, maybe most, were untrue. 'You must remind them we're not the police,' Jackie told him. 'We're not reporting them to anyone. They can tell us the truth without fear of consequences.'

But everyone feared consequences, Kit included. And the reason this organisation existed was to help create stronger dossiers for immigration cases. The 'story sheets', as they were told to call them, went on to another agency, bigger and sturdier, that could check information with NGOs in the home countries, and verify the information lawyers needed. Jackie and Kit and all the others who took their turns at the much-fingered computers needed to get actual, useful information in some kind of chronology. True, they weren't the police, but they needed to be detectives, in their own earnest and shambolic way. God knows they didn't have the training to be therapists.

The Nigerian woman said her name was Ndudi and that she was from Lagos. Her market stall had been demolished by government bulldozers just after Christmas, and that was it for her. 'We have no power,' she said, and it took Kit a moment to understand she was talking about electricity. 'No petrol, no power. No water. We cannot pump water without the generator. How can we live this way? You tell me. No business, no goods, no light, no water. You write this down.'

'I am,' Kit reassured her, typing to catch up. She was his fifteenth client that week from Lagos. Lagos had twenty times the number of people as Brussels. Kit had never visited a city so vast; there was nothing on that scale in Europe. His Lagos clients spoke in loud, confident voices, as though they were all market traders, bold and savvy.

'Would you say you've been persecuted in any way?' he asked. 'Boko Haram?'

Often these were the magic words, the key to frantic stories of fear and kidnap, escape and terror. But Ndudi just looked irritated.

'I am not thinking about Boko Haram. They are not the only problem in Nigeria. I am Igbo. We have never been welcome in Lagos.' She said it as though Kit should have known.

He wanted to tell her that he knew much more than he once did – just in time to finish this temporary job and walk away into the cold, as the clients did every day. Every week he'd learned more things about the world, more of its unknown places and convoluted skeins. One client had explained that Benin was the world capital of the illegal petrol trade. From the stories he recorded, he now knew about cities like Zaria in northern Nigeria, a city bigger than Christchurch or Edinburgh, where stubby bushes of cotton and tobacco grew and the walls seemed to be made from sand and where, just last year, hundreds of local Shiite Muslims had been gunned down in the street. One of them was a client's son. She cried every time she mentioned his name.

Kit now knew a little about Abuja, too, the dry and half-empty capital of Nigeria, where one of his clients had been crushed unloading slabs of Italian marble for a gated estate of villas and pools, losing his right leg; nobody bought the houses, he'd told Kit, and he didn't know why. The rich were still awash in oil money, even if everybody else had to queue for hours for petrol.

Kit liked to think of himself as educated; he'd been to university, after all. But until last month he'd never heard of Abuja. He'd thought Lagos was the capital of Nigeria. He hadn't even heard of Maiduguri in the country's northeast, Boko Haram's spartan fortress. A client, his face pockmarked with shrapnel wounds, had described it in dramatic strokes: young women blowing themselves up in the bus station and the marketplace, grenades flung at the thatched roofs of village houses, tanks rumbling past the mosque when it was all too late. Blood and flames and screaming, he said. He'd reached for Kit's hand, to guide it over the rock pools of his face.

Ndudi told him the name of the market was Oshodi. He asked her to spell this, trying to imagine the shrill spread of it, the reef of women like her, bright and hard, at its centre.

'And what did you sell?' he asked.

'Rice, cereal, chocolate, Milo.'

'So, food. Groceries.'

'Sometimes CDs or perfume. Other beauty things – hair wax and nail polish. Whatever I can sell. But what does this matter, what I used to sell? What does the past matter?'

'We're just trying to tell your story.'

'I am telling you my story,' Ndudi insisted. She was looking at Kit now, glaring at him. 'Everything was smashed up. Everything is gone.'

'Afterwards – I mean, after the demolition – did you move to another market?'

'There is no afterwards,' she said. The whites of her eyes were streaked with red. 'There is just the money we have saved, and the money my uncle could give us, and then we came here on the plane.'

'On a plane,' Kit said. The day before another client had listed the places he'd passed through, largely in the back of trucks, after he left Benin City – Ouallen, Agadez, Qatrun – on his way to the Mediterranean. The distance was endless, maybe 5000 kilometres of road. Nowhere in Europe was that far. The man had been robbed one night in Niger. The sea was just another desert to cross.

'We are not going back,' Ndudi told him.

'Of course not,' he said, and then wondered if he should have just nodded. They were not to give clients promises or false hope; they were not to comment on legal processes or the machinations of the state. They were not a welfare agency, and they could neither help nor advise. They were just there to listen to people's stories and write them down.

'I had lots of boat testimonies today,' Jackie told him when he was closing down his computer, brushing his lunch crumbs into the worn carpet. 'So hard.'

Hard to listen to, he wondered, or hard to capture? Their job wasn't really hard at all; if it was that difficult, he'd have been given more training. He and Jackie and the others who drifted in for their shifts weren't the ones who'd trekked overland and squeezed into a boat to get spewed up somewhere, half-dead and freezing, in a foreign place that felt like a prison camp. When Kit came to Europe he'd taken two long flights, Auckland to Los Angeles to London. Nothing about it had seemed frightening or foreign. He'd experienced no hardships greater than stiff legs and a few days of jetlag.

He had a sense of Lagos now, from the stories he'd been told, and it seemed like a science-fiction set rather than a city. There was a green island, where the wealthy and powerful lived, reachable by a long, curving bridge; there was a lagoon of some kind where the poor lived in shanties-on-stilts above water that was black with oil and filth. The traffic stretched for miles and some days, whether you were walking or driving, any movement was impossible. Much of the city was clogged and misshapen, and Dickensian in its alleys and slums, its smells of paraffin and candle wax, the slow-moving gurgle of its rusting buses.

Kit wouldn't last five minutes there, he knew; he would be slit open and emptied out within moments of arriving. He wasn't hard or wily enough, not for Lagos, not for London, not even for the job in Brussels typing other people's stories.

The foyer of Kit's building was always dark, whatever the season. Mr Smets, the self-appointed unpaid concierge, was busy at the mailboxes as usual, shuffling promotional flyers from Carrefours and peering at stray letters addressed to past tenants. He was stocky and sallow, and Kit couldn't remember ever seeing him outside.

'*Goeienamiddag*,' Kit said, nodding but avoiding eye contact. If he was lucky, he'd be able to wriggle up the stairs without being asked to comment on packages, or commiserate on some issue of foyer disarray.

'*Is nog weg uw vriend*?' Mr Smets asked. Kit smiled and nodded again. Although Jules had lived in this building for years, Mr Smets always called him 'your friend'. Two steps up the stairs. Three steps. It would be impolite to bolt, especially as Mr Smets was still talking, in rapid Flemish.

'*Ik ben droevig*,' Kit said – fourth step now, then fifth. That might have been the first Flemish phrase he learned: I'm sorry. I don't understand. I don't speak Flemish.

'You hear this story,' said Mr Smets, who refused to speak a word of French, and ignored any hapless visitor or delivery person who dared to address him as Monsieur, but didn't mind switching to English if it meant capturing Kit on the stairs. 'It is unbelievable. But true. My friend told me.'

It took Kit a moment or two to realise the story was taking place in the country of Nepal, because Mr Smets pronounced English as though it were a lesser dialect of Dutch. The main gist of it seemed to be that someone, not the friend himself, was riding a motorbike in Nepal when he was attacked by a tiger.

'The tiger, he jump from the trees and onto the man. The man ride his bike! He speed up! But the tiger, he hang on. The man feel the tiger's breath. The tiger rip, rip, rip at the man with his . . . his . . . '

'Claws?'

'Yes, claws. He bite the man's shoulder and scratch his back. And still the man and the tiger ride the motorbike! It go here and there on the road. And then, they fall off, the man and the tiger. The bike is there, on its side. The man do not run away. Perhaps the fall onto the road kill him. Or the tiger kill him and then eat him.'

'Horrible,' said Kit, and took another step.

'But wait.' Mr Smets held up a Carrefours flyer. 'Do you know what they found? There on the road?'

Kit shook his head. A mauled body, he suspected. The blood of a tiger who'd fallen off a motorbike. Maybe a Carrefours flyer – he had no idea where this was going.

'Nothing,' said Mr Smets, relishing the word. 'Nothing at all. But one thing. What do you think?'

Kit was about to say 'the motorbike', but sensed this was not the correct answer. Also, he wanted to say, if nothing was found, how could anyone know about the leaping tiger, the breathing and the clawing, the speeding up?

'It was the head,' Mr Smets said in triumph, clearly pleased to have outwitted his listener. 'The head of the man, still wearing his motorbike helmet. Every other piece of his body is gone, but the head is still there. You see? The tiger cannot break the helmet. He cannot eat the head! So on the road there is only the bike and the man's head, in its helmet. The neck, the body, the arms, the legs – all gone.'

'Horrible,' Kit said again. It *was* horrible.

Mr Smets had returned to shuffling the mail, his back to Kit. He was humming to himself. When Kit reached the landing, he heard Mr Smets exclaim, '*Een tijger op een motor!*' Kit paused, door key in hand, and waited for something else, like a laugh. He was sure Mr Smets was about to laugh. But downstairs everything was quiet. Kit couldn't even hear the rustling of paper anymore.

He wondered where Mr Smets' friend had heard this story. It was one of those stories that might be true or might be an urban myth, if something that allegedly happened somewhere in Nepal with tree-obscured tigers and no bystanders could be urban. Maybe it was just another racist story, a warning to anyone venturing from home: bad things could happen in faraway places.

Shirley Simmonds

Earth, Ocean

They met at a café. She drove by the day before, paused across the road, peered out the window at customers coming and going, couples meeting and greeting. Were they meeting for the first time too? There were seats and tables arranged in the garden. It was humble and cosy, it looked like a place that provided good, wholesome, satisfying food, served by staff with warm smiles.

He knew the café, was the one to suggest it. It took exactly thirty-five minutes to get there from the coast, over the mountain range. He arrived just before 1 pm, expecting she would be late, ordered an orange juice, and sat at a table that would allow him to watch the café entrance.

She parked outside the café, after circling the block one more time so as not to arrive too early, not to appear too eager. She spotted him straight away, his head down, thumb busy with his mobile phone. Texting, perhaps? Or just appearing occupied so that he didn't seem too eager perhaps?

'Kia ora.'

A slight pause before he looked up.

'Oh. You're here. Kia ora.'

(Not the spark of the first meeting, not the tingle all over, not the skip of a heartbeat, not the intuitive gut feeling that he was the one.)

She fixed her smile. They kissed cheek to cheek. They ordered, they talked a bit. They ate, they laughed a bit.

He talked of his work with the rangatahi, and their waka ama club on the coast. From beneath her eyelashes, she observed him as he spoke: his face, his mannerisms, gestures, expressions.

His shirt was taut across his chest. She watched it move as he moved, slacken then tighten. She envisaged running her palm across that chest, following the curve to where it dipped in the centre. She would curl her hand there and feel the warmth, tuck her face in that hollow and listen as the heart gently patted her cheek, as he whispered into her forehead –

The shock of her thoughts jolted her back to this reality. She surprised herself with the strength of this physical lure. She hadn't felt anything like this in a long time. She felt a stir, an awakening. She grasped for something to talk about, to cover her thoughts. She spoke of the bumper crop of tomatoes she grew this summer. Of chutney, relish and warm jars of pasta sauce.

He noticed the shift in her and wondered at it. He observed her while she chatted. A quick smile, a true laugh. Her hands talked when she talked; palms splayed then clasped, a dismissive flick over the shoulder, a waving finger to punctuate a point. When she listened, her chin rested in one of those hands, fingers curled, and he felt her entire focus in his direction, and it was thrilling. Her nails were short and she wore no nail polish, no rings or jewellery. He noticed a scratch on the back of her wrist and envisaged taking the scratched hand from her chin in both of his and drawing it to his chest, pulling her near. The impulse surprised him. He liked to think he had good control over his physical desires. He shifted in his seat. Sought something to talk about. He spoke of early morning trainings, fund-raising activities, trips to regattas.

It was three o'clock. The lunch had been 'okay', the conversation 'okay', but she wasn't sure if it was enough for another date. Wasn't sure what he thought either.

'How bout Thursday?' he said.

'Thursday? Thursday would be great,' she replied.

She had to admit she knew that they would sleep together at this, the next meeting. And she knew that he knew. But they both went through the day pretending that the evening and all it entailed wasn't approaching. She didn't know if she felt thrilled or apprehensive. Excited or afraid.

They took her girls to the beach. She glanced around. He'd gone further up the shore to chat with someone. She unwrapped her towel to her togs underneath and eased into the water, gasping at the cold, but revelling in the chilly tingle all over her body. She glided in the shallows to where her daughters were paddling. The water felt great, sensual, the waves buffeting her gently.

While catching up with his cousin, he watched her from behind his sunnies. She was comfortable in the water, at ease. More than he was. He preferred to be on the surface, riding the waves and the surges of the ocean, easing his waka with the currents of the sea, turning with the wind. He wasn't that keen on being in the water itself. Too exposed. Too vulnerable. She wore togs. Most women he knew wore shorts and t-shirts in the water. He could see each ridge of her spine, skin sparkling with seawater. Found himself wondering what it would be like to run a finger slowly down the centre of her back . . .

They got pizza and ice cream for the girls, and iced coffees for themselves. She watched his hand lift his coffee to his lips, fingers curved around the glass, and found herself wondering what it would be like to feel a finger run slowly down her spine.

Back at his place she put the girls to bed; sandy, exhausted and sun-kissed. As they drifted off, the aroma of grilling steak wafted in from the kitchen. She slunk out of the room, closing the door gently. Steak, salad, red wine. They ate fast and silent. Then he was behind her chair and his lips were on her ear, her cheek, her neck. Then she was off the chair and leading him by the hand, and they ran up the carpeted stair to his bedroom. She undressed. He undressed. God, he was beautiful. His skin was dark and glossy. She could see the definition of every contour in the dim light. Her eyes roved the intricate detail of his tā moko, chest, shoulders, hips, thighs. The whorls and patterns indented in his skin. She wanted so much to trace it with her fingers, her tongue. Beautiful. So sexy.

Their bodies came together, her thighs, his thighs. Her breasts, his chest. They kissed, desperately. And she inhaled, burying her face in his neck. Hā ki roto. Long and slow, taking him all in. She smelled through the layers of his life, detected boot polish, something like baby lotion. The fresh sweat of the day, salt and seaweed, hot sand and barbecue smoke.

Then the deeper, manly musky smell. He reached a hand to her breast. For a moment she resisted, holding his arm at bay, her heart thumping. Then relented, and nearly cried out at the touch. They tumbled onto the bed, their bodies already entangled. She burned for him. Yearned.

She knew she should be sensible, but – oh! She couldn't stop.

He tried.

'Are you on anything? Do we need to be careful?'

Oh damn.

'No, I–'

'Shall I–'

'Yes.'

With some effort, he got off the bed and delved around in a drawer. Handed her a little silver packet.

'You do it.'

'No, you do it.'

'No, you do it. It's more sexy if you do it.'

Gah. She hated putting condoms on, could never do it right. She tore the packet open and stifled a laugh.

'What?' he said, catching the edge of her giggle.

'Blue! Why do you have a blue condom?'

'Well, I don't know. They were freebies.'

She giggled some more, and tried to unroll it. What was that? She sniffed delicately. *Bubble gum!* He had bubble gum scented condoms? Wait a minute – on impulse she put out the tip of her tongue to the blue rim. They were bubble gum *flavoured*!

Her laugh burst out as a snort, then overflowed, uncontrolled.

He was mystified, embarrassed. 'Well, they were freebies,' was all he could think of saying.

She hiccupped and tried to swallow her laughter and it took a massive effort. She only managed it because she so dearly wanted to go there now. Wanted his body on her body. In her body. Ached for him now.

Loved him even.

She let herself in the front door of his house, with the key he'd given her. At one and the same time feeling familiar, yet intruding. The girls tumbled in after her, running around to explore their surroundings. Lifting this and that, climbing on furniture, pressing buttons. She hefted them onto a stool each and plonked a plate of crackers in front of them, then busied herself with dinner preparations. She had promised to cook for him, something special. So she fished out the precious package of whitebait from the chiller bag, barely defrosted.

She was whisking eggs when he came home.

'Hey girls!' He went to each of them, a kiss, an awhi, all the while, his eyes darting in her direction. He came up behind her and nuzzled her ear.

'Hey you.'

She tilted her head to the side to tuck her face into his neck. Inhale. Boot polish, baby lotion, that musky manly smell. She breathed deep. He pulled back a little and looked into her face.

'You look happy. But —'

She ducked her head quickly before he could see into her eyes. Buried her face back into his neck. Inhaled again, now so familiar. Salt and seaweed, sand and smoky barbecue.

'I'm pregnant.'

She didn't mean it to come out like this. Not with the girls so near, despite the whispered tones. He pulled back again to look into her face.

'How do you know?'

'I know.'

'Yes, but how?'

'I just know.'

'But *how*?'

She knew. But to satisfy his need for evidence she did a test the next morning. Then a second test. Both results positive. Now he knew.

They lay on the bed of the upstairs room, moonlight through the open curtains, gilding the edges of their bodies, still glistening. It was hot. She couldn't sleep, and knew he didn't either. They had talked it out all they could. What to do? Where to live, his town or hers? She couldn't imagine him ever leaving his rohe. She couldn't envisage herself ever leaving her garden. What to do? She needed to think of the girls. How would they react? Would they understand? She knew this whole situation had rocked him, his routine, his life. She knew he had plans that needed him to be free, available. To travel. She knew that deep down –

– he really didn't want this.

She lifted up onto one elbow. Feeling her eyes on him, he stopped pretending he was asleep, and turned to her. Did they need to talk about it some more? They'd been round in circles. This was heavy stuff. He didn't know what to do. He felt trapped and cornered. He needed to think about his plans, his mahi. He couldn't envisage leaving his home, the coast, but maybe he'd have to. He was acutely aware that they had known each other for just a matter of weeks, but he knew she would make the best of this, despite being unexpected. She would dote on this child as she did her girls. He knew deep down that –

– she would love this.

'Sooo . . .' he cast around for something to talk about. 'Sooo – do you do any sport?'

She frowned slightly. He was avoiding the Big Topic. Okay. 'Nah, not really.'

'Oh.'

He thought of his world of rugby league, marathons and half marathons, basketball, paddling. Early morning runs and damp training shoes, sweated t-shirts and liniment, gym workouts and the clink of iron. The shriek of the whistle and the roar of the crowd. He thought of the paddle in his hands as he dipped and pulled it through the water and the waka scudding along the surface, rising and tilting with the surge of the ocean.

'I've never been sporty.' she said. 'Although I used to run a bit. Not for a while though, not since the girls.'

'Oh. Um, and . . . you've got a big garden at home?'

Sheesh, this was starting to sound like an interview!

'Yeah, I love gardening.'

'Yeah?'

'Well, it's so satisfying, pulling up a carrot, or digging up spuds, chopping silverbeet that you know was only tiny seeds a matter of weeks ago. The girls love it too, hanging out with me and looking for strawberries and worms, eating flower petals and collecting caterpillars.' She thought of her trowel plunging into the fertile, fertile soil, and the pleasure of the sun on her neck, the ache in her arms from pruning, cutting, hauling loads of clippings. She thought of the thrill of the first blossoms on the fruit trees after Matariki. Of unearthing taewa or picking plump tomatoes, snapping beans from their vines and snipping a lemon from the tree. The smell of fresh earth, damp compost, orange blossoms, the hum of bees and the scent of pollen on a warm spring day.

'Never really gardened myself,' he said. 'Can't say I've got green hands at all.'

She smiled into the night at his misuse of the phrase. What a mental image! Green hands, blue condom.

'Hey, what are you laughing at?'

'Nothing.' She swallowed a giggle.

'Yes, I can see your teeth!'

He tackled her and tickled her, and she laughed outright. He laughed too. They loved.

Afterwards they lay again, a new sheen to their glow in the rounded moonlight. She sensed him start to drift off, his breaths deepening. She whispered softly, lightly into the depth of their night:

'Are you not even a little bit excited about it all?'

His breath stilled. So long that she thought maybe he hadn't heard, maybe he slept.

Then, 'Yeah I guess. Yeah, a bit.' He paused, breath held. 'But it's a very tiny bit.'

His mouth set in a straight line, but with a slight up-curve to it that could have almost been the tiny edge of a smile. Just a very tiny bit.

The following weekend she went back to the Pā, looking forward to the peace and stability that returning to the marae always brought for her. Although a part of her was apprehensive. They weren't 'telling' anyone yet. It was the sensible thing to do, to wait till around the twelve-week mark. But would anyone see? See it in her āhua? This was her whānau. They knew her well. Surely someone would know something was up. Those nannies, they had a way of detecting these things. She felt fake, false, nervous. Heck, no one even knew she was going out with this guy!

On the morning of her cousin's wedding, the dawn covered the marae ātea with a blanket of unseasonable mist that gently burned off to produce a glorious day – filled with the aroma of hāngī and steam pudding, kids running in and out of the wharekai, waiata and hoots of laughter. Her cousin beaming and radiant, a bride happily, heavily pregnant with their first child.

She sat on the cool grass in front of her whare tipuna and watched her cousin pledge her life to her love, and she cried behind her sunnies. Cried hot tears that streamed straight down her cheeks and dripped to her chest, her breast. Tears of unfettered self-pity. She felt a twinge below her puku, noticed it but thought nothing of it, dismissive.

Then later a spot. Then more spotting.

She travelled home. The next day there was more bleeding, and now she was certain.

That night saw her waking suddenly at around eleven, with an urgent need to go to the bathroom. The strangest physical sensation came through her lower belly, and as it came out, she cupped her palms around it, and held it close. She felt a curious detachment, a numbness, yet a sense of protectiveness. With an odd clarity, she noted sharp irrelevant details: the blue-grey patterned lino, the ingrained dirt in her cuticles, the healing scratch on the back of her wrist, the *smallness* of it, this thing in the palm of her hand, the absence of blood (now, was that strange?), the slightly tacky, visceral feel to its membranous wrap.

She may have even slept for a brief moment, curled up right there on the blue-grey lino, for the world closed in and went dark, then she woke, and *ached* and wished she slept still.

With a cruel polar irony, she recalled the first detection of her elder daughter's heartbeat, the muted *whump-whump-whump* of the ultrasound machine. She remembered blinking back sudden tears as the words arrived in her mind: *I never knew I was lonely until I realised I was no longer alone.*

And now, crouched here, cupping this small sad bundle in her hands, her body centred around it, she felt so utterly, *utterly* alone.

After a time (how long?) she rose. She thought of Māui, once swathed in his mother's hair. She wrapped the tiny bundle in a soft muslin lavalava, one of the ones she used to once swaddle her girls in, round and round. The gentle folds of muslin made it almost substantial. She tucked it snug into the front of her waistband. Nearly where it should be. Then got a torch and her garden trowel, pulled her dressing gown around her and stepped out into the night, one arm curved protectively, tenderly, around her middle.

The moon was nearly full again. At the bottom of the garden, she dug in the nearly full moonlight. In the fertile, fertile soil. A small hole in the earth, a small hole in her soul. She piled a heap of rocks over the area.

Two strands of whakapapa, joined for a moment, and then . . . nothing. She felt empty. Stood and paused, feeling that a karakia should be said, but nothing came. So she returned to the house, crawled into bed between her two girls, who automatically wrapped themselves around her.

She slept.

He felt a numbness. Her words on the phone last night lay like rocks in his soul. He felt he had lost something he didn't know he'd even had. He felt lost.

She drew a deep breath. Sat on the edge of her bed and knew she needed to do something. Something to shake this feeling. Something to lift her.

He drove down to the shore, hefted his waka from the roof rack and readied it. Paused to look out across the bay. Across there, the mountains. The other side of the mountains, *her*.

She spied the tip of a running shoe at the bottom of the wardrobe. Pulled them out from beneath the pile of fallen clothes and shoes, rummaged around for socks. Sports bra, shorts, tank top. It had been so long, years even.

He dragged the waka to the water, clipped on his lifejacket and positioned himself in the seat. Steadied the canoe with his paddle. Took a deep breath. One more glance across the bay, then in a deliberate motion, turned his back towards the mountain range and began to paddle in the other direction. Steady, even strokes. Faster, smoother, swifter. The waka skimmed across the ocean.

She let herself out the front door. Down there, to the right, was the little mound of lonely rocks. She lifted her gaze to the mountains. The other side of the mountain range, across the bay, *him*. Then, in a deliberate motion, she turned to the left, turned her back to the pile of rocks and the mountains, and began to run.

Anton Blank

Kai

Kana met Kahungunu at a te reo Māori class at Unitec. Being a new migrant and having read so much about te iwi Māori before she came to Aotearoa, Kana wanted to learn the language. She'd read how there was a veritable revival of te reo Māori, and Kana had to put her name on a waiting list for the Unitec gig. After six months, Kana received the email to say that her class would start in three weeks.

The tutor was a plump brown wahine Māori, in her thirties Kana guessed, with a big personality that more than matched her physical presence. Her name was Sonya, a whānau name she explained to the class – because Sonya had a Dutch father. And yes, I have been to Holland, Sonya said to the class. The houses there are so tiny, she laughed, I could barely get my backside through the front door. Kana couldn't take her eyes off Sonya's moko kauae, which kept an eye on proceedings, surveilling the class, ensuring there was a requisite respect for proceedings. You will find, Sonya went on, that te reo Māori, it's like food for the soul. Sonya's face relaxed as she held her gaze at middle-distance, inhaled for a second before she returned her attention to the class.

Kahungunu and Kana worked in the same small group, using the coloured Cuisenaire blocks to practise their faltering new vernacular. Kana didn't find the pronunciation difficult, the sounds were very similar to Japanese. She held back though. Kana didn't want to overstep the mark by out-performing her classmates. The millennial Kiwis were confident, assertive, most of them had some learning from high school. When Kana talked to them during class break they told her that they supported Māori rights. They explained the history of the Treaty of Waitangi.

On the other hand, Kahungunu stood by himself when the class had their cup of tea. He lowered his head, in an effort to make himself smaller, Kana thought to herself. When it came time for Kahungunu to repeat sentences after Sonya, he was faltering. At one point Kana thought he would cry. Jeez, I was so dumb at school, Kahungunu said. Kana felt a lump in her throat, and her eyes watered. She dabbed at the corner of her eye with a tissue. Kana approached Kahungunu after the class to tell him he'd done well. I went to Tokyo with my high school volleyball team, Kahungunu told Kana.

Back at Kana's apartment, Kahungunu stroked his enormous penis in front of her. I just want you to watch for a while, he told Kana. I've never been with a Japanese woman before. Kana took her clothes off slowly, an item at a time as Kahungunu masturbated and filmed his appendage on his iPhone. After he came, he wiped himself with a paper towel that Kana brought to him from the kitchen. He said goodbye without touching Kana. This was a weekly ritual until Kana told Kahungunu that she wanted him to touch her. Kahungunu was tense when Kana first kissed him, and as she massaged his biceps with her fingertips, his mouth opened and he moaned appreciatively. Later when Kahungunu was inside her, Kana's thoughts drifted back to Sonya's moko kauae and blood rushed to her extremities.

I'm calling the baby Kai, Kana would later tell her Instagram fam. She had over 100,000 followers. In Japan it was easy because she'd been on a popular game-show on television – it wasn't difficult to feel famous there. She'd been posting about her life in Aotearoa, and Japanese followers in Tokyo and New Zealand said they admired the way she could speak te reo Māori. She'd been a guest speaker at an end-of-year function at the Japanese society in Auckland. We owe it to the indigenous people of Aotearoa to learn the language, Kana declared. I've become a revolutionary for the language.

As Kana advocated for te reo Māori, the tone of the comments on her Insta feed changed, she noticed. It was occasional at first, young white women telling her she was appropriating Māori culture, you need to check your privilege one of them said. One morning she woke up to a string of comments from followers she had to assume were Māori from their pictures and the description in their profiles. HANDS OFF OUR LANGUAGE. STAY IN YOUR LANE. Further down, a muscular, tattooed Australian, told Kana she was yellow peril.

Kana went to Kai's cot, where he lay on his back, chortling and gurgling. He was an easy baby and as Kana stared at Kai, she felt at peace with herself, secure in her motivations, brave even. She'd called the baby Kai as a reference to her te reo Māori teacher Sonya, the language, it's kai for the soul. Kana could hear Sonya whispering in her ear softly. And in Japanese kai means restoration, I love this duality, Kana told her followers. She'd had no contact from Kahungunu for a month or two, I don't get that you have no interest in your son, she said in her last text message.

As she suckled Kai in her favorite armchair, Kana started to think about her post for today's social media. I haven't learned te reo Māori for you, she would say to everyone, I've done it as a sign of respect and to preserve a language that will not survive if more of us don't learn it. It's an amends too, to the countries that the Japanese have colonised, and the indigenous cultures we have eroded and damaged. And as the mother of an indigenous child, I am proud to say that I can communicate with him in his mother tongue. Kana will sign off the post with kua mutu! and within a week she will have thousands more followers and be interviewed by famous New Zealand journalists.

Jessie Puru

Fuccboi

He puts the M in mana
and the aui in māuiui
yeah he's sick alright, in the head
it's too big for his own good

every night he was in my DMs
talking about how he just wished we could meet
even though I've heard he has slid
up between the scariest of thighs
on this motu
just one of these days he's going to get himself killed
but still I just let him ramble on until 3 am
it's entertaining, what can I say?

he spent months, even years to butter me up
talking about how I am such a beautiful wahine
and I think wow, this man is really putting in the hours
surely, he doesn't do that to everyone

my mate used to go with his brother
and all he did was talk shit about him,
about who was better at this and that,
'just because this fulla was whangai'd by some rich Māori
that he thinks he's better than the rest of us'
yeah, he looks a bit up himself
but that smile, man

he's always saying some cheesy shit
like one day I was complaining
about there not being enough hours in the day

'I'd slow down time for you if it were up to me'
like calm down smooth guy

I finally gave in
the morning after I dropped him off at the boat ramp
so he could meet his brothers for one of their regular
fishing trips or 'their regular pissing contests'
as my mate described it
before he got out of the car
he kissed me hard and his lips were salty
and sucked all the moisture out of me
I couldn't wait for the next time
I said 'bring me back a big one'
and he said 'I'll bring you back the biggest'

when I got home
his thread was gone from my inbox.

Vaughan Rapatahana

Ngā whānau

'Jenny, don't be late home from school today, please. We have to get your ballet gear organised for Saturday.'

Jenny's mother repeated herself and then added, 'Didn't you hear me the first time?'

'Yes, Mum,' was all Jenny had to say, as she grabbed her bag and closed the front door behind her. Jenny already had a bit of a headache, and it was only Tuesday morning.

School went pretty much the same as any other day. The usual lessons. The usual stupid boys with smirky faces. The usual homework tasks set. The only thing that was different was that Jenny, now a senior, was asked to go to a lunchtime meeting with the other prefects.

Ms Gilhooley smiled at them all and went right to her point. 'I won't keep you long because I know some of you have other duties. But we would like some of you to help with the new students this term. We would like some of you to volunteer to be mentors, please.' She glanced around the prefects. One or two put their hands up straight away. Jenny was not one of them.

'Thank you for volunteering, Isaiah.' Ms Gilhooley smiled again.

'Miss, I wasn't volunteering. I wanted to ask when we were meant to mentor these new kids?' Isaiah said in a rather patronising tone. 'I mean, I have sports practice most days after school . . .'

A few affirmative nods and a 'yeah' or two greeted his comment.

'We were thinking Tuesdays and Thursdays during term one. Perhaps for half an hour at this stage. We would like you to get to know some of the new students who we think may need a little bit of support at school. You could ask them if they had any questions and give them assistance with studies perhaps – and definitely give support if they feel lonely . . .'

Isaiah was sighing, and one or two others looked supremely uninterested.

Joanna Skipper and Gerald Hope, however, did volunteer.

'What about you, Jenny? Can you help us, please?'

Jenny was reluctant, but she was also aware that she 'should set an example' because her mother always said so.

'OK I will help,' she replied softly.

At 3.15 that afternoon Jenny was introduced to Charm. Charm's family had recently returned to the district. They were nearly seven years apart in terms of their ages and their year level at the small area school.

Charm lived up to her name: she beamed at Jenny when the two were introduced and told her she was very happy to have a 'senior' to help her settle into the school.

Jenny asked if the younger girl had any questions, to which Charm immediately responded, 'My form teacher is Mr Sellars. He is trying to be a funny guy because he keeps on telling us jokes all the time. But his jokes aren't funny.'

Jenny did not know what to say. Mr Sellars had never taught her. So, she smiled and said nothing.

'Do you play any sports?' Charm asked.

'I used to play netball . . .' Jenny trailed off. She wasn't going to tell the younger girl that her mother had nagged Jenny about quitting netball, because 'it takes up too much of your time'.

Charm was waiting for the rest of the sentence, but all she received was, 'How about I meet up with you tomorrow at lunchtime and you can tell me about anything at school that you need help with?' Jenny knew her mother would probably berate her for not going home straight after school, so she was attempting to scale down the conversation.

'OK,' smiled Charm. 'But where?'

'How about I come and find you in Mr Sellar's room when the lunch bell goes?'

'Sure,' Charm said.

Jenny found her mother drinking wine on the front porch. Their small car was out on the driveway.

'You are late,' snapped her mother, somehow sipping at her glass at the same time. 'We agreed that we had to go and pick up your gear from Mrs Marriner's this afternoon.'

Jenny slipped past her mother's irate eyes and went into her bedroom to change. 'Ballet,' she thought. 'I don't even like ballet.'

She must have been speaking out loud to herself, because her mother was at the doorway asking, 'What did you say?'

Jenny was not going to repeat herself. She knew her mother too well, especially when she had been drinking. 'Nothing,' she replied, turning on a smile at the scowling woman. 'I'm ready,' she said, knowing her refusal to say more would have annoyed her mum.

'By crikey, girl, you are stubborn,' muttered Mother from the passenger seat. She had lost her licence some months ago and now relied on her daughter to transport her everywhere.

Jenny could feel the next phrase coming; it was inevitable.

'You are just like your father. Stubborn. Wouldn't listen. Wouldn't talk half the time. Just buggered off and left us. The bastard.'

Jenny concentrated on her driving. Besides, she couldn't really remember her father. There were no photographs of him in their home either. She wondered if there ever had been. Still, even though she did not recall his presence, there was a gap in her life.

At 12 minutes past 12 the next day, Jenny strolled up to the door of Mr Sellar's classroom over in the far block. She waited until the lunchtime bell rang, reading through the students' names typed on the list outside.

'Charm Te Rito. Tui house' she spied halfway down. Jenny wondered if Charm spoke te reo Māori, because she had been learning the language herself for the last five years. Despite her own mother going on and on with, 'Why do you want to learn that for? It won't help you get a job, girl. Waste of time,' and so on and on.

While she was wondering, the class squeezed out of the room like toothpaste: all at once and all over the place.

'Kia ora, Jenny,' smiled Charm Te Rito.

'Kia ora, Charm,' responded Jenny, 'Matekai koe?'

'Āe, tika tō kōrero e hoa.'

The pair strolled across to the school's small tuck shop, where Charm bought a drink and a sandwich. 'Me koe hoki?' she asked Jenny.

'Kāore ahau he pīrangi he kai mai i tēnei wāhi,' answered Jenny, showing Charm her pre-packaged lunch.

As they went to sit outside in the sun, Charm spoke first, 'You speak pretty good reo . . . '

'Tēnā koe, e hoa. I have been learning Māori for several years now.' Jenny thought about saying, 'even though my mother thinks it's a waste of time,' but she shelved the comment.

Charm chewed on her sandwich silently.

'My mum speaks reo around home sometimes. My dad is dead,' she added.

'I'm sorry to hear that,' said Jenny as she munched her apple.

'He was a Pākehā,' said Charm in her forthright fashion.

So was mine, thought Jenny, again not sharing the information; although she did quickly reflect that both had no father figure around them.

'Well, do you have anything that you want me to help with?'

Charm had finished eating and was back to beaming. 'Not really . . . although I wonder what house you are in?'

'Tūī,' Jenny said between bites of the apple, 'it's the best house!'

The two girls continued to see one another sometimes over the next few weeks. On one occasion, Jenny's mother had come to the school on foot to accompany her daughter home – probably to break her daily monotony – and had spied the pair chatting outside the school gates.

'Who was that Māori girl you were talking to today?' she asked later, handing Jenny a dish to dry when they were both at the sink.

'Oh. Ms Gilhooley asked us prefects to mentor some junior students for a while. To help them settle into the school. Especially if they are new to the area.'

'What is her name?' her mother asked bluntly.

'Charm. Charm Te Rito.'

Jenny couldn't understand why her mother was screwing up her face.

'Te Rito. Used to be a family of them up in the valley. Troublemakers. Keep away from them, girl. You won't get any thanks from them, I'm telling you.'

Jenny said nothing much as a response. 'OK,' she muttered as she stooped to place the plates under the sink. Jenny liked Charm Te Rito because the younger girl made her laugh with her constant good humour and frankness of delivery. Besides, they seemed to get along well, especially when both were practising their reo.

'We will have to start preparing for the competitions next month,' Jenny's mother announced. 'More practice.'

Jenny turned toward her mother. 'More practice?'

'You want to win this year, don't you.' Her mother stated as an edict.

Jenny literally bit her tongue to stop herself from replying. More practice was about the last thing on her mind.

A couple of weeks passed. Jenny saw Charm less and less and saw piles of homework more and more. Ballet practice came and went in increasing waves, as the regional competition date neared.

Jenny struggled to keep up with the combined demands of school and plié. Neither were of great interest to her, despite her mother's constant entreaties about 'getting a good job' and 'coming first, so the family will be proud of you'. Jenny was more interested in reading her own books and going online whenever she could escape being nagged. She could only fully relax when she was searching even though she was scanning nothing in particular. Somehow doing that helped to fill her lonely inner self, although Jenny never articulated this.

Thankfully, as term one wore on, Ms Gilhooley was not pressing for more mentoring by prefects; not that many would have been keen then anyway. Isaiah used to roll his eyes whenever he saw Charm walking and talking with Jenny, while Gerald Hope had already told Ms Gilhooley that he 'just didn't have any time to help now'.

On the Saturday of the competitions Jenny performed as well as she was able, which was nowhere near good enough for her mum. A highly commended didn't cut it with her. On the way back home that afternoon, Jenny had to listen to a tirade. 'You could have done better than that, Jenny. I don't know what has happened to you recently. Too much silly stuff at school.' And on and on and on, getting ultimately to, 'You're just like your damned father. Never listen to someone who knows better.'

Jenny felt like saying, 'My father left us when I was a baby. How can I be just like him?' but merely sighed as she drove into the rapidly gathering dusk sprinting toward the windscreen.

A couple of days later, she chanced across Charm out on the netball court, where she was practising for the junior school team.

'Heya, Jenny,' she glowed, just as she was passing the ball way down court. 'Pēhea koe, e hoa?'

Jenny had to grin back. 'Kei te pai,' she lied a bit, 'kei te pai.'

'Bout time we caught up, eh,' yelled Charm as she shot down the court in pursuit of the other team.

'Yes,' replied Jenny, far too quietly for anyone to hear her.

Term one was sinking fast. Jenny's mother was drinking faster these days. The holidays were going to be a rest time for Jenny, she hoped — despite the assignments which did not interest her much. She found herself sighing far too often.

'Jenny,' her mother was calling out from the kitchen. 'Come and help me, please.'

Jenny slowly walked into the kitchen. What now? she mused.

'Yes Mum?'

Her mother's hand was bleeding slightly onto a spanner. Blood was also on the sink tap, which she had obviously been trying to adjust, because it was askew, turned around to face the back of the sink.

'Get me a towel, please. I don't want to get blood everywhere.'

Jenny did as she was told and grasped her mother's bloody hand in the towel, wiping away the residue and placing a sticking plaster on the small cut.

'What are you trying to do?' she asked.

'To fix the leak, girl. This hot tap has never been any good.'

'I think you will need a new washer, Mum,' said Jenny, well aware from her technical classes how to fix a leaking tap.

'I know, I know. I just thought I could tighten this because we don't have any washers.'

'I can go down to the store and see if they have any . . .'

'OK, OK,' said her Mum, as she reached for a glass and a bottle all at the same time. 'Get me some Port Royal.' She shouted, 'Better get some cigarette papers too,' as Jenny was getting into the car.

Jenny grinned as she drove away from home. Good to get a break. She pressed her foot down to speed the car a bit faster and to feel the wind blow through her long black hair.

Outside the local all-purpose store, Charm Te Rito was sitting, eating an ice cream; smiling as soon as she saw her schoolmate.

'Kia ora anō, Jenny. He aha tō kōrero?'

Jenny smiled back. 'Got to buy some stuff for home.'

She went inside and soon found a set of washers — enough to fix an army of leaking taps.

Back outside, Charm was standing up, her ice cream gone. 'How about a ride home? You can come and meet my mum, eh,' suggested Charm.

Jenny did not even think about saying 'no' and soon the two of them were driving out into the countryside, down the rocky driveway to the farmhouse where Charm lived with her whānau.

Inside the cottage, Charm introduced Jenny to her mother, a petite and pretty wahine with a wide smile. She grinned even more widely when Jenny replied to her i te reo Māori.

'E noho, girl. Pīrangi koe he inu?'

'Kāo.'

'Pīrangi koe he kai?'

'No thank you, I'm good,' said Jenny, not wanting to be a bother.

Mrs Te Rito had already put down some buttered rēwena in front of the guest anyway, as well as a large glass of soft drink she had taken from the refrigerator humming away in the background.

'Tēnā koe,' said Jenny, tasting the bread, and the honey Mrs Te Rito added, with pleasure. She looked around the kitchen and at the old wood stove and older wooden cupboards. There were quite a few photos spread about, including a couple of a white man who was laughing away at everyone who looked at him.

'That's my dad,' said Charm, following Jenny's eyes. Surprised eyes because Jenny couldn't help but think that the man seemed familiar.

Her expression must have interested Mrs Te Rito too, because she asked, 'Ko wai tō ingoa whānau, Jenny?'

'Mikkelson,' said Jenny.

'I thought so,' said Mrs Te Rito quietly. She looked right into Jenny's face and then carefully clasped her own daughter's hand. 'Charm. Come closer, girl . . . sit next to your sister.'

Iona Winter

Portal to the stars

There was a time when I'd lie in my bed,
and look out the window above it
to the whetū. I never knew
what the brightest ones were called.

Venus or Mars?
On clear nights I'd say to myself,
'I should ask him when he gets here,'
but I had other things on my mind by then.

The next morning he'd be gone.
Back to his other love,
taking the winding road
where Papatūānuku was reclaiming her skin.

In brief moments before sleep,
eyes open to a thick blanket of secrets,
my breath and limbs were always
the same hefty stone.

Carin Smeaton

Bird-peoples make it to ngā Rangi-i-Totongia-a-Tamatekapua

david blaine where r u now cos i havent seen u since the symonds street off-ramp where i showed u a card trick or two & u recommended youtube talking boutfriction levitating us back into the 90s our tūrangawaewae our stomping-ground bridge it was still open-access back then barrier free from glass fast & escape was way easy or at least inevitable visible to the naked eye an express flight to rangitoto 4 hauraki-healing if u made it that far (& not all bird-peoples did) tho when we did we all got the same dead gorgeous view same as any prophet who got lured away from her exodus hell by such dazzling balancing-acts stretchin it out till kingdom come & that is how u take yr mind off an emergency says david blaine on grafton bridge u dont see the drop see the vision the mission of possibility a future on valium vs a life at the lights stuck on red in the rain when u cross david blaine he got a way of possessing u watching u he'll tap on yr window wit his deck o split spades he'll take it away bleed into the fluorescent night of moon where my birdwoman once flew my rona in blu rising above rangitoto

Emma Hislop

Cure

It was late afternoon when Miri arrived at James's friends' place in the King Country. There was another car in the driveway she recognised as Charlotte's. Charlotte was James's younger sister and Miri's friend from art school. She had a lot of opinions. It would have been better to wait and come with James. It wasn't the first time he'd let work commitments affect their plans. But she was here now, and he was flying up tomorrow. She should go in. The front door opened. They must have heard the car. She waved, took the keys out of the ignition.

'Miri. It is Miri, right? Not Miriam or Miriama? Please come in. I expect you're thirsty after that drive. Of course, you already know Charlotte.'

Linley was an artist, too. Her partner Andre was an architect. Inside, the house was all glass and gigantic white walls – asking to be filled with something. Out towards the garden, a separate work studio adjoined the house. Miri's weakness for rich white guys meant she already knew what this weekend looked like. Linley and James went to university together, back in the stone ages.

'Miri! Is that the new Ruby dress?' Charlotte said. 'You look incredible.' Miri knew it, and smiled to herself, avoiding Charlotte's gaze. Miri wondered how long she could make the James situation last. A lot of people said that Capricorns only opened up if they liked you, but it was deeper than that. A lot of it was reassuring James that he wasn't alone anymore. It had been a welcome distraction from the boredom of lockdown, but lately it was getting to be a drag.

'It's so light,' Miri commented. And then, because it seemed awkward to stop there, 'What a lovely space.'

She wondered if they even realised what they were living on top of. James hadn't mentioned it. Driving in, there were rock walls and remnants of takuahi, on the slopes terraced gardens lined with rocks still visible. She'd spotted Kawakawa cultivations still growing there. It wasn't called the King Country for nothing.

'You can follow the light around the house, starting with the snug in the morning and ending in the lounge,' Linley explained, making a circular gesture with one hand. 'Although you're living at Ocean Parade with James at the moment, aren't you?'

Miri nodded, cradling her Balenciaga bag. She wasn't sure how much James had told them. She reminded herself to keep the conversation low stakes. People misunderstood the situation if they thought James was just helping Miri.

'You'll know all about fabulous light, then,' Linley said. She laughed exaggeratedly. 'That must be great,' she said. '*You go girl!*' James's place was on the seafront and along with the incredible views it had excellent light. Miri's last flat had looked out at a brick wall. 'Please sit. I'll bring you a drink.' She was blonde, with a good figure, seemed at ease in herself.

Miri had realised she could basically live with James, if she wanted to. She told him her landlord put the rent up, and she'd stay with him till she found somewhere cheaper. If she was honest with herself, she would probably break up with him, but he let her drive his Audi, which she liked. She hadn't been in one before. She hadn't had her licence long, less than a year.

They sat on the deck, with a cheese board and a selection of wine. It was easy to forget what a huge week she'd had, a major assignment and two double shifts. Miri finished her first glass faster than she could admit to anyone. Mostly it was them asking questions.

'You're an artist too, right?' Andre said, other questions in his eyes. They might be unaware of the arrangement, but she was clearly young enough to be James's daughter and they knew James had separated from his wife and son a few months before.

Charlotte had introduced them at an art opening and he contacted her a week later to ask if he could include her work in an exhibition for ten emerging Māori artists he was curating. He'd used the word *showcase*. The show wasn't just about installing. They all stayed together for a week, and James took care of them. It was a whole entire experience, they stayed together in a villa that he had rented out. It was really spacious. Everyone had their own rooms and double beds. He made them delicious blackberry and fresh-mint mocktails and they drank Rosé and ate pistachios. It felt like James was both the director, and a person that really looked after them. Like a really caring friend.

Art school was incestuous – everyone had fucked everyone. One night at a party, Miri vibed with James. They'd hugged before – when she caught up with Charlotte and him together, or said goodbye at events – but that night was the first time Miri didn't let go. It was too easy to let him believe she'd caught feelings. This was how she could become somebody.

'Yeah, I graduated last year. And I'm part way through a teaching Diploma.'

She wondered if it had been a mistake to come. She'd failed the last assignment, due to the fact she had disagreed with the treaty principles, as outlined by the course conveners. As though she was messing with them, ridiculing the guidelines. James was the one who encouraged her to take the course, offering to pay half.

'Get your teaching qualification,' he told her. 'Then you can do what you like.' If she passed, he'd give her a job at his company doing the accounts. They had a casual dress code, a chill-out room, free massages, and it was a short walk from James's apartment.

'I do a lot of other cool stuff. I make art videos and TikToks. My friend Hana and I have this pop-up shop in the weekends sometimes. And I've got a waitressing job.' She had nearly 10,000 Instagram followers and more since the art show. There was her reo class. Sometimes she had to collect James's shirts from the drycleaners. She was pretty much doing the job of four people but she was still broke. At least she didn't have to worry while they stayed together.

'Baby,' he'd say. 'How did I get so lucky?' And recently, 'My home is your home.' The way he saw it, Miri was the thing that made him better. She was used to men like James, but the fact he was artistic, and didn't want to own her meant the arrangement worked for her. And he could hold a conversation. Although it was always the same with rich white guys. It was like she was exploring the world from a place they just weren't able to access. But they were going on holiday to Europe in a month, when she finished her studies. He was paying but the price was symbolic.

'It will be a relief to leave hospitality, I imagine, Miri,' Linley said. 'Now, who needs freshening up?' Miri's glass was refilled as Linley asked the question. They were good at entertaining. There was something in the way Linley talked about James, like a protective parent. Not that Miri knew what that was like.

'You're still waitressing though, aren't you?' Charlotte asked, nibbling on a piece of cheese. There was an array of things on the platter: grapes, nuts, crackers and blue cheese.

Miri nodded. Her goal was to make insufficient funds a thing of the past. She didn't think she could take a third job, but it had crossed her mind. 'Evenings and weekends mostly, now I'm doing the course. But it's not sustainable. I'd rather be doing paid promotions on Insta, but James has zero faith in me being an influencer.'

'Can't imagine why,' Andre laughed. He had the kind of tan that told Miri he didn't know the meaning of a day's work.

Miri shrugged. He picked up a bottle of red and then the corkscrew. 'Remind me where you grew up, again Miri. Which suburb of Wellington?'

'Northern suburbs,' she said not really wanting to give him the specifics but not prepared to lie, trying to work out how she could change the subject.

'And to think, this time last year, you and James were in *Florence*,' Charlotte said. It had been Miri's first trip overseas, but it wasn't all first-class flights and five-star hotels. James had wined and dined clients while she hung out in the hotel room.

'Which suburb? Kelburn's not North, is it, Charlotte?' Andre poured the wine, his eyes on Miri. Like a dog with a bone. It amused Miri how much importance rich people put on certain things. Like they were living life at a different frequency.

'Moera. In the Hutt. Do you know it?' What he hoped to prove was anyone's guess. They had already made their assumptions about her. 'I hardly recognise it now, to be honest.' The stretch of road she'd grown up on was currently being dug up for more gentrification. The family in the corner dairy evicted to make way for another shopping mall.

'Right, right. Nothing a fresh coat of paint won't sort out. Goes to show it's more about drive and ambition than education.' Seeing the racism in him was unsettling. It was right there in his mind. Every time this kind of thing happened, Miri normally called it out. But she wasn't always sure if she imagined it. And here it was, not imaginary, and not hidden, but right here, out loud, to her face. She decided to try out her recently acquired knowledge on him. This guy could do worse than to listen to voices other than his own.

'Interesting opinion, Andre. I'd have to disagree. My high school brought a perspective on truth to the table that only we knew and one everyone needed to hear.'

'Sure,' Andre said. He looked like he was trying to unpack it. Miri wasn't certain how to suggest to him that this should be a joke, and yet wasn't. What even was that? Some misplaced sense of duty? She didn't owe him any explanation.

They ate in silence for a minute. Thinly sliced celery and fennel, and dressed with a bit of fish sauce, lots of lemon and shaved Parmesan. Miri thought about her assignment, her last chance to resubmit. She thought of her shared studio space, with its leaking ceiling and no loo. She wished she could check her email and her phone. She couldn't wait to text Hana. Briefly, she rethought her situation, again.

'That's a very attractive quality. No doubt it's the reason you've managed the course and a job on top,' Linley said. She'd missed the point entirely, but Miri felt instant relief at the break in the silence. She was careful, she didn't really talk about the James situation, except to Hana. Mostly how disappointing the sex was.

'Being in debt is hard,' Charlotte said. They were halfway through the steak and potatoes. Miri remembered how disorganised Charlotte had been at art school. It was like she lacked drive.

'Who said anything about debt, Charlotte? Being financially responsible is hard, too.'

'Oh.' Linley's lipstick marked the rim of her wine glass. 'I didn't mean to imply . . . it will be worth it in your case, Miri.' She was probably sincere, but they had no idea. Sometimes it was a sixty-hour week. The longer she worked at the restaurant, the more her ability to make art seemed to be slipping away.

'Your student loan repayments must be killing you now you're working,' Charlotte said, stabbing her fork into the steak. Charlotte and James's parents had covered Charlotte's art-school fees. 'I hear it's brutal.'

Opening the bottle of wine she'd brought felt like a good idea, but Miri couldn't see it anywhere. Asking felt like too much of a statement at this point.

'Another reason I plan to quit waitressing soon,' Miri said. 'For me, it'll be about getting the balance right, at the right time.' Don't go to work, James said. You should quit. Stay here with me. There was a new waiter at the restaurant, his name was Ari, and she couldn't stop looking at him. They were the same age and had a lot in common.

'Work and home life have always been connected for us,' said Andre. 'The studio was well worth the investment, cheaper than a divorce!' he laughed, flashing perfect teeth. Miri recognised the same certainty in

Andre that was in James, that just about *everything* would work out to their advantage.

'I'm certain you'll figure it out, Miri. You're obviously smart, an asset to your people,' Andre said.

Charlotte gave him a look. 'Oh, that's embarrassing, Andre. Why would you say that?'

Andre flushed. He seemed genuinely embarrassed.

'What?' he said.

'You might benefit from a crash course on the treaty. It's called being an ally. We all have blind spots.'

Miri felt conflicted. Andre was annoying, but Charlotte was being more annoying. The confidence of Charlotte couldn't be underestimated.

'I have you to thank, actually, Miri,' Charlotte said. 'What I was hearing from you at art school was completely different to my experience of growing up. My understanding of being Māori was non-existent.'

She used the past tense. Charlotte was actually hilarious.

'Recently I realised, oh my God, if there's one, there's two . . . what else am I blind to?' Charlotte said. 'If we're taking up space as Pākehā laughing at white supremacists and saying, shame on you, and having a good time in the space, I need to change.' Charlotte wanted to be a part of something that changed the conversation.

'That's a beautiful thing to say, Charlotte, we're all entitled to be who we are without judgment,' Linley said.

The fact that they'd said '*we*'; it suggested a shared responsibility, which seemed to include Miri. But how did you talk about what you just couldn't talk about? If you get the message you're not good enough then you spend all your time trying to be good enough by being nice to people. By never saying how you feel because they might not like how you feel.

'I noticed the remnants of a kāinga, driving in. Would that be right, Andre?'

'It's name was Killer Hill. That's what they called it anyway.' Miri would understand after the climb up tomorrow, Andre laughed. If the weather improved. They took all their visitors up.

'That can't be the real name, though,' Miri said. 'What's the Māori name?'

'I'm not sure of the specifics. The people who look after it now do a good job,' Andre said. He hadn't denied it was there, it was just his version of the story. On the other hand, James must have at least known about it. Hadn't he? Had he avoided mentioning it?

James kissed her hard at Arrivals in the morning, then they found the car. Her hands gripped the steering wheel, as he put his suitcase in the back, before settling into the passenger's seat.

'I hope Andre and Linley looked after you last night?' he said. 'And Charlotte behaved herself?' He'd recently limited his alcohol consumption to a bottle of wine a day.

She forced a smile, could already feel the anger. 'Everyone seemed to have a good time. How did the work thing go?' At first, it seemed easy to write off the differences. But not this.

'The weekend's bound to be awash, with these guys. You might want to slow down a bit.' She carried on at fifty down the residential road. He trusted authority, which annoyed her. 'Oh, fine. We signed the deal,' he said. He was a natural manager, unfazed by having to make decisions that affected others. When she met him, she was impressed that he owned his own place. He did his taxes on time. But mostly he believed he could achieve things. She used to think by working hard at school she could achieve anything.

Her phone vibrated. She glanced at the cracked screen. At the beginning, James lavished her with gifts, but not so much since the divorce. The only person to ever leave a voice message on her phone anymore was Miri's mum. She'd never got the hang of texting.

But it was Hana. Miri stopped at the lights, and quickly read the text. Hana had found the perfect flat. It was within their budget and they could do what they wanted with it, because it was going to be bulldozed in a year to make way for apartments. It even had a gallery space.

'The way your friends were describing everything,' she said. She couldn't keep these impressions to herself. She added after a minute, 'It was like they had no idea of history.'

James laughed, then added, darkly: 'Andre's memory's probably been diluted by red wine. Some of it'll be fantasy. Some of it never happened at all.'

'That's it. It's like it never happened.' She was louder and more accusatory than she'd meant to sound. She watched the rain fall on the windscreen and figured out what she wanted to say. Lately, she'd been more critical of him. They'd started to argue about everything, especially politics. She felt disappointed by the government's response to lockdown, but he wasn't bothered. It weighed on her mind. She had friends who had been directly affected by Covid. It seemed to Miri that these other things were too hard to speak about.

'There is a kind of social amnesia in this country where people conveniently forget what happened in the past,' he said.

'I went into a school last week and the deputy principal – who's British – pulled me up on my Greek pronunciation,' she laughed. 'I was taking an art workshop on Matariki and talking about the nine stars and he said, "Miri, I'm disappointed you can't pronounce Pleiades properly." I'm trying to reclaim my native language, like claw it back and he's talking about fucking Pleiades.'

He put a hand on her knee. 'You seem upset.'

She concentrated on driving.

'It's like . . . they've given themselves permission to view the world with the eyes they've grown up with,' she said quietly.

'I mean, if you're doing post-grad, you should know how to pronounce Pleiades. And how can you know what you don't know? Or what you don't see?' he said. He laughed but he wasn't joking.

The passing lane was approaching. Miri flicked the indicator on, and accelerated out into the right lane to pass the truck, but as the Audi drew parallel the truck sped up.

'Asshole.' She floored the accelerator. 'Yes, but the country they think they're living in isn't the country they're living in. I just –' she was aware of James leaning over, checking her speed. 'It's just difficult to exist within a system that wasn't designed to support your people.'

A car coming towards them in the distance flashed its lights as Miri passed the truck, and pulled back into the left lane.

'I feel like you want me to say something and I don't know what you want to hear,' he said. 'And, Christ, can you slow down a bit?'

'Andre actually said to me last night I was a credit to my people.' The first few times this sort of thing happened, she might have reacted differently. Perhaps it was possible, from his perspective, to feel blamed. Who else was there to blame? They occupied her mind, that was tiring enough.

She reacted like this, partly because she felt like shit, and she wanted to take her mind off the assignment. She wasn't used to working under pressure like James was. Her next assignment was due in a fortnight. She'd have to make sense of all those readings before then. If she failed again, she was off the course.

'I think I'm just – Yeah. I have some course stuff – going on.' She spoke slowly and deliberately. 'It's like, they have to make sure I'm fit to teach, which seems to mean repressing the ugly parts of this country's history.'

James was nodding, moving his head up and down – showing he understood the complexity of what she was saying, but did he really? There was such a thing as too much nodding. 'Can I just say something, though?' He wasn't finished, apparently. He reasoned that this stuff had nothing to do with him, not directly. And being contemptuous only made people defensive.

'I mean, if you direct hate into something long enough, that's what you'll get,' Miri said, looking out the window.

'What does *that* mean?' he asked.

None of her answers felt appropriate so she didn't say anything.

Miri watched them from the car, wanting to see what they were like when she wasn't around, how James moved through the world with these people. They hadn't talked since the conversation in the car. Linley was smart-casual, in fitted dark jeans and a shimmery blouse. James in his lived-in clothes: V-neck jumper almost the same grey as his hair, striped shirt and rumpled black chinos. The divorce had cost him a lot. And he was generous. Sometimes you had to agree to disagree.

'How was your flight?' she heard Linley ask.

'Fine,' he said, getting his bag out of the boot. He kissed Linley on the cheek, pulling her in close for a hug. 'Looking very well, Lin.' Linley leaned in and whispered something to him, and they both smiled. Miri had always felt she was leading this, but, for a single moment, she felt annoyed. But she didn't feel like having any more arguments. Already, the day felt long. She'd let it go, for the weekend anyway. She needed to stop thinking about the assignment.

The mirrors in the hallway were a good distraction – similar to a changing room where you're surrounded by your own reflection. She admired the ruched fabric of her new dress and the way her hair fell over her bare shoulders. Miri tried out the different angles, taking a few pictures on her phone and sending them to Hana. She retouched her lip gloss before posting the best one to her Insta stories.

'Sit down whenever you're ready, Miri,' Linley said, placing everything in the middle of the table. Miri wanted to stay looking at herself, but went and took a seat.

Brunch. Eggs on toast, crusty bread, chorizo sausage.

'Amazing,' Miri said, feeling more generous now. The eggs looked perfectly cooked, the sausages spattered with sea salt and rosemary.

'Loving the new table, you guys,' Charlotte said.

'We couldn't believe our luck when this turned up on Trade Me,' Andre said, sitting opposite Miri. 'Early twentieth century.' Miri had no interest in tables.

James sat beside her, pulling his chair closer. He had changed out of his plane clothes. He put his arm around her waist, letting his fingers rest on the studs in her dress. Miri could tell he was trying not to let the cracks between them show.

'Food is always within reach at a round table.' Linley put a carafe of orange juice down for the mimosas. 'Every time I clear plates, I think about who has sat here over the years.'

'As long as the mimosas are within reach, Lin,' James laughed, pouring himself a large one. Miri's phone was in her bag, and she could feel it vibrating. It stopped, then started again. She'd applied for the weekend off but the restaurant sometimes still called.

'We drove a couple of hours to pick it up,' Andre said. 'Turned up at this big storage facility and this elderly couple are trying to sell everything. We masked up and got talking and the old guy said their retirement had failed. They needed to shift the lot.'

'This is boring. Let's talk about something else,' said Miri, glancing at the clock on the wall. She was missing the latest episode of *Love Island*.

'I'd like to propose a birthday toast, to my old friend, James,' Andre said, lifting his glass, and looking at Miri.

James paused, then held his hands up as though he was being shot. 'Don't remind me,' James said jokingly, like he always did when his age came up in conversation. He raised his glass, making eye contact with Miri. 'Cheers.'

'May you enjoy your *little pleasures* a bit longer.'

They all raised their glasses. Linley looked so uncomfortable that Miri had to bite her lip to keep from laughing. Andre was such an asshole.

Her phone vibrated again. Was she one of those people now? Is that who she was? Refusing to answer her friends' calls? This wasn't right. Leave or stay, leave or stay. Maybe it was this that made Miri's mind up, maybe it was something else. There was something different inside her in that moment, like a moving forward. She looked at her phone. There were photos of the flat from Hana. Miri still had an eye for a bargain.

They ate, looking onto the garden, talking about the new offices at James's company. Recently, James installed a set of inbuilt bunks at the office so that staff could nap or stay over if they were working late. Rest was essential for thinking big thoughts.

'We're floating the idea of an office in Venice,' James said. Miri had always wanted to go to Venice.

'It was after Venice that I decided to read Deleuze,' Linley said. 'And Camus. And I started to ask how art serves me. My father taught English at the university there. The library was the first public space that felt like mine.' Miri pictured Linley as a child, lying on the floor under the shelves, with a book in one hand. Miri made a mental note to google Camus later.

'This is delicious, Lin. Farmers market sausages, I assume?' James said. Miri cut through the sausage. She rarely cooked. James taught her how to make gnocchi from scratch. He introduced her to oysters.

'We're getting all our meat there these days. Do you enjoy cooking, Miri?'

Miri usually ate dinner at the restaurant. She was starting to think her biggest problem was time. The less time she spent in the studio, the more she worried about what time had gone. 'Truthfully, I'm just not excited by cooking.'

'Miri's hours aren't sustainable. She won't mind me saying that.'

'It's not that I want to work so much,' Miri said. She was sick of working late shifts. 'I want to make art. But I need a reliable income. It's –' What did any of them know about anything? Being his own boss, James could work the hours he chose. No one ordering him around, or asking him to work late.

'I just –' If she could just have one job instead of three, she thought. James had called her ambition into question and now she couldn't stop thinking about it. Was wanting to be an artist selfish? In the beginning, he'd championed her work. Miri drank some orange juice to give herself something to do.

Linley started clearing the plates, saying something about coffee and Danishes and moving into the lounge where they'd be more comfortable.

'Any plans today?' Charlotte said. 'The hill I guess?'

After another cup of coffee, Miri would be ready to leave. No, not up the hill today, or any day. She picked up her Balenciaga bag, with the car keys inside.

Ana McAllister

My Grim Reaper

I kiss the Grim Reaper on the lips and he tells me I'm a goddess.
I say of course, I am Hine-nui-te-pō.
I am your equal.
I look up from my knees and read death across his gut.
I take no issue being on my knees for my grim.
He's a sweetheart underneath that heavy black hood.
His skin stained with the stories of his ancestors, just like mine.
Black hair, black nails, black eyes. I stare into them and fall down.
Bones grinding against one another.

Naturally grim returns the favour.
He's good like that.
He enters like Māui and I gift him immortality over and over again.
Tell him to bow down to me after I bowed to him.
We are the perfect couple, death and death.
Bowing to each other because no one bows to us anymore.
When he's away from me, I reach down for him. My fingernails longing for his skin underneath them.
And he's so often away from me.
Gathering souls one at a time.
My souls come to me that is the gift of my people.

Everytime one of my souls comes to me I orgasm. Don't tell me my pussy isn't sacred.
My grim knows that. And even when I'm on my knees. He's on his knees too.

Kelly Joseph

Obsidian Dream

They stopped in the small city of Bend for a quick lunch at a diner and then drove south to Paulina Lake through the high desert. Theirs was the only car for miles – it was mid-week and the tourist season was long over. Olly sat in the back of the rented SUV, cringing as Emily shot questions at him from the passenger seat.

'So, do you know Peter Jackson?' she said, her face turned slightly towards him so he could see her profile. Her forehead was prominent, like a toddler's.

'What do you watch on TV over there? Or do you guys like, still run around in grass skirts? Didn't I hear that the May-or-ees are cannibals?'

Dan adjusted the rear-view mirror. Olly knew it was so that Dan could see him squirming at his sister's inane questions. Dan's aviators reflected the road ahead but hid his unnerving amber eyes.

'It's pronounced Māori,' Olly said quietly.

'Mouldy?' she said, giggling. Olly resisted the urge to open his door and roll onto the highway to get away from her. He had endured her questions for three days. It was confusing why Dan even invited her along. They had become friends at the Northwest Film Center where Olly taught experimental film and video. Dan was the screenwriting tutor.

A couple of months earlier Amy, Olly's American girlfriend, had dropped him for a bearded vegan who worked with her at the local wholefoods store. Because of the break-up, Olly's fiancé visa was about to run out and this coincided with his family telling him they needed him to come home. This trip was a last hurrah before he had to fly back.

He had been looking forward to the road trip with Dan, imagined a fun and perhaps even debauched boys' getaway. He'd bought several packs of beer in preparation. It was disappointing when Dan had come to pick him up and Emily was perched in the passenger seat.

Olly didn't even know Dan had a sister. They didn't look related. She had dark wide-set eyes and a gamine haircut that revealed elfin ears.

For a split second he thought she was kind of hot but then she opened her maddening trap.

The goal was to do a loop and end up in the Columbia River Gorge. They had spent the previous day at the Warm Springs Reservation. While Dan and Emily played the slot machines at the Casino, Olly drove to a nearby shantytown.

He stopped at a thrift store run by a pair of aged Native American women.

Their faces were carved with deep wrinkles, like the canyons he saw when he first flew over the States.

The thrift store was just a small room in a prefab building and there wasn't much on offer except for handbags, belts and old t-shirts. The store reminded Olly of his mum who used to volunteer in her church charity shop before she got sick. He felt a twang of something in his gut as he thought of her, a mixture of guilt and sadness.

He found a Peanuts t-shirt with Charlie Brown talking into a CB radio saying, 'I never get a break', that he took up to the women to buy. They were engrossed in gossip about a fight that had taken place at a recent powwow. When he politely cleared his throat to get their attention, one of the women scrutinised him with cloudy cataract eyes. One of her brows went up and the other down, trying to figure him out.

'What nation you from?'

'I'm not . . . I'm from New Zealand.'

She whistled. 'Is that so? You're a long way from home, Honey,' she said.

'You're sure handsome enough to pass for one of us you know,' said the other woman, laughing gruffly. This wasn't the first time Olly had heard this. On different occasions he'd been asked if he was Hispanic, Greek, Armenian or Jewish. Olly liked the confusion his looks created. It made him feel like he could fit in almost anywhere as long as he kept his mouth shut.

They had left the reservation that morning. On their way out they stopped on the crest of a butte so that Olly could get some Super 8 footage. He walked a little distance from the car to a fence line where he could see for miles — clumps of sagebrush, twisted junipers, rocky outcrops, a cluster of restless horses, a distant curtain of rain moving across the ochre landscape, and an expansive sky above. There was so much sky that he felt almost untethered from Earth and gravity. He felt alert and buzzed, almost electric.

The camera whirred as he pulled the trigger of the Super 8. Then he felt a pressure on the back of his knees. He spun around with a sick feeling that he was being attacked. It was a dog leaping up on him. His heart thumped as two other dogs surrounded him. Then he realised it was just a mother and two pups, husky-type dogs with friendly eyes and black lips that appeared to be smiling.

They continued to bound around his legs. Olly shot footage of them at his feet.

Their friendliness stirred something in him that he hadn't felt for ages, maybe years. He felt normal, happy even.

When Olly got back to the car Dan was leaning on the door watching him. Dan tossed away a cigarette and ran a hand through his oily blond hair.

'When we saw those dogs running towards you, we hopped back in the car and closed the doors,' he laughed. 'We thought you were going to be torn to shreds.'

'Why didn't you call out a warning?' asked Olly.

Dan shrugged. Olly was swiftly depressed again; he felt utterly alone.

Signs declared that the Newberry National Volcanic Monument was up ahead.

'Fuck, I'm so bored. This samey-same landscape is driving me nuts,' said Emily.

Something splatted against the windscreen leaving a blob of yellow juice. Then there were more light thumps on the glass and more fluid. Olly leaned between the seats to peer out the front window.

A cloud of pale, yellow butterfies hovered over the road. The trio were quiet as more butterflies kamikazed into the glass. The juice got so thick Dan had to switch on the wipers to see the road. Emily turned up the volume on her Sleater-Kinney CD and sang tunelessly along. Olly was disturbed enough that he didn't even think to capture the strange moment on film.

Hairpin turns led to the Paulina Peak Outlook. Eventually, the cloud of butterflies disappeared but Olly felt suddenly carsick, so when they reached the summit he hopped out quickly. For several minutes he leaned against the car gulping in the fresh mountain air. Glancing down he saw papery wings caught in the wipers and on the SUV's grill.

There was a view across Paulina Lake and Eastern Lake to a distant mountain range with a few patches of snow. You could also see an undulating grey area where there were no pines growing. It reminded

Olly of a giant cowpat and an interpretive sign said this was the Big Obsidian Flow.

Paulina Lake itself was the hue of an aquamarine swimming pool, flanked by spiky pines. Feeling less queasy, Olly pulled out his Super 8 camera again, popped in a new film cartridge and swung around to capture his surroundings.

An enormous log floating near the edge of the lake caught his eye and he zoomed in on it.

'Hey, look at that weird log,' he said pointing.

'And it's weird because why?' asked Dan.

'Dunno. There's just something weird about it.'

'*You're* fucking weird,' said Emily from the car, tapping her feet on the dash impatiently.

For a brief moment he imagined his hands around her slender neck, choking the living shit out of her. Dan laughed and got Olly in a playful headlock and rubbed his hair before they hopped back in the car.

They drove for another five minutes to a tollbooth at the park entrance where they paid a camping fee. Inside were four shuttered historic cabins sheltered under the pines. Further along was a car park and campground. There were a few sites on the grey sand at the lake edge and they parked up on one of these.

As he stretched his legs Olly read a sign tacked up on a post warning that they were in black bear country. It suggested not surprising bears by hiking in noisy groups during the daytime. It also recommended hanging food from a tree or storing it in the car.

Later, after they set up their tents, he saw Emily carrying pretzels and cookies into the tent she shared with Dan.

'Didn't you see the sign?' he asked.

Emily snorted defiantly. 'It's exaggerated. I grew up in Oregon and I've never heard of anyone being mauled by a bear.'

When Emily went off to the toilets Olly moved his tent a few feet farther away from hers.

Pine trees loomed over the campsite, an army of straight-backed sentries. Pinecones were scattered everywhere like hard little turds. The scent of pine needles reminded Olly of the trees his parents used to buy at the local service station at Christmas time, with their new shoots that would inevitably droop in the summer warmth, and branches that bowed under the coloured baubles, blinking lights and tinsel his mum piled on.

Dan called Olly over and pointed upwards.

'See that there,' he said. There was a heavy looking branch hanging precariously from a few shreds of bark. 'That there's a widow-maker. My father got brained by one of those a few years ago on his property.'

'God, that's awful,' said Olly.

'He deserved it, the old cunt,' said Dan kicking a few pinecones towards the lake.

He didn't elaborate and Olly didn't ask. Olly had known Dan for over a year and he still couldn't work him out. When they met, he thought Dan was just another aloof Portland hipster but as he got to know him, he found Dan was an oddity because even though he wore the mandatory horn-rimmed glasses and stove-pipe jeans, he was more jock than geek.

When Olly arrived in Portland, he didn't know anyone except Amy and when she began working nights, he got quite lonely. Then for some reason, Dan began inviting him to have lunch together at the downtown food carts. At the time, Olly felt that he couldn't be too fussy about who he made friends with.

These past couple of months Dan had been pretty good at helping him take his mind off things — they went to several gigs and bars together. Dan even took Olly to Nicolai Street Clubhouse, a local strip bar, and as they watched a skinny blonde with tiny tits writhe on a pole, Dan told Olly he was better off without Amy. She was wrong for him — far too earnest.

He suggested Olly fuck a whore, maybe two, to get her out of his system. Olly quite liked this idea, but of course he didn't put the plan into action. He didn't know any whores and he wasn't going to pay for one. That was cheating. Besides, he just wanted to be back with Amy. Yes, she was totally overly earnest, but he liked that. She had integrity. She had made him feel sane.

It was Dan's idea to take the road trip. He had sorted everything out to Olly's surprise. Looking back to when they first met, it wasn't like Dan had a heap of friends either. In fact, it seemed like Dan repelled people. No one at work could stand his inappropriate sarcasm and the constant smirk on his lips. When Olly thought about it, Dan was probably more of a loner than he was.

There were only a few other people staying at the campground. An older couple were parked up in a Winnebago. There was also another tent set up under a thick cluster of pines but no sign of who set it up. Olly, Dan and Emily situated their tents facing the lake. They drank a few beers and made smores as the sun went down. Two deer appeared from the pines then disappeared silently. Dan and Emily decided to take a walk by themselves.

Olly stood at the water's edge looking across, licking chocolate and sticky marshmallow off his hands. The setting sun illuminated criss-crossing vapour trails in the sky above. The water was clear enough to see the rocks beneath the water.

A motorboat headed back to the boat launch after a day's fishing. Water rippled from the boat's wake creating small waves that lapped near his feet. They died away.

Then strangely, ripples appeared from a different direction, but this time he couldn't tell where they were coming from. The waves that rolled in were bigger than before.

He was surprised to find his shoes suddenly submerged in freezing water. He cursed and walked backwards to dry sand. As he bent down to take off his wet shoes and socks, the hairs on his head began to stand on end. He looked out onto the water.

The light was fading quickly. He shivered. Something was moving out there.

Moments later when he heard Emily's shrill laughter and Dan's low voice, he was actually relieved. He tried not to think of all the horror movies he had seen as a kid involving lakes and stupid, inevitably doomed youths. Later. Dan slunk off to bed early and left Emily and Olly sitting on a log watching the embers of the fire die down. Emily was relaxed and slightly drunk. She scooted over to his side. She closed her eyes and laid her head on Olly's shoulder. Feeling awkward, Olly looked up to the sky. The stars were hidden behind clouds.

'Mmm, you smell nice,' she said. Suddenly she had both hands on his chest. She nuzzled her head in his armpit and began kneading at him like a kitten.

'Sooooo nice,' she said. Her hands began to move towards his crotch. He tried to resist but felt horny despite himself. It was a monumental effort to stand and shuffle to the other side of the fire. Since the beginning of the trip, she had constantly made him feel like he was falling from a skyscraper. He couldn't fuck her. There was something very wrong with Emily.

'I think we should try to get some sleep,' he said roughly.

She looked a little wounded, but then she shrugged and stood. She disappeared into her tent and he heard her whispering to Dan. Olly thought it was weird Dan wanted to share the tent with his sister. Dan said it was because Emily might get scared in the middle of the night, which was a laugh. She didn't seem the type to be afraid of anything.

Around 4 am, Olly woke up with freezing toes and fingers. Then he heard heavy breathing and pawing outside his tent. He held his breath, pulled his sleeping bag around his ears, and thought about how the thin tent fabric would pull apart like cobwebs under a sharp claw. The noises lasted ten long minutes before he heard footsteps receding. He couldn't get back to sleep, and he wasn't keen to get out of the tent to ask if Dan had heard anything. When he did finally fall asleep, he had a dream about an eruption.

It was his greatest fear as a kid, greater than his fear of tsunamis. Throughout his childhood and teenage years, he'd had recurring dreams of his local mountain, Mount Taranaki, erupting. Clouds of grey smoke would billow into the sky, and then the summit cracked apart, spitting fiery fountains. It always ended with molten rivers flowing deadly towards the sea, his house and his family. Since he had moved to the States, he hadn't had the dream but as he slept in the tent by the lake, he had the most vivid one yet.

He could see red-hot pyroclastic rocks being thrown from a crater — this time not from Taranaki, but from the Newberry caldera. Paulina Lake sizzled and disappeared into a crack. A wall of lava rose from the fissure. Of course, he couldn't move. All around the air shimmered from the heat. The pine trees melted into surrealistic green puddles. The lava was a garnet wave towering over his tent, and then slowly it folded over to consume him.

He woke sweating and trembling. He had burrowed himself deep inside his sleeping bag. He unzipped it and took in deep breaths of cool air. Rolling over to his side and bending his legs towards his chest, he waited for the birds to start singing to signal a safe new day.

In the morning his breath hung smoke-like in the freezing air. The grass sparkled with frost and crunched beneath his shoes. He found prints in the rime leading up to his tent. The prints were odd, not what he imagined bear claws to look like, but longer, spikier, and there was also a streak like the bear had been dragging something behind it. The sun came over the pines and melted the prints away before he could ask Dan's thoughts about them.

He hadn't heard it drive off, but the Winnebago was gone, and the other tent had been packed up along with its mysterious occupants. When they woke, he told Emily and Dan about the night's events. They said they hadn't heard anything, and Emily in particular was nonchalant about the nocturnal visit.

'It was probably just a coon or groundhog,' she said.

'You still up for staying another night?' Dan asked.

'Yeah, definitely,' said Olly. He had been looking forward to doing the loop track around the lake, seeing the obsidian flow up close and taking a dip in the hot pools – maybe even getting some footage to use in his class.

They packed their swimsuits, towels, water, trail-mix and as many beers as they could carry into their backpacks. The track was narrow in places and there were rocks protruding on the path. Olly, not exactly the most physically coordinated, tried not to trip.

Near a barbeque area they came across two chipmunks lingering under empty picnic tables. They were the first chipmunks Olly had seen. Tamed by hundreds of visitors who came through with food, they hopped from beneath a table right to his shoes and stood on hind legs sniffing the air.

Olly was surprised by how small they were, and how cute, especially with the little racing stripes down their sides. Even so, there was something about them, their cuteness or their tininess, that made him want to scoop them up and squeeze the life out of them or toss them against the nearest tree.

They walked for about an hour before they came to the Interlake Obsidian Flow. A path zigzagged through mounds of the sharp, brittle rock. Razor shards were scattered everywhere. They were mostly glistening grey but there were large chunks of the black, glass-like rock that Olly knew well.

His parents used to have a large polished piece of obsidian amongst their succulents at home, along with glass buoys they had found on the beach, conch shells, spiky coral, and round pieces of pumice. Back then the black volcanic rock used to make Olly whimper with fear because it reminded him of his eruption dreams. Eventually his mother gave the rock away to a relative because she knew it upset him.

He was alwavs an anxious kid. He cried a lot. Small things triggered his tears: soap suds, false teeth, stick insects, cuckoo clocks, crucifixes, moustached policemen, sunflower heads. His mother fussed over him when he cried. She rocked him and stroked his forehead. She coddled him more than his siblings. She prayed for him.

When she dropped off his lunch at school every day, he would go hot with shame as she beckoned him over to the gates. Her great hulk quivered from the effort of walking up the hill, large wet marks under her armpits, wheezing breath. He never asked for her attention – he just wanted to fit in, not stand out. He was teased for being the weird Māori kid who cried at anything, whose mother was like his wide shadow.

When he was at high school, he grew out of the crying but began to have panic attacks instead. One day he found himself shaking and gasping for air in a school assembly, and he was so overcome with an impending sense of death he began pulling clumps of his hair out. He couldn't wait to leave school to get away from all the mocking he got from his classmates.

He took off to art school in the South Island, and when he met Amy, who was there on a scholarship, he was happy to leave the country with her. He had tried everything to treat the panic episodes, from St John's Wort to Celexa, but nothing had worked. As soon as he left New Zealand, they stopped.

When his brother rang to say their mum was sick, and that Olly should come home, Olly felt his pulse race, pains in his chest, his throat closing up. He hung up the phone so he could do his breathing exercises to calm himself down. He knew he would have to go home eventually, but he didn't intend to move back to his home town.

The last time he walked down the main street he had a panic attack, fearing he would see someone he went to school with. It was expected that Olly would be the one to look after their mum. Their dad had died several years ago, she was alone, and all the other siblings had kids, jobs, partners and responsibilities. Olly was going to be jobless, homeless, unattached. It made sense he would be her caregiver. Plus, his brother said on the phone that Olly had always been their mum's favourite.

He had been looking forward to moving to Wellington when he got back. He still wanted to do that. He hadn't even rung his mother to talk to her, to see how she was feeling. Every time he thought about ringing her, he felt the chest pains, the rising panic. He was guilt-ridden, but he knew he couldn't look after her when he got home, couldn't go back to that house where he grew up, or return to that town. He could almost believe that his mother got cancer just so he would come home to look after her. He couldn't help it — he resented her for getting sick.

Dan and Emily were walking a fair distance ahead amongst the obsidian rocks. Olly was shooting footage of their silhouettes. Emily hopped onto a boulder and struck a pose. She lost her balance and slid to the ground, falling on her hands. Olly kept filming as Dan went to her aid, lifted her up and gently kissed her grazed palms.

Through his scratched viewfinder Olly saw her return Dan's kiss directly on his mouth. Olly, flushed and bewildered, turned his camera away from them, towards clumps of shiny rocks nearby. A few moments later when he had recovered, he looked up. Emily and Dan were walking apart like nothing had happened. Olly trailed behind them trying to process what he had seen.

They ambled for another twenty minutes until they came to a hot pool dug into the sandy edge of the lake. Someone had placed logs around the makeshift pool but they were lopsided and the edges were caving in. There were charred circles next to the pool where fires had been lit, and crushed empties were strewn about.

The boys stripped down to shorts, Emily to her bikini, and they hopped into the pool. The temperature of the water was like a bath, which felt good as the sun weakened and lowered in the sky. But the pool had slimy sides and when they sat, small particles of furry goop floated into their laps. It made Olly feel unclean. They drank the beers they had brought. After a while Dan got quiet and his face turned red.

'Too hot,' he said as he shambled from the pool and dressed. Lying on a towel, he soon nodded off.

Olly had a beer buzz. The slime no longer bothered him. Emily sidled up and sat close to him.

'Who are you?' said Olly.

'What do you mean?' she asked, slurring.

'I mean, I saw you two kissing,' said Olly, nodding towards Dan.

'Oh. We do that sometimes. Our relationship is kinda complicated.' She lifted a beer and drank thirstily. 'It's not officially incest. He's my adopted brother — blah blah. It's a boring story.' Her beer bottle slipped from her hands into the water. It sunk, and when she reached in to retrieve it, her hand found Olly's thigh. Her fingers quickly slid up and into the top of his shorts. His dick was limp but with a few cursory tugs she had him hard. She jerked him off in an efficient and expert way. Just before he came, Olly thought drowsily that he'd heard something behind them.

'What the fuck's going on Em?' asked Dan.

Emily laughed, her hand still in Olly's shorts.

Dan pulled Olly out of the pool and had him in a headlock before he knew what was happening. Olly couldn't breathe, he felt dizzy. Reality began to warp as Dan began to punch him in the kidneys. Olly couldn't catch a breath. He felt faint.

Everything turned white around him. He did a few teetering steps like a baby and soon he was falling towards the green-blue of the lake.

He opened an eye to find he was alone. Face against damp sand. It was dark and freezing. Dead quiet. They were gone obviously.

After a while he made a weak attempt to get up but then his head felt close to imploding and his body was a heavy sack of tenderised meat. So he just lay there, ear on sand, eyes towards the water.

There was a wedge of moon above, enough to illuminate the sand and reflect prettily on the water. There was the slight lap of water against the shore, but other than that it was silent. No calls or snuffles of night creatures. No wind. But then there was something. He pressed his ear against the sand a little more. He heard a steady beat, almost like a heartbeat. Something deep in the Earth's core.

He raised himself slowly, to his knees and looked out towards the centre of the lake. The moon reflected a smooth surface like polished obsidian. After a few minutes though, he saw ripples emanating outwards in increasing circles. His body became electric with fear. His breath came quickly. He couldn't get enough into his lungs and he thought he might pass out again.

'Breathe, you stupid prick, breathe,' he thought, forcing himself to breathe though his nose, then slowly let it out of his mouth. Again and again till his heart stopped thudding in his chest. He gulped the cold air deeply and let out one long breath.

Then he stepped into the water to his ankles and stopped. The ripples made little lapping waves against his legs.

Looking up, he searched the heavens for familiar stars, but of course his favourite, the Southern Cross, wasn't there. He missed that little diamond shape.

One night when he was small, he had found his dad under the

rotary clothesline in his pajamas riding out a panic attack. When he had recovered and his breath became quiet, he scooped Olly up, held him close.

He eventually pointed up to the Southern Cross and said, 'See there, Son. Our people call it Te Punga; it's the anchor for a great sky canoe.' Olly imagined great canoes sailing out there amongst the stars, and even greater celestial creatures at the helm. He was never afraid of the night sky.

Alice Tawhai

Perfect Circle

Pinky didn't really know anyone except the birthday girl, Lou, and she'd thought twice about attending her party. But in the end, she'd decided, what's life for if you're too scared to live it? She drove down the long beach road in a haze of sunset and sea salt. It seemed to go on forever, but nothing did.

Later that night they sat around a fire pit. Down at her feet, orange beach daisies with flat petals lay like fallen suns in the sand. Her feet made white holes where the rain had wetted it brown. Scuffing her heels made a mess of white powder. No one cared if they had sand in their blankets. That sort of consideration seemed irrelevant. The pink and white umbrella reminded her of circuses or popcorn. The white tassels hanging from it were blushed pink by the flames. Lounging underneath, Saul held his wine glass casually, idly watching the wine as it glowed like a rose in the light.

Saul was a friend of Lou's husband, Levi. Pinky assumed that they were both welders because they both wore the same black t-shirt that said 'welders make good connections'. He wore black wrap-around shades that absorbed the light from the fire and made it impossible to know what sort of expression was in his eyes.

'Where did you get that fire pit?' Pinky asked Levi. She'd always wanted a fire pit.

'I got it from work,' said Levi. 'It was an old tank I found out the back, and I brought it home and cut off the end and blasted the lead paint off. It's a perfect circle, just the right size for a fire pit.'

Saul shuddered. 'Did you get those arsenic flowers, Bro?'

'Nah, not this time.'

'Arsenic flowers,' Pinky said, thinking of purple flowers glowing as they burned. 'What are those? They sound nice.'

'Arsenic fevers,' clarified Levi. 'You definitely don't want those. You feel awful. Not right in yourself.'

'You wake up sweating,' said Saul. 'And you know there's something really wrong. I've had them a few times. And I'll probably get them again.'

'What do you do about it?'

Levi shook his head quickly, as if to ward them off. 'Nothing, there's nothing you can do. You just have to wait for them to go away and hope that they do.'

'I'm never sure if I'm completely rid of them,' said Saul.

They drifted into silence again.

'Whatcha been up to lately, Bro?' asked Levi.

'Nothing. Who's got a story?' said Saul.

'I dunno, Bro, I'm a few in.'

'Tell us how your hair went white,' said Saul. 'I reckon you witnessed a murder. You just don't see snowy white hair like that on a brown man.'

'Lol, Bro. I woke up one morning in my twenties and it'd gone white overnight. My father was the same. There's no story.'

'That's a story.'

Pinky regarded Saul's jet-black hair. She tried to imagine that happening to him. He looked ageless.

He stared at the embers. 'Fire. The whole world is on fire. We're fiddling while Rome burns. Do we really think that there's gonna be taxis to Mars for all of us? Those'll be reserved for the billionaires who got us into this mess in the first place. The rest of us seething masses are just gon fight each other to death as our population explodes while our liveable habitat gets smaller.' Pinky nodded. It was a true story but what could they do.

They were somewhat sheltered by being in a dip. The driveway rose on one side while the sand dunes encircled them on the other. She could hear the sea crashing beyond their rim. The sky was black and fuzzy while the smoke from the fire crackled upwards with thin lines of bright orange sparks. It was as if they were sitting in the shallow crater of a volcano. There was a boom as someone let off loud fireworks nearby, followed by a rustling and dozens of birds shooting up into the sky in tukutuku patterns lit by the glow in the sky above their fire. They settled as quickly as the noise subsided. 'Our planet used to be covered in birds but now they've mainly been driven to our margins. We've blocked out birds so much that even when we see them, we don't,' said Pinky, thinking out loud.

'Have you seen all the fantails around this year though?' asked Lou.

'I don't want to see them,' said Saul.

'What, you don't believe the old wives' tales?' asked Levi. 'If I believed in those, I'd have been dead long ago, there's that many around.'

'Not here at the beach,' said Saul, 'and I don't really go far from here. I go to work and then I come home again. That's about it.'

Someone tried to light a paper lantern. It was supposed to glow and hang in the sky full of birthday happiness, but it caught alight and had to be flung onto the fire by the person holding it. 'Oh well, we tried,' they said. Sometimes you did just have to let things go when they didn't work out, and let them be what they were, rather than what you thought they might have been, thought Pinky. The fire popped with the light rain and bits of lantern soared up from the flames like birds on fire.

'Still a show,' said Lou.

Embers were falling onto the ground from the overhanging ends of the wooden pallets. Saul stood up and picked the bigger ones up by the parts that weren't yet glowing.

'It's a wonder you don't get burned,' said Pinky.

'I work with fire so I know what I'm doing,' he said. 'But it's a great converter. Everything goes back to carbon. Ashes to ashes . . .'

'It's burning blue!'

'That piece must be tanalised. Tanalised bits do that. Fire burns differently depending on what you add.'

His glasses shone like the back of a shiny black beetle crawling through the sun. Or perhaps he had flames in his eye sockets and the lenses just kept them in check. Who knew, she thought. Anything was possible.

'What's your story?' he said.

'Mine?' said Pinky. 'I suppose I've got a lot of stories.'

He gazed at the fire pit. 'How about one about a perfect circle?'

'Um. Specific. But okay. So, this one time, my brother broke up with his girlfriend of 13 years. And it was like a one-sided knife fight; she burned his stuff, reported him to the Police, lay in wait for him at his job trying to get him fired. And she had to be the one to move out of the house, cos our parents own it. Honestly it was a relief. She'd been an absolute psycho bitch. But then my best friend, who was friends from school with someone who worked with this girl, told me that her school friend had complained to management that my brother's ex had been stealing from the till for ages. And my friend told me that I was no way to tell her because they were installing cameras to catch her in action. Made me promise. And I agreed. But then later my brother's ex messaged me to say thank you for something I'd done, and I did end up telling her. Poor chick was about to lose not only her partner and her home but also her job. She never wanted to break up even though they were toxic together. And I know my brother, and I wouldn't be surprised if she'd been stealing for him because he has expensive tastes.'

'Good on you, I would have too,' said someone.

'How's that a circle though?' asked Lou.

'Well, the thing is, I told her not to tell anyone I'd told her about the cameras. But she probably didn't think that included the chick she worked with who she thought was her friend. So long story short: the school friend told my friend who told me who told her who told the school friend. Everything's a circle in the end. I felt bad for letting my friend down for a while, but then I realised that I was no worse than anyone else in the circle. All of us sworn to secrecy and all of us breaking our promises.'

'That's how it goes. We've all done things.'

One by one people drifted off to bed to dream of white powdery sand and the glow of flames, even the birthday girl. 'Our perfect circle has dwindled away,' Saul said. 'And with only two people, that's just a line. You can't make a circle without three points. You may as well come and sit over here with me.' Pinky looked at him. Her body felt heavy with heat, and for some reason she didn't know whether that was an invitation that she wanted to accept.

But before she could think it through, a woman skipped through the embers and plonked herself down next to him under the umbrella. Pinky was surprised that she didn't burn herself. She was barefooted like a dark-skinned female Jesus. But perhaps the devil also wore no shoes. There was no point in making assumptions.

The creamy inner of the umbrella behind her caught the apricot glow from the fire while the wheel of silver spokes glinted gold as the light hit them. 'Kia ora, my name's Hine,' she said, crossing her legs as if she didn't expect any answer, and immediately it was as if she'd been there the whole time.

'The sun's rays are just our star twinkling,' Pinky said absently, surprised to hear her words in the air, because really they'd just been a thought, and if anything, what she should have been doing was introducing herself. No one answered her.

Hine pulled a woollen blanket with a coconut ice pattern of big pink and white squares across her knees. It went perfectly with the pink and white umbrella, and both things were now two shades of pink because the fire had risen again. She shook her effortless curly black hair across her shoulders, and Pinky might have thought she was an Islander, but she obviously wasn't, because of her name.

'I've got a story,' said Hine. Pinky wondered how she knew they'd been telling stories. Perhaps it was something that everyone did in the firelight. 'So I was working in New York, and I was told that whatever happened I should never get into a black cab. Only a yellow one. But I was right out in the suburbs acting in a small theatre. And this one night I was the last to leave and I mucked around by the stage door talking to this man who took off on his bike when we finished. I told him not to wait cos I'd flag down the next cab, and what do you know, the only one in sight is a black one. So what do I do?'

'Of course you get in,' said Saul.

'How well you know me already,' said Hine. 'Wouldn't you?'

'Yeah,' said Saul. 'There's some invitations that shouldn't be resisted.'

Pinky could imagine Hine acting out different characters and she wasn't surprised to find that she was an actress. 'So what happened?'

'As soon as I got in and told him where I wanted to go, I heard the doors locking, like the whole lot of them clicking at once from central locking. And my windows wouldn't go down. I told him to let me out a heap of times, but he didn't seem to speak English, or perhaps he didn't want to, and he just kept on going. And then we started going along streets I wasn't familiar with.'

'Omg, what did you do?'

'Well eventually it seemed to dawn on him that I wanted to stop, probably because I was shouting, and he let me out. He was angry because he seemed to think I didn't have enough money. I had to go into a shop and get some out with my card. But at least he let me out to get it. Out there in the middle of the Badlands where he'd driven us.'

'And then what?'

'I caught a yellow cab home.'

'So nothing happened,' said Pinky.

Saul laughed. 'Some stories nothing happens. Some stories something does.'

'In some stories people get out alive and in some stories they don't,' said Hine.

It was all in the choices, thought Pinky.

She took her black jersey off. One moment the fire had been too cold because it had burned down and she'd needed to move her chair closer, and the next moment Saul had put more pallets on it, and it had leapt up again making it too hot. The new rose tattoo on her shoulder was peeling. She remembered that she'd brought a red velvet cake for Lou's birthday breakfast the next morning, thick with cream cheese icing, and it was still in the car. She knew she should do something about that, but maybe later.

'When did you get that?' he asked. Her tattoo was glowing bright blood red in the firelight.

'Last week,' she said. 'Gutting 'cos I can't swim, but I've always dreamed of having a rose tattoo here.'

'Nice,' said Saul.

'I've got a tattoo story,' he said, 'but it's a short story.'

'Bring it.'

'So, I was getting a tattoo done, just a cover up . . .'

'What was it covering up?'

'An old story. And anyways, me and June, who was doing the inking, were talking about cover ups. And she said the only one she wasn't able to do was for this woman who came looking for a cover up of a black panther. It was just too black. And I said couldn't you just do a bigger black panther around the first one? But June just shook her head and said it was really bad art. And I got caught up trying to picture a panther so big and bad that it couldn't be swallowed . . .'

'I've got a tattoo too,' said Hine. She threw off her blanket and stood up, rolling her tight black tube dress up her legs.

'Oh, look at that,' he said. 'I've avoided them for so long . . .' Hine turned so that Pinky could see her tattoo as well. The feathers of the bird's tail fanned out across her butt cheek as if it was gesturing to her pussy. Saul leaned towards Hine. 'Looks like a perfect circle to me,' he said, making a circle of his own with his thumb and forefinger and giving her arse a long cool stare that started with one lifted eyebrow.

'Is that an invitation?' said Hine.

'Best I leave you guys to it,' said Pinky. She probably needed to get that cake out of the car anyway.

'Getting up early, like the dawn maiden?' asked Saul.

'Maybe. Things come to an end, and I'll have to leave, so yinno.'

Lou messaged her. 'Hey, I thought you might want to know . . .'

'Know what?'

'Saul walked into the fire at his job. And didn't come out. Just out of nowhere. I thought you might want to know since you two had a thing recently . . .'

'Omg that's terrible. But we didn't have a thing.'

'Oh. Levi went out to check if he needed to put the fire out that night and he said it was just you and Saul. He said yous looked cosy.'

'No, that wasn't me.'

'Oh, well I thought you might want to know . . . he seemed pretty certain that it was just you two. Thought he said Saul said something about it at work. But whatevs. Cool that you could come.'

'Yeah, definitely,' Pinky messaged back. 'It was an invitation I couldn't resist accepting.'

Fabian Waenga

Māori Homelessness in New Zealand

183 years
Still counting

K-T Harrison

That Last Summer

The last week of that fourth-form year limped towards its end. My restless legs wanted to race out of that stuffy classroom and leap into the rest of summer. My wound-up desk-cramped body ached, just ached; surely, surely, and truly; ached to burst out of the too tight and too short school uniform that was keeping me in. Wait, I told myself, be patient. Ever since Monday it had seemed that the clock on the wall had been holding on to time, holding it back, holding it up, holding it still and holding it to ransom. So I waited as patiently as I could – I glared at the clock – I willed it to go the same speed as the thumping noise my racing heart made in my ears, but it only tick-tock, tick-tock, tick-tocked at its own sweet pace.

By eight minutes past nine each morning, the sweat that glued my white blouse to my back and stunk-up my armpits had dried and become wet again, dried and become wet again, and dried, leaving the salty residue to sit on my skin, prick at it and make it itch. But I wasn't the only one with itchy-prickly skin. My friends – Jo, Max, Frankie, Georgie and Belinda – itched too. Ever since the end of October we'd been moaning to one another about having to breathe in the fried-onion pong that radiated out of our heating-up sweaty bodies. And although we washed thoroughly each day before school, dusted our skins white with talcum powder, sprayed ourselves silly with anti-perspirants, rolled on yards and yards of roll-on deodorant and dotted our face spots with anti-pimple cream, at fourteen years old it seemed we could do nothing to stop the hormonally predetermined sweat, stink, itch, and pimples that plagued us all. All except for the rich girls. They always looked so, so cool. So very cool.

At interval on Tuesday, I'd overheard Diana, Michelle, Paulina and Jacqui talk about the holidays they would have at their family baches at Whangamatā, Whitianga or the Mount.

'Again,' Diana said as Michelle nodded her head and Paulina and Jacqui rolled their eyes. In loud whispers, they shared their dreamed-up imaginings with one another — what they would look like in their new bikinis with their bronze tans, their sun-bleached golden hair — and the summer boys they would attract.

'Those boys,' Michelle said. 'They make those six weeks almost bearable.'

'Shhhh,' Paulina said. 'Big Ears is listening.'

'Oh, let her,' Jacqui said. 'Let her dream a little. God knows the dreary lives her and her lot must lead.'

'Oh yes indeed,' Diana said. 'Have you ever been down Rata Avenue? They live in such pokey little box houses. My driving instructor made me drive along that godawful street. They don't have cars, you see — can't afford them, so what better place to practise? Of course, you have to mind out for the umpteen children playing on the street.'

'Really?' Michelle said.

'Oh yes,' Diana said.

'The actual road?'

'Yes.'

'It's a wonder they don't get run over.'

'Yes, isn't it?'

The houses on Rata Ave were mill houses, and we were mill children. Our fathers all worked at the paper mill in this timber town we all lived in. Number six Rata was our house, number eight was where the twins, Jo and Max, lived, and next door to them at number ten was Frankie's house. Georgie was across the road at number nine, and next door at number seven was where Belinda and her family lived. We'd all grown up together on Rata, and we called each other's parents Aunty and Uncle. In all our growing-up years, we'd never known holidays at the east coast places of Whangamatā, Whitianga or the Mount, or at any beach we'd gathered seafood from, east or west.

For us, those times were day trips. We'd all pile into whichever vehicle had a space to sit in — we had a blue van, so we had heaps of room for lots of people. At low tide, we dug in the sand for pipi, and we collected pūpū — sea snails. Initially, as youngsters, we felt around in rock pools for pāua and kina and mussels, and with hammer and screwdriver we chiselled oysters from the rocks. As we grew we learned how to free dive, leaving the rock pools for the kids. And we went deeper. And all the times we gathered food, others sunbathed, and like pink pork sausages on a hot barbecue, they browned. Then they turned over to brown on the other side.

Sometimes a few of them gathered seafood too. And when the tide was in and our bags were full of what the sea gave us, we devoured the food our mothers had prepared and packed the night before, while those others swam, or splashed at each other and squealed as prettily as they could. But sometimes, instead of swimming, splashing and squealing, those others cooked and ate their seafood right there on the shore. We turned our backs on those people. They didn't know the lore we lived by. And, as in the classroom, it seemed we had nothing to contribute to their learning because all the learning we got came from them. So we ate the food brought from home and hoped nothing bad would befall us – because of them. We'd enjoy the sweet pipi and relish the pūpū that we'd dig out of their shells with safety pins, and feast on all the other shellfish gathered that day as we'd always done – when we got home. But only after they'd been shared out between all of us, including those on Rata who could not be at the beach that day.

As much as we all enjoyed those times at the beach, and as much as we relished the food that appeased our hunger at each meal we had at home, there was a hunger in us that far surpassed the need to fill our empty stomachs. At fourteen years old, we had the rest of our lives before us, and the dreams we shared had nothing to do with the flimsy stuff of bikinis, or the fleeting summer boys of the rich girls' desires. That we were all born with brown skins had everything to do with it – we had neither time nor necessity to oil ourselves and burn for the sake of affectation. We'd reckoned on how to pursue our dreams in the third form. With help from the guidance counsellor, we'd worked out how we were going to make them come true. Had we not, our ambitions would have been as insubstantial and as transitory as a rich girls' summer. We had to work hard to pass our exams well. We knew that we'd have to work twice as hard to get half as far and be treated half as fairly as them. But in order for us to take ourselves out of where we were with what we knew, we needed money – we'd decided we were all going to the university in Hamilton.

At the end of that year, that fourth-form year, I'd come first in maths, English and science with a second in French. Jo and Max had come second equal in maths, English and science and first equal in French. Frankie was first in tech drawing, woodwork and metalwork, Belinda was first in cooking and sewing and Georgie was first in accounting, typing and commercial practice. At prize-giving on Wednesday, after I'd received the prize for overall excellence in achievement, I looked for my parents amongst the sea of politely clapping mothers and fathers. They were not there to clap for me. Nor were Jo and Max's, Frankie's, Georgie's or Belinda's parents there to clap for them. So we clapped extra hard and extra loud for each other.

'We beat them,' Georgie said.

'We haven't finished yet,' I said.

With letters of recommendation from the principal, Mr Ryan, we all got holiday jobs. I was hired to help out at the town dump, Jo and Max were to work at the Stevens's Dairy in Kelso Street, Frankie got a job mowing lawns up Grandview Heights where the mill bosses lived, Georgie would deliver meat orders on Syd the butcher's bike, and Belinda got a job at the fish and chip shop down Roseberry Street.

So while the fried onion stink of our adolescence sweated out of our armpit pores, and the over-boiled cabbage stench of the paper mill wafted in and around the classroom, filling our nostrils with the putrid air it spewed out all day, every day, in our minds we were already out of there. When the bell screamed out our release on Friday, I froze, and then I was up and sprinting towards the rest of my life.

I spent all of my first pay. I bought Christmas presents for my brothers and sisters and my mother and father. Jo, Max, Frankie, Georgie and Belinda did the same. We also bought gifts for one another. 'Merry Christmas,' we all said, and that was the end of our first pays. My second pay went towards our power bill. So did Frankie's, Georgie's and Belinda's. Between them, Jo and Max had enough to pay their family's whole bill. So, despite knowing that after two weeks none of us had yet saved towards our futures, we all knew we'd contributed to bringing Christmas joy to the people we loved and who loved us, and that the lights would stay on in our homes for at least another month.

All through the rest of that last summer, we worked at our jobs and we saved as much of the money we were paid as we could. On our days off, we walked the roads of our growing up. And, along all the roads we went up and down, we roamed through our memories and we sorted through remembered stuff from earlier times. We rediscovered — for there was nothing new for us to discover in those places — the times we'd shared when we were younger.

'That's where . . . remember?'

'You fell in.'

'You saved me from drowning.'

'We got chased by a boar.'

'Lucky for you a hunter from the club was there to shoot it.'

'You got stuck in the fence.'

'You waited for me.'

'Mr Scarlett thought we were sheep rustlers . . .'

'We set fire to that hill.'

'We tried to.'

'Yeah.'

'You fell off your bike.'

'You laughed.'

'You kissed me.'

'You kissed me back harder.'

'I did too.'

'Kiss me now.'

'Nah.'

Once, on a Friday night, at Frankie's suggestion, we ventured up Grandview Heights. Diana, Michelle, Paulina and Jacqui all lived there.

'I'll show you my houses,' Frankie said. 'I mean, the ones I do.'

'Hey,' Jo said. 'All their streetlights go.'

'Holy Moses,' Georgie said. 'They do too.'

But no lights shone out from the houses themselves. At one of them, we gripped the bars of the wrought iron fence and peered in through the narrow gaps. A security light flashed on and displayed a white concrete driveway that curved through a manicured lawn and continued around towards the back of the house. Palatial splendour from out of a Mediterranean tourist guide magazine stood before us.

'Wow,' said Max and Belinda.

'That's one of mine,' said Frankie.

'All that space and they grow their flowers in pots.' I said. 'And their animals are concrete. How dumb is that?'

'It's beautiful,' said Jo.

We let go of the bars, backed away from the fence, and then the light went out. We stood at the white overstuffed mailbox and turned to look out over the town.

'I can see Rata, I can see my house,' Belinda said. 'See, down there.'

'There's ours,' Jo said. 'There's Mum's gumboots at the back door.'

'There's Dad, head beneath the bonnet of our old bomb, as usual,' Frankie said.

'There's mine,' Georgie said. 'I can see into my parents' bedroom.'

'What are they doing?' Max said.

'How should I know? The door's always locked.'

'Don't you ever wonder, though?'

'We'll know soon enough.'

'Stop being dumb,' I said.

Looking down from our elevated positions, we picked out the bits of our homes that we could see. I saw the potato and kūmara plants that grew in our front yard. I thought the corn waved. I thought I could see my only school blouse hanging out to dry; I thought I could see my mother at the kitchen table, counting out one- and two-cent pieces to buy a bottle of milk. I could see the family-sized talcum powder we all shared; I could see my mother's roll-on that I used, and I could see the cracked mirror that I squeezed my pimples at each morning. I saw how rickety and old our van really was and, leaning up against it, saw my baby brother Bobbie's rusted-up old bike with the wobbly back wheel that came off when he hit a bump or a rut in our crunched-up pipi-shell driveway. I could see us, all of us.

'Let's go home,' I said.

'Not yet,' said Max. 'I can see our garden. The tomatoes are red roses.'

'There's all our parents on the piss at yours,' said Georgie.

'Again,' Frankie said. And she rolled her eyes.

'There's our mum dancing with your dad. She's singing that old people's song,' Jo said.

'What song?' I said.

'You know, the one they always sing.'

Then, with Belinda in the lead, they began to sing.

Halfway through their singing they began to dance with each other. They sang, they danced and they pretend-felt each other up. They laughed, they sang, they danced.

'Stop making things up,' I said. 'Fools.'

Then a security guard came. 'Go back home, you fellas – go on, you know you shouldn't be here. Get, before I call the cops.'

We walked towards town, down that well-lit street with the darkened windows – we walked back down to Rata in silence. And even though nothing more was said that summer about what we imagined they could see at ours from up at theirs, I thought it – every day, I thought about it.

One day some of the kids from down John Street, where the forestry workers' homes were, joined us at the lake. We smoked the Buddha joints they offered us. It wasn't that the weather was particularly hot, or that the water was exceptionally warm; it might have had something to do with the heat in our bodies and the uncontrollable urge to cool them down, it may have been at the insistence of the John Street kids, or it may have been because we were stoned out of our Rata Ave heads – we took our clothes off. Where through the cold days of winter we only dabbled our fingers in the chilly water, that summer we plunged in, smarting at the first hit of cold that smacked our sizzling bodies. And hissed the water warm.

'It only hurts at first; after that it's nice.' Belinda said.

We floated through what was left of the days – and nights. We laughed – screamed indecent and immodest loud laughter, our mouths wide open, too, too afraid to close them in case the uncouth joys of childlike boisterousness became swallowed up by grown-up manners and matters. We'd yearned for the knowledge of locked-door adult secrecy, so we ached our way through ignorant experiments to rid ourselves of innocence. So in the too-few nights and times that were left of that last summer, we frolicked beneath the waxing January moon, and then too soon the nights were over.

The driving-school car crawled its way along Rata. Bobbie had been bumping his way up and down our driveway all morning. The car sped up. A bike wheel rolled onto the road, the car swerved to miss it, accelerated, hit Bobbie, kept going, ran him over. The ambulance attendants rushed to the driver, who sobbed in the car as Bobbie lay dying on the road.

We took him home to our pā in our blue van. The grown-ups did what grown-ups do at a tangi. We helped the cooks to feed the people who had come to farewell Bobbie. We gathered pipi and pūpū, mussels, kina, pāua and oysters. Others from the town helped out with food. Mr Stevens brought milk and bread every day, Mr Scarlett gave three sheep, Syd the butcher gave a whole cow, the hunters' club gave a deer and a wild pig, and the fish and chip shop up Roseberry Street gave two bins crammed full of fish heads.

As Bobbie's body went into the ground beside where our grandparents were buried, Jo and Max, Frankie, Georgie and Belinda sang. And time stood still.

The learner driver was discharged without conviction. Judge Geary said that this unfortunate mishap should not impact adversely on one so young. 'And may I add, one from such a prestigious and upstanding family who dedicate their lives to and are committed to building up this town. Let us not condemn one with such a promising future.

Had young Bobbie not been playing out on the road, had he been appropriately supervised, we would not be here today.

'I strongly advise that the family of Robert (aka Bobbie) Jacob King reflect upon the joy that he brought to everyone who knew him in the four short years of his life. I exhort the family of Robert (aka Bobbie) Jacob King to extend kindness and understanding towards the young lady who will no doubt suffer the trauma of this horrific tragedy for the rest of her life. What occurred on the sixth day of February in this year, 1970, was indeed a tragedy of utmost proportions. We are all of us – all of us – victims here.

'Order – order in the court,' Judge Geary said. My mother and the Rata Avenue aunties ceased their wailing. I wanted to bang his stupid gavel down on his pompous ass's head and tip him out of his high-up-there throne, stomp on him and all he stood for. I didn't, but I hadn't finished yet – later, though.

For some time afterwards, I grieved the losses of that summer.

'It only hurts at first,' Belinda had said. Afterwards I recalled the sting, but I couldn't remember where it hurt the most – or if it hurt at all. Had time already begun to heal the wounds of our loss of innocence? What then were we guilty of?

What?

Anaru Eketone

Go back to the pā/Hoki ki tōu maunga

Go back to the pā she said
Puzzled, but I don't live at the pā
I went there to see my grandfather's grave
Eight I was looking at statues of angels
The mausoleum with the cracks in the wall
Telling people I saw bones
Go back to the pā

Go back to the pā she said
Puzzled, that a Māori was here
White-collared jobs are for white-collared people
Not for the likes of you
Labouring or the dole
That is where you should be
Go back to the pā

Go back to the pā she said
Puzzled, here we don't have a pā
There is the kaik down the harbour
Shining red on the hill
Memorial window and polished floors
The silent carved church
Go back to the pā

Go back to the pā she said
Puzzled, what did she mean?
Eyes and moko kauae focused
When did you last go home?
Stand on the land
Let the wind cleanse you
Go back to the pā

Go back to the pā she said
Puzzled, where has the noise gone?
Why am I at peace?
Cleansed by the wind
Feet on the ground
Eyes on the mountain
Go back to the pā

Aziembry Aolani

Parking Warden

My colleague says my skin colour shows that I like rugby.
I tell him, 'I don't follow rugby . . .'
He says, 'Your skin tells *me* though . . .'
My skin has never spoken to anyone.

A man yells from a moving vehicle,
'Get a fucking real job!'
He extends one of his fingers towards me.
That. Is. Talent.

A woman says the job I do is ridiculous.
Despite paying for the wrong space,
she continues to question my presence.
'Like why do you even?'
Is that even a question?
'I'm actually quite odd,' I reply –
awkward and triumphant silence.

I am called a fat shit.
The driver isn't in the best shape himself.
'Why don't you go for a run, ya fat shit!'
He snatches the fresh white print.
I try to catch laughter in the middle of my throat.
I walk almost 30 kilometres a day,
and I'm Polynesian.

At a pedestrian crossing,
I overhear a woman tell her child,
'You see, Son. If you work hard at school, you won't have to do a job like that.'
She points to me.

I turn to the child, 'And I have a walkie-talkie!'
The child smiles.
To his mother's evil eye,
I pull a thumbs up.

Two elderly ladies ask for directions.
One lady says, 'Darling, you don't speak the way you look . . .'
The other: 'You're a very polite young man . . . Good for you . . .'
I pity them.

I see taxis on broken yellow lines
double-parked on a one-way street.
A driver spots me and alerts his companions.
'Go, go! The brown one is here!
The brown one is there!'
I see panic spilling out of their ears and exhaust pipes.

'Does anyone give you shit, Bro?'
asks a man gripping a can of beer.
'Why would they? Look at you . . .'
I attach a printed headache to a vehicle.
'You're a big dark-skinned brother. No one will give you shit, my kill!'
I have a sudden vision of myself, as fresh kill, on the roof of a parked vehicle.

A mechanic spots me checking resident and coupon zones.
He screams,
'Warden! Warden!'

Just another white jaw rattling to remind me of what I am.

Amber Esau

A poem (,) of course

(flatmates, then walls) membrane and then some.

Viscous and sad before the walls open.
The ending is continual glue, each layer hiding noise bubbles
in the plasterboard then pink batts fuzzy and blind between them rock

the ripples, bear the cave walls that hang conch somewhere in the
fur, lovers spin sons but get caught amongst the leaves and start
to settle in a rhythm as fast or slow as birth
making.

(the line, wet sheets) shrivelled fingers and the bath.

Soaked first then steamed, sand contours
thirst to salt before it sets to skin. Easy to scrape the underside
of a giant ripple
unused, the bottom of the tub gargles and stirs

the backwash, loose grains hidden in water
like Koko, muddy and tin, the darkest gold-panning this side of the
Pacific, like cliff banks squeezing the creek bed this is what it means
to fuck in silence

(stovetops, spillage) the dusty and the dirt.

What's land without a little spill? The drama of the elements fished
out of Papa and chucked at the pop of a balloon dipping lower
to the ground, running out

of breath, out of belonging

the land bends down to the pressing of metal. Chicken wire fence and
shrapnel spilling tomato on the stove, spitting the hybrid wetness out
a lid less pot left for someone
else to tidy.

Aroha Awarau

The African Stars

Dear Sahara,

I took your diary from your desk before the cops could get to it. I didn't read it, but I probably know most of the stuff that's in it 'cause we're BFFs and everything. I'm writing in it because you'd want to know everything that's been happening while you've been sleeping. I know the newspapers say you're in a coma, but I like to think that you're taking a very long sleep.

It was funny when the cops came into class today because you could tell Miss Hall liked one of them. She went all red like a plum. I turned to you to laugh and forgot that you're not here. That happens a lot. It was good to see Miss Hall in a good mood 'cause she's been very sad lately. I think she blames herself for what happened to you. I overheard her tell the cops that she should've picked up on the signs. But you know that we're good at hiding what's been happening to us — you with your bruises and me with my stuff. Derek hasn't touched me since you went to hospital. I suppose he's feeling sorry for me 'cause of what's happened. It won't last though. I miss you. We always knew the right things to say to each other to make things better.

I wish I could come to the hospital to see you, but only family members are allowed to see you. That makes me angry 'cause we know it was those mongrels that put you in there in the first place. I tried to sneak in by telling the nurse that you were my sister, but she didn't believe me. Maybe because you're dark and I'm a waka blonde. It was worth a try. I can't wait until you wake up so you can tell everyone who did this to you. Mum and Derek are being weird too. They are hiding the newspapers from me and making sure the TV is off when the news is on. Your picture is everywhere. What's worse, the picture they're showing on TV and in the newspapers is the one where you're wearing that pink Pokemon shirt. The one your mother had as her Facebook profile pic and you begged her to take it down 'cause you didn't like the way you were smiling. I try not to read about what you went through. I don't need to know the gory details. I can only imagine what happened from all the stories that you've shared with me. All I need to know is that you're asleep and soon you'll be waking up.

I'm at the park at the moment. I'm writing this at our spot just behind the swings. I've been doing this every night since you've been gone. Soon the stars will be out and I can continue our nightly ritual of looking up to the night sky and dreaming of Africa. It was still light when I spotted the first star of the night. I got so excited that I turned to you and forgot that you weren't here. That happens a lot.

Sweet dreams.
Tunisia xox

Dear Sahara,

The cops returned to the classroom today and wanted to question us. Miss Hall wore a new outfit. You would've liked it, although it didn't have any Pokemon pictures on it . . . haha. They wanted to speak to me first 'cause I'm your best friend. Miss Hall was really supportive and told me to be honest. Derek really wanted to come into the room with me, but I told the cops I only wanted Miss Hall to be my support person. She was extremely happy since the cop she fancied was the one doing the interview. He asked how we became friends. That brought back memories. I told him how we met when we were five years old at kōhanga. How we were the only two in the class without Māori names. Actually, not only did we have non-Māori names, but we were also both named after African deserts. He asked if our parents loved geography, but I told him we got our names because our parents thought they sounded cool, not because they had a connection to Africa. I told him how the other kids who lived in Marmite Village wouldn't play with us because of our weird names. He asked me why I called our neighbourhood Marmite Village and I told him that's what everyone calls it. He must be new in town. Then he started asking me really hard questions. I didn't want to answer them, but Miss Hall told me that anything that I said might help bring the mongrels that did this to you to justice. I can tell you what I didn't tell him. I didn't tell him about the first time I saw the bruises on your thighs and how you told me that your mum's boyfriend did that to you. How when you mentioned your stepdad, it made me open up to you about what my stepdad was doing to me. How you were being hurt a different way to how I was being hurt and how we had a lot more in common than being named after African deserts. How the things that we shared with each other, we had never shared with anyone else before and that's why we were lucky to have found one another. I didn't tell him about how we both love Africa and how we loved the stories about the exotic and faraway land. How we would sneak out at night and lie at our spot in the park, right behind the swings. How we would gaze up to the stars and dream of Africa, sharing our hopes, our dreams and our pain. How your mum's boyfriend and his mongrel relatives would do horrible things to you. How Derek would come into my room and treat me like the woman that I've yet to become. How they left scars on your body that were getting harder to hide. How what Derek was doing to me didn't leave any physical scars but I was still able to know the pain that you had endured. How at only nine years old we were going through stuff that no one our age should be going through. How we would look up to the stars and dream of Africa. Imagining that there'd be other little girls just like us in villages in Kenya or Zimbabwe. Imagining that they would look up at the exact same night sky and think of us. Sahara and Tunisia from Marmite Village — we found each other and discovered a way to connect to the world.

You're probably thinking what information I did share. Don't worry, I only told them enough to help their investigation and didn't tell them anything that would break our bond and betray your trust. I told them that you were living in an unsafe home and that the mongrel that was probably responsible for putting you in hospital was your mum's boyfriend.

Miss Hall said she was proud of me for what I did today. After the interview she gave me — and the cop — a big hug. Derek picked me up afterwards. He kept asking questions about the interview, but I didn't tell him much. He's starting to be touchy feely again. Mum still hasn't noticed, even when I think he's being obvious.

After this long day I went back to our spot in the park. I looked up to the stars. They were shining brightly. It's going to be a good day tomorrow.

Sweet dreams!
Tunisia xox

Dear Sahara,

The cop who interviewed me yesterday pulled some strings and let me and Miss Hall come and see you. Did you feel me hold your hand? You looked peaceful. You looked safe. Miss Hall told me that sometimes people in a coma are still conscious but they just can't respond. It was nice because Miss Hall and the cop left the room so we could have some private time. I'm not sure if you heard me, but I really needed to talk to you, 'cause you are the only person I could talk to about these kinds of things. I told you how last night Derek came into my room again. I knew it wouldn't last. But this time it was different. It was like he knew I was sad, that I was vulnerable and that seemed to make him more determined. When he does it now, it hurts less. He even told me last night that when I start getting my period he'll stop. I can't wait until that happens.

When it was night, I opened the curtains and lay next to you. The stars were out in full glory. I closed my eyes and I dreamed of Africa. I pictured us on a safari. I pictured us watching elephants and lions. I pictured us cruising down the Nile and fighting over who was going to be Cleopatra. I realised that you are in a safe place, asleep in this hospital. No one can get to you, especially those mongrels. When you wake up, you're going to be protected. You're going to be happy. You deserve it. We deserve it.

Sweet dreams
Tunisia xox

Dear Sahara,

Great news. They arrested the mongrels that did this to you. There were five of them! They even arrested your mum because she knew what was happening to you and didn't do anything about it. Miss Hall said she was proud of me because everyone who gave interviews helped the cops. I avoided reading the newspaper and watching the news because I didn't want to know the gory details. I saw you in hospital and saw how you suffered. The police also said they have enough evidence to charge the mongrels. You don't have to testify in court. So you can sleep as long as you need to. By the time you wake up, it will be over.

I looked up a new word today, shujaa, it's the Swahili word for hero. That's what you are Sahara. A true shujaa.

Tunisia xx

Dearest Sahara,

I can hardly hold the pen to write this. I'm feeling numb as I try to find enough courage to write these words.

My dear, Sahara. You died today.

I thought writing those words in your diary would make it easier for me. But it doesn't. Miss Hall told the class you passed peacefully in your sleep last night. The pain must've been too unbearable for you to handle. Weirdly, I knew the exact moment when you died. It's hard to explain, but I could feel it inside of me, like you were giving me a nudge, like you were asking me for my permission to leave this earth. I resisted, and I didn't want to let you go, but I realised that it was selfish of me to hold onto you — that I had to let you go.

I was lying on our spot in the park, behind the swings. I felt you lying next to me and I didn't feel so lonely. I looked up at the stars. I noticed one star that was shining more brightly than the others. Sahara, I can feel your presence.

Rest in peace my shujaa.
Tunisia xx

Dear Sahara,

Your tangi is tomorrow. I've decided this is going to be my last entry 'cause I'm going to place the diary in your coffin tomorrow. There'll be a little piece of both of us with you when you take your final journey.

I haven't been able to sleep since your death. It's weird, Sahara, but I can feel your presence and know that you're watching over me.

Everyone has been paying tribute to you — our school, the newspapers, our town. The entire country is in mourning. You've moved and inspired so many, but I can't help but feel that I've been the only one who has truly been by your side, that we've been through our struggles together. That's why I did what I did today, because of you.

I told Miss Hall today what Derek has been doing to me. I should've told my mum first, but I had this feeling that she wouldn't believe me. Besides, Miss Hall has been very supportive during this time. Miss Hall was shocked and very upset. I told her that's why me and you were best friends. How we kept each other's secrets. She told me that I was brave to open up to her. She called the cops and social services, and I've been staying with her since. They won't let me stay at home until they feel that it's safe for me. The cops questioned me about everything. Miss Hall told me that this is just the start and that it will get harder. Mum's upset and Derek? Well, I don't care what he thinks. He can rot in hell and hopefully I won't have to see him ever again.

Throughout this I could feel you next to me. I could feel you holding my hand and showing your support. Although you're gone, I can feel your presence more than ever before.

I went to our spot tonight, right behind the swings. The stars looked perfect. I closed my eyes. I thought of Africa. I thought of you, and I knew that everything was going to be okay.

Tunisia x

Miriama Gemmell

Family Tree

1.1.1 cousin wants the whakapapa
1.1.2 cousin played reps back in the day
1.1.3 cousin bringing the leftovers
1.2.1 cousin baby four on the way

1.2.2 cousin gone to the tangi
1.2.3 cousin overtime pretty busy
1.2.4 cousin one more month of curfew
1.2.5 cousin moving back to brizzie

1.3.1 cousin trying to learn the reo
1.4.1 cousin raffle for the touch trip
1.4.2 cousin got the korowai
1.4.3 cousin always had a lip

1.5.1 cousin tryna straighten out
1.5.2 cousin makes a mean fry
1.7.1 cousin too shame to do your song
1.7.2 cousin got a DUI

1.7.3 cousin had another miscarriage
1.8.1 cousin separated now
1.8.2 cousin wants to work the land
1.9.1 cousin just doesn't know how

1.9.2 cousin pretty into church
1.9.3 cousin bringing extra mince
1.9.4 cousin knows who broke in
1.9.5 cousin not been quite right since

1.10.1 cousin is the spit of nan
1.10.2 cousin kinda got the blues
1.10.3 cousin owes a bit of money
1.11.1 cousin tidied up the shoes

1.11.2 cousin never leaves the house
1.11.3 cousin is a skinny miss
1.12.1 cousin being a bloody nuisance
1.12.2 cousin come give us a kiss

Reihana Robinson

Jealousy or the main highway

was born in a small town
destined for the dole queue

parents moved away from here split
up I have no roots at all

in the garden with my brother
I threw potatoes split

by the spade — tail tilted to the sprung earth
in the house with my real mama

I danced and danced
there was only one escape route

only one way out of there
we called it the main highway

grew up on the volcanic plateau
never knew the taste of snow

knew the stink of the mill
rotten cabbages in the wind

tall pines losing their personalities
scarring a sacred land

company town mapped out
wild horses

galloping inside my dreams
wanna be a baby again

I danced and danced
there was only one escape route

only one way out of there
we called it the main highway

now I have a baby of my own
fixing to live in a small town

bet you're screwing that whore again
mirror overhead in some motel

there's a G-string tying up my emotions
I'm lost again – Jeezus deserted me

all the missions I've hungered after
left me starving

what's left can't feed the baby

Witi Ihimaera

Tāwhaki

E Ara Mai

I'm dozing in my crew cabin when the video link tells me, 'Tāwhaki, wake up.'

It's Dad of course. Other people prefer electronic wake-up calls, but I prefer my father's voice and face. 'Mōrena,' he smiles. 'Good morning. E ara mai, rise up!'

I pull the sleeping bag around me, yawn, and cock one eye at him. Dark weathered face. Big head and high forehead like mine, but lots of thick black hair whereas I have a military fade. Crooked teeth, one grazing his bottom lip. A quizzical, teasing expression. And he always calls me Tāwhaki even though my name is really Branson. Mum's choice, but it's too up itself, he reckons.

'You haven't got a girl . . . or boy . . . in bed with you?' he teases.

'As if,' I give the usual snort. No room, and nobody I'm attracted to! Would I admit to my father that nobody is attracted to me? Hell no.

Dad's face goes into his pretending-to-be-sad look. 'You better watch out, Son,' he says. 'You're 23, your gears must be in perfect working order, but they could go rotten.'

I turn my back on him.

'Don't roll over and poke your bum in my face. Time for you to do your mahi. Is Pōhutukawa looking beautiful this morning?'

The World in the Sixth Extinction.

Pōhutukawa is one of the Māori names for the Earth. And it's just like Dad to prefer the Māori description. Earth has no beauty to it, being monosyllabic and inert.

I wash and brush my teeth, take a dump into the collection bag and an air current sucks my urine into the waste compartment. I suit up and listen as *Ranginui-14* groans around me, whining like a cantankerous god.

Heigh-ho, it's off to work I go, floating my way through the connecting corridors of the space station to the observation cupola. I'm one of the weathercasters on board. Early morning shift today, so there's only a few military boys at their posts and a couple of fliers chatting up Anahera, one of the shuttle captains. 'Mōrena,' she grins.

I wink at her, grab what passes for breakfast – coffee to go and a sandwich – and float on by to the lookout to take over from Nigel, my American counterpart.

'Hey,' I say to him.

Changeovers of shifts are always monosyllabic and Nigel's in a hurry to get to bed. 'Did you change the sheets?' he quips as he vacates the chair.

I strap myself in, do the usual instrument check, and then surrender to the lyrical beauty of a sea of stars. The panoramic vista always takes my breath away. Space is studded with light, twinkling diamonds strewn on a velvet cloth all the way back through the twelve heavens. To Io, God of all gods, in the topmost bespaced rangi tūhāhā. And further back to Te Pō, the night even before stars, to Te Kore, the nothing before that.

But that's the view in front of me. I pull the visor down across my face and rotate the cupola to the view behind and beneath. The shadow side of an enormous dark globe wearing a corona of radiance. Patch my father back into the comms. He looks eagerly over my shoulder at the world below.

'Yes, Dad,' I say, trying to keep the sarcasm from my voice. 'There she is! Your beautiful Pōhutukawa! She was once the daughter of Rangi Tamaku, the eleventh heaven, wasn't she?'

'You remember my old stories?' Dad asks, delighted. 'Her other name was Papatūānuku and she married Ranginui, the Sky Father. There was nobody more glorious than she was in all the firmament, Moko. Glowing like pounamu, with blue oceans the colour of a whale's dreams.'

I turn my father off. 'You're too sentimental, old man.'

Because below me is the brutal reality. The night is retreating over the Americas – or what is left of it. By the 22nd century, global warming had melted both ice caps and raised the sea levels over 200 feet. In what used to be the USA, the entire Atlantic seaboard, gone. The Rockies as well as the Sierra Nevada and the Appalachian ranges, the primary high dry regions. A cluster of islands where San Francisco was. Further north in Canada, the bare bones of the Canadian Rockies-extension, the St Elias and Laurentian chains. And southward, what was once Central America has been washed away. And the accustomed shorelines of South America have long disappeared, its people clambering up the stark backbone of the Andes.

If that hadn't been enough, Earth's rising heat made much of the surface uninhabitable. And during the daytime, with the sun at its apex, nobody could survive in the open. No wonder all humankind went underground, working at night and sleeping during the day.

'Tāwhaki,' Dad warns. 'Pay attention.'

The corona has burst a flaming red over Pōhutukawa below. I can't help it, I take a deep breath. It's an unconscious gesture, a flinch against the awesome power of the sun. I want to scream. My instrumentation starts to go crazy, the panel flashing all kinds of signals.

And I start my daily transmissions. 'Get underground, people,' I warn everyone, here comes Te Rā! I broadcast the readings to the relay stations below. Count down the sun's advance, 'T-minus 10, 9, 8,' for the north-west sector. As the ground temperature starts to rise, 'T-minus 7, 6, 5,' for the central sector. Back to that edge of sun scything through the north-east, 'T-minus 4, 3, 2 . . .'

There's the usual adrenalin rush of fear. Uncle Sam is on fire and there's just a few seconds for any stragglers to reach the scattered silos and batten down the hatches. Quick. Now. *Get the kids to safety.*

Ranginui-14 is on a high Earth and geosynchronous orbit. It's in a sweet spot, some 35,000 kilometres above the equator, where the space station can match the rotation of the earth on its axis. From the cupola I have views north and south of the arc.

Behold, the world below, a burning fiery furnace. It's been a long time since anybody lived at 0° latitude. The parts of those countries in Africa, South America and Asia that once straddled the equator had the sun directly overhead and were the first to fall victims to it, pretty much. And Kiribati, Maldives, São Tomé and Principe were among the early island states to succumb to rising sea levels.

The next casualties were all the countries between the Tropic of Cancer (latitude approx. 22° 27 north of the equator) and the Tropic of Capricorn (latitude 23° 26 22 south). Once upon a long-ago time the zone between was called the Tropics, holiday destinations associated with waving palm trees, smiling natives, suntans and sex in the sand. Among the countries in the zone were Mexico, Egypt, Saudi Arabia, India, southern China, northern Australia, Chile, southern Brazil and northern South Africa. We call it the Scorch Sector now. Anybody left in the open will be burnt to cinders.

But, hey, my geographical references are coming from the old tattered early-21st-century map pasted on the roof of the cupola. It's like a treasure map to a lost time, because everybody knows that's not the world we live in any longer.

'Satisfied now?' I ask Dad. 'What would all your Māori gods of creation think of this? I reckon God of all gods, in his uppermost first heaven, would be truly pissed off.'

I'm baiting him, pushing the envelope, but he pushes back. 'So would Rehua in the third heaven,' he says, 'and don't refer to the gods with such disrespectful language.'

'All their work for nothing!' I mock him. 'Not to mention the other creation gods and goddesses of the time-space continuum, eh, like Mahorahora-nui-a-rangi, her husband Te Mangu and their four sons. They kept the wā, the energy of the universe, flowing from the past into the present, and what do we do with it? We abuse the taonga tuku iho, the gifts of life, they gave us.'

Dad is getting riled with me. 'Are you trying to pick a fight, Son?'

'Just saying, Dad. Somebody sure messed up. And it wasn't me or my generation.'

He searches for a rejoinder, trying to lighten the mood. 'Maybe you can reboot creation for us,' he says after a while. 'You could do a Māui.'

I cock an eyebrow at him and throw my what do you mean look at him.

'Don't play the dumb ass,' he grumbles. 'You know full well, the story about how, i ngā wā o mua, Te Rā went so fast across the sky that the people didn't have time to work the vegetable gardens. No sooner had the sun come up and they had started planting than, e hika, down he went and it was night-time already . . .'

Yes, I remembered the story, it had been a favourite when I was a boy and Dad told it to me at bedtime. He was the well-loved supervisor of the engineering team which kept Rarohenga – that's the nickname we have for our very own underground city in New Zealand – operational. You've heard of Rarohenga, haven't you? It lies at the base of Hikurangi Mountain, the first point on the earth's surface to be touched by the new day. If ever you are lost in space, all you need to do is wait until the sun comes up. What would you be waiting for? Why, the flash of sunlight on the sacred mountain! Once you see that sword of light, then you can calibrate your position. Ah, ko Hikurangi, there, and mark.

'. . . Anyhow, it was up to Māui, the demi-god, to come up with a solution,' Dad continues. 'He gathered his brothers together, and they travelled to the ends of the Earth where Te Rā lived. They wove a magic net and, when he started to rise, Māui trapped him in it. He used a magic jawbone to belabour the sun into submission. And when Te Rā pleaded for clemency, Māui made him promise to go slower across the sky.'

'The point being?'

'Maybe it's time for a modern Māui to give Te Rā a hiding but, this time, to make him go faster?'

'Yeah, right, well don't look at me, Dad!' He's always thought I should rise above my current position forecasting weather. 'Māui was half-god, and that story's just a myth. I don't have a magic jawbone either.'

I ignore him and get back to my instrumentation. I try to push back on the reality of a China that is now flooded. All Bangladesh gone along with coastal India. What's Cambodia now? Just an island with its Cardamom Mountains the peak.

What happened to their billions of population? Don't ask.

I really don't have time to continue arguing with Dad, as Australia is looming up below. 'I'm putting you on hold,' I tell him.

The space station starts to judder and groan as corrections are made to adjust its orbit. They bring mathematical focus to the fires that have been burning day and night. Time to broadcast the specific coordinates for the roaring conflagration so people further south can get out of harm's way.

And then I receive a transmission from Earth. It's my Auntie Kui, She-Who-Must-Be-Obeyed, Dad's sister.

'Kia ora, Branson,' she says.

She looks across my shoulder and sees Dad behind me.

'Still talking to your father, I see. Are you on track for arriving home this weekend?'

'Yes, Auntie!' She thinks I'll do a runner. 'My leave's been approved.' Suck that up.

'So you'll be on the shuttle, arriving home on Saturday? Ka pai?'

She's just about to sign off except that she hesitates and looks at me with tenderness. 'You have to let him go someday,' she says.

Pōhutukawa, Who Used to be Blue Once

The shuttle screams like the hokioi, the fabled bird of prophecy, as it hits the main air of Earth's atmosphere.

'Good morning, Vietnam,' the captain, Anahera, says. The five grunts in the cabin go ape at the retro affirmation of a safe entry. *Ranginui-14* has a primary military surveillance operation, safeguarding the ANZUS Quadrant. The infantrymen are transferring to comms duties at ground stations in Antarctica.

'Here, Bud, have a beer,' one of the grunts offers.

I pretend to join in the revelry but I'm not feeling it. I've been living on *Ranginui-14* for an entire year. The bubble up there has been cosy, safe, above the dying planet, not in it. But now that the shuttle is descending through the realm of Tāwhirimātea, god of winds, I realise that soon I will have to face the realities of ground zero.

And I can't stop the rage that I was always able to suppress on *Ranginui-14*. Medievalists had defined humanity as *animal rationalis*. What the fuck happened? Jonathan Swift, author of *Gulliver's Travels* satirically defined us as *animal rationalis capac*, capable of acting rationally – which he didn't actually believe, and the evidence proved devastatingly otherwise. Because in the mid-20th century the Anthropocene epoch arrived and humankind became the defining agent in changing the ecology of the environment. Mass exoduses of humankind out of war-torn Africa and the Middle East had already placed pressure on nations on their perimeters. Then came the climate refugees.

'Hold on tight, boys,' Anahera says to us. 'We're in for a rocky ride.'

The shuttle is being thrown all over the sky. No need for Anahera to generate drag and thereby dissipate speed. Jet streams are smashing against the craft and doing that for us. They are voluminous with thick, dark, detritus pelting the bodywork with the shattered bones and cartilage of Earth.

'We're through,' Anahera says as she angles the descent into something resembling a glide path.

And the world turns a virulent red. This is what hell must look like. The atmosphere swirling with tornadoes and twisters. Lightning strikes close to the shuttle, let us in, let us in. The air stinks. Rotten. Below is the sea. It looks as if all the gods of the twelve heavens have vomited their guts out into a bowl. The waves are froths of bilious blood-veined sick.

Oh Pōhutukawa, you used to be blue and green once.

A Kōrero with My Father

I can't help it. I mouth the words to myself, What have we done to you? What have we done to us?

'You mustn't be so hard on humanity,' my father answers, eavesdropping on me as usual.

'The clear signal,' I reply angrily, 'was the creation of a blanket of definable man-made radioisotopes around the earth. Why didn't humankind see it?'

'You're talking about them,' Dad says. 'We did take notice, Son.'

'But you couldn't stop their actions. And when the refugees fled in terror from the Scorch Sector north or south to the Pole sectors, they were turned back. To face certain death?'

A massive stasis had occurred in all the world's governments. The situation of the world's dispossessed, the homeless, the starving became too big to fix. The United States, unapologetic about not signing up to the goals of the 2015 Paris climate agreement, fast-tracked its 'America First' policy. Then chaos . . . temperature trends in the troposphere shot into the red red red . . . there was ozone depletion . . . massive emissions from the ocean of hydrogen sulphide. The destruction of the ceiling above let the sun in, and thus began the rise in fatal levels of UV radiation . . . all symptoms of the collapse of the biosphere.

Auē te mamae, there was a confluence of mounting catastrophic events . . . famine . . . severe droughts . . . earthquakes . . . melting ice caps . . . viruses. The four horsemen of the Apocalypse came *riding, scything souls, bring out your dead* . . .

International and trade blockades went up up up . . . and the entire system of international cooperation broke *down down down* . . .

In the early 21st century the world population had peaked at almost 8 billion, and it was already overcrowded. By the 22nd century, 5 billion had been wiped off the slate. The human brain cannot contemplate the magnitude of such losses.

Wherever people survived, they were left to sort out a future for themselves. The world writhed in all the agony attendant upon the sixth extinction. 'Auē, taukiri . . .

'Stop this,' my father says.

He has always been the voice of sanity, bringing everyone back into the room.

'We're still here,' he continues. 'We've muddled our way through. The old verities are gone, but humanity still holds. No use crying over spilt miraka. Here at the bottom of the world we do not go gently into the night, we go raging at the light.'

It's a nice little kōrero, no wonder Dad has always been a leader of men. But I am not about to let his clever turns of phrase divert me. I haven't finished with him yet.

'Dad,' I say to him. 'The worst is we weren't just killing ourselves. Look at what else humankind destroyed. The only way to see the big whales, cats, lions and cheetahs is to watch them via the feeds that play into our dreamworlds when we sleep. The biomass of birds. The skies are empty. The total mass of insects, gone, and wasn't the state of bugs the state of the world?'

'There's always hope,' Dad answers with his usual refrain. 'If you can't do a Māui, you might have to do a Tāwhaki. You remember your namesake, don't you?'

'How can I forget? You told me often enough when I was a boy.'

My father is persistent, his voice riding through my words. 'It was Tāwhaki who climbed from the twelfth heaven through all the rangi tūhāhā to make a special request of Io, God of all gods, in the uppermost level.'

Dad is gentling me, calming me down, cutting me off from the terrible pass that I sometimes plunge into. 'He was just a young man like you, and he went by way of the aka matua, the parent vine, climbing through the eleventh, tenth, ninth heavens. He was transformed by the task from corporeal to spiritual, from unschooled to literate, from human to superhuman. Oh, his climb took him a long time, Son . . . up the poutama, the stairway, he ascended, eighth, seventh, sixth, fifth . . . and on the way he tested the parameters of life and death, the parameters of creation . . . where did space begin and end? Where did time begin and end? He came to the fourth heaven, the third, the second.'

My father's voice rises to a level of heightened ecstasy. He makes me imagine Tāwhaki kneeling before Io.

Tāwhaki has come to ask for three baskets of knowledge, though some people say there were four. In the first basket, Te Kete Aronui, is the knowledge to help all humankind. Te Kete Tuauri, the second basket, contains the ancient rites and ceremonies to ensure the tapu reinforcement of the knowledge of Te Kete Aronui. The third basket,

Te Kete Tuatea, has examples of the lessons of history to learn from. Although divisible, the ultimate power of the baskets multiplies exponentially when they are operated together for the benefit of all.

'E Io,' Tāwhaki asks. 'Humankind seeks enlightenment.'

He is surrounded in a dazzle of illumination. The heavens begin to sing.

Let the baskets of knowledge be theirs.

City Beneath the Mountain

A pattern of lightning strikes. Not heavenly song but the screaming sound of a world *in extremis*.

'We're approaching Hikurangi,' Anahera tells us. 'We'll be at the landing zone in five minutes and counting.'

'Tāwhaki had magic karakia to help him, Dad,' I say to him as I check my seatbelt. 'And where would I find the aka matua in a world like ours?'

Anahera is in a race with the sun. Although we're coming in on the mountain's shadow side, we must drop down into Rarohenga before Te Rā rises above the summit.

Dad snorts. 'Don't you know anything? The story of your namesake is a metaphor. You have to find the aka matua in yourself, Son, as we all must, and find the way from death back into life.'

'Just in time,' Anahera says. The deflector shields part, the earth opens up, and she steers the shuttle into the arrival dock. Everything happens quickly after that. Customs and security clearances. Descending by lift into the bowels of the city. When the doors open, Rarohenga blazes with light.

The city carries its military function lightly. Stripped down. Functional. A people who can build a space station surely had the expertise to create an underground complex. And after all, in our mythology there were two primary worlds, one was Te Ao Mārama and the other Rarohenga, the world below. The parents of the demi-god, Māui, lived there. Like we do now, when the day dawned, down they would go to the cool world beneath.

Around the world there are many underground cities like ours. Built by the survivors of the precipitous decline in the world's populations. But even now there are still too many people for the cities to service. And so while the cities still maintain a quasi-governmental and military function, the society is divided into Essentials on one side and the Non-Essentials (NEs) and Olds (Os) on the other.

'At least at Rarohenga,' I say to Dad as we step from the shuttle, 'you may be old but you're still essential.' In some cities around the world the NEs and Os are in permanent lockdown. Stacked on top of each other in enforced hibernation. They are fed dreams of what the world used to be like, a home where the buffalos roam.

'I love you too,' Dad says in response to my sarcasm. But his voice is shadowed and his eyes are glowing. 'Ah, there's Kui!'

And I feel a darkness descending all around me. A huge sense of impending loss.

She waits in the arrival concourse to greet me. My three sisters are with her. I recognise other whānau as belonging to agricultural crews which supply the city with kūmara, the staple food that Rarohenga depends on. They were with Dad and me when . . .

'Nau mai, haere mai ki te wā kāinga,' Kui smiles. You have arrived, you are here, welcome home. Home?

She looks across my shoulder to my father. 'E te Rangatira . . .'

I follow her gaze. Dad looks at me, tenderly.

'This had to happen some time, Branson.'

Why is everyone weeping?

'Goodbye, Son.'

It happens so quickly. One moment Dad's there. The next moment he is gone. It's the moment I have dreaded. Because I have not only been running away from reality. I have also been running away from this particular moment.

'Thank you for bringing your father back,' Aunt Kui says. 'I didn't think you would be able to do it!'

I am terrorised, gasping. The sense of loss overwhelms me. 'I . . . I . . . I . . .'

I am in psychic shock. 'Dad, don't leave me.' And I fall in a faint into my aunt's arms.

Kete o te Wānanga

A year ago. I am with Dad and his work crew. It is night and we have driven to the outer perimeter of the plantations to fix some of the sun-filtering shades. Some of the louvres aren't functioning, not closing, and the harsh sun is shrivelling the kūmara below.

It is dark when we leave Rarohenga. When we arrive at the plantations, we see that some of the kaimahi ahuwhenua, the farmers, are working the fields with their wives and a group of small children. Dad goes to greet them. 'The women wanted to bring the kids into the fresh air. Have a picnic before we go back. And the tamariki like to play in the cool night.'

'Ka pai,' Dad answers. 'All good.' He pats the little ones on the head. 'You are the future,' he says to them. 'Your ancestors came from a place called Hawaiki. You are royal children.'

The engineering team work speedily. Overhead, the sky turns, a few scattered stars.

After we've fixed the shades we sit around with the farmers enjoying each other's company. The kids scamper around, enjoying themselves. Someone has brought a guitar, so we sing some of the old songs.

'Me he manu rere, auē . . .' That was Mum's favourite before she died. I was still a baby and Aunt Kui brought me up. It's basically been just Dad and me after that, really.

How did it happen that we left our return to Rarohenga too late? The dawn is already lightening the sky, but we think we have time. We travel back to the city in convoy, the two crews, engineers and farmers in four transports. Hikurangi mountain doesn't look too far away.

Then one of the farmers' transports breaks down. 'You three go on,' Dad tells the others. 'You go with them, Tāwhaki.'

'No,' I answer. 'You might need me here.'

We watch the other transports as they depart. Then Dad says, 'Haere ki te mahi,' rolls up his sleeves, and tries to figure out what the problem is. There are fifteen of us waiting around, Dad, two engineers, me, six farmers, two women, and three children — two of them are babies being breast-fed.

'We should have put the women and children in the other vehicles,' Dad says.

'They didn't want to leave their husbands,' one of the farmers says.

'I should have forced them to go. They are my responsibility.'

The problem is found and can't be fixed. Three batteries damaged. 'I'll radio base,' Dad says, 'and ask them to send an extraction unit. Not a problem.'

And we still think that we're okay except that sometimes it's not the sun you need to be aware of. The rising sun has kick-started the morning wind. Before we know it, the currents are swirling an eviscerating blast of heat. The world becomes an oven and begins to cook us. Before we know it, we are gasping and falling to the ground.

'Tāwhaki,' Dad yells, 'break out the fire blankets.'

The blankets are fire-resistant wingsuits that might win us some time. We huddle beneath, the men forming a protective rim for the women and children in the middle.

Above us, the sound of an extraction unit. 'Get the kids to safety,' Dad says to me.

'What about you?'

'Me and the other men have to keep the blankets up and around you as you leave. The women and children are in your care. Go, Son.'

Every second counts. Stepping beyond the blankets, we are already burning. The children are screaming. The wind is a fiery maelstrom. We fall into the arms of our rescuers.

'What about my dad!'

'We have to go.' The rescue transport wheels away. The wind whips the blankets away from Dad and the men. Dad raises an arm.

He bursts into flames.

The women, children and me were in the burns unit at Rarohenga for over a month. I embraced the pain of the skin grafts, I felt I should have died with my father. We all recovered and, when I was well enough to return to duty, I applied for transfer to *Ranginui-14* and got it. But I had loved Dad so much that I couldn't let him go. I took his wairua, his spirit, with me, whether he wanted to come or not, whether others wanted me to take him or not.

They could go to hell. He was mine and I would not let anybody have him.

And now, over a year has passed. I have returned for the hura kōhatu, the unveiling ceremony for Dad and the other men who died. Unveilings usually take place a year after the tangihanga, the mourning ceremony.

I stand with Aunt Kui and the mourners in front of the memorial stone in the family urupā. It's outside Rarohenga, within a cleft of Hikurangi mountain. Among the attendants are the wives and children who survived with me.

'Shall we begin, Nephew?' Aunt Kui asks.

I nod my head and the tributes start. Not only to Dad, but also to the other men, the engineers and farmers, who died with him. And, contrary to my expectations, the commemoration is not as sad as I was expecting. In fact, some of the memories are hilarious and others are, well, quite salty. In other words, human. 'I didn't know Dad was such a ladies' man,' I whisper to Aunt Kui.

She rolls her eyes. 'Let's just say my brother's gears never went rotten, and leave it at that.'

Everyone begins to sing songs in celebration of the lives that were taken so that we can go on. One cheeky kuia starts doing a hula.

'She was one of your father's er . . .' Aunt Kui begins, leaving me to connect the dots.

'Oh, Dad. You were always talking about my namesake Tāwhaki.

'I will try to find a way. For the sake of the children, I will climb to the uppermost heaven, yes, I will find the aka matua, I will do it. But, Dad, when Tāwhaki brought back the baskets of knowledge the first time, look what humankind did with all those taonga. We trashed them.

'My father, we don't deserve a second chance. And the real question is: if we are given it, and if Io grants us the baskets of knowledge again, will we get over our self-destructive nature and obsessions and do better this time?

'Will we?'

Tru Paraha

Borderline

-... . -.-- --- -. -.. | -.-. ..- .-.. - ..- .-. .

ki tua

-... . -.-- --- -. -.. | ... .-.. . . .--.

ki tua

-... . -.-- --- -. -.. | -... .-.. --- --- -..

ki tua

-... . -.-- --- -. -.. | -.-. .. ...- .. .-.. | -.. ..- .. - . ...

ki tua

-... . -.-- --- -. -.. | -.. --- --. -- .-

ki tua

-... . -.-- --- -. -.. | . -. - .-. .--. .-. .. ... .

belong

-... . -.-- --- -. -.. | .-.. . --. . -. -..

beyond

-... . -.-- --- -. -.. | - . .-. .-. --- .-.

beyond

-... . -.-- --- -. -.. | .... --- .- -..-

beyond

-... . -.-- --- -. -.. | . -.-. --- -....- .--. .-. --- -.. ..- -.-. .

beyond

-... . -.-- --- -. -.. | -.. --- ..- -... -

-... . -.-- --- -. -.. | -... --- -.. .. . ...

be gone

-... . -.-- --- -. -.. | .... --- .--. .

beyond

-... . -.-- --- -. -.. | --.- ..- .- -. - ..- -- | .--. .... -.-- ... .. -.-. ...

beyond

-... . -.-- --- -. -.. | .- -- -... .. ...- .- .-.. . -. -.-. .
-... . -.-- --- -. -.. | - .- .-.. -.- .. -. --.
-... . -.-- --- -. -.. | .--. --- ...- . .-. - -.--
-... . -.-- --- -. -.. | --. . -. -.. . .-.
-... . -.-- --- -. -.. | - .- .-.. . -. -
-... . -.-- --- -. -.. | .. -. ...- .- ... .. --- -.
-... . -.-- --- -. -.. | .-.. --- ...- . | ... --- -. --. ...
-... . -.-- --- -. -.. | .--. --- .-.. .-.. ..- - .. --- -.
-... . -.-- --- -. -.. | .-- .- .. - .- -. --. ..
-... . -.-- --- -. -.. | .- .--. .--. .-.. .- ..- ... .
-... . -.-- --- -. -.. | ..-. ..- -. -.. .-. .- .. ..-. ...
-... . -.-- --- -. -.. | .--. --- . - .-. -.--
-... . -.-- --- -. -.. | .-. . ..-. ..- --. .
-... . -.-- --- -. -.. | .--. --- .-. -. --- --. .-. .- .--. .... -.--
-... . -.-- --- -. -.. | .-.. .- .--
-... . -.-- --- -. -..

zerow

ki hea

;;;

Ruby Solly

Eulogy

As a child
whenever I was angry,
inconsolable,
my father would tell me to write a eulogy
to the person who had caused me pain.
He said that by the end of it
I would see
that even those who cause us pain
are precious to the world.

  My father was an exceptional man,
  he was blessed
  with a gentle soul.
  He walked in step
  with the many animals he adored
  and he treaded lightly on this earth.
  He taught me
  to tread as he did
  and to leave the world as you found it.
  Ideally, improve it.

One day I will read this
to a room of faces I barely recognise.
I will look out on a world
no different with him gone
as it was
with him here.

Apirana Taylor

taku toa

ehara taku toa i te toa takitahi
engari taku toa he toa takitini
my strength is not the strength of one
my strength is the strength of many

ehara taku toa i te toa takitahi
engari taku toa he toa takitini
my hand is not the hand of one
my hand is the hand of many

ehara taku toa i te toa takitahi
engari taku toa he toa takitini
my stand is not the stand of one
my stand is the stand of many

ehara taku toa i te toa takitahi
engari taku toa he toa takitini
my call is not the call of one
my call is the call of many

Interview: Five Māori Novelists

Interviewed by Vaughan Rapatahana

AD – Alan Duff
PG – Patricia Grace
CH – Cassie Hart
WH – Whiti Hereaka
JP – Josh Pomare

Of late, there has been a noticeable increase in the number of novels written by Māori. Such new novelists include Becky Manawatu, Michael Bennett, Rebecca K Reilly, Monty Soutar and Coco Solid.

I asked five established Māori novelists – who write across several genres – a set of searching questions about writing in Aotearoa as a Māori author. I was especially interested in their views regarding the term 'Māori writer'. I am extremely grateful to all for their willingness to be interviewed, and for their cogent and informative responses.

Could you write a bit about your early influences and reading regarding fiction written by Māori? What drew you to becoming involved in the novel genre, that is, why did you begin writing novels?

PG The answer to the first part of your question is, simply: there were none – no influences regarding fiction written by Māori. In those early days I had never read, or seen anything written by a Māori author. If there was such writing, it had never come my way. By the time I came across other writing by Māori, I was already writing myself.

I was in my early twenties, living in a remote farming area of Northland where my husband and I were teaching and raising a family.

While there, I joined, as a country member, a Penwomen's Club which was based in Auckland. The club ran monthly writing competitions, one of the yearly categories being for a 'Māori Short Story'. I don't know how many entries this attracted (there were no other Māori in the club). I only knew that every time I entered, I came out the winner. (I was disqualified once because of a late entry. The post office was miles away.) This was in the early sixties. I still had not seen any writing by other Māori.

Previously, during my teacher training years, I read, for the first time, short stories, novels and poetry by New Zealand Pākehā writers. For the first time I 'heard' the New Zealand voice in literature, the Kiwi vernacular. I began to learn about 'voice', about having one's own voice.

In those early competition stories, I was experimenting, finding my way – my own voice, storylines, characters, themes, settings. What a great thrill it was to learn of, and eventually to have a copy of, Hone Tuwhare's *No Ordinary Sun* (1964). This was the first time I had read a book by an author who was Māori. What an experience it was. At about the same time – late 60s, early 70s – I came across stories and poetry by Māori in *Te Ao Hou* magazine. This was the official journal of what was then the Māori Affairs Department. I began to send work there myself. Most unforgettable for me at the time, and always, was Arapera Blank's story, 'One Two Three Four Five'.

My competition stories were published in various papers and magazines and eventually collected by Longman Paul Publishers, becoming my first book, *Waiariki*, which came out in 1975. It was my editor at Longman Paul, Phoebe Meikle, who gave me a push towards longer fiction when she said, 'Now, we want a novel from you.' I set about the writing of *Mutuwhenua*.

WH I read *Whale Rider* when I was around eleven because Taupō-nui-a-Tia College had adapted the story into a play and I loved it. Later, when I went to that college, we studied *Pounamu Pounamu* in English. Around that time *Once Were Warriors* came out and my sister auditioned for Grace (she didn't get it!) so I read that too. I read *The Bone People* as a teenager too, but a lot of that went over my young head.

I started as a playwright, so reading novels wasn't really an influence on my decision to write. I started to write novels after a short film script of mine won its category in the E Tuhi (now Pikihuia) Awards. Brian Bargh from Huia Publishers called me and asked if I had a novel manuscript (I didn't). Eventually, after a few more calls, I decided to try writing a novel.

CH I grew up in a big family of readers – not just my immediate family but extended as well. We lived rurally, with an aunt, uncle and cousins a kilometre up the road, and my grandparents just a little further on from them. There was a lot of book sharing going on in those days!

I can't say that I read a lot of Māori fiction when I was younger, though – plenty of our myths and legends via school, and then I was exposed to more engaging texts when my mother dug into our heritage when I was a teen, but there was never a push for reading more of our indigenous work either at home or at school. In fact, I don't think it was until I was in my later teens that I realised there was even such a thing as Māori fiction. The vast majority of what we had was science fiction, fantasy and horror, with the occasional crime or mystery novel thrown in the mix. It was the literary diet I grew up on and I still lean this way heavily with my reading.

JP Alan Duff, that's about it to be honest. There weren't too many Māori writers that were taught to us at school, even at Western Heights in Rotorua. Indirectly Witi Ihimaera too, given *Whale Rider* was such a hit. My father was probably the main Māori storyteller who influenced me. Growing up with him I was always drawn to his stories and storytelling. He is one of the great storytellers, and I recognise a strong tradition of oral storytelling in our whakapapa. These days when you get the whānau together you can barely get a word in.

It has been stated that in recent years there has been an explosion of Māori writers writing and publishing in the novel genre, with more types of novels – crime, fantasy, historical, romance, 'real life' and so on. Do you agree? If you do agree, why do you think this is happening?

PG The production of novels by Māori began with the publication of *Tangi* by Witi Ihimaera in 1973. The 70s saw three further first novels, by Heretaunga Pat Baker, June Mitchell and myself. In the 80s came Keri Hulme's *The Bone People*. The 90s brought forward first novels by Renée, Alan Duff and Apirana Taylor, while the first decade of the new century gave us firsts by Katerina Mataira, Paula Morris, Lisa

Cherrington and Isabel Waiti Mulholland. Katerina Mataira's novel *Makorea* was a double first, being also a world first – the only published novel written in the Māori language. Then in the 2020s came firsts by Whiti Hereaka, Olivia Aroha Giles, Tina Makereti, Tīhema Baker, Helen Waaka and Becky Manawatu.

Most of these writers have continued to write novels, so the count is continuing upwards. (I would like to enter a count-up into this interview but I'd be worried about accuracy. Someone may have researched the number and titles.) Themes and storylines have broadened in the way that you have mentioned. An explosion of novels by Māori? I would have to agree with that. I expect it is all part of the expansion into many areas of writing by Māori in Te Reo and English – of short and long fiction, non-fiction including biographies, essays, specialist texts, writing for children and young adults. We have our own publishing house in Huia Publishers, which will account for much of this burgeoning of published work. Mainstream publishers are now sensing that there has been a shift in the market place and wish to further expand into titles by authors who are Māori.

WH I think there are more Māori novelists being published across genre, yes. I believe that some of this is down to the work of the Māori Literature Trust (Te Waka Taki Kōrero, of which I am a board member) and our programme Te Papa Tupu. I wrote my second novel *Bugs* as a participant in the programme in 2012, and have continued to be involved as a mentor for writers like Steph Matuku and Cassie Hart. The programme helps to tautoko emerging Māori writers not only by teaching them the skills they need but also in creating a community around them.

CH I do! And I think it's wonderful. For so long it felt like that in order to be a Māori writer you had to write a certain way. The books I did read as an adult all had this beautiful way with language, and were quite grounded in being Māori, and in Māori settings. For so many people these days, the experience of being Māori is different – we can't and should not be boxed into writing in specific settings or themes because of our heritage. Māori culture is rich with story and creativity, so it's wonderful to see that expressed.

That said, maybe it's not necessarily that Māori are writing more novels. Maybe it's more to do with a change in publishing, a push for more representation, the smaller presses that have emerged in Aotearoa, as well as easier access to overseas publishers and readers. Maybe Māori have been writing novels for a long time and it's just that we're seeing more of them being published now.

JP I have certainly noticed many more Māori novelists coming through, although it may be more to do with the fact that as someone within the industry now, I pay more attention to what is happening around me. There is a long list of very strong writers, the likes of Becky Manawatu, Michael Bennett, Monty Soutar; it's hard to imagine a time when so many Māori novelists are in the local best seller lists. I also think we are seeing more interest in genre fiction as opposed to literary or 'real life' fiction (not to mention short stories, and poetry). I see not just more Māori writers but more Black, Indigenous and People of Colour (BIPOC) writers from a range of cultures are these days finding audiences in crime, romance, historical and fantasy fiction, which we didn't see so much twenty years or even a decade ago.

If indeed Māori are writing more novels, is there any such thing as 'the Māori novel' with a 'Māori world view' incorporating Māori mythology and tradition, and whānau, identity, social and environmental issues?

PG There are novels written by Māori that incorporate the Māori world view as outlined in your question. There are novels by Māori that do not. There are many different ways of being Māori. We are as various as any other people. It is important that our literature shows this diversity. One thing that all the writers will have in common, is a whakapapa Māori. In *Te Ao Mārama* series of writing by Māori, editor Witi Ihimaera gives recognition to this by including writing by Maōri of diverse backgrounds.

But, auē! This question takes me back to the 70s, 80s, 90s when we writers were plagued with questions, from people who were not Māori, both here and abroad, which I for one had put no thought to until then: Who is Māori? Why do you call yourselves Māori writers? Why do you choose to write when you actually come from an oral culture? Why do you write in English? What have you gained from your European (nobody used the word Pākehā in those days) heritage? The thing is, the Māori Writer label was not devised by the writers themselves — I know because I asked them – though we had given iwi affiliations as part of our bios. It seemed to be a requirement. We were just writing. Not that we rejected the label either, though some later writers did, believing that this description restricted them. As for the question, which was usually a statement rather than a question: 'You're half Māori and half Pākehā', it always gave the questioner problems when I said I was not *half* anything. I was wholly Māori and wholly Pākehā, but identified as Māori, having had little choice about that. Also, what I am not, is 'a person of colour' unless everyone else is. I have to wonder who thought that one up. I'm always taken aback that people would want to tell me who I am. I was aware of other writers, who were not Māori, being more free to answer questions about their works rather than their identities. Labels were/are put on our writings as well: post-colonial, hybrid. Again, Auē! However, because I'm happy to have my work examined and discussed every which way, in any forum, some descriptives are unavoidable.

WH I'm of the opinion that if a Māori author writes a novel then it is a Māori novel – it doesn't matter what its content might be.

CH I think there are – and there is definitely a place for that. It felt like, for a long time, unless your book fitted that niche, it wasn't really a Māori book. These days there is a lot of push back on that.

Māori are not all the same. We come from different backgrounds, we approach our culture in different ways, and I think it's so important for fiction to explore and reflect this.

But also, I think that te ao Māori can come through in so many more ways than the general public might pick up on. For example, my book isn't specifically Māori, though there is a character who is part Māori and hasn't really connected with that side of his heritage as much as he possibly should have. Aside from that, it's a book very connected to the land, to nature. There are so many tohu in it. I guess you could say that I am less interested in the politics and social constructs of what it means to be Māori, and more interested in whānau, identity and mythology.

JP Sure, the traces of the author can be found in all fiction – all Māori writers' world views are largely informed by lived experience so in this way their world view finds its way into the work – but I think there is a distinction here between a person of Māori heritage incorporating their own lived experience into the fiction, and a novel that is overtly tackling

Māori mythology and history. My world view is informed in part by my experience of growing up and living in New Zealand as a Māori tāne, so this is the water I swim in, this is the only world I know and in this way, it informs my politics and world view, but I'm yet to tackle Māori heritage, history, mythology head on.

Are there difficulties getting novels (and indeed other fiction pieces) published because the themes are Māori and/or because the authors are Māori? That is, are there issues of being pigeonholed 'a Māori writer' and being expected to write about 'Māori themes'?

PG I have not had difficulty being published. I would think that publishing for Māori would be easier now, especially with the new history curriculum in schools and the need for complementary material. I have been told though, by one writer, that work was sent back to her by an editor wanting the piece to have a more Māori focus. She resisted this.

WH I haven't experienced this! And I don't really pay mind to what people expect of me – I write what I need to write.

CH I used to feel like there was very much a need to do things in the 'right way' in order to be considered a Māori writer. This changed dramatically when I was accepted into Te Papa Tupu, which is an amazing mentorship programme for emerging Māori writers.

It was there that I met the amazing Whiti Hereaka, who was my mentor, and other greats like James George, Paula Morris and Jacquie McRae, as well as the awesome folks who run Huia Publishing.

That experience really opened my eyes to the fact that there were so many different ways to tell Māori stories, and mine was just as valid as anyone else's.

I felt like novels in particular had to be a certain way in order to be Māori, but during the mentorship I really soaked up the reality that any novel written by Māori is Māori, just by its very nature. It doesn't have to have te reo, or a marae, or anything specific to our culture to make it so.

Before then, I'd never considered myself a Māori writer, because I was writing science fiction, fantasy and horror, and those never felt like they could be Māori fiction. Now, I am proud to call myself a Māori author, and I can see all the ways in which my writing is informed by te ao Māori.

On the topic of other forms of fiction, I think that since the world really opened up via the internet there are so many more opportunities out there. The world is hungry for good stories, and hungry for diversity. There are so many markets out there for writers to explore. The shores of Aotearoa are beautiful, this is the best place in the world to be, but I don't think anyone should limit themselves to only publishing within our country.

JP I think there are real issues with being pigeonholed 'a Māori writer' but it tends to begin much earlier in a writer's journey/career than people expect. I think those with 'minority experience' – that is to say, those who come from diverse or marginalised backgrounds – in the world of books and publishing are expected to write about that experience. This begins at school, and in tertiary education – competition judges for short story prizes want to see these *diverse* stories, and so the publishing industry serves as both the mechanism and incentive for diverse stories. Which is great, but it means we are often pushed down one path to write certain types of books, dealing with certain themes. This idea, that our only cultural value is to provide insight into another experience, is reinforced via every cultural institution and touchstone along the way. We are told our story is important, we must tell the story of our people, which works well for some but not all.

What advice would you give Māori writers just getting started on their first novel manuscript? You might mention, for example, the continued doubt and strain about publisher, reader and media expectations, even when you've sold thousands of copies. Yet, you might also comment more positively about how great it is seeing your novel in print and how this could well encourage other Māori authors to write novels.

PG I think that new writers who are Māori should ignore the expectations of others, write what they want to write, in the way they want to do it. This does not mean that they should not take heed of good advice or look objectively at criticism of their work, but, in the end, having considered everything, it is up to them. They will need to work hard, know who they are at a deep level, and what their experiences in life have been – always including the life of imagination and dreams. They will need to read heaps. They will want to strive, always, to become better writers.

WH If you're just getting started writing a manuscript, focus on that process – worries about publication and how it might be received just use up energy that is better used now in writing your story. Those things are future problems.

What has helped me in getting through a project is having a support network: other writers or a writing group, friends and family who might not have any idea about writing but will support you in other ways – perhaps taking some of your responsibilities so that you have the time to write.

It's also helpful to remind yourself *why* you need to write this story – whatever that reason might be – so when it does get hard you have a bit of motivation to push through.

Set yourself up for success. Plan some time to devote to your work. Remember to eat well. Go out for a walk from time to time. Be kind to yourself, it is difficult work at times.

CH My advice would be – focus on your book. Write stories that you love and let that love come through on the page. Your early work might never see the light of day, but it's the only time in your writing life when you don't have any external pressures on it. You can make it as wild and wonderful as you want while you find your way with story and pacing and structure. Your process will change over time, maybe your genre, you might play with tense and point of view, and that's all wonderful. Enjoy it, roll around in it. Make the most of this beautiful time in your journey. Hold your story close and pour your passion into it.

Things do change once you accept that publishing contract and the story is no longer just your own – it's for the publisher, and the readers, and the world at large. And that's wonderful too! When you hold that book in your hands and feel the weight of those pages and words and you know that someone out there will be reading it soon. That not everyone might love it, but that it will find those who love it as much as you do. It's so amazing.

Once that first book is out, there is new pressure and new weight on you. It's a different thing and sometimes worrying about whether you will be able to strike lightning can make it feel a whole lot harder.

JP I would say write what you like to read. It's simple. And to do that you need to read widely, find books that speak to you, or entertain you, or affect you, and recognise what each book does for you. Don't write to the expectations of your teachers, or friends, or peers. Just write for yourself first.

Finally, please let us know about any upcoming writing projects you have relating to the genre. Once again, this may well encourage more Māori to write fiction.

PG I have completed a set of stories, for which I will soon complete the editing, but have no thought of writing another extended work, as yet. I can't wait to see what new novels, and novelists, this decade will bring.

WH I have two more novels that are related to *Kurangaituku* in development. The first of those is currently called *Ariā* and follows a young woman's life and her burgeoning career as an artist as she is slowly taken over by Kurangaituku. It is a ghost/haunting story so will probably end up as horror.

The novel after *Ariā* is very early in its development, so much so that I don't have a name for it. I do know that it will be set in the future and that Kurangaituku will again influence the story.

CH I am always — always — working on books, but right now my focus is on getting ready to start a sequel to *Butcherbird*, which was my first traditional publication with Huia. It feels weird to be coming back to it after so much time away, but the pieces of the novel that I needed have started falling into place in my brain, so I'm excited to return to Jena and Will, and see how their stories unfold. Speculative fiction, fantasy, science fiction, horror are always going to be my home, and I love how naturally my heritage weaves into those genres and adds layers.

JP Sure, I've got a bit on my plate at the moment. I'm writing a couple of novellas for Audible. One is due out at the end of the year and the other in 2024. Plus, I've got to get stuck into my next novel. I'm planning a story set between Cambridge, Rotorua, Edinburgh and London. It's a crime novel, but it will likely contain my views on colonialism, the justice system, and many other things.

Alan Duff responded holistically to the pātai, as here:

AD My first advice is, unchain yourself from being 'a Māori writer'. We are from an oral culture, not a written one. Personally, I owe my writing career to my Pākehā dad's side. I grew up with books and got taught to love the written word. If you are going to write then just write. Forget the me-Māori. That will anyway come through in your natural-born cadences.

Before you write, read. And keep reading till your eyes bleed. Or you'll never be a writer. Like playing sport: you don't start hitting aces for quite a few years.

Draft. Draft. Draft again. And again. And again. I wrote 12 drafts of *Once Were Warriors* and it was the last that got me published. Around the world. The other 1.1 million words were practice. Golfing great Gary Player said, 'The harder I practise, the luckier I get.'

I love being Māori. But unless you are writing in te reo, then it is not Māori writing. Just writing. I found the richness of Māori EXPERIENCE helped inform so much of my writing. The tangihanga ceremony; the group singing; the vitality and animation of everyday verbal exchange; the humour; the pride; and yes, even the fighting.

I love our instant rapport; the social obligation to greet everyone in a room no matter who we or they are. But writing itself is a discipline requiring the highest standards of creative excellence, true grit and refusing to give up. And remember, we all stand on the shoulders of the giants who preceded us.

Originality. My first attempts at writing a book were just awful attempts at imitating published authors. Instead of being myself. I owe my former agent, Chris Else, who told me to take my authorial voice out of it and write in the immediate. It was like being let out of prison. And I know the feeling!

Where you can and if you must, push things Māori. But never in the reader's face. Everyone has suffered. Every race and tribe, throughout human history, has been colonised, massacred, treated like shit. Better to gain a reader's empathy by coming at them from the side, so to speak, using a setting laid with benign traps to tweak their heartstrings, not pluck and plunk wildly demanding they listen.

At Duffy Books in Homes, we have put 15 million books into the hands of mostly Māori and Pasifika children from low-income homes. Why? Because I knew that one of our biggest problems is that there are no books in our homes. I know we've made a difference.

But on no account try and convert a non-reading adult to a reader. Like asking a smoker to stop. If you do have writing ambitions, keep company with people who love reading. They don't have to be writers. I hardly know any. And I have many friends who do not read much, yet whose company I love. So don't be snobbish about it. Just a bit picky!

Know your grammar, spelling, punctuation, and always aim for a manuscript as faultless as you can get it. Called presentation and professionalism. Without which you will surely fail.

My last note. Remember you are descended from seafarers who navigated the vast Pacific Ocean discovering islands using the stars as guides. We were and are warriors. Of a new and exciting kind.

Kia kaha!

Tēnā koutou katoa ngā kaituhi Māori.

Interview: Children's and YA Novel Writing

With: Ataria Sharman and Shilo Kino
Interviewed by Kiri Piahana-Wong

In recent years, increasing numbers of Māori writers have published books in the young adult and children's novel genres. These genres afford the writer the opportunity to variously delve into mythology and the supernatural, tackle political issues, address social concerns, and even empathise with and inspire their young readers. Writers like Lauren Keenan, Steph Matuku, Tania Roxborogh, Lani Wendt Young, Hirini Moko Mead, Fraser Smith, Tim Tipene, Whiti Hereaka, Pamela Morrow, Shilo Kino and Ataria Sharman have been making their mark in these genres.

In this interview I asked Ataria Sharman (AS) and Shilo Kino (SK) to describe their experiences as new authors starting out in children's and YA fiction.

Ataria, you are the author of children's novel Hine and the Tohunga Portal *(2021) and Shilo, you wrote YA novel* The Pōrangi Boy *(2020). What drew you to the children's/YA novel genres and why did you choose to tell the particular story you told?*

AS I spent my formative years reading children's and YA books. When you're reading a book as a kid, you are experiencing things for the first time, and everything feels new and exciting. There are many aspects of life like romance, responsibility and independence you haven't yet experienced; it's all unexplored terrain. Writing in that genre, the main characters are often younger. They have an innocence and naivety that feels energising for the reader experiencing the fictional world through their tellings.

It felt like my imagination was more potent when I was younger. After all, I wasn't (yet) weighed down by the world's worries, which, although essential, are also boring to me because they're real-world worries. I like magic powers and big battle worries. Not like my-boss-at-work-sucks and I-can't-pay-my-bills worries. Even today, I mostly read children's and YA fantasy fiction. I'm not a huge fan of adult literature. I am an adult, and I live that life. I enjoy escaping into something I can't experience in this reality.

There are two atua wāhine in *Hine and the Tohunga Portal*, Mahuika and Hineteiwaiwa. I wanted to write it to raise awareness of our atua wāhine while completing my master's thesis on that same kaupapa. Of course, children's fantasy fiction is the perfect vehicle for that as it reaches our tamariki. I enjoyed creating a world where everything is Māori. In *Hine and the Tohunga Portal*, there are no non-Māori characters. It's inspired by Māori narratives and belief systems, including pre-colonial flora and fauna. It was a lot of fun writing about that kind of world.

SK Our history is shaped by injustice and the fight for land back, but the sad reality is the majority of people in Aotearoa don't know our history. I learnt about the 506-day occupation at Takaparawhau (Bastion Point), the Tūhoe raids, the Parihaka invasion, and the protest at Ngāwhā prison as an adult.

I grew up in Waipu, a small town in Te Tai Tokerau that was predominantly Pākehā. I learnt more about the Scottish settlers than rangatira within my own iwi. It is a common story for many of us. I lived away from my marae and whenua, I had no grandparents alive to teach me about my culture, and my parents were busy doing their best to survive in a Pākehā world. I grew up reading and consuming stories that told me that Māori were destined to fail. Māori were the criminals, the baby killers, the gang members, the underachievers, the prisoners, the drug and alcohol addicts. This kind of narrative is destructive and harmful to children. This is what ultimately inspired me to be a writer and journalist and write a book like *The Pōrangi Boy*.

The Pōrangi Boy is about a young boy called Niko who is bullied and called 'pōrangi' for fighting to stop a prison from being built on sacred land, inspired by the protest at Ngāwhā. There are a lot of layers within the story but I hope Niko and his story is able to whakamana (empower) tamariki and rangatahi.

I grew up reading children's and YA novels like Tamora Pierce's Alanna *series, Sherryl Jordan's* Winter of Fire, *Maurice Gee's* The Halfmen of O *trilogy, and C S Lewis's* Narnia. *Of course, these books all feature white characters in the lead roles and often draw on medieval English history for their setting. It blew my mind as an adult to discover Lani Wendt Young's* Telesa *series, and finally read a YA story with brown characters, setting and mythologies. Could you talk about your early influences and reading in children's/YA fiction and how this may have changed over time?*

SK I grew up on stories such as *The Babysitters Club*, *The Famous Five*, *Narnia* and I still love these stories now because of the nostalgia they hold. However, I remember stumbling across Maya Angelou and it was a feeling like no other! The feeling of being seen. The feeling of your soul rising. Someone finally could speak to your mamae. *I Know Why the Caged Bird Sings* was my introduction to stories about identity and belonging that was the beginning of my journey into writing.

Now as an adult, I find there is often a disconnect and sometimes frustration when I read stories written by Pākehā writers. The writing might be amazing but I feel myself wanting and needing more. I notice the gaps, the cultural differences, the privilege, the trauma porn. Maybe it's because I've spent the majority of my life mostly consuming stories with a Pākehā lens and now I'm hungry for more indigenous stories or stories that speak to me. Therefore, I'm more intentional now with the books I read. Last year I read mostly books written by indigenous authors. It was a lot more effort having to source particular books but it also made me feel hopeful that there is a wide option of books available now that are written by people of colour.

AS I grew up with *Narnia*, *Northern Lights* by Philip Pullman and J R R Tolkien's *Lord of the Rings* and *The Hobbit*. I don't think I thought deeply about the characters in the books I read growing up until later in life, but they were almost exclusively white characters. Then *Harry Potter* by J K Rowling came along, which has tokenistic inclusion of people of colour.

As a child, you don't understand racism. You can experience racism but not realise the word to describe that experience is 'racism'. When you only read white characters, do you know that brown characters can also be included on the page?

Although back then I didn't critique the stories I read, that doesn't mean it didn't feel like something was missing. Reflecting years later, I realised I never felt seen in the books I read. I never thought that the characters were like me or represented me and my skin colour or my way of being in the world. This is the reason I wrote *Hine and the Tohunga Portal*. It's a book I needed when I was younger.

I found stories I felt more connected to in Japanese manga and anime. I loved *Ranma ½* by Rumiko Takahashi, which I happend on at Wellington City Library, and the movies *Nausicaä, Princess Mononoke* and *Spirited Away* by Hayao Miyazaki. All feature strong female characters and storylines with interwoven Japanese belief systems. Perhaps I resonated strongly with these stories because the characters and narratives aligned more with Māori culture. Or maybe they just stood out as something vastly different to the European novels I was overexposed to.

In recent years there has been an explosion of Māori writers writing and publishing in the children's and YA novel genres. The judges for the 2022 New Zealand Book Awards for Children and Young Adults say that: 'there is a growing strength of books with a te ao Māori world view and titles in te reo Māori' (Te Ao Māori News). Please comment. In your opinion is this statement correct?

AS When I was studying postgrad in Māori Studies I remember one of the lecturers advising me to be careful using the overarching term 'te ao Māori'. My understanding of this was that the Māori world view is the collective viewpoints of everyone who has Māori heritage. We're a diverse people; we have different cultural backgrounds and upbringings. As you can imagine, the world view of everyone who is Māori differs hugely across cultural, societal, political and ideological viewpoints.

Suppose 'te ao Māori' is the collective world view of all Māori people. In that case, the only requirement for the statement 'there is a growing [number] ~~strength~~ of books with a te ao Māori world view' to be true is for more published books to be by Māori authors. I've taken the word strength out, and I'll return to that later. If you have Māori heritage, any writing you publish is growing the literal number of texts from the world view of a Māori person.

In recent years, we've seen investment into kaupapa to support and grow Māori writing talent. For example, Shilo and I went through the

Te Papa Tupu programme by the Māori Literature Trust. I believe this targeted support has led to an increase in published books by Māori and their recognition at awards such as the New Zealand Book Awards for Children and Young Adults. It certainly is the case for Shilo and me.

It's hard to comment on the use of 'strength' in that statement because we don't know the judges' criteria. Perhaps a clue can be found in the same press release, in a sentence in the following paragraph: 'Māori language and world views are taonga unique to Aotearoa.' From this, one of the criteria could have been an increase in the quality of books using the Māori language.

I would say there has been an increase in finalists this year and in recent years that use Māori words, including those completely in te reo. My thoughts are, therefore, that the statement above is correct.

SK There is a growing number of books being published with a te ao Māori world view and titles in te reo Māori. However, Māori writers have always existed. Māori stories have always been in the world. Huia Publishers have been publishing Māori writers and children's and YA stories for over 30 years. Has there been an 'explosion' of Māori writers or is it because mainstream publishers and other platforms are finally choosing to publish more of our stories? So, while I am optimistic and excited about the growing number of books from Māori being published, we still have a long way to go. For example, I would like to see more of our books on the front stands and windows at mainstream book stores. A big shout out to McLeods Booksellers in Rotorua for their range of books written by Māori! By seeing the diversity of stories within our culture, more of our rangatahi will be encouraged to write our stories.

Please let us know about any upcoming writing projects you have relating to the genres under discussion.

SK My next book is an adult fiction book titled *All That We Own Know*. The title of the book is alluding to the fact that as tangata whenua, we once owned all the land in Aotearoa. Now we own less than 5 per cent. All that we have left now is all that we know — which isn't a lot.

All That We Own Know follows the life of a strong-headed wahine and activist who is navigating life, relationships, identity and whānau here in Tāmaki Makaurau. Colonisation isn't a one time event. The spiritual wound left from the loss of land impacts whānau for generations. How does it affect a young wahine navigating the modern world today?

It is very different to *The Pōrangi Boy*. I would say *The Pōrangi Boy* is a book I would have wanted to read as a child. *All That We Own Know* is a book I would have wanted to read in my 20s.

AS I'm writing the sequel to *Hine and the Tohunga Portal*. The working title is *Hine and the Sacred Huawhenua*, a reference to a quest Hine and her brother Hōhepa must go on to restore balance in a world corrupted by a particular evil sorcerer. It's taking me longer than the last book. I think it's because I've improved at writing now, so my first drafting is better and I have more awareness of things like plot issues or introducing too many characters. It's slower going, but I'll probably get through the editing and other aspects of the process quicker than when I didn't know what I was doing!

What advice would you give Māori writers just getting started on their first children's/YA manuscript?

AS I learnt how to write by writing, and I wasn't good when I started. So, if you'd like to give it a go, it's critical to give it a try! Start writing, find places to publish your work, and look out for mentoring and opportunities for editorial feedback. It's called learning on the job, and you can make it happen. There are tertiary studies in creative writing but no straight pathway to finish your first novel. I can tell you that the more you write, the better you'll get.

SK Me maumahara koe, he kākano koe i ruia mai i Rangiātea. You should remember, you are a seed sown in the heavens and born of greatness.

Our stories are unique and have the power to heal the world. We are the vessel and instrument for many untold stories. I draw strength from my tīpuna who were the greatest storytellers.

Also remember what Whaea Toni Morrison once said: 'if there's a book you want to read, but it hasn't been written yet, then you must write it.' For Māori writers, there are many many stories that have not been written yet. Therefore, we must write them! Some of the greatest stories come from a deep yearning. I'm fascinated by where that yearning comes from and what happens when you follow that prompting and draw it out from you until it becomes words and then a story. That yearning will turn into your purpose for writing your manuscript and it is what you need to remember when you feel like giving up. Writing to me will always be a spiritual experience.

Finding a community of writers was also helpful for me as writing can be isolating. I'm grateful for Te Papa Tupu programme and the writers who I met on that programme. It gave me the encouragement and support I needed to carry on with *The Pōrangi Boy.* Also, get your friends and people around you to read your draft so they can give you good, honest feedback.

Writing looks different to everyone. I try to follow the Maramataka and my ikura cycle and write according to the phases. During Whiro and when I have my ikura is when I do some of my heaviest and emotional writing. During the Ovulation phase is when I write my funniest words (or I like to think it is funny). I often write the best when I'm not at my desk but instead outside and going about my day. Something might happen and I'll write it on my notes app. Writing is one hundred per cent about observing people and what they *don't* say. Find what works for you.

Shilo and Ataria, thanks so much for sharing your time and knowledge. Ngā mihi nui.

Biographies

Hana Pera Aoake (Ngaati Mahuta, Ngaati Hinerangi, Waikato-Tainui, Ngaati Waewae) is an artist and writer from Te Wai Pounamu. In 2020 they published their first pukapuka, *A bathful of kawakawa and hot water* with Compound Press. They are the curator at the Sir James Fletcher Kawerau museum and a mum.

Aziembry Aolani (Ngāpuhi / Kānaka Maoli) is an emerging writer and mad gamer. Some of his work can be found in *Turbine | Kapohau* and Anton Blank's *Ora Nui* journal.

Aroha Awarau (Ngāti Maru, Ngāti Porou) is of Māori, Niuean and Samoan descent. Born and raised in Taranaki, he is an acclaimed storyteller who has enjoyed success in playwriting, film writing and journalism. He has won multiple media awards as a writer for *Woman's Weekly, New Zealand Listener* and Māori Television, and has been a finalist in the Adam NZ Play Awards and NZ Scriptwriting Awards. His short films have been shown at festivals in New Zealand and overseas including the ImagineNATIVE Film Festival in Toronto and the Hawai'i International Film Festival.

Hinemoana Baker (Ngāti Raukawa, Ngāti Toa Rangatira, Te Āti Awa, Kāi Tahu) is a poet, musician and performer. She lives in Berlin, Germany, where she is currently completing a PhD in Cultural Studies. Her latest collection of poetry, *Funkhaus* (Te Herenga Waka University Press, 2020), was shortlisted in 2021 for the Ockham New Zealand Book Awards.

Anton Blank works in the public sector, developing strategies to mitigate unconscious bias and its impact on Māori. Anton is also the editor of the Māori literary journal *Ora Nui*.

Marino Blank (Ngāti Porou, Ngāti Kahungunu) is a qualified teacher. She has been published in the Māori literary journal *Ora Nui, Puna Wai Korero* (Auckland University Press, 2014) and *Flash Frontier*. Her first book of poetry, *Crimson*, was published in 2014. Her mother Arapera was a poet and writer, and her father Pius was a photographer.

Shelley Burne-Field (Sāmoa, Ngāti Mutunga, Ngāti Rārua) is a fiction and non-fiction writer from Te Matau-a-Māui. She completed the University of Auckland Master of Creative Writing in 2020 and is a graduate of the Te Papa Tupu writing programme. Her short story 'Speaking in tongues' was named as the only finalist from Aotearoa New Zealand in the Commonwealth Short Story Prize 2022. Shelley's short stories have appeared in print, online and in anthologies around the world. Her short story 'Pinching out Dahlias', which is included in this anthology, is the most read story ever published on *Newsroom*. Her new novel for middle grade readers — a fantasy adventure about kāhu — will be published by Allen & Unwin in 2024.

Jacqueline Carter (also published under Jacq Carter and Jacqs Carter) is Ngāi Tūkairangi of Ngāi Te Rangi on her paternal grandfather's side and Te Patuwai and Ngāi Te Hapū of Ngāti Awa and Waitaha on her paternal grandmother's side. She is also of English, Irish, and Scottish descent through both of these grandparents and her mother. She started writing poetry in her teens while at Epsom Girls' Grammar School, after a visit by Paki Cherrington, and started composing waiata when she was little. Her poetry has been published in various anthologies, including Robert Sullivan, Albert Wendt and Reina Whaitiri (eds.) *Whetū Moana* (Auckland University Press, 2002) and its sequel *Mauri Ola* (Auckland Univesity Press, 2010), as well as all editions of Anton Blank's *Ora Nui*.

Jack Remiel Cottrell (Ngāti Rangi) is an itinerant flash fiction and short story writer with a sideline as a volunteer rugby referee. He also runs workshops teaching the art of flash fiction to students in rural secondary schools. Jack won the 2020 Wallace Foundation Prize for best manuscript, and was shortlisted for a Sir Julius Vogel Award in 2020 and 2022.

Alan Duff was born in Rotorua in 1950. He has written novels, including *Once Were Warriors, One Night Out Stealing* and *What Becomes of the Broken Hearted?*, a novella (*State Ward*), several children's books and a number of non-fiction works. *Once Were Warriors* won the Pen Best First Book of Fiction Award and *What Becomes of the Broken Hearted?* won the Montana New Zealand Book Award for Fiction. Both novels were made into internationally acclaimed films. Duff was the driving force behind the Books in Homes scheme, which, with commercial sponsorship and government support, aims to break the cycle of illiteracy, poverty, anger and violence among underprivileged children by providing books for them to own.

Anaru Eketone belongs to the Ngāti Maniapoto and Waikato iwi and lives in St Leonards, Dunedin, with his wife, Margaret. They have two adult children, Heramaahina and Te Ao Marama.

Amber Esau is a Sā-māo-rish writer (Ngāpuhi, Manase) from Tāmaki Makaurau. She is a poet, storyteller, and professional bots. Her work has been published both in print and online.

Rangi Faith (Kāi Tahu and Ngāti Kahungunu) was born in Timaru to English and Māori parents and brought up in Temuka, South Canterbury. He is retired from teaching schools on the east and west coasts of Te Waipounamu and is currently living and writing in Rangiora. His work explores the history of both European and tangata whenua – and has a keen interest in the resurgence of te reo in Aotearoa. He is widely published in anthologies and publications throughout the motu.

Miriama Gemmell is from Ngāti Pāhauwera, Ngāti Rakaipaaka and Ngāti Kahunugnu ki Te Wairoa. Her poetry has been published in *Awa Wahine*, *Kapohau*, *Landfall* and *Te Whē*. Miriama lives in Te Matau-a-Māui with her hoa rangatira Richard, and tamariki, James Rewi (9) and Hana Tirohia (7). Miriama washes yoghurt pots and feels closer to her tīpuna.

James George is a novelist and short story writer of Ngāpuhi, English and Irish descent. He is author of *Wooden Horses* (Hazard Press, 2000), *Hummingbird*, *Ocean Roads* and *Sleepwalkers Songs* (Huia Publishers, 2003; 2006; 2016). Amongst his awards and prizes, his second novel *Hummingbird* was a finalist in the Montana New Zealand Book Awards 2004, and the Tasmania Pacific Fiction Prize 2005. *Ocean Roads* appeared on the 2007 Commonwealth Writers' Prize Shortlist as one of the Best Books in the Southeast Asia and South Pacific region and was shortlisted in the fiction category of the Montana New Zealand Book Awards 2007. James was also a recipient of the Buddle Findlay Sargeson Fellow in 2007. James teaches creative writing at the Auckland University of Technology, on both the Bachelor of Arts and Master of Creative Writing programmes. He is currently working on his fifth novel, *Two Rivers*.

Anahera Gildea (Ngāti Tukorehe) is a poet, short story writer, essayist and 'artivist'. Her first book *Poroporoaki to the Lord My God: Weaving the Via Dolorosa* **was** published by Seraph Press in 2016 and her collection, *Sedition* was published by Taraheke | Bushlawyer in 2022. She is the co-editor of the bilingual literary journal *Te Whē*, holds an Master of Arts in Creative Writing from the International Institute of Modern Letters, Graduate Diplomas in Psychology and Teaching, and is completing doctoral research at Te Herenga Waka—Victoria University of Wellington, developing critical literary theory based on Māori intellectual traditions.

Patricia Grace (Ngāti Toa, Ngāti Raukawa and Te Ati Awa) is one of New Zealand's most celebrated writers. She has published over 35 titles, including novels, short-story collections, works of non-fiction and books for children, a number of which have been translated into te reo Māori. Among numerous awards, she won the Goodman Fielder Wattie Book Awards in 1986 for the much-loved *Potiki*, which also won the New Zealand Fiction Award in 1987. She was longlisted for the Booker Prize in 2001 with *Dogside Story*, which won the Kiriyama Pacific Rim Fiction Prize. *Tu* won the 2005 Montana New Zealand Book Awards Fiction Prize and the Deutz Medal for Fiction and Poetry. Her children's story *The Kuia and the Spider* won the Children's Picture Book of the Year and she has also won the New Zealand Book Awards For Children and Young Adults Te Kura Pounamu Award. Patricia was born in Wellington and lives in Plimmerton on ancestral land, in close proximity to her home marae at Hongoeka Bay.

Mihi ki te Atua
Mihi ki te Kingi
Mihi ki nga Aitua
Mihi ki a koutou, tēnā koutou, tēnā koutou, tēnā koutou katoa
Ko Hapuakohe tōku maunga
Ko Mangawara tōku awa
Ko Tainui tōku waka
Ko Ngati Pāoa tōku iwi
Ko Ngati Pāoa tōku hapū
Ko Waiti tōku marae
Nō Te Hoe-o-Tainui ahau
Kei Rahui Pokeka ahau e noho ana
Ko **K-T Harrison** tōku ingoa
Tēnā koutou, tēnā koutou, tēnā tātou katoa.

Cassie Hart (aka *J.C. Hart* and *Nova Blake*) is a Māori (Kāi Tahu, Makaawhio) writer of speculative fiction. She has published over ten novels and novellas and has had her work printed in various anthologies. She also co-edited and contributed to the Sir Julius Vogel winning benefit anthology *Tales for Canterbury*, has been a finalist for the Sir Julius Vogel awards many times and won it in 2022 with her novel *Butcherbird*. In addition, she has been a finalist for short fiction for the Australian Shadow Awards and in 2021 she was a Hugo finalist for Best Related Work and Best Collected Work. She lives with her husband, three children, and assortment of animals in Taranaki.

Nicole Titihuia Hawkins (Ngāti Kahungunu ki Te Wairoa, Ngāti Pāhauwera) is a writer, home-baker, red lipstick enthusiast, aunty and proud māmā. She teaches high school English and Tikanga a-Iwi and runs side hustles with her besties in her spare time. Her collection *Whai* (Tender Press, 2021) won the Jessie Mackay Prize for best first book of poetry at the 2022 Ockham New Zealand Book Awards.

Hāora Hema (Ngāti Kahungunu ki Te Wairoa) grew up in Wairoa and moved to Australia in his teens. From a young age Hāora has been hyper-aware of the racism and inequalities that exist in Aotearoa. After a career as a teacher, Hāora is now working in the public service to develop Māori-Crown relations capability. Hāora lives in Te Whangaui-a-Tara with his two children Irirangi and Rohan.

Whiti Hereaka is an award-winning novelist and playwright of Ngāti Tūwharetoa, Te Arawa, Ngāti Whakaue, Tuhourangi, Ngāti Tumatawera, Tainui and Pākehā descent, based in Wellington. She holds a Master of Creative Writing (Scriptwriting) from the International Institute of Modern Letters. She is the author of four novels with Huia Publishers: *The Graphologist's Apprentice* (2010), and the award-winning YA novels *Bugs* (2013), *Legacy* and *Kurangaituku* (2021). *Legacy* won the New Zealand Children's and Young Adult Book Award for YA fiction in 2019 and *Kurangaituku* was awarded the 2022 Jann Medlicott Acorn Award for fiction in the Ockham New Zealand Book Awards and was long-listed for the Dublin Literary Award 2023. She is also co-editor, with Witi Ihimaera, of an anthology of Māori myths, *Pūrākau* (Vintage, 2019). Whiti has been involved with Te Papa Tupu, an incubator programme for Māori writers, as a writer, a mentor and a judge. She also sits on the boards of the Māori Literature Trust, the Michael King Writers Centre and Playmarket NZ.

Emma Hislop (Kāi Tahu) lives in Taranaki. Her debut collection of short fiction, titled *Ruin and Other Stories*, was published with Te Herenga Waka University Press in March 2023. She is currently working on her first novel.

Nadine Anne Hura (Ngāti Hine, Ngāpuhi) is a creative non-fiction essayist and zine-maker based in Porirua. Her writing weaves themes of language, identity, equity and climate justice, and can be found online and in print in a number of publications. She is a regular columnist for *The Spinoff Ātea*, an active member of Te Hā o Ngā Pou Kaituhi Māori, and is passionate about grassroots Māori writing and collective publishing.

Rangimiria Ihakara (Ngāti Pikiao, Ngāti Tuwharetoa, Ngāti Konohi, Ngāti Kurī) is a short story writer with a passion for writing about te ao Māori. With mentorship from Ataria Sharman she published her story 'Kua Ngū' in *Tupuranga*'s second issue *Lua: A Whole New World*.

Witi Ihimaera (Te Whanau a Kai, Te Aitanga a Mahaki, Rongowhakaata, Ngāti Porou) is an Indigenous author and anthologist. His recent work includes the 50th Anniversary edition of *Tangi*, *A Kind of Shelter: An Anthology of New Writing for a Changed World* (co-edited with Michelle Elvy), *Pounamu, Pounamu* (te reo edition) and *Witi's Wahine* (written by Nancy Brunning) in an acclaimed three-week season at the Auckland

Theatre Company. He recently embarked on a 50th Anniversary tour to Australia (Brisbane Writers Festival), Sweden and Finland (NZ Studies Association), Germany (Eine Unl-Ein Buch "Big Read" of The Whale Rider), Canada (Presence Autochtone Indigenous Film Festival), USA (International Congress of Children's Literature) and will shortly tour France and French Polynesia where four of his novels have French editions. His novel *White Lies* is soon to appear in an Amharic Semitic language edition. He is taking next year off to learn te reo at Te Wananga Takiura, Auckland.

Teoti Jardine (Waitaha, Kāti Mamoe, Kai Tahu, Irish and Scottish) attended Hagley Writers Institute in 2011. His poetry has been published in *London Grip*, *Te Karaka*, *Te Rūnaka*, *Ora Nui*, and *Catalyst*. His short stories have appeared in *Flash Frontier*. He lives with his dog Amie in Riverton Aparima, New Zealand.

Hinemoa Jones is of Māori (Te Arawa, Tainui) and Pākehā descent. She is a storyteller, writer, educator and facilitator of wānanga and the traditions of the whare tapere: Māori games, raranga, and karetao (Māori puppetry). Hinemoa has worked alongside James Webster in the revival process of karetao Māori and has performed nationally and internationally.

Kelly Joseph (Ngāti Maniapoto) is a writer and artist currently living in Kirikiriroa with her daughters. Her work has been included in anthologies such as *Huia Short Stories, Black Marks on the White Page* (Vintage, 2017) and *Pūrākau: Māori Myths Retold by Māori Writers* (Vintage, 2019). She has had stories broadcast on national radio, written poetry for the *School Journal*, and published essays on contemporary Māori art. Kelly was a Tau mai e Kāpiti Māori Writer in Residence, as well as a recipient of an Emerging Māori Writers Residency at the Michael King Writers Centre.

J. Wiremu Kane (Ngāpuhi, Ngāti Toro, Ngāti Manu, Te Māhurehure) (he/him/ia) lives and writes on the unceded ancestral lands of Ngāti Hei. He was the 2022 Emerging Māori Writer in Residence at the International Institute of Modern Letters, and winner of the 2022 Surrey Hotel Writers Residency. He has been widely published in print and online including *Middle Distance: Long Stories of Aotearoa New Zealand* (Te Herenga Waka University Press, 2021), *Landfall*, *Mayhem*, *New Zealand Listener*, *School Journal*, *Newsroom*, and *bad apple*. He likes to put words together in ways he's been told not to, and aims to make colonists regret forcing the English language on him.

Ben Kemp works as a primary school teacher in Canberra. He also worked as a teacher in Papua New Guinea for the three years with his diplomat wife and three children. Gisborne-born Kemp arrived in Australia after living ten years in Japan. Tokyo was where he discovered his passion for Kabuki theatre and Japanese film and literature. Between 2003 and 2010 he recorded three studio albums with his band Uminari and toured in Japan, Australia and New Zealand. His artistic work has often explored the nexus between Japanese and Māori/Polynesian culture. He credits the late Taupo-based Māori writer and mentor Rowley Habib with helping him tap into poetry and original writing in his twenties.

Raina Kingsley (née Tutaki) is of Ngāi Tahu, Ngāti Momoe, Ngāti Kahungunu and Rangitāne descent. She lives in Christchurch with her husband. She has had poems published in the *Poetry New Zealand Yearbook*, *Leaving the Red Zone* and *Catalyst*.

Shilo Kino (Ngāpuhi, Waikato-Tainui) is a reporter and writer. She released her debut novel *The Pōrangi Boy* with Huia Publishers in 2020 and undertook a year-long full immersion journey at Te Wānanga Takiura. She writes about social issues, justice and identity. Twitter: @shilokino

Hinewirangi Kohu-Morgan (Ngāti Porou, Ngāti Kahungungu ki Nūhaka, Ngāti Ranginui ki Tauranga Moana) was an artist, poet, healer and taonga pūoro practioner. She taught in New Zealand and abroad, conducting workshops on all aspects of Māori philosophies of mental, physical, and spiritual wellbeing. Hinewirangi was a Board Member of the International Indian Treaty Council and a Representative for the Nuclear Free and Independent Pacific movement. On 15 February 2023 Hinewirangi passed away peacefully, surrounded by her whānau.

Kahu Kutia (Ngāi Tūhoe) (she/her/they) is a haututū storyteller and writer currently based in Te Whanganui-a-Tara. She is also an artist and maker with Kauae Raro Research Collective. Much of her work is informed by an upbringing in Waimana, amongst her people and within matemateāone. Her work explores themes of whakapapa, intergenerational vision, climate change, colonisation and takatāpuitanga from a contemporary Māori world view.

Arihia Latham (Kāi Tahu, Kāti Māmoe, Waitaha) is a writer, creative, and rongoā practitioner. Her poetry collection *Birdspeak* was published by Anahera Press in 2023 and her short stories, essays and poetry have been published and anthologised widely. She was an arts columnist for the *Dominion Post* and presents often at arts and writers festivals. She lives with her whānau in Te Whanganui-a-Tara.

Colleen Maria Lenihan (Te Rarawa, Ngāpuhi) is a fiction and TV writer. Her first book *Kōhine*, a collection of short stories, was published by Huia Publishers in 2022 and received rave reviews. Colleen has been awarded several residencies: Michael King Writers' Centre Emerging Māori Writer 2019; Surrey Hotel Winner 2019; Dan Davin Literary Foundation Residency for a Short Story Writer 2019, and Te Herenga Waka—Victoria University of Wellington International Institute of Modern Letters Emerging Māori Writer 2023.

Tina Makereti (Te Ātiawa, Ngāti Tūwharetoa, Ngāti Rangatahi-Matakore) is author of *The Imaginary Lives of James Pōneke* (Vintage, 2018) and co-editor of *Black Marks on the White Page* (Vintage, 2017), an anthology that celebrates Māori and Pasifika writing. In 2016 her story 'Black Milk' won the Commonwealth Writers Short Story Prize, Pacific region. Her first novel *Where the Rēkohu Bone Sings* (Vintage, 2014) won the 2014 Ngā Kupu Ora Aotearoa Māori Book Award for Fiction, also won by her short story collection, *Once Upon a Time in Aotearoa* (Huia Publishers, 2010). In 2022, while she was an Ursula Bethell Writer in Residence, she won the Landfall Essay Competition. She convenes one of the MA creative writing workshops at Te Herenga Waka Victoria University of Wellington.

Steph Matuku (Ngāti Mutunga, Ngāti Tama, Te Ātiawa) writes stories for the page, stage and screen. Her junior fiction book *Whetū Toa and the Magician* and picture book *The Eight Gifts of Te Wheke* (Huia Publishers, 2018, 2021) were both finalists at the New Zealand Book Awards for Children and Young Adults. Steph likes coffee and zombie movies, and has two children who inspire her every day.

Ana McAllister is a kiritea Māori whose iwi are Te Aitanga-a-Māhaki and Ngāti Porou. She also has ancestry to England, Ireland, Scotland and Poland. Ana is a 'sometimes writer', reformed artist and always tutū. She has been called an 'elite Māori' by her adversaries and a mana wahine by her friends.

Kay McKenzie Cooke (Kāti Māmoe, Kāi Tahu) lives and writes in Ōtepoti Dunedin. She has had four books of poetry published. Her book, *Feeding The Dogs* (Otago University Press, 2002) won Best First Book of Poetry, 2003. She has independently published two novels, both set in Murihiku Southland. Born in Western Murihiku Southland to parents of Māori, Scottish, English and Irish ancestry, much of her writing reflects the landscape and stories of her birthplace and heritage.

Donna McLeod (Te Ātiawa) lives on McLeod Bennett papakāinga in Motueka. As mana whenua her life is about kaitiakitanga and telling the stories of her people. She is a poet, a playwright, a writer, a creative and a strong advocate of Māori art. As a member of Te Oro Hā, she has told stories of Parihaka for 20 years, Matariki, unveiling for those who passed during Covid and is currently working on Te Ramaroa and Nelson Tenths' for Nelson Arts Festival. She is a past member of Te Ohu Whakaari, has been published in several anthologies and on the day her poem 'Ihumatao' was published in *The Spinoff*, Donna was there to tautoko the protest with her daughter and mokopuna.

Atakohu Middleton (Ngāti Māhanga) is an Auckland-based journalist who has worked for national and international print media, including *Mana, New Zealand Herald, New Zealand Listener, Sunday Star-Times* and, in England, *Guardian*. She is now communications adviser to a family infrastructure company, Middleton Group, and a Māori-language reporter for Radio Waatea. Middleton holds a PhD in Māori journalism practise from the Auckland University of Technology, and her doctoral dissertation was the basis of her first book, *Kia Hiwa Rā! Māori Journalism in Aotearoa New Zealand* (2023).

Kelly Ana Morey (Ngāti Kurī, Te Rarawa, Te Aupōuri) is an award-winning writer of both fiction and non-fiction. Her first novel *Bloom* (Penguin, 2003) won the Hubert Church Prize for Fiction at the 2004 Montana New Zealand Book Awards; her second, *Grace is Gone* (Penguin, 2004), was a finalist in the 2005 Kiriyama Prize. Morey's most recent novel, *Daylight Second* (Penguin, 2016), was a finalist in the NZSA Heritage Awards and the Ngā Kupu Ora Māori Book Awards in 2017. Morey wrote *Service from the Sea*, the Royal New Zealand Navy's history, during her tenure as oral historian at the RNZN Museum. Morey's poetry has appeared in *Whetu Moana: Contemporary Poetry in English* (Auckland University Press, 2002) and as part of Phantom Billstickers Poetry Poster Series. Her short fiction has been published in numerous anthologies, including *Huia Short Stories* (1997 and 2001); *Black Marks on the White Page* (Vintage, 2017); and *Pūrākau: Māori Myths Retold by Māori Writers* (Vintage, 2019).

Paula Morris MNZM (Ngāti Wai, Ngāti Manuhiri, Ngāti Whātua) is a novelist, short story writer, editor and essayist from Auckland. Much of her work explores issues of race, diaspora and displacement, and cities around the world as locations of transformation and transgression. An Associate Professor at the University of Auckland, where she directs the Master of Creative Writing, Paula is the founder of the Academy of New Zealand Literature; Wharerangi, the online Māori literature hub; and the Aotearoa New Zealand Review of Books.

Born and raised in Pātea, **Airana Ngarewa** (Ngāti Ruanui, Ngārauru, Ngāruahine) writes about Māori affairs for *The Spinoff*. His writing has also been published in *Radio New Zealand, New Zealand Herald, Newsroom*

and *Landfall*. He won the short story and poetry competitions at the Ronald Hugh Morrieson Literary Awards in 2022. His debut novel, *The Bone Tree*, was released by Moa Press in August 2023.
E kore e kā te rākau rewarewa
E kore e kā te ngākau Ngarewa

Zeb Tamihana Nicklin (Ngāti Pāhauwera, Ngā Tokorima a Hinemanuhiri, Ngāi Tūhoe, Ngāi Tāmanuhiri, Rangitāne) has been teaching te reo Māori for 17 years. He is a licensed translator under the Māori Language Commission and an award-winning short story writer in te reo Māori with Huia Publishers.

Kōtuku Titihuia Nuttall (Te Ātiawa, Ngāti Tūwharetoa, _WSÁNEĆ) is a PhD student at the International Institute of Modern Letters. Her first book, *Tauhou,* was published by Te Herenga Waka University Press in 2022 and in Canada by House of Anansi Press in 2023. She won the 2020 Adam Foundation Prize and was runner-up in the 2021 Surrey Hotel–*Newsroom* writer's residency award. She lives on the Kāpiti Coast of Aotearoa New Zealand.

Michael O'Leary was born in Auckland in 1950 and is from Te Arawa and Irish ancestors. He is a novelist, poet, artist, and publisher, having published over 200 titles of Aotearoa New Zealand literary works. His own writing includes six novels, most recently *Apocrypha Scripta*, in 2021, and ten volumes of poetry, most recently *The Ballad of the Triple Track* with HeadworX in 2022. His writing has been published in anthologies and his artwork has been shown in galleries. He has a BA in English from the University of Otago, and an MA in English from Te Herenga Waka—Victoria University of Wellington for which he wrote a thesis on *Alternative Small Press Publishing in New Zealand*, which was published as a book by Steele Roberts in 2002. O'Leary has owned several bookshops, the latest of which is Kakariki Books, situated at the Paekakariki Railway Station. He lives in Paekakariki, for which town he has written six books of local history, the latest published in 2023.

Tru Paraha is a performance writer and poet based in Auckland, with whakapapa ties to Ngāti Hineāmaru, Ngāti Kahu o Torongare, and Israel/Palestine. She has a PhD with Creative Practice from the University of Auckland and is a lecturer in the English Department. Her interests and teaching specialty include transcultural writing, ecopoetry, and Aotearoa literature. Tru's poetry has appeared in numerous forms, including sound recordings, theatre, print, galleries, and online literary journals and magazines. Her recent collection, 'in my darkling universe', features in *AUP New Poets 8* (Auckland University Press, 2021).

Kiri Piahana-Wong was born in Taumaranui. Her Chinese grandfather emigrated to New Zealand from Maktin Village, Guangdong, China in the early 1930s. He met Kiri's Māori grandmother working in market gardens in Tauranga. She was the daughter of paramount chief, Te Hare Piahana (Ngāti Ranginui). After their marriage, Kiri's grandparents moved to Auckland. Kiri's father was the eldest son of nine children; her mother is NZ-born of English heritage. Kiri is a poet and editor, and she is the publisher at Anahera Press. Her poems have appeared in over forty journals and anthologies, most recently in *A Clear Dawn: New Asian Voices from Aotearoa New Zealand (Auckland University Press, 2021), A Kind of Shelter Whakaruru-taha (*Massey University Press, 2023), and *Vā: Stories by Women of the Moana (Tatou Publishing, 2022).* Her first poetry collection, *Night Swimming*, was released in 2013; a second book, *Give Me An Ordinary Day*, is due out soon. Kiri lives in Whanganui with her family.

J.P. Pomare (Ngāpuhi) is an award-winning and bestselling author whose debut novel, *Call Me Evie* (Hachette, 2018), won the Ngaio Marsh Award for Best First Novel. *In the Clearing* and *The Last Guests* (Hachette, 2019; 2021) were critically acclaimed bestsellers, with *In the Clearing* now a Disney+ Original Series. *Tell Me Lies* (Hachette, 2020) was a #1 Audible bestseller and was shortlisted for the Ngaio Marsh Award for Best Novel and the Ned Kelly Award for Best Crime Fiction and his fifth book, *The Wrong Woman* was an international best seller and *Home Before Night* (Hachette, 2022; 2023) is his sixth novel and was first published as an Audible Original. J.P. was born in Rotorua, and now resides in Melbourne with his wife and daughter.

Brian Potiki has published work including *Aotearoa: poems & songs* (Steele Roberts, 2003); *Te Wai Pounamu, your music remembers me: 4 South Island history plays* (Steele Roberts, 2007); *Hey Maori people: radical Maori theatre in the 1980s* (2010); and *Exile on Tombleson Rd* (Blurry Lines, 2021).

Jessie Puru (Ngāti Te Ata, Tainui, Ngāpuhi) is a mother, poet, and writer. Her poetry has been published in Aotearoa and the USA. In 2019, Jessie was runner up for the Emerging Poets Competition. She has a Bachelor of Creative Arts from the Manukau Institute of Technology and a Master of Creative Writing from Auckland University of Technology, where she was the 2019 recipient of the Copyright Licensing NZ Master of Creative Writing Scholarship.

essa may ranapiri (Ngaati Raukawa, Te Arawa, Ngaati Puukeko, Clan Gunn, Horwood) is a person who lives on Ngaati Wairere whenua. They are the author of *ransack* and *ECHIDNA* (Te Herenga Waka University

Press, 2019; 2022) and a PhD student looking at how poetry by taangata takataapui enhances our understanding of atuatanga. They are also a co-editor of *Kupu Toi Takataapui / Takataapui Literary Journal* with Michelle Rahurahu. They have a great love for language, Land Back and hot chips. Thanks as always goes to their ancestors, who are everything. They will write until they're dead.

Frazer Rangihuna (Ngāti Porou): The first person to tell me I had the knack for anything good was the wonderful Mr Reynolds, my fifth-form English teacher, who wrote in my school report: 'Frazer has a distinct gift as a writer. If only he wasn't so easily distracted.' And after 30-something more years of distraction, I'm up to the 75,000th word in my first novel. I have degrees, just not in creative writing. I'm self-taught with three published works. My story 'Piro', included in this anthology, was the winner of the *Sunday Star Times* Short Story Competition in 2017. My other works are 'The Dance' and 'Īhe & Her'. I live in Auckland with my dear partner Tim and I'm a professional teaching fellow in mental health nursing at the University of Auckland.

Vaughan Rapatahana (Te Ātiawa, Ngāti Te Whiti) commutes between homes in Hong Kong, Philippines, and Aotearoa New Zealand. He is widely published across several genre in both his main languages, te reo Māori and English and his work has been translated into Bahasa Malaysia, Italian, French, Mandarin, Romanian, Spanish. He is the author and editor/co-editor of well over 40 books.

He earned a PhD from the University of Auckland with a thesis about Colin Wilson and writes and lectures extensively about Wilson. More, Rapatahana is a critic of the agencies of English language proliferation and the consequent decimation of indigenous tongues, inaugurating and co-editing *English language as Hydra* and *Why English? Confronting the Hydra* (Multilingual Matters, 2012; 2016) and several academic papers accordingly.

He is a poet, with nine collections published in Hong Kong SAR; Macau; Philippines; USA; England; France, India, Australia, and Aotearoa New Zealand. *Atonement* (UST Press, 2015) was nominated for a National Book Award in Philippines in 2016; he won the inaugural Proverse Poetry Prize the same year; and was included in *Best New Zealand Poems* (2017). He also writes short fiction and has had two novels published.

Rapatahana is one of the few World authors who consistently writes in and is published in te reo Māori. It is his mission to continue to do so and to push for a far wider recognition of the need to write and to be published in this tongue. His latest poetry collection is written exclusively in te reo Māori (with English language 'translations') is titled *te pāhikahikatanga/incommensurability* and was published by Flying Islands Books in Australia, 2023.

Reihana Robinson (he tamaiti whāngai) is a writer, artist, and environmental researcher. Her first poetry selection is part of *AUP New Poets 3* (Auckland University Press, 2008). *Auē Rona* (Steele Roberts, 2012) and *Her Limitless Her* (Makāro Press, 2018) are her first two poetry collections. She received the inaugural Te Atairangikaahu Poetry Award. She lives near Moehau.

Te Kahu Rolleston (Ngāi Te Rangi) is a poet, spoken word performer, actor and battle rap artist. In 2014 he won the National Poetry Slam Competition. Te Kahu is an alumnus of the Banff Centre's Indigenous Writing Programme and hosted the 2021 E Tū Whānau Spoken Word Competition.

Tania Roxborogh (Ngāti Porou) is a veteran secondary English teacher and award-winning author. She is passionate about teaching, books, Shakespeare, training her dog, and learning te reo Māori. These things influence her writing and research even though she has to work hard to make progress at them.

Ataria Sharman (Ngāpuhi, Tapuika) is a writer and editor. Ataria holds a Master of Arts, and her research focused on mana wahine and the atua wāhine. Her novel, *Hine and the Tohunga Portal*, was published by Huia in 2021 and a finalist in the 2022 New Zealand Book Awards for Children and Young Adults. She is the creator of Awa Wahine, a platform dedicated to celebrating and promoting the voices of wāhine Māori. Formerly, she was the editor of *The Pantograph Punch.*

Shirley Simmonds is a mother of two young sons, Tamihana and Raukawa, and is dedicated to raising them with the language and values of their ancestors. As a health researcher, much of her writing is technical, therefore she revels in the opportunity to write creative pieces and finds this writing practice a way to make sense of the world. When not at her computer, Shirley can be found in the garden, at the marae, exploring new places, or creating in the kitchen.

Carin Smeaton lives in Tāmaki Makaurau. She is proud to have both Māori and Moana connections through Muaūpoko and Safune. Her first book *Tales of the Waihorotiu* was published by Titus in 2017. She is still trying to write the second while raising her teenage boys and working at a research library in the city.

Ruby Solly (Waitaha, Kāi Tahu, Kāti Māmoe) is a writer, musician and taonga pūoro practitioner living in Pōneke. She has been published and exhibited around Aotearoa as well as in the USA, Antarctica and Europe. Her first book *Tōku Pāpā*, a mihi to her Kāi Tahu whakapapa, was published by Te Herenga Waka University Press in 2021. Her second book, *The Artist*, a poem novel about southern Māori cave art, was released in May 2023.

Robert Sullivan (Ngāpuhi Nui Tonu, Kāi Tahu) is an academic, editor, former librarian and award-winning poet. Since the 1990s he has authored several critically recieved collections of poetry including, most recently, *Tūnui | Coment* (Auckland University Press, 2022) and co-edited the Auckland Univerty Press collections *Whetu Moana*, *Mauri Ola* and *Puna Wai Kōrero* (2002, 2010, 2014). Robert is currently an Associate Professor in Creative Writing at Massey University and previously worked as an academic at the University of Hawaiʻi and the Manukau Institute of Technology.

Ariana Sutton is of Waitaha, Kati Mamoe, Kāi Tahu and European descent and comes from Murihiku Southland. Home and whakapapa have often inspired her work. Global handshakes and the hierarchies of bats find home in her poems, too. First published in Melbourne's *Work and Tumble*, her writing feature in several journals and anthologies throughout Aotearoa. In 2020 she won the Dan Davin Adult Poetry Prize and is currently completing her first collection. Ariana is a Māori healing clinician by day currently residing in the Tairāwhiti East Coast with her partner and son.

Alice Tawhai is the pen-name of the author of three collections of short stories and a novel. She avoids photography, biography and all forms of personal advertisement.

Apirana Taylor is a nationally and internationally published poet, playwright, short story writer and novelist. He's been Writer in Residence at the University of Canterbury and Massey University. He tours globally presenting his poetry and taking creative writing workshops. He's written and published poetry, plays, short stories and novels and his work is included in many anthologies. His work is studied nationally and internationally. He tours schools, tertiary institutions, universities, marae, galleries and prisons throughout the country reading his poetry.

Stacey Teague (Ngāti Maniapoto, Ngāpuhi) is a writer, editor, and teacher living in Te Whanganui-a-Tara. She is a publisher at Tender Press and has a Master of Arts in Creative Writing from the International Institute of Modern Letters. She has one book, *Takahē* (Scrambler Books, 2014) and two chapbooks, *not a casual solitude* (Ghost City Press, 2017) and *hoki mai* (If A Leaf Falls Press, 2020).

Gerry Te Kapa Coates is a published author and has been a consulting engineer with decision-making, governance and directorship experience. He has expert knowledge in sustainability and renewable energy issues and technology and has also been the Managing Director of his own consultancy firm. His writing experience includes work on the Ngāi Tahu claim in 1978–79 and much work for Ngāi Tahu and the EPA.

kani te manukura (Ngāi Tūhoe) is a hunter/gatherer/grower/cook/storyteller. He lives a life of quiet rebellion in a small seaside town. This is both better and worse than it sounds. kani also finds writing about himself in the third person quite odd.

Alice Te Punga Somerville (Te Āti Awa, Taranaki) is a scholar, poet and irredentist. She writes and teaches at the intersections of literary studies, Indigenous studies and Pacific studies; she is a professor at the University of British Columbia in the Department of English language & literatures, and the Institute for Critical Indigenous Studies. Her publications include *Once Were Pacific: Māori Connections to Oceania* (University of Minnesota Press, 2012), *250 Ways To Start an Essay about Captain Cook* (Bridget Williams Books, 2020) and a book of poetry *Always Italicise: how to write while colonised* (Auckland University Press, 2022).

Anne-Marie Te Whiu is a Māori-Australian writer, weaver, facilitator, editor, cultural producer and festival director. She was a 2021 Next Chapter Fellowship recipient, and her writing has been shared broadly both in Australia and in Aotearoa New Zealand. Her two debut poetry collections, titled *Mettle* and *These Are The Bodies I Have Found,* will be published with Taraheke | Bushlawyer.

Tayi Tibble (Te Whānau-ā-Apanui, Ngāti Porou) is a writer from Te Whanganui-a-Tara. She is the author of two books *Poukahangtus* (THWUP, 2018; Knopf, 2022; Penguin UK, 2022) and *Rangikura* (THWUP, 2021; Knopf, 2024; Penguin UK, 2024). She works as a publicist at Te Herenga Waka University Press.

Ariana Tikao (Kāi Tahu) is an artist of the sound and word variety. Her practice is often inspired by kōrero relating to her tīpuna. Her first book *Mokorua* was published by Auckland University Press in 2022, and her second book *Te Rā: The Māori Sail* (illustrated by Mat Tait) was published in July 2023 by the Christchurch Art Gallery. She has a Master of Arts in Creative Writing from the IIML, and has been published in *Takahē, Swamp, Turbine | Kapohau, Awa Wahine,* and a chapter in *Bill Hammond: Across the Evening Sky* (Christchurch Art Gallery, 2021). She is an Ursula Bethell Writer in Residence at the University of Canterbury in 2023 and is a New Zealand Arts Foundation Laureate.

Kahu Tumai descends from Waikato-Tainui iwi. She is a māmā based in Ōtautahi Christchurch originally from Whangārei. Her writing is a confluence of mana wāhine/takatāpui, queer intersectional feminism, and her passion for community centred work. Mentored by Tusiata Avia, her writing has been published in *The Pantograph Punch*, *Tupuranga*, *FIKA Mai Le Moana* and *Mayhem*.

Peta-Maria Tunui (Ngāti Kahu, Ngātikahu ki Whangaroa) is a writer and creative who weaves words to form the shapes of her world – the connections, strength, surprises and frayed edges. This poem was her first foray into poetry film under the mentorship of Charles Olsen and Lilian Pallares and the resulting product was screened at festivals around the world. Peta-Maria is married to the handsome, patient Ihaka and she is māmā to a curious cheeky whirlwind – Tākiri.

Anne Waapu is a mokopuna of Rongomaiwahine, Ngāti Hinemanu, Te Āti Haunui-a-Pāpārangi and Ngāti Kahungunu. Living in the sovereign lands of Te Āti Awa, Ngāti Toa Rangatira and Raukawa ki te Tonga, Anne is a haututū who loves to give things a go. A kaupapa Māori researcher and justness advocate (IYKYK), Anne is focused on the transformation of New Zealand's colonial justice system and so is interested in constitutional transformation, prison abolition and healing historical and intergenerational trauma. A kaitautoko of related kaupapa, Anne is also a tauira of Ahunga Tikanga at Te Wānanga o Raukawa and first had her writing published in *Te Whē*.

Fabian Waenga Ki runga i te taha o Pāpā nō Te Tai Rawhiti ahau. Ko Te Whānau a Apanui tōku iwi. Ki runga i te taha o Māmā nō Te Tai Tokerau ahau. Ko Ngā Puhi tōku iwi.

Arielle Walker (Taranaki, Ngāruahine, Ngāpuhi, Pākehā) is a Tāmaki Makaurau-based artist, writer, and maker. Her practice seeks pathways towards reciprocal belonging through tactile storytelling and ancestral narratives, weaving in the spaces between. Her first chapbook, '*river poems*', was recently published as part of *AUP New Poets 9* (Auckland University Press, 2023), and her writing can be also found in *Tupuranga*, *Sweet Mammalian*, *Turbine | Kapohau*, *Oscen: Myths*, and *No Other Place to Stand: An Anthology of Climate Change Poetry from Aotearoa New Zealand* (Auckland University Press, 2022).

Iona Winter (Waitaha) is a widely published poet and short fiction writer. She was the 2022 CLNZ/NZSA Writers' Award recipient for *A Counter of Moons*, a creative non-fiction project addressing the complexities of being suicide bereaved. In 2023, Iona launched Elixir & Star Press, a dedicated space for the expression of grief in Aotearoa New Zealand.

Poet, fiction writer and essayist **Briar Wood** (Ngāpuhi Nui Tonu) grew up in South Auckland, Aotearoa. She worked extensively as a lecturer in Britain and teaching writing in Aotearoa New Zealand. Her poetry collection, *Rāwāhi* (Anahera Press, 2017), was shortlisted in the 2018 Ockham New Zealand Book Awards. *A Book of Rongo and Te Rangahau* was published by Anahera Press in 2022.

Credits

Hana Pera Aoake, 'My body is made from many' published in *Mai i te poo ki te ao maarama,* Kei Te Pai Press, 2021

Aziembry Aolani, 'Parking Warden' published in *Turbine | Kapohau*, International Institute of Modern Letters, 2020

Aroha Awarau, 'The African Stars' published in *Huia Short Stories 12*, Huia Publishers, 2017

Hinemoana Baker, 'He Kanohi Kitea' and 'December' from *Funkhaus*, Te Herenga Waka University Press, 2021

'He Kanohi Kitea' features a well-known Māori kīwaha, 'December' was first published as a poetry poster by Phantom Billstickers

Anton Blank, 'Kai' published in *Flash Frontier*, August 2021: KAI, 2021

Marino Blank, 'Tūrangawaewae' published in *Flash Frontier*, May 2020: WATER, 2020

'Porotaka Circle' published in *Ora Nui 4,* Oranui Press, 2021

Shelley Burne-Field, 'Pinching out Dahlias', *Newsroom*, 17/7/2021

Jacqueline Carter, 'Our tūpuna remain' published in *Te Rito o te Harakeke – A collection of writing for Ihumātao*, Rangatahi o te Pene, 2019

Jack Remiel Cottrell, 'Reasons why I called in sick rather than go to the mihi whakatau for new employees last Friday' from *Ten Acceptable Acts of Arson*, Canterbury University Press, 2021

Anaru Eketone, 'Go back to the pā' published in *Ko Aotearoa Tātou: We Are New Zealand*, Otago University Press, 2020

Amber Esau, 'A poem (,) of course' published in *Poetry New Zealand Yearbook 2022*, Massey University Press, 2022

Miriama Gemmell, 'Family Tree' published in *Landfall* 238, Massey University Press, 2019

'gimme a bone' published in *saltwater love,* https://saltwaterlove.weebly.com, 2020

James George, 'Whenua to Whenua' published in *Scorchers: A Climate Fiction Anthology*, Eunoia Publishing, 2020

Anahera Gildea, 'Black Shroud' published in *i got you, babe*, Taraheke | Bushlawyer, 2021

'Speaking Rights' published in *Manifesto Aotearoa: 101 Political Poems*, Otago University Press, 2017

K-T Harrison, 'The Last Summer' published in *Stories on the Four Winds: Ngā Hau e Whā*, Huia Publishers, 2016

Nicole Titihuia Hawkins, 'Titihuia's Moko' and 'Tuia' from *Whai*, Tender Press, 2021

Hāora Hema, 'The Whitests of Nan's Mokos' published in *Ora Nui* 4, Oranui Press, 2021

Whiti Hereaka, 'Papatūānuku' published in *Pūrakau: Māori Myths Retold by Māori Writers*, Vintage, 2019

Emma Hislop, 'Cure', excerpt from forthcoming novel

Nadine Anne Hura, 'The Garage Party' published in *Sport* 47, Te Herenga Waka University Press, 2019

Rangimiria Ihakara, 'Kua Ngū' published in *Tupuranga Lua: A Whole New World*, 2020

Witi Ihimaera, 'Tāwhaki' published in *Scorchers: A Climate Fiction Anthology*, Eunoia Publishing, 2020

Teoti Jardine, 'Kuihi' published in *Ora Nui* 3, Oranui Press, 2017

Hinemoa Jones, 'Kaikaranga' published in *Ora Nui 4,* Oranui Press, 2021

Kelly Joseph, 'Obsidian Dream' published in *Ora Nui 4,* Oranui Press, 2021

Ben Kemp, 'Kūmara' published in *AUP New Poets 6,* Auckland University Press, 2020

Raina Kingsley, 'Museum Ethnographic Case No. 1', *Catalyst* Vol. 18, 2021

Hinewirangi Kohu-Morgan, 'Five kuia/grandmothers ago', *New Zealand Poet Laureate,* 29/7/2021

Kahu Kutia, 'kids' published in *Ora Nui 4,* Oranui Press, 2021

Arihia Latham, '(i) rui ruia, (ii) kapakapa, (iii) tui tuia' published in *Te Whē ki Tukorehe*, Te Whē Press, 2020

Colleen Maria Lenihan, 'Nerissa' from *Kōhine*, Huia Publishers, 2022

Steph Matuku, 'Homesick' published in *Vā: Stories from Women of the Moana*, Tatou Publishing, 2021

Ana McAllister, 'My Grim Reaper' published in *Stasis* 1, 2020

Kay McKenzie Cooke, 'Tuturau' from *Upturned,* The Cuba Press, 2020

Donna McLeod, 'Ihumātao' published in *Te Rito o te Harakeke – A collection of writing for Ihumātao*, Rangatahi o te Pene, 2019

Atakohu Middleton, 'Wairua' published in *Huia Short Stories 14*, Huia Publishers, 2021

Airana Ngawera, 'A metropolitan tangi' published in *Mayhem* 8, University of Waikato, 2020

Zeb Tamihana Nicklin, 'Iti te Kupu, Nui te Kōrero' published in *Huia Short Stories 14,* Huia Publishers, 2021

Kōtuku Titihuia Nuttall, 'Food' from *Tauhou*, Te Herenga Waka University Press, 2022; House of Anansi, 2023

Tru Paraha, 'Borderline' published in *AUP New Poets 8,* Auckland University Press, 2021

Kiri Piahana-Wong, 'New Year' published in *Ora Nui 3*, Oranui Press, 2017

Brian Potiki, 'Rowley's Tangi Down the Road' published in *Landfall* 234, Massey University Press, 2018

essa may ranapiri, 'knot-boy ii' published in *Out Here: An Anthology of Takatapui and LGBTQIA+ Writers from Aotearoa New Zealand,*

Auckland University Press, 2021
'Māui Becomes Who S/He Was Meant To Be' from *ECHIDNA*, Te Herenga Waka University Press, 2022
'One of the Great Ocean-going Canoes' from *ransack*, Te Herenga Waka University Press, 2019
Frazer Rangihuna, 'Piro', *Sunday Star-Times*, 7/1/2018
Vaughan Rapatahana, 'hā pīwakawaka' from *ināianei/now*, Cyberwit, 2021
'Ngā whānau' published in *Antipodes* Vol. 33, Wayne State University Press, 2019
'Rangiaowhia, 1864' from *ngā whakamatuatanga/interludes*, Cyberwit, 2020
Reihana Robinson, 'Jealousy or the main highway' from *Her Limitless Her*, Mākaro Press, 2018
Te Kahu Rolleston, 'Te Rārangatira' published in *Solid Air: Australian and New Zealand Spoken Word*, University of Queensland Press, 2019
Tania Roxborogh, 'Rapurapu/Searching' published in *Flash Frontier*, April 2019: Historical Fiction, 2019
Shirley Simmonds, 'Earth Ocean' published in *Vā: Stories from Women of the Moana*, Tatou Publishing, 2021
Carin Smeaton, 'Bird-peoples make it to ngā Rangi-i-Totongia-a-Tamatekapua' published in *Mayhem* 6, University of Waikato, 2018
Ruby Solly, 'Eulogy' and 'Untitled' from *Tōkū Pāpā*, Te Herenga Waka University Press, 2021
Robert Sullivan, 'Declaration of Independence', 'Rock Art' and 'Ruia' from *Tūnui / Comet*, Auckland University Press, 2022
Ariana Sutton, 'The Right Whale to Talk to' published in *Sweet Mammalian* 8, 2021
Apirana Taylor, 'karanga' published in *Ora Nui* 3, Oranui Press, 2017
'to write' published in *Ko Aotearoa Tātou: We Are New Zealand*, Otago University Press, 2020
Stacey Teague, 'Hineteiwaiwa' published in *Atua Wāhine: A Collection of Writings by Wāhine Māori*, 2020
kani te manukura, 'Tricks of a treaty' published in *Manifesto Aotearoa: 101 Political Poems*, Otago University Press, 2017
Alice Te Punga Sommerville, 'Kupu rere kē' from *Always Italicise: how to write while colonised*, Auckland University Press, 2022
Anne-Marie Te Whiu, 'Blood Brothers' published in *Ora Nui* 4, Oranui Press, 2021
'Smells Like Colonial Spirit' published in *Tupuranga Tahi*, 2019
Tayi Tibble, 'Identity Politics' from *Poukahangatus*, Te Herenga Waka University Press, 2018; Knopf, 2022; Penguin UK, 2022
'4 the Dead Homies' and 'Hine-nui-te-pō' from *Rangikura*, Te Herenga Waka University Press, 2021; Knopf, 2024; Penguin UK, 2024
Ariana Tikao, 'To'u reo' published in *takahē* 101, Takahē Publishing Collective, 2021

Kahu Tumai, 'A Karakia' published in *Mayhem 9*, University of Waikato, 2021
'Tūrangawaewae' published in *Tupuranga Tahi*, 2019
Peta-Maria Tunui, 'Noho Mai', https://loveinthetimeofcovidchronicle.com, 2021
Anne Waapu, 'a series of never ending beginnings' published in *Te Whē ki Tukorehe*, Te Whē Press, 2020
Fabian Waenga, 'Māori Homelessness in New Zealand' published in *More Than a Roof: Housing, in poems and prose*, Landing Press, 2021
Arielle Walker, 'Here are all the ways the story is the same' published in *AUP New Poets 9*, Auckland University Press, 2023
Iona Winter, 'Portal to the stars' from *gaps in the light*, Ad Hoc Fiction, 2021
Briar Wood, 'Kuramarotini' from *Rāwāhi*, Anahera Press, 2017
'Skep' published in *Turbine / Kapohau*, International Institute of Modern Letters, 2019

Published for the first time

Rangi Faith, '. . . no one thing we wanted'
Emma Hislop, 'Cure'
Witi Ihimaera , 'Te Hau Puru'
J. Wiremu Kane, 'Tha Ara Rīpeka (Crossroads)'
Tina Makereti, 'Whare Tangata'
Kelly Ana Morey, 'I'm So Happy I Could Die'
Paula Morris , 'Brussels'
Michael O'Leary, 'The Burst Pipe'
Kiri Piahana-Wong, 'Nō hea koe?'
Jessie Puru, 'Fuccboi'
Alice Tawhai, 'Perfect Circle'
Apirana Taylor, 'taku toa'
Gerry Te Kapa Coates, 'The Promised Lands'

Interview: Children's and YA Novel Writing
Interview: Five Māori Novelists